GOOD
TASTES

GOOD TASTES

The SHERRY GOLDEN
COOKBOOK

ILLUSTRATED BY MADELINE SOREL   ALFRED A. KNOPF   NEW YORK   1985

This is a Borzoi Book published by Alfred A. Knopf, Inc.

Copyright © 1985 by Sherry Lazar Golden

Illustrations copyright © 1985 by Madeline Sorel

All rights reserved under International and Pan-American Copyright Conventions.

Published in the United States by Alfred A. Knopf, Inc., New York,

and simultaneously in Canada by Random House of Canada Limited, Toronto.

Distributed by Random House, Inc., New York.

Library of Congress Cataloging in Publication Data

Golden, Sherry.   Good tastes.

Includes index.

1. Cookery.   I. Title.

TX715.G6135   1985   641.5   84-48656

ISBN 0-394-53181-7

ISBN 0-394-73857-8 (pbk.)

Manufactured in the United States of America

First Edition

FOR JAMIE

CONTENTS

Introduction   ix

BREADS:
YEAST BREADS
AND QUICK BREADS   1

SOUPS   35

APPETIZERS   53

SAVORY PIES, QUICHES,
TARTS, AND OTHER
PASTRY DELIGHTS   73

CRÊPES, BLINTZES,
PANCAKES AND
WAFFLES   105

PASTA   125

STIR–FRY   165

POULTRY, MEAT, FISH
AND SEAFOOD   191

WITH–MEAT COOKING:
CO-STARRING VEGETABLES, GRAINS,
DAIRY, AND LEGUMES   203

PASTA, GRAIN,
VEGETABLE, AND
BEAN SALADS   219

SAUCES, FILLINGS,
AND MARINADES   239

DESSERTS   259

Index   291

INTRODUCTION

Food has always been an important part of my life. To my mother it was a marker of stability and abundance. No matter how difficult things might be, good food, she insisted, would always be on our table. I grew up near two adoring aunts who cooked in a skillful, earthy Jewish tradition. I would stand on a stool next to them as they worked in their warm kitchens, rolling out my scraps of dough which they fussed over and baked with great to-do, linking food forever with well-being and love.

And I enjoyed baking for my father, offering up to him special gifts and treats, in the same way that I twirled before him in a new outfit or dress, waiting for the delighted and approving smile that always came. Whenever I return to the city where I grew up, I head for my mother's kitchen. It's a different kitchen than the one I practiced and learned in; my aunts are now guests at the table; and my father is no longer alive. But the wish to gather people I care about together, to cook for them and create some special harmony of feelings and tastes, is an enduring part of my life.

Good food is a sensual experience, one that is both richly personal and social. It is satisfying to prepare, gratifying to serve, and a joy to eat—alone and shared with others. It is a source of playfulness and creativity that is grounded in the everyday and the suggestions of pocketbook, imagination, and mood. Food is truly for *all* the senses; it reverberates in experience through anticipation and memory, nourishing the whole person.

Food is magically both part of our daily lives and a medium for rare pleasure experienced often. For me this can be the earthy pleasure of a dense homemade rye bread, fragrant with caraway or dill, cut thick to hold a slice of Cheddar, and savored with a cup of hot tea. Or it can be an intricate pastry lattice loaf of seafood, spinach, and eggs, with alternating whites and oranges of yolks and deep spinachy green—an elegant pleasure to produce, to look at, to serve others, and to eat.

It is these harmonies of diverse elements and style that I love to celebrate through food. Elegant and earthy, subtle and intense, grand and informal, meaty and vegetarian, health-conscious and lush—cooking is most complete when I allow for all of these and cook to express at different times all of who I am.

I hope these recipes create this kind of experience and expression for you. Receive, share, and enjoy them. For isn't this what food—and life—is all about?

ACKNOWLEDGMENTS

I am profoundly moved when I think of all the people who have contributed to me and therefore to this book. I can't acknowledge each of you appropriately in this brief space. But if you have worked with me, laughed with me, danced with me, dreamed with me... in some way nourished me with your love ... then you have helped make all things possible, including this book.

In the six years since I began this project, there have been many who, in both large and small acts, shared their time, ideas, encouragement, and spirit, or made a connection for me that moved me farther or more easily along the path. I think of you and thank you from the bottom of my heart.

There are a few who helped so directly to make this book possible that I want to mention them.

Faye Snider, seeing how much I loved to create with food, suggested I write a cookbook and thereby nudged me toward a new and joyful chapter of my life. Nancy Nicholas, my editor, and Barney Karpfinger, my agent, believed in this book enough to stand behind it and speak for it; each has been an unfailing source of support and good ideas. Finally, there are those at Knopf, many unknown to me, who tested and enjoyed these recipes and helped move the book through the editorial and design process to the form you now hold in your hand.

I thank you all.

BREADS

YEAST BREADS

Easy Processor Brioche

Whole Wheat Processor Brioche

Buttery Brioche Twists

Onion Caraway Twists

Lemon Poppy Seed Twists

Herb Cheese Twists

Brioche with Savory Cheese Filling

Rich Herbed Brioche with Whole Grains and Seeds

Farmhouse Fruit and Nut Bread

Three Grain Loaf

Rich Sweet Swirls

Savory Bread Swirls

Garlic Tahini Filling

Cheese and Herb Filling

Honey Sesame Filling

Honey Poppy Seed Filling

Jam and Praline Filling

Braided Rye

Wonderful Raisin Bread

Oatmeal Dill Bread

Herbed Walnut Cheese Swirl

Buckwheat Honey Raisin Bread

Whole Wheat and Rye Rolls

English Muffins

QUICK BREADS

Master Recipe: Best Ever Banana Bread

Best Ever Almond Raspberry Bread

Best Ever Poppy Seed Banana Bread

Best Ever Three Seed and Nut Bread

Best Ever Caraway Rye Banana Bread

Best Ever Sesame Banana Bread

Best Ever Buckwheat Banana Bread

Best Ever Peanut Banana Bread

Best Ever Cornmeal Banana Bread

Best Ever Cranberry Banana Bread

Best Ever Blueberry Banana Bread

Best Ever Cream Cheese Banana Bread

Best Ever Chocolate Banana Bread

Best Ever Carrot Bread

Best Ever Zucchini Bread

Four Season Fruit Bread

Velvet Pumpkin Bread

Nutted Soda Bread with Herbs

Fruited Soda Bread with Nuts and Caraway

Cranberry Raisin Bread

Blueberry Bread

Cottage Health Loaf for Faye

Maple Corn Bread

Prune Marvel Muffins

Buckwheat and Maple Walnut Muffins

Cranberry Raisin or Blueberry Muffins

Extraordinary Blueberry (or Cranberry) Muffins

Raisin and Bran Muffins for Jack

Bread, not dessert, is my downfall. I can pass up all kinds of desserts, though sometimes with a tug. But I'm helpless to refuse a slice of crusty chewy bread, flecked with whole grains and spread with butter. When I make bread, I know by now to time the baking to coincide with lunch. Fresh-baked bread, still warm and smelling of grain, is irresistible to me. I'm going to eat 2 or 3 thick slices at least, so I may as well make a meal of it.

By and large I surrender to this passion graciously, for I think of bread as health-giving, good for me. I feel nourished, too, by the process of making bread. The slow fermentation of yeast and the expansion and transformation of the dough put me in touch with deeper rhythms and the livingness of foods. Although flour, water, yeast, and salt are all that are needed to make a good bread, the variety of grains, cereals, sweeteners, liquids, fruits, nuts, herbs, and seeds that can be added to breads suggests wonderfully creative bread variations; and the flexibility of forms that breads can take nourishes my aesthetic sense as well. And finally, there's the delicious pleasure of offering friends or dinner guests slices from a homemade bread—a loaf not available in any bakery or store.

I think of bread making as a simple earthy process rather than a complex or delicate one. Like a good baby who plays contentedly once its needs have been met, bread will quietly do its thing and respond with amazing flexibility once certain needs and schedules have been acknowledged and taken care of. Above all, bread needs gentle warmth, and time, for the yeast to grow and expand and lighten the dough. It helps to know that a little extra warmth can speed up the process. Too much warmth (as in baking) will kill the yeast and end the process. Cold retards the growth of yeast, but does not kill it. Refrigeration and even freezing can be used to slow or temporarily halt the rising process, which is useful when unexpected events or a complicated schedule preclude a normal rising progression.

Rather than worry about whether or not my dough has risen enough or too little, if I've added too much flour or kneaded for a long enough time, I've learned to see the subtleties and vagaries of bread making as lending interest and individuality to the loaves. I've actually found that I prefer a slightly underrisen loaf, being of the dense-munchy-chewy school of bread eating. Even a serious bread-making mistake can reward you with a curiously satisfying result. One time I put my oiled bread into the oven for its first rising. I turned the oven on to provide just a gentle push of warm air, but then forgot to turn it off again. The bread responded to the initial warmth by rising slightly, then of course began to bake, luckily in an aluminum bowl. The bread that was "meant to be" never happened, but a delicious, dense, earthy loaf came out of the oven instead.

Let me take you through a typical bread-making process.

I use dry yeast purchased in bulk rather than in individual packages and store it in the refrigerator. It doesn't seem to matter whether the yeast is cold or at room temperature. What is important, however, is to use water that is pleasantly (but seriously) warm to the touch. Water that is too hot will kill the yeast; water that is too cold will slow the yeast and interfere with the dissolving process. Should a phone call or other digression call me away to return later to a madly bubbling yeast mixture, I simply stir it down and add it to my ingredients. But undissolved or unbubbling yeast says "try again"—a good start is very important here.

The first thing I do when I begin a loaf is stir together yeast, water, and a small amount of sugar in a measuring cup. This procedure is called "proofing." When the yeast has dissolved and bubbles have formed on the surface of the mixture, it proves that the mixture is active and ready to go to work. The sugar is food for the yeast and encourages its growth. This growth and the throwing off of the carbon dioxide that is trapped in the bread's gluten network (developed by kneading) are what cause the expansion of the dough.

If milk is the liquid called for, I heat it until little bubbles form around the edge of the pan then add oil or butter (I often use unrefined corn oil for its lovely flavor), sugar or other sweeteners, and any other flavoring ingredients called for. I stir this mixture well then let it cool down to a temperature that won't harm the yeast.

Next I place the proofed yeast and other liquids in the work bowl of the food processor with enough unbleached all-purpose flour to give me a batterlike mixture. (Begin with 1-2 cups of flour—the amount will depend on the volume of liquid in the recipe.) I then run the processor for a minute or two, really encouraging the gluten development in this first batch of flour and giving the kneading process an extra-good base or push. If you don't have a food processor, this stage can be done in an electric mixer on a stand. And if you prefer to leave out this batter-beating stage, you can just combine all the ingredients in a mixing bowl and then really give your all to the hand kneading.

After this preliminary kneading I add most of the remaining flour called for in the recipe and process briefly. The kneading of a single loaf can be completed in a large-capacity processor, but generally there is just too much dough for the machine to handle well; I just remove about two thirds of the dough to a floured spot on my counter and knead each third in turn in the processor. I add just enough flour to give me a smooth, satiny, but still soft and pliant dough, and at the end knead the thirds together briefly by hand.

If you are hand kneading from the start, mix the wet and dry ingredients together in a bowl until a coherent dough is formed. Turn this onto a floured surface and knead, adding flour as necessary, until a nonsticky elastic but flexible dough results. (This will take anywhere from 10-15 minutes.) Some people prefer kneading by hand, considering this one of the basic pleasures and releases of bread making. I, on the other hand, am grateful for the excellent and speedy job done by the processor.

Whichever method you choose, I find it helpful to start with the high gluten flours, such as unbleached all-purpose then whole wheat bread flours, and to add the lower gluten flours like rye or buckwheat later, since they contribute the least to the important gluten network.

When kneading is completed I place the dough in a well-oiled or well-buttered bowl large enough to contain the dough when it is doubled in size. I turn the dough in the bowl so that all surfaces are greased and place a dampened dish towel or several thicknesses of damp paper toweling over the top of the bowl. The greasing and the dampness keep the surface of the dough soft and pliant as it expands. One caveat: make sure the toweling remains damp throughout the rising. If it dries out, the surface of the dough may dry or, worse, rise up to the paper or towel and stick to it. If this should happen, moisten the towel with warm water (a mister works well) and peel it away very gently.

The dough is now placed in a warm, draft-free environment. A very lightly preheated oven that has been turned off is my choice. Let the dough rise until it is doubled in bulk. Forty-five minutes to an hour is an average rising time, but the length of time depends on several factors: the temperature of the rising environment, the temperature of the ingredients, the amount of yeast being used, and the density of the dough. Heavier doughs with cooked cereals and whole grains added to them sometimes never quite double in size. These also take longer to rise, as do doughs rich in sour cream and butter. You can tell when bread is doubled by just looking. If you have used a bowl the size of about double the volume of your unrisen dough, you'll know the bread is ready when it has rounded over the top of the bowl. You can also tell by sticking 2 fingers into the dough. If the finger holes fill up after a minute or two, there is still more expansion—and therefore rising time—left in the dough.

When the first rising is finished, punch the dough down once in the bowl, whooshing out all the trapped gas. One or two gentle kneadings return the dough to its original size, and then it is ready to be shaped. If you wanted to, you could give the dough a second rising in the bowl. Each rising adds somewhat to the fineness of the bread's texture.

Bread can be shaped into a simple freestanding round or a more complicated braid or it can be fitted into a loaf pan. The dough can also be rolled out and spread with sweet or savory fillings then rolled up into a loaf or more sophisticated braids or swirls. Sometimes I bake bread in a large-capacity ring mold to create an unusual shape; a 9-inch springform pan contains the elegant large round of cheese-stuffed brioche described in the chapter on appetizers.

The formed bread is placed in a buttered baking pan or on a sheet that has been sprinkled with cornmeal or rolled oats. Brush the surface of the bread with oil or melted butter, or even warm water as needed, to keep it pliant during rising. The bread can also be covered with a light damp towel. Then it is once again placed in a warm, draft-free environment. I use my oven again, removing the bread to the back of the stove top for the last 5–15 minutes of rising time while the oven preheats for baking.

Bread is ready to be baked when the loaf appears doubled in volume and when a finger pressed gently into the still elastic loaf nevertheless suggests that the dough's capacity to expand is becoming depleted or, when the dough is in a loaf pan, when it is gently rounded over the top of the pan. Just before I bake the bread I brush it with an egg wash (1 egg beaten with a little water or milk—a beaten egg white works just as well if that's what I have available in the fridge). Poppy, sesame, or caraway seeds are more likely to stay on the loaf if they are sprinkled on right after glazing. Breads bake for an average of 30–45 minutes, but the length of time depends on the type of dough and the size of the loaf. Bread is done when it is an appealing golden color and makes a hollow sound when rapped on the bottom. Remove your finished bread from its pan, let it cool on a rack, and see how long you can resist cutting into it.

Breads freeze beautifully. If I'm preparing 2 loaves, I'll wrap 1 just-cooled loaf in heavy-duty foil and freeze it for a special dinner or a time when I want fresh-baked bread but am unable to allocate the time to produce it. A bread pulled from the freezer makes a wonderful and most welcome house gift. Warmed in the oven no one will know you didn't bake it that very morning.

Following are some of my favorite breads: a light brioche; special-occasion brioche rolls; a flavorful herb brioche; a densely fruited and nutted whole-grain loaf that I love to slice thick and toast and eat with butter and cups of hot tea; a three grain loaf lightly crunchy with steel-cut oats and sunflower seeds; sweet and savory swirl breads with fillings that color and flavor delicately from within; unique and delicious breads that use banana puree as a subtle

flavoring and superior potatolike starch addition; an airy buckwheat raisin loaf; English muffins; and whole-grain rolls. I hope that you will find favorites among the recipes and also that you will use them to create your own uniquely personal loaves.

Note: Unbleached all-purpose flour is the flour of preference for yeast bread making because of its higher gluten content. When choosing whole-grain flour, whole wheat *bread* flour (as opposed to whole wheat *pastry* flour) should be used in yeast bread baking. Bread flour is coarser and grainier than pastry flour and is milled from strains of wheat that have a higher gluten content.

EASY PROCESSOR BRIOCHE *yields two 8 by 4-inch or one 9 by 5-inch loaf*

I like this egg- and butter-rich bread best in its supporting role in the following recipes, and in Cheese in Brioche, Brioche Lattice Loaf, and Picadillo and Brioche Loaf.

1 1/2	Tablespoons yeast
1/4	cup warm water
2	Tablespoons sugar
3 1/2–4	cups unbleached all-purpose flour
3/4	cup scalded milk, cooled to lukewarm
2	eggs
8	Tablespoons (1 stick) butter, melted and cooled
2	teaspoons salt

Combine yeast with the water and sugar in a measuring cup and let stand until the yeast is dissolved and bubbly. Place 1 cup of the flour in a food processor work bowl. Add the yeast mixture and with the machine running add the milk. Process well then let this sponge rise in the machine for 30 minutes. With the processor running add the eggs, one at a time, then the melted butter in a thin stream, and the salt. Add the remaining 2 1/2 cups of the flour, processing until the machine slows down. Remove two thirds of the dough and process each third in turn, adding just enough flour (if necessary) to give a soft but unsticky dough. Knead the portions together briefly by hand, then place the dough in a buttered bowl, turning the dough so all sides are greased.

Cover the bowl with a damp kitchen towel or damp paper toweling and let rise in a warm place until doubled—50–60 minutes. Punch the dough down.

Divide the dough in half, form into loaves, and place in two buttered 8 by 4-inch loaf pans, or one 9 by 5-inch loaf pan. Or form into a long cylinder and place in a buttered 10 or 12-cup ring mold, pressing and joining the ends together. Butter the top of the dough, cover with damp toweling, and let rise in a warm place until doubled—about 40 minutes. (If you like, you can use egg wash to brush the top of the bread and sprinkle with poppy or sesame seeds.) Preheat the oven to 350°F.

Bake the bread for about 35 minutes, or until the loaves are golden and have a hollow sound when rapped on the bottom. Remove the bread from the pans and let cool on a rack.

WHOLE WHEAT PROCESSOR BRIOCHE

Substitute 1 cup whole wheat bread flour for 1 cup of the all-purpose flour added after the sponge has risen.

BUTTERY BRIOCHE TWISTS *yields twenty-six to twenty-eight 7-inch twists*

1 recipe Easy Processor Brioche
(preceding recipe)

ONION CARAWAY TWISTS

2 Tablespoons dried minced onion
1 Tablespoon caraway seeds

LEMON POPPY SEED TWISTS

Finely grated rind of 1 large lemon
1 Tablespoon poppy seeds

HERB CHEESE TWISTS

1 Tablespoon rosemary or dill or herb of choice
1/4 cup grated Parmesan cheese
4-6 Tablespoons (1/2-3/4 stick) butter, melted

Prepare according to the directions for Easy Processor Brioche. When the milk is scalded, add the dried minced onion, lemon rind, or herbs to it. Add the second flavoring when you combine the milk, yeast, and flour and process or beat well. It is not necessary to allow this sponge to rise. Add the eggs, melted butter, salt, and the remaining flour and

process or knead until a soft but unsticky dough results. Let rise according to the directions for Easy Processor Brioche.

Preheat the oven to 375°F. Punch down the dough (do not knead it), divide it in half, and roll each half out to a rectangle about 6 by 16 inches and about 1/4 inch thick. Brush with some of the melted butter.

Using a pizza cutting wheel or a sharp knife cut about 13-14 strips, each about 1 inch wide. Grasp each strip at the top and a few inches down, then twist your hands in opposite directions 3 or 4 times to form a corkscrew effect. Place each twist on a baking sheet, pressing down slightly on the ends if necessary to secure the twist. Allow 1 inch between each twist.

Brush twists generously with the rest of the melted butter and bake for 18-20 minutes, or until lightly golden. Remove to racks to cool.

You can brush the twists with egg wash instead of butter and sprinkle with additional seeds or with coarse salt.

Twists freeze well; defrost as many as you need and warm briefly.

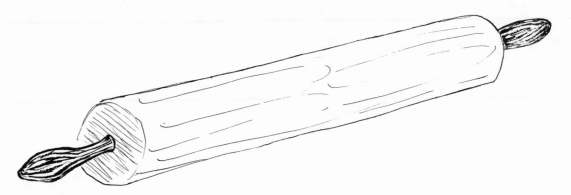

BRIOCHE WITH SAVORY CHEESE FILLING *serves 8–15 people or more*

Choose this when you want a stand-out, more-filling-than-usual bread. For other cheese-filled brioches, see Cheese in Brioche and Brioche Lattice Loaf.

  1 recipe Easy Processor Brioche (p. 7)
  1 small clove garlic, minced
  1 medium onion, diced
  2 Tablespoons (1/4 stick) butter
  1/2 cup minced fresh parsley
  1 1/2 pounds grated cheese*
  2 eggs, beaten
     Egg wash (1 egg beaten with 1 Tablespoon water or milk)
     Poppy, caraway, or sesame seeds

While brioche dough is rising (first rise), sauté the garlic and onion in the butter until onion is translucent and tender. Add parsley and stir. Let cool. When dough is ready to be punched down, combine the cheese, beaten eggs, and onion mixture, stirring well.

When brioche is fully risen, punch it down. Let it

*Use one kind of mild white cheese like Havarti (also dilled Havarti or other Havarti variations) or Muenster, or try a combination of cheeses such as 1 pound Havarti, 1/4 pound Bruder Basil (smoked cheese), and 1/4 pound Cheddar.

rest 5 minutes, then roll it out to a circle approximately 20 inches in diameter, lightly flouring as needed the surface you are rolling on. Fold the dough into fourths, to facilitate moving it, and fit it into a well-buttered 9-inch springform pan. Let the excess hang over the sides.

Turn the cheese mixture into the dough-lined pan, then bring the dough up over the cheese. Begin at any point, then, moving around the pan, form neat folds or pleats with the dough as you bring it up over the cheese. When you have finished folding or pleating, take the excess dough at the center with thumb and fingers, pinch it together, and twist—swirling the folds slightly.

Place the springform pan on a baking sheet and let the dough rise in a warm place for 20 minutes. (It will not rise much; do not be concerned.) Brush the top with egg wash and sprinkle generously with seeds. Release the springform lock. Place the pan in a preheated 350°F oven and bake 50–60 minutes, or until the dough is deeply golden. (If I plan to freeze and reheat the loaf, I might bake it a little lighter.) Remove the bread from the oven to a rack to cool. Serve warm. Bread can be refrigerated and reheated, or frozen, defrosted, and reheated.

RICH HERBED BRIOCHE
WITH WHOLE GRAINS AND SEEDS *yields two 9 by 5-inch loaves*

Subtly textured with seeds, herbs, and whole-grain flours—a delightfully balanced loaf with no one taste predominating.

1½ Tablespoons yeast
1 cup warm water
1 teaspoon sugar
1 cup unbleached all-purpose flour
2 eggs
8 Tablespoons (1 stick) butter, melted and cooled
1 cup quick oats, or rolled oats that have been ground to a coarse powder in a processor or blender
1 cup cottage cheese
¼ cup honey
1 Tablespoon salt
1½ Tablespoons poppy seeds
1½ Tablespoons sesame seeds
1 Tablespoon caraway seeds
1 Tablespoon dill seed
1 Tablespoon dried dill
1 Tablespoon tarragon
1 Tablespoon minced chives
1 teaspoon thyme
½ cup whole wheat bread flour
½ cup rye flour
About 4 cups unbleached all-purpose flour

Prepare according to the directions for Easy Processor Brioche (p. 7), combining the yeast mixture with the 1 cup all-purpose flour in a food processor or standing electric mixer. After the sponge has risen, beat it down by processing. With the machine running, add the eggs and melted butter. Then add the oats, cottage cheese, honey, and salt, processing well. (If you are not using a processor, you should grind even the quick oats to a powder in a blender.) Add the poppy seeds, sesame seeds, caraway seeds, dill seed, dried dill, tarragon, chives, thyme, and the whole wheat and rye flours. Process. Add the remaining all-purpose flour, processing in batches or mixing and kneading by hand. Place the dough in a buttered bowl, turning it so the top is buttered. Cover with a damp kitchen towel or damp paper toweling and let it rise in a warm place until doubled, about 60–90 minutes. Punch down the dough. Divide it in half, form into loaves, and place in two buttered 9 by 5-inch loaf pans. Or form the dough into long cylinders and place in two buttered ring molds. (You can use two 10-cup molds or one or two 12-cup molds, depending on whether you want small cocktail-size or large, high slices.) Butter or oil the top of the dough. Cover with damp toweling and let rise again in a warm place until doubled, about 1 hour. Preheat the oven to 350°F.

Bake for 30–35 minutes, or until the loaves are golden and have a hollow sound when rapped on the bottom. (Loaves baked in ring molds require less baking time. Two 12-cup rings will bake in 20–25 minutes.) Remove the bread from the pans and let cool on a rack.

FARMHOUSE FRUIT AND NUT BREAD _yields 2 round loaves_

Attractive with bright bits of apricot and other fruits, rich and crunchy with nuts, moist with cooked cereal, this is a hearty, subtly sweet loaf. It's also a heavy loaf and will not rise much. If you prefer a lighter loaf, use a higher ratio of all-purpose flour and/or more yeast.

Because this is a stiff dough I find the rolling and folding technique the easiest method for adding and distributing the fruit and nuts evenly.

   1 Tablespoon yeast
  1/2 cup warm water
   3 Tablespoons sugar
 1 1/2 cups water (use potato or bean cooking water
       if you have it)
  1/2 cup cornmeal, preferably stone ground
   2 Tablespoons oil or butter (1/4 stick), melted
   2 Tablespoons sesame seeds (optional)
 1 1/2 Tablespoons salt
   1 egg, beaten
   2 cups unbleached all-purpose flour
   2 cups whole wheat bread flour
       Additional 1 1/2–2 cups flour, either
       all-purpose or whole wheat
 1 1/2 cups coarsely chopped mixed dried fruits
       such as apricots, figs, prunes, raisins,
       or currants
  1/2 cup coarsely chopped walnuts and almonds

Combine yeast with the warm water and 1 Tablespoon of the sugar in a measuring cup and let stand until the yeast is dissolved and bubbly. Combine the 1 1/2 cups water and the cornmeal in a saucepan. Bring the mixture to a boil, whisking until it begins to thicken—another 2–3 minutes—then remove it from the heat. Add the oil or melted butter, the remaining 2 Tablespoons of the sugar, the sesame seeds, and salt. When cooled to lukewarm, stir in the yeast mixture and the beaten egg. Add this mixture to the 4 cups of combined all-purpose and whole wheat flours. Knead by hand or process in batches in the food processor, adding enough additional flour to yield a smooth, elastic dough.

Place the dough in an oiled bowl, then turn the dough so all sides are oiled. Cover with a damp towel or damp paper toweling and let rise in a warm place until almost doubled, about 1 hour.

Punch the dough down, knead it very slightly, then divide it in half. Roll each half out into a rectangle and spread each rectangle with some of the fruit and nut mixture. Roll it up like a jelly roll, then roll it out again, spreading it again with more of the fruit and nuts. Repeat 2 more times to distribute the fruit and nuts throughout the dough.

Form each piece of dough into a round and place both on a 10 by 15-inch baking sheet sprinkled with cornmeal. Oil the tops of the dough and let them rise 45–60 minutes, or until doubled. Preheat the oven to 350°F.

Bake for 45–50 minutes, or until the loaves are golden and have a hollow sound when rapped on the bottom. Let cool on a rack.

THREE GRAIN LOAF *yields 1 large or 2 small loaves*

This is an earthy but mellow bread with sweet nutlike nuggets of oats and sunflower seeds adding texture and taste. I especially like it for sandwiches, although it's great for serious bread-and-butter eating too. You can decide what ratio of all-purpose to whole wheat flour you prefer.

1 Tablespoon yeast
1/2 cup warm water
2 Tablespoons sugar
1 cup milk
1/2 cup steel-cut oats
2 Tablespoons oil
1 Tablespoon salt
1 egg, beaten
2 cups unbleached all-purpose flour
1 cup whole wheat bread flour
1 cup rye flour
  Additional all-purpose or whole wheat flour as needed
  Generous 1/4 cup lightly toasted sunflower seeds

Combine yeast with the water and 1 Tablespoon sugar in a measuring cup and let stand until the yeast is dissolved and bubbly. Scald the milk and add the oats, oil, remaining Tablespoon of sugar, and salt. When the mixture has cooled to lukewarm, add the yeast and the beaten egg. Combine this mixture with the 2 cups all-purpose flour and beat or process well. Add the whole wheat and rye flours and knead by hand or in batches in the food processor, adding enough additional flour as needed to give a smooth and elastic dough. Knead in the sunflower seeds by hand.

Place the dough in an oiled bowl then turn the dough to oil all sides. Cover with a damp towel or damp paper toweling and let rise in a warm place until doubled, about 1 hour. Punch down.

Knead the dough gently and form into 1 large round loaf (or 2 small loaves). Place the loaf or loaves on a baking sheet that is lightly greased or is sprinkled generously with quick oats or cornmeal. Oil the top of the loaf or loaves and let rise in a warm place until doubled, about 50–60 minutes. Preheat the oven to 350°F.

Bake the large loaf for 40–50 minutes, the smaller loaves for 30–40 minutes, or until golden with a hollow sound when rapped on the bottom. Let cool on a wire rack.

This series of swirl breads presents an exciting way to hold and distribute a flavorful filling within a bread and create a visually beautiful pattern as well.

RICH SWEET SWIRLS *yields 2 swirls or 12 rolls*

- 1 Tablespoon yeast
- 1/4 cup warm water
- 2 Tablespoons sugar
- 1/2 cup milk
- 4 Tablespoons (1/2 stick) butter
- 1/4 cup sugar
- 1/4 cup sour cream
- 2 teaspoons salt
- 1 egg plus 1 yolk, lightly beaten
- 3-4 cups unbleached all-purpose flour
- 1 cup whole wheat bread flour
  Honey Sesame Filling or Jam and Praline Filling (p. 15)
  Egg wash (1 egg beaten with 1 Tablespoon water or milk)
  Sesame or poppy seeds (optional)

Combine yeast with the water and sugar in a measuring cup and let stand until the yeast is dissolved and bubbly. Scald the milk then add the butter, sugar, sour cream, and salt; when the mixture has cooled to lukewarm, add the egg and egg yolk and the yeast mixture. Combine this mixture with 2 cups of the unbleached all-purpose flour in a bowl or food processor and beat or process well. Add the whole wheat bread flour and enough more unbleached all-purpose flour to form a cohesive dough.

Knead, or process in batches, adding additional flour as needed to yield a smooth and softly elastic dough. Place the dough in a buttered bowl then turn the dough to coat all sides. Cover with damp toweling and let rise in a warm place until doubled, about 75-90 minutes.

Punch down and divide the dough in half for 2 swirls or into 12 pieces for rolls. Follow the method for forming Savory Bread Swirls (p. 14) but make the rectangle slightly larger and the cylinder coils somewhat longer. Spread with filling as directed for Savory Bread Swirls. Rub softened butter on the tops of the formed swirls. Let rise on a buttered baking sheet until doubled, 50-60 minutes. Brush with egg wash and sprinkle with sesame or poppy seeds, if desired. Preheat the oven to 350°F.

Bake for 35-40 minutes, or until the swirls are golden and sound hollow when rapped on the bottom. Let cool on racks.

SAVORY BREAD SWIRLS *yields 2 small swirls, 12 rolls, or 1 large swirl*

1 Tablespoon yeast
3/4 cup warm water*
2 Tablespoons sugar
2 Tablespoons oil
2 teaspoons salt
1 egg, beaten
2 cups unbleached all-purpose flour
1 cup whole wheat bread flour (you can
  substitute all-purpose flour)
  Additional unbleached all-purpose flour
  Garlic Tahini Filling or Cheese and Herb
  Filling (following recipes)
  Egg wash (1 egg beaten with 1 Tablespoon milk
  or water)
  Sesame or poppy seeds (optional)

Combine yeast with the water and sugar in a measuring cup and let stand until the yeast is dissolved and bubbly. In a bowl or food processor combine the yeast mixture, oil, salt, egg, and 1 cup of the unbleached all-purpose flour, then beat or process well. Add the remaining cup of the all-purpose flour and the whole wheat flour and knead, or process in batches, adding additional unbleached all-purpose flour to yield a smooth and softly elastic dough. Place the dough in an oiled bowl, turning to coat all sides with oil, then cover with damp toweling and let rise in a warm place until doubled, about 1 hour. Punch the dough down and divide in half for 2 swirls, in 12 pieces for rolls, or leave as is for 1 large swirl.

To form the swirls, roll one half of the dough into a rectangle about 6 by 15 inches. Spread half of the Garlic Tahini or Cheese and Herb Filling over the dough, leaving a 1-inch border on two of the short and one of the long sides. Starting with the long side on which the filling comes to the edge, roll the dough into a cylinder, pinching the dough at the seams to seal. Roll the cylinder gently along the counter top with the palms of your hand to seal and elongate further. Form a swirl by coiling up the cylinder, stretching the dough as you coil and keeping the seam on the side of the coil. When you get to the end of the dough, stretch it again and tuck the end under. Repeat with the other half of the dough. Place the swirls on a greased 10 by 15-inch baking sheet. Rub the top lightly with oil and let the dough rise in a warm place until doubled, about 45 minutes. Preheat the oven to 350°F. Brush the swirls with egg wash and sprinkle with sesame or poppy seeds, if desired.

Bake for 30 minutes, or until the breads are golden and sound hollow when rapped on the bottom. Let cool on a rack.

To form rolls, roll the 12 small pieces of dough into rectangles measuring roughly 3 by 6 inches. Divide the filling equally among the 12 pieces, spreading it over the dough but not quite to the edges. Roll up the dough as with the larger rectangles, pinching the edges to seal. Roll the cylinders to elongate and seal and form the coil shape in the same manner as for larger swirls. Place on a greased 10 by 15-inch baking sheet. Brush or rub lightly with oil and let rise until doubled. Preheat the oven to 400°F.

Bake for 15–20 minutes. Let cool on a rack.

If preparing a single swirl, roll dough out to a larger rectangle. Baking time will be increased.

*Sometimes I use only 1/4 cup water to dissolve the yeast and add only a portion of the sugar. For the balance of the liquid I scald 1/2 cup milk and add the rest of the sugar and the oil and salt to this, combining the 2 mixtures when the milk has cooled to lukewarm.

GARLIC TAHINI FILLING

1/4 cup sesame tahini
  2 Tablespoons minced fresh parsley
  2 Tablespoons minced chives or finely
     minced scallion
  1 Tablespoon butter, softened
  1 Tablespoon lightly toasted sesame seeds
  1 clove garlic, minced fine or crushed
1/4 teaspoon salt
2-3 dashes Tabasco sauce

Combine the ingredients in a small bowl and mix
until smooth.

CHEESE AND HERB FILLING

  4 ounces Cheddar, Havarti, or a
     combination of mild cheeses, grated*
  2 Tablespoons minced fresh parsley
  2 Tablespoons minced chives or finely minced
     scallion, or other fresh herbs
  1 egg yolk
  1 small clove garlic, minced fine or crushed
1/4 teaspoon salt
2-3 dashes Tabasco sauce

Process or beat the ingredients together until smooth.

*Adding 1-2 ounces of a smoked cheese lends a particularly nice
flavor.

HONEY SESAME FILLING

1/2 cup lightly toasted sesame seeds, ground in a
     blender or processor
1/2 cup Praline (p. 286)*
1/4 cup honey
  2 Tablespoons rum
  1 Tablespoon butter, softened
  1 teaspoon (or more) finely grated orange rind
     Pinch of salt

Mix together or process the ingredients. If you like
raisins, sprinkle some over the filling.

HONEY POPPY SEED FILLING

Follow method for Honey Sesame Filling, substituting poppy seeds for the lightly toasted and ground
sesame seeds.

JAM AND PRALINE FILLING

1/2 cup raspberry or strawberry preserves
1/2 cup Praline (p. 286)*
  1 Tablespoon kirsch or brandy

Mix together the ingredients.

*You can substitute 1/4 cup chopped walnuts and 1/4 cup sugar for the
Praline, but you will lose some of the wonderfulness of the caramelized
nuts.

By a curious but fortuitous route I began to use banana in my yeast breads. I found that banana puree provided a natural sweetness and a depth of flavor that fascinates and delights the palate. Unlike other starches more commonly added to breads, bananas need only the quick whir of the processor or the mash of a fork to add their special magic. The puree produces an exceptionally elastic dough and a moist loaf that keeps its just-baked freshness for a surprising length of time.

BRAIDED RYE *yields 1 large or 2 small braids*

This is my favorite "banana bread." Try it and see if you feel as I do that banana and rye were meant for each other. I love this bread sliced thick and spread with butter or topped with a hunk of sharp Cheddar or creamy dilled Havarti. It is also spectacular toasted, the toasting bringing out an unusual buttery taste and texture.

    2   Tablespoons yeast
 1/2   cup warm water
    2   teaspoons sugar
    1   cup banana puree (about 2 large bananas)
 1/2   cup unflavored yogurt
    2   Tablespoons oil, preferably unrefined corn oil
    2   Tablespoons lightly toasted sesame seeds
        (optional)
1 1/2 Tablespoons salt
 1-2   Tablespoons dill or caraway seed, or
        a combination
3 1/2 cups unbleached all-purpose flour*
    2   cups rye flour

*If you prefer a denser loaf, substitute 1 cup whole wheat flour for 1 cup of the all-purpose flour; form this denser bread into a round loaf.

Combine yeast with the water and sugar in a measuring cup and let stand until the yeast is dissolved and bubbly. Combine the yeast mixture with the banana puree, yogurt, oil, sesame seeds, salt, dill or caraway, and 2 cups of the unbleached all-purpose flour. Process or beat well. Add the whole wheat (if used—see note) and rye flours, processing in batches or kneading by hand. Add additional all-purpose flour as needed to yield a smooth, *softly elastic* dough.

Place the dough in an oiled bowl then turn the dough to oil it on all sides. Cover with damp toweling and let rise in a warm place 70–90 minutes, or until the dough is *slightly more than doubled.*

Punch the dough down and knead it gently once or twice. Divide the dough into thirds. Roll each third into a cylinder about 16 inches long. Press the 3 pieces together at one end, then form them into a braid and place the braid on a 10 by 15-inch jelly-roll pan that has been sprinkled with cornmeal. Rub the bread with oil and brush lightly with water. Let rise in a warm place for 60–65 minutes, or until doubled. Preheat the oven to 350°F.

Bake for 45–50 minutes. Cool on a rack.

WONDERFUL RAISIN BREAD *yields 9 by 5-inch loaf*

One of the best raisin breads. You can vary the filling: before sprinkling on the raisins, brush the dough with melted or softened butter and sprinkle on crushed nuts, toasted sesame seeds, and/or cinnamon and brown sugar.

½ cup raisins
1 Tablespoon yeast
1 teaspoon granulated sugar
½ cup banana puree (about 1 large banana)
½ cup sour cream
2-4 Tablespoons brown sugar (packed)*
2 Tablespoons (¼ stick) butter, melted*
1 egg, lightly beaten
2 teaspoons salt
1 teaspoon almond extract
3 cups unbleached all-purpose flour
½ cup whole wheat bread flour
  Additional all-purpose or whole wheat flour
  Egg wash (1 egg beaten with 1 Tablespoon milk or water) (optional)

Soak the raisins for 5 minutes in boiling water to cover. Measure out ¼ cup of the warm raisin water and combine with the yeast and sugar. Let stand until the yeast is dissolved and bubbly. Drain off any remaining water and set the raisins aside. Combine the yeast mixture with the banana puree, sour cream, brown sugar, melted butter, egg, salt, almond extract, and 2 cups of the unbleached all-purpose flour. Beat or process well. Add the remaining all-purpose

*If you would like a richer coffee-cake taste, use 4 Tablespoons brown sugar and increase the butter to 4 Tablespoons (½ stick).

and whole wheat flours and knead by hand or process in batches, adding additional flour as necessary to yield a smooth and softly elastic dough.

Place the dough in a buttered bowl then turn the dough to grease all sides. Cover with damp toweling and let rise in a warm place until *slightly more than doubled,* 60-90 minutes. Punch down and knead the dough gently once or twice.

Roll the dough out to a rectangle about 9 by 12 inches. Spread the drained raisins evenly over the dough and roll it up jelly-roll fashion from a long side, pinching the seam to seal. Place seam side down in a buttered 9 by 5-inch loaf pan. Rub the top lightly with oil or softened butter. Let the dough rise in a warm place until doubled, 45-60 minutes. Preheat the oven to 350°F.

Brush with egg wash if you like and bake for approximately 45 minutes, or until the loaf is golden and sounds hollow when rapped on the bottom. Let cool on a rack.

OATMEAL DILL BREAD *yields 9 by 5-inch loaf*

This is a light-flavored, fine-textured bread with good body—a lovely all-purpose loaf. The rolls make delicious hamburger buns.

1 1/2 Tablespoons yeast
 1/2 cup plus 2 Tablespoons warm water
  2 teaspoons sugar
 1/2 cup banana puree (about 1 large banana)
 1/2 cup cottage cheese
 1/2 cup rolled oats*
  2 Tablespoons oil
  1 Tablespoon salt
 1-2 Tablespoons dried dill
  1 Tablespoon dill seed
  2 cups unbleached all-purpose flour
  1 cup whole wheat bread flour
     Additional unbleached all-purpose flour

Combine yeast with the water and sugar in a measuring cup and let stand until the yeast is dissolved and bubbly. Combine the banana puree, cottage cheese, oats, oil, salt, dried dill, and dill seed and set aside. Add the yeast and 1 cup of the unbleached all-purpose flour and beat or process well. Add the remaining cup of the all-purpose flour and the whole wheat flour and knead, or process in batches, adding a small amount of additional all-purpose flour if needed, to yield a smooth and softly elastic dough.

Place the dough in an oiled bowl then turn the dough to oil all sides. Cover with damp toweling and let rise in a warm place until slightly more than doubled, about 75-90 minutes. Punch down, kneading gently once or twice. Form into a loaf shape and press into a buttered 9 by 5-inch loaf pan. Oil

*If you are hand kneading, use quick oats or grind rolled oats to a coarse "flour" or powder in a blender.

or butter the top of the dough, cover with damp toweling, and let the dough rise in a warm place until *slightly more than doubled,* about 60-80 minutes. Preheat the oven to 350°F.

Bake for 35 minutes, or until the loaf is golden and sounds hollow when rapped on the bottom. Let cool on a rack.

OATMEAL DILL ROLLS

Prepare Oatmeal Dill Bread. After punching the dough down after the first rise, divide it into 10-12 pieces. Knead each piece lightly and roll into a 7-inch cylinder. Form each cylinder into a small knot. (You can also knead into a simple round shape.) Place rolls on a greased baking sheet. Brush each roll with water or rub lightly with oil. Let rise until doubled. If using water, brush again and bake in a preheated 400°F oven for 15-20 minutes. Makes 10-12 rolls.

BUCKWHEAT DILL BREAD

Substitute 1/2 cup medium kasha (buckwheat groats) for the rolled oats.

OATMEAL DILL BREAD WITH ONION

Dice 1 medium onion fine and sauté it in the 2 Tablespoons oil called for in the recipe until the onion is golden brown. Add it to the dough after the first major processing or beating, along with the whole wheat and all-purpose flours.

HERBED WALNUT CHEESE SWIRL *yields 1 swirl about 9 inches in diameter*

1 1/2 Tablespoons yeast
 1/2 cup plus 2 Tablespoons water
  1 teaspoon sugar
 1/2 cup banana puree (about 1 large banana)
 1/2 cup ricotta cheese
  2 Tablespoons olive oil
  1 Tablespoon salt
  3 cups unbleached all-purpose flour
  1 cup whole wheat bread flour
     Olive oil or 1 Tablespoon butter, softened
 1/3 cup coarsely chopped walnuts
  2 Tablespoons grated Parmesan or other hard
     grating cheese
1-2 teaspoons basil, or herbs of choice

Combine yeast with the water and sugar in a measuring cup and let stand until the yeast is dissolved and bubbly. In a bowl or food processor combine the banana puree, ricotta, the 2 Tablespoons olive oil, salt, dissolved yeast mixture, and 1 cup of the unbleached all-purpose flour. Beat or process well. Add another cup of the all-purpose flour and the whole wheat flour and knead, or process in batches, adding additional all-purpose flour as needed to yield a smooth and softly elastic dough. Place the dough in an oiled bowl (use olive oil), turning the dough to oil all sides. Cover with damp toweling and let the dough rise until doubled, about 75–90 minutes.

Punch down, kneading very gently once or twice. Roll out the dough into a rectangle measuring about 10 by 18 inches. Spread the rectangle lightly with olive oil or softened butter and sprinkle with the walnuts, cheese, and herbs of choice. Beginning at a long side, roll up as for a jelly roll. Pinch the edges to seal well and continue rolling and stretching the cylinder on the counter, elongating it to about 25 inches. Follow directions for forming swirls on page 14. Place the swirl on a greased baking sheet, rub with olive oil, then let rise in a warm place until doubled, about 45–60 minutes. Preheat the oven to 350°F.

Rub the swirl again with oil and bake for 35–40 minutes. Let cool on a rack.

BUCKWHEAT HONEY RAISIN BREAD *yields 9 by 5-inch loaf*

This is a good bread if you're partial to a high, light loaf but enjoy the hint of a deeper grain flavor. This bread makes great French toast—and a super peanut butter sandwich!

    1 Tablespoon yeast
 1/4 cup warm water
    1 teaspoon sugar
 3/4 cup milk
 1/2 cup raisins
 1/3 cup medium kasha (buckwheat groats)
    2 Tablespoons (1/4 stick) butter, softened*
      Generous 2 Tablespoons honey*
    2 teaspoons salt
    1 egg, beaten
    1 teaspoon ground cinnamon
    3 cups unbleached all-purpose flour
      Additional unbleached all-purpose flour
      as needed
      Additional kasha for sprinkling
      the pan (optional)

Combine yeast with the water and sugar in a measuring cup and let stand until the yeast is dissolved and bubbly. Scald the milk, then add the raisins to it. After 5 minutes, strain the milk and set the raisins aside. Roast the kasha in a hot skillet until it is fragrant. Add the butter, honey, salt, and kasha to the milk, stirring until the butter is melted. When the mixture has cooled to lukewarm, add the beaten egg, cinnamon, and yeast mixture.

In a bowl or food processor combine the yeast mixture with 2 cups of the unbleached all-purpose flour and beat or process well. Add the remaining

*For a sweeter, more coffee-cake taste, add an additional 2 Tablespoons (1/4 stick) butter and 2 Tablespoons honey.

cup of the flour and knead, or process in batches, adding additional flour as needed to make a smooth and softly elastic dough. Place the dough in a buttered bowl then turn the dough to butter all sides. Cover with damp toweling and let rise in a warm place until doubled, about 60–80 minutes.

Punch the dough down and knead in the raisins. Let rest for 5–10 minutes. Form into a loaf and place in a well-buttered 9 by 5-inch loaf pan that has been sprinkled lightly, if desired, with the additional kasha. Cover with damp toweling and let rise until doubled, about 45–60 minutes. Preheat the oven to 350°F.

Bake for 35–40 minutes, or until the bread is lightly golden and sounds hollow when rapped on the bottom. Let cool on a wire rack.

WHOLE WHEAT AND RYE ROLLS *yields 12 rolls*

1 Tablespoon yeast
1½ cups warm potato or bean cooking water
2 Tablespoons sugar
½ cup leftover cooked cereal such as oatmeal or Cream of Wheat
2 Tablespoons oil
1 Tablespoon salt
1 cup unbleached all-purpose flour*
2 cups whole wheat bread flour
1 cup rye flour
¼ cup lightly toasted sesame seeds
  Additional unbleached all-purpose flour
  Egg wash (1 egg beaten with 1 Tablespoon milk or water) (optional)
  Dill, caraway, poppy, or sesame seeds (optional)

*If you would like a lighter roll, reverse the proportions of unbleached all-purpose and whole wheat flours and let the rolls rise until fully doubled.

Combine yeast with the water and sugar in a measuring cup until the yeast is dissolved and bubbly. In a bowl or food processor combine the yeast mixture with the cooked cereal, oil, salt, unbleached all-purpose flour, and 1 cup of the whole wheat flour and beat or process well. Add the remaining cup of the whole wheat flour, rye flour, and sesame seeds and knead, or process in batches, adding more unbleached all-purpose flour as needed to give a smooth and softly elastic dough.

Place the dough in an oiled bowl then turn to coat all over with oil. Cover with damp toweling and let rise in a warm place until doubled, about 1½ hours.

Punch the dough down and divide it into 12 pieces. Roll each piece into a cylinder and form into a bow knot, or any shape you like. Place on a baking sheet sprinkled lightly with cornmeal and brush or rub each roll with a little oil. Let rise for 30 minutes, or longer if you would like an airier roll. If you like, brush the rolls lightly with egg wash and sprinkle with seeds. Preheat the oven to 400°F.

Bake for 15–20 minutes. Let cool on a rack.

ENGLISH MUFFINS *yields 12-15 muffins*

Imagine serving and eating English muffins that you made yourself—I always have this incredibly proud-of-myself feeling. They also freeze beautifully.

    1 Tablespoon yeast
    1/4 cup warm water
    1 Tablespoon sugar
    1 cup milk
    2 Tablespoons (1/4 stick) butter
    2 Tablespoons sugar
    2 teaspoons salt
    1/2 cup unflavored yogurt
    1 1/2 cups unbleached all-purpose flour
    1 cup whole wheat bread flour
    1/2 cup barley flour*
    3 Tablespoons semolina or farina**
    3 Tablespoons lightly toasted sesame seeds
      Up to 1/2 cup additional unbleached all-purpose flour
      Additional semolina or farina

Combine yeast with the water and the Tablespoon of sugar in a measuring cup and let stand until the yeast is dissolved and bubbly. Scald the milk. Add the butter, the 2 Tablespoons sugar, and salt and stir until the sugar is dissolved and the butter melted. Stir in the yogurt. When the mixture is lukewarm stir in the yeast mixture. In a bowl or food processor combine the yeast mixture with the unbleached all-purpose flour and beat or process well. Add the whole wheat and barley flours, semolina or farina, and sesame seeds and knead, or process in batches,

adding only as much additional unbleached all-purpose flour as is necessary to give a soft but unsticky dough.

Place the dough in a buttered bowl then turn the dough to coat all sides. Cover with damp toweling and let rise in a warm place until doubled, about 1-1 1/2 hours. Punch down the dough and roll it out to a thickness of 1/2 inch. Cut out 3-inch rounds, rerolling scraps as necessary. Have a mound of semolina or farina on the counter and press the muffin into it gently so that both sides are coated lightly and evenly with the cereal.

Place the muffins on an ungreased baking sheet, leaving space between them. Cover with damp paper toweling and let rise until doubled, about 40 minutes. Heat 2 griddles and/or sauté pans over medium heat. Transfer the muffins carefully with a narrow spatula to the griddles or sauté pans and cook them, turning them over once, until they are a deep golden color on both sides, about 7-10 minutes per side. The amount of time will depend on the thickness of the muffins and the type of pan. If the muffins seem to be browning too fast or too slowly, lower or raise the heat. When the muffins are cooked, transfer them to a rack to cool. Place cooled muffins in a plastic bag and store in the refrigerator or freezer.

You now have a muffin much superior to what you can buy—ready to split and toast.

*Barley flour is available in health-food stores.
**You can substitute cornmeal (*not* stone ground) for the semolina or farina used to coat the muffins.

QUICK BREADS

I love to create company bread baskets filled with quick breads and muffins: deep amber slices of pumpkin bread; an unusual and beguiling banana bread (poppy seed? chocolate? rye?); and muffins, golden and specked with cranberries, blueberries, raisins, or nuts. For a party brunch this is a glorious celebration of morning hunger, and the abundant, sweetly satisfying ways to fill it.

Quick breads are for any time, though. A quick bread can be *the* touch for an intimate breakfast, or become a light lunch (spread with peanut butter or filled with cottage or cream cheeses), a hunger-appeasing snack, an accompaniment to soups and salads, a less-sweet dessert, and a most welcome house gift. Quick and easy to make (especially using the processor), mouth-watering to look at and slice into, quick breads can also be filled with lots of high-protein and whole-grain goodness.

Here you will find quick breads in many delightful forms, beginning with a moist and tender master recipe for the best-ever banana bread—and variations that I hope will startle and excite your taste imagination. Feel free to experiment. Nuts seem to be wonderful in all quick breads, whether or not they are called for. If raisins are your pleasure, add them. The banana bread variations especially showed me how I could use ordinary kitchen ingredients to create an exquisite assortment of breads. I hope you will try them all, have fun in the doing and the tasting, and evolve other possibilities for quick and creative breads and muffins.

Note: I prefer to use unbleached all-purpose flour, but any all-purpose flour is acceptable. I also use whole wheat *bread* flour, but whole wheat pastry flour, which has less bran, can be substituted. The ratios of all-purpose to whole wheat flours are my preferences, what I think works best in the loaf, but feel free to follow your own tastes in this matter. Also, I generally use extra-large eggs in all my cooking and baking.

It never ceases to amaze me how much a moist, subtly banana-tasting loaf was meant to be combined with so many different flavors. Almond Raspberry is beautiful to look at with its pink center swirl and almond topping. Three Seed and Nut Bread is gloriously nutty and quietly unique, with its hint of cumin and other seeds. Make sure to try it. Chocolate is subtle—1 ounce gives the bread an indefinable something. Poppy seed was made to be combined with banana. (Add ground nuts if you like them.) And rye and banana are a particularly auspicious match, with caraway adding a wonderful zing. This and Three Seed and Nut or Sesame Banana are particularly good choices for dinner breads, or accompaniments to quiches and crêpes. Blueberry Banana, Almond Raspberry, or Chocolate Banana may be your choice for brunch or breakfast loaves. Match them to your menu and your personal tastes. Check out, too, your preference for yogurt or sour cream. I find the yogurt loaf slightly lighter and more delicate, the sour cream loaf richer, a touch more dense in texture.

MASTER RECIPE: BEST EVER BANANA BREAD *yields 9 by 5-inch loaf*

1/2 cup quick oats, or rolled oats that have been ground to a coarse powder in a processor or blender

3/4 cup unflavored yogurt*

1 cup banana puree (about 2 large bananas)

4 Tablespoons (1/2 stick) butter, softened

1/2 cup sugar**

1/4 cup oil

2 eggs

1 teaspoon vanilla extract

3/4 teaspoon salt

2 teaspoons baking powder

1 teaspoon baking soda

1 1/2 cups unbleached all-purpose flour

1 cup whole wheat bread flour

1/2 cup chopped walnuts to top or add to bread (optional)

*Substitute 3/4 cup sour cream for a richer loaf.
**I sometimes use 1/4 cup packed brown sugar in place of 1/4 cup of the sugar called for.

Preheat the oven to 350°F. Butter a 9 by 5-inch loaf pan.

Combine the oats, yogurt, and banana puree and set aside. Process or beat the butter and sugar until smooth. Add the oil in a stream then the eggs, one at a time, while continuing to process or beat. Add the banana mixture and the vanilla and salt and process just to mix through. Sprinkle the baking powder and baking soda over the batter. Add the flours and process or beat just until the ingredients are well blended, being careful not to overbeat or overprocess. (If you are using the processor, 2 quick on-off pulses and a couple of mixes with a rubber spatula will usually do it.)

Spread the batter evenly in the prepared pan and bake for 55–65 minutes, or until a toothpick inserted into the center comes out dry. Let cool for 5 minutes, remove the bread from the pan, and complete cooling on a rack.

BEST EVER BANANA BREAD VARIATIONS

BEST EVER ALMOND RASPBERRY BREAD

Add 1/2 teaspoon almond extract and, if desired, 1/2 cup finely ground almonds to the batter. Melt 1/2 cup raspberry preserves, stirring over low heat. Spread about two thirds of the batter in the pan then make a shallow indentation lengthwise down the center. Spread preserves in the indentation and smooth the remaining batter over the preserves. With a sharp knife marble the batter back and forth several times down the length of the pan. Top the bread with 1/2 cup coarsely chopped unblanched almonds. This variation requires additional baking time (about 10 minutes) because of the preserves.

BEST EVER POPPY SEED BANANA BREAD

Add 1/4 cup poppy seeds with the oats, yogurt, and banana puree mixture. Top the bread with additional seeds.

BEST EVER THREE SEED AND NUT BREAD

Omit the vanilla extract and add to the batter 1/2 cup finely ground walnuts, 2 Tablespoons sesame seeds, 2 Tablespoons poppy seeds, and 1 Tablespoon cumin seeds.

BEST EVER CARAWAY RYE BANANA BREAD

Omit the whole wheat flour and substitute rye flour. You will still need a total of 2 1/2 cups flour for this recipe, but you may prefer to use 1/2–1 cup rye flour and the rest all-purpose. Add 1/2 Tablespoon caraway seeds to the batter and sprinkle an additional 1/2–1 Tablespoon caraway seeds on top of the bread before baking.

BEST EVER SESAME BANANA BREAD

Substitute 1/4 cup sesame tahini for the 1/4 cup oil and add, if desired, 1/2 cup dried currants to the batter. Coat the entire buttered baking pan lightly with sesame seeds and sprinkle sesame seeds generously on top of the bread before baking.

BEST EVER BUCKWHEAT BANANA BREAD

Substitute 1/2 cup medium kasha or buckwheat groats for the oats. Add 1 teaspoon ground cinnamon and, if desired, 1/2 cup raisins.

BEST EVER PEANUT BANANA BREAD

Substitute 1/4 cup peanut butter (smooth or chunky) for the 1/4 cup oil. Also add 1/2 cup finely or coarsely chopped roasted peanuts to the batter. (Reduce the salt to 1/2 teaspoon if you are using salted nuts.) Sprinkle additional chopped peanuts on top of the bread before baking, if desired.

BEST EVER CORNMEAL BANANA BREAD

Substitute 1 cup stone-ground cornmeal for the 1 cup whole wheat flour. (If you prefer a heavier loaf you can substitute the cornmeal for 1 of the cups of all-purpose flour.)

BEST EVER CRANBERRY BANANA BREAD

Add 1 cup chopped cranberries and 1/2 cup coarsely chopped pecans or walnuts to the batter.

BEST EVER BLUEBERRY BANANA BREAD

Add a generous 1 cup fresh blueberries to the batter. If you would like to change the bread's flavor slightly, reduce the vanilla extract to 1/2 teaspoon and add generous gratings of fresh nutmeg or 1/2 teaspoon ground nutmeg.

BEST EVER CREAM CHEESE BANANA BREAD

Substitute 4 ounces softened cream cheese for the 1/4 cup oil. Add 1/2 cup raisins or currants and, if desired, 1/2 cup chopped walnuts or pecans.

BEST EVER CHOCOLATE BANANA BREAD

Add 1–2 ounces finely grated semisweet chocolate to the batter.

Best Ever Banana Bread becomes carrot or zucchini bread with a few small recipe changes.

BEST EVER CARROT BREAD

Substitute 1 1/2 cups finely chopped or grated carrot for the banana puree. Use 1/2 cup light brown sugar (packed) instead of granulated sugar and add 1 teaspoon ground cinnamon. Add 1/2 cup (or more) finely or coarsely chopped walnuts, if desired. You can also substitute 1/2 cup maple syrup for the sugar called for in the recipe.

BEST EVER ZUCCHINI BREAD

Substitute 1 1/2 cups lightly packed grated zucchini for the banana puree. Use 1/2 cup light brown sugar (packed) instead of granulated sugar and add 1 teaspoon ground cinnamon. Add 1/2 cup (or more) finely or coarsely chopped walnuts, if desired.

FOUR SEASON FRUIT BREAD *yields 9 by 5-inch loaf*

Fruit that is both pureed into the batter and added in chunks gives this bread a wonderfully moist texture. If you don't have a processor, you can puree half the fruit separately in a blender, adding the yogurt if necessary.

1 1/2 cups sweet plums or pears or peeled peaches or peeled apples*

1/2 cup quick oats, or rolled oats that have been ground to a coarse powder in a processor or blender

3/4 cup unflavored yogurt**

4 Tablespoons (1/2 stick) butter, softened

1/2 cup plus 2 Tablespoons sugar

1/4 cup oil

2 eggs

1 Tablespoon kirsch, rum, brandy, or sherry (with apples), or Amaretto (with pears)

1/2 teaspoon vanilla extract

1/2 teaspoon salt

2 teaspoons baking powder

1 teaspoon baking soda

1 1/2 cups unbleached all-purpose flour

1 cup whole wheat flour*

1/4-1/2 cup coarsely chopped nuts for topping

*If the peaches or apples are not peeled, mold forms very quickly in the bread. This doesn't seem to happen with the pears or plums. Also, the peaches and plums are wetter fruits, so breads made with them will require a slightly longer baking time.

**Substitute 3/4 cup sour cream for a richer loaf.

*I generally use whole wheat bread flour in all my bread baking, both yeast and quick. If I have it on hand, I sometimes choose to use whole wheat pastry flour in this particular bread for a somewhat finer result.

Preheat the oven to 350°F. Butter a 9 by 5-inch loaf pan.

Dice the fruit and set aside. Combine the oats and yogurt and set aside. Process the butter and sugar until smooth. With the processor running add the oil in a stream through the feed tube then the eggs one at a time. Scrape down the mixture if necessary. Add the liqueur or wine of choice, the vanilla, salt, the yogurt and oat mixture, and one third of the fruit. Process well—the fruit should be reduced to a coarse puree. Sprinkle the baking powder and baking soda over the batter. Add the flours and process in 2 quick on-off pulses. Fold the remaining diced fruit well into the batter with a rubber spatula.

Turn the batter into the prepared pan, sprinkle with chopped nuts, and bake for 60-70 minutes, or until a toothpick inserted into the center comes out dry. Let cool in the pan for 5-10 minutes then remove from the pan and complete cooling on a rack.

VELVET PUMPKIN BREAD   *yields 9 by 5-inch loaf*

A beguilingly rich bread with a delicate, moist, tender crumb. I sometimes add a handful each of golden raisins and roughly chopped pecans. A double recipe can be baked attractively in a 12-cup ring mold or in a 9 by 13-inch pan.

```
 8  Tablespoons (1 stick) butter
1/2  cup sugar
 2  eggs
    One 15-ounce can pumpkin
 1  cup unbleached all-purpose flour
 1  cup cornmeal*
 1  teaspoon baking powder
 1  teaspoon baking soda
3/4  teaspoon ground cinnamon
1/2  teaspoon salt
```

Preheat the oven to 375°F. Butter a 9 by 5-inch loaf pan.

Process or cream together the butter and sugar. Add the eggs one at a time while processing or beating then add the pumpkin and process or beat until well combined. Add the flour, cornmeal, baking powder, baking soda, cinnamon, and salt and process or beat just until ingredients are well blended, being careful not to overmix. (If you are using the processor, 2 quick on-off pulses and a couple of mixes with a rubber spatula will do it.)

Turn the batter into the prepared pan and bake for 50-55 minutes, or until a toothpick inserted into the center comes out dry. Let cool for 5-10 minutes then remove the bread from the pan and complete cooling on a rack.

*I use white or yellow degerminated (Quaker) cornmeal. Stone-ground yellow cornmeal works well too, but gives a grainier, less finely textured bread.

NUTTED SODA BREAD WITH HERBS *yields 1 round loaf*

This superb bread, in its savory or sweet version, can accompany and enhance just about any meal. Serve with eggs for breakfast, soup or salad for a special lunch, or as a wonderful dinner bread when you want something fresh made and warm from the oven.

- 1 cup unbleached all-purpose flour
- 1 cup whole wheat bread flour
- 1½ teaspoons salt
- ½ teaspoon sugar
- ½ teaspoon baking soda
- 3 Tablespoons butter, cut into pieces
- ¼ cup chopped or finely chopped pecans or walnuts
- 4 Tablespoons minced fresh dill or fresh basil, or 4 teaspoons dried dill or 3 teaspoons dried basil
- 1 cup buttermilk, or half milk and half unflavored yogurt

Preheat the oven to 375°F. Butter a baking sheet lightly.

Combine the flours, salt, sugar, and baking soda in a bowl or the work bowl of a food processor. Cut in or process the butter until the mixture is the consistency of fine meal. Add the nuts and herbs (I pair the pecans with the dill and the walnuts with the basil). Stir or process to mix through. If you are using the processor, transfer this mixture to a bowl. Add the buttermilk or combination of regular milk and yogurt, stirring well with a fork, until the mixture coheres. Turn out onto a lightly floured surface and knead gently a few times, adding a little additional flour if the dough is on the sticky side. Form into

a ball and place on the buttered baking sheet. Cut an X in the top of the dough with a razor or sharp knife. Bake for 45–50 minutes. Cool on a rack.

FRUITED SODA BREAD WITH NUTS AND CARAWAY

For a sweeter variation, add instead of the herbs ¼ cup snipped figs, dates, apricots, raisins, or dried fruit of choice, and 1 Tablespoon caraway seeds. Chop the nuts on the medium to coarse side.

CRANBERRY RAISIN BREAD *yields 8 by 4-inch loaf*

Beautiful and delicious with bits of red tart cranberry and brown sweet raisin.

1½ cups unbleached all-purpose flour*
 ¾ cup sugar**
 2 teaspoons baking powder
 ¾ teaspoon salt
    Grated rind of 1 lemon
 6 Tablespoons (¾ stick) butter
 1 cup coarsely chopped cranberries
 ¾ cup quick oats, or rolled oats that have been
    ground to a coarse powder in a processor
    or blender
 ½ cup raisins
 1 cup milk
 1 Tablespoon unflavored yogurt
 1 egg

*If desired, use whole wheat bread flour for part of the flour.
**Reduce the amount of sugar if you prefer a less sweet loaf.

Preheat the oven to 375°F. Butter an 8 by 4-inch loaf pan.

Combine the flour, sugar, baking powder, salt, and lemon rind in the work bowl of a food processor or in a mixing bowl. Cut in or process the butter until the mixture is the consistency of fine meal then stir in the cranberries, oats, and raisins. Beat together the milk, yogurt, and egg. Add to the cranberry and raisin mixture and stir until the ingredients are just combined, being careful not to overmix.

If you are using a processor, you can beat the liquid ingredients in a mixing bowl, transfer the cranberry mixture to the bowl, and stir them together. Or you can add the liquid to the processor work bowl, processing only once or twice in quick on-off pulses and using a rubber spatula for most of the mixing.

Turn the mixture into the prepared pan and bake for 50–55 minutes.

Let cool 5–10 minutes in the pan. Then remove bread from the pan and complete cooling on a rack.

BLUEBERRY BREAD

Substitute 1 cup fresh blueberries for the cranberries and omit the raisins. Sprinkle the top of the bread with cinnamon-sugar, if desired.

COTTAGE HEALTH LOAF FOR FAYE *yields 9 by 5-inch loaf*

Earthy, high in protein, and densely delicious—1 or 2 slices make a wonderful breakfast or quick lunch.

1 1/2 cups cottage cheese
1/2 cup medium kasha (buckwheat groats)
1/2 cup oil
1/2 cup honey
3 eggs
1 1/2 teaspoons ground cinnamon
1 teaspoon salt
2 teaspoons baking powder
1-1 1/2 teaspoons baking soda*
2 cups unbleached all-purpose flour
1/2 cup walnuts, broken up or chopped coarse
1/2 cup raisins
1/4-1/3 cup medium kasha for coating the pan (optional)

Preheat the oven to 350°F. Butter a 9 by 5-inch loaf pan.

Combine the cottage cheese and kasha and set aside. Beat together or process in a food processor the oil, honey, eggs, cinnamon, and salt. Add the kasha and cottage cheese mixture and beat or process until well combined. Add the baking powder, baking soda, and flour to the batter and mix through or process in 2 quick on-off pulses. Add the walnuts and raisins and continue beating just to combine the ingredients or, if you are using the processor, complete the mixing with a rubber spatula.

Turn into the prepared pan (which you can sprinkle and coat with additional kasha, if you like). Bake for 60-65 minutes or until a toothpick inserted into the center comes out dry. Let cool 5-10 minutes in the pan. Remove bread and complete cooling on a rack.

MAPLE CORN BREAD

1 1/4 cups unbleached all-purpose flour
1 cup cornmeal, preferably stone ground
1 Tablespoon baking powder
1 teaspoon salt
1 cup milk**
1/3 cup maple syrup
4 Tablespoons (1/2 stick) butter, melted
1 egg

Preheat the oven to 375°F. Butter a 10-inch pie plate or a 9-inch square baking pan.

Combine the flour, cornmeal, baking powder, and salt in a mixing bowl. Combine the milk, maple syrup, melted butter, and egg and stir them into the dry ingredients, mixing gently with a fork just until the ingredients are combined. Turn into the prepared pan and bake for 30 minutes, or until the corn bread is golden and tests done when a toothpick is inserted into the center. Let cool 5-10 minutes in the pan. Remove bread from the pan and complete cooling on a rack. To serve, cut in wedges if using pie plate; in squares if using 9-inch square pan.

*The smaller amount of baking soda will give you a slightly more dense, grainy loaf. I like it both ways and so leave the experimentation and option up to you.
**I sometimes place a heaping Tablespoon of unflavored yogurt in the measuring cup then add enough milk to measure 1 cup.

Is there anything more appealing than a basket of fresh-baked muffins? Well, maybe just 1 muffin, taken from the freezer when you're hungry and warmed in the oven until it's soft and ready to eat. Here's an assortment of these easy-to-prepare individual quick breads: Prune Marvel Muffins, faintly orange and almond flavored with a surprise center; Buckwheat and Maple Walnut Muffins, dark and grainy; Cranberry Raisin or Blueberry Muffins; and Raisin and Bran Muffins for the raisin lovers.

PRUNE MARVEL MUFFINS *yields 15–16 muffins*

1½ cups unbleached all-purpose flour
½ cup whole wheat pastry flour
⅓ cup sugar
1 teaspoon baking powder
¾ teaspoon baking soda
½ teaspoon salt
   Grated rind of 1 orange
1⅓ cups buttermilk, or half milk and half
   unflavored yogurt
6 Tablespoons (¾ stick) butter, melted
1 egg
½ teaspoon vanilla extract
½ teaspoon almond extract
¼ teaspoon orange extract (optional)
1 recipe Orange Prune Filling (following recipe)

Preheat the oven to 400°F.

Combine the flours, sugar, baking powder, baking soda, salt, and grated orange rind in a mixing bowl. Combine the buttermilk, melted butter, egg, vanilla and almond extracts, and optional orange extract and add them to the dry ingredients, stirring gently with a fork until just mixed.

Line muffin pans with paper baking cups and fill the cups one-third full with batter. Make a well or indentation in the batter with the back of a teaspoon and fill each well with 1 teaspoon Orange Prune Filling. Cover with enough additional batter to fill baking cups three-quarters full. Make a cross through each muffin with a small knife. Bake for 15–20 minutes, or until a toothpick inserted into the center of the muffin comes out dry. Cool on a rack.

ORANGE PRUNE FILLING

4 ounces pitted prunes
   (½ cup well packed)
3 Tablespoons orange juice
2½ Tablespoons honey
   Pinch of salt

Bring the ingredients to a boil in a small saucepan. Cover, turn off the heat, and let sit for 15–20 minutes. Puree.

BUCKWHEAT AND
MAPLE WALNUT MUFFINS *yields 12 muffins*

1 1/2 cups unbleached all-purpose flour
1/2 cup buckwheat flour*
1/2 cup finely chopped or grated walnuts
1 teaspoon baking powder
3/4 teaspoon baking soda
1/2 teaspoon salt
1 1/4 cups buttermilk, or half milk and half
   unflavored yogurt
4 Tablespoons (1/2 stick) butter, melted,
   or 1/4 cup oil
1/4 cup maple syrup
1 egg

Preheat the oven to 400°F.

Combine the flours, walnuts, baking powder, baking soda, and salt in a mixing bowl. Combine the buttermilk, melted butter or oil, maple syrup, and egg and add them to the dry ingredients, stirring gently with a fork until just mixed.

Line a muffin pan with paper baking cups and fill cups about three-quarters full. Bake for 15–20 minutes, or until a toothpick inserted into the center of a muffin comes out dry. Cool on a rack.

*If you are really fond of buckwheat and want a denser muffin, use equal parts all-purpose and buckwheat flour or substitute whole wheat flour for part of the all-purpose flour.

CRANBERRY RAISIN
OR BLUEBERRY MUFFINS *yields 12 muffins*

Preheat the oven to 400°F.

Prepare batter for Cranberry Raisin or Blueberry Bread (p. 29). Line muffin pans with paper baking cups and fill cups three-quarters full. Bake for 20 minutes, or until a toothpick inserted into the center of a muffin comes out dry. Cool on a rack.

EXTRAORDINARY BLUEBERRY
(OR CRANBERRY) MUFFINS

Prepare the recipe for Cranberry Raisin or Blueberry Bread (p. 29) but reduce the sugar to 1/2 cup and add 1/4 cup walnuts or pecan halves to the batter. Sprinkle the tops of the muffins generously with Praline (p. 286) before baking.

RAISIN AND BRAN
MUFFINS FOR JACK *yields 12 muffins*

1 1/2 cups buttermilk, or half milk and half
    unflavored yogurt
  1 cup raisins
1/2 cup whole bran flakes (available in health-
    food stores)
    Several gratings of fresh nutmeg*
1/4 cup oil or 4 Tablespoons (1/2 stick)
    butter, melted
  1 egg, lightly beaten
  1 cup unbleached all-purpose flour
1/2 cup whole wheat bread flour
1/4 cup sugar
  1 teaspoon baking powder
3/4 teaspoon baking soda
1/2 teaspoon salt

Preheat the oven to 400°F.

Combine the buttermilk, raisins, bran flakes, and nutmeg and set aside for 30 minutes.

Stir the oil or melted butter and egg into the buttermilk mixture. Combine the flours, sugar, baking powder, baking soda, and salt. Add the buttermilk mixture and stir gently with a fork until just combined. Line muffin pans with paper baking cups and fill the cups three-quarters full. Bake for 15–20 minutes, or until a toothpick inserted into the center of a muffin comes out dry.

*You may flavor these muffins with grated orange rind and/or ground cinnamon instead of nutmeg.

SOUPS

SOUPS

Multi-Bean Soup

Lemon Lentil Soup

Favorite Split Pea Soup

Gingered Carrot and Pear Bisque

Cream of Broccoli Stalk Soup

Cream of Broccoli Stalk Soup II

Curried Butternut Bisque

Cream of Cauliflower and Cheddar Cheese Soup

Spinach Walnut Bisque

Nantucket Scallop Chowder

A Simple and Simply Beautiful Fish Soup

Hot Beet Soup with Dilled Meatballs

Scotch Broth

Won Ton Soup

Aunt Clara's Fruit Soup

Summer Blueberry Grape Soup

Chilled Fresh Beet Borscht

Quick Beet and Orange Soup

Fresh Tomato Borscht

Summer Chilled Dilled Green Soup

STOCKS

Stocks and Stock Making

Soup is something I can count on, like a hug from an old friend. Unthinkingly I have undervalued it with the apology, "We're only having soup..." And yet, soup is one of the most warming and comforting meals I can think of to eat and to serve to others. Like a thought remembered, or a need responded to, soup is a delicious sense of well-being, captured in a bowl.

There are times when only soup will do. A cold winter night with no time to cook makes me grateful for soup. I take it out of the freezer that morning, or straight from the fridge that night. If it's bean soup, all I need do is heat it, add fresh-cooked pasta, and sprinkle on plenty of freshly grated Parmesan cheese. Steamy aromas travel to my nose, soft chewy textures and subtle flavors awaken my palate, and warmth fills my body. This is a soup experience, elemental and evocative, of the very best kind.

There are many different ways to enjoy soup. I love hearty, earthy lentil and split pea soup rich with slightly melting chunks of cheese and tender bites of pasta or spaetzle. These soups are meals in themselves, and I can elaborate on them with crusty breads and crisp salads. Easy-to-prepare fresh-baked soda breads are wonderful with soup: Nantucket Scallop Chowder or Cream of Broccoli Stalk Soup with a fruit and nut soda bread, Curried Butternut Bisque or Gingered Carrot and Pear Bisque with an herbed and nutted soda bread. These are meals elegant in their simplicity, satisfying to both diner and cook.

And then there are light, refreshing cold soups. Quick Beet and Orange Soup served with elegant Seafood Mousse Turnovers, or Summer Chilled Dilled Green Soup served with oversize Mexican Empanadas or Cheese Bean Turnovers, make unusual special lunches or filling light suppers. Although I rarely serve soup as a course preceding a meal, Aunt Clara's Fruit Soup or Summer Blueberry Grape Soup has a fresh sweet clarity that enhances any meal. Whether served with savory pastry, breads or muffins, or eaten alone, chilled soups capture the flavors of the fruits and vegetables of the season.

Following are a rich variety of favorite soups: earthy bean, pea, and lentil soups; chowder and vegetable "cream" soups, which you can prepare with either milk or cream to suit your caloric and nutritional "budget"; aromatic broths; and chilled fruit and vegetable soups.

Although soups can be prepared in vegetarian versions utilizing vegetable broths and vegetable cooking water, flavorful chicken, beef, and fish stocks add immeasurably to a soup's depth. The information on stock making should increase your soup (and sauce making) skills and success.

MULTI-BEAN SOUP *yields about 3¹/₂ quarts*

Many beans, many colors, many textures—this soup is similar to a minestrone, but earthier and beanier. It's a wonderful way to clear out small amounts of beans you have accumulated in your pantry. One of my favorite uses for this soup is as a wonderfully tasty and high-protein meatless sauce for pasta. I ladle a thick and garlicky version of this soup/sauce over al dente linguini or spaghetti topped with cubes of Jack, Muenster, or Havarti cheese. Sprinkle generously with grated Parmesan and dig in. Whether you enjoy it as a soup or sauce, thick or thin, feel free to add your own choices of vegetables and herbs. Just make sure the final result is a deeply flavored herb-scented mix.

About 2 cups at least 4 kinds assorted dried beans such as kidney, navy or pea beans, small limas, chick-peas, whole green peas, or pinto beans

2 cups diced onion

2 large carrots, cut into ¼-inch slices

2 ribs celery, cut into ¼-inch slices

3-4 Tablespoons olive oil or rendered prosciutto or bacon fat*

3-4 large cloves garlic, minced (be generous)
One 35-ounce can tomatoes**

2 cups rich chicken or beef stock
(see pp. 50-51)
Herbs: plenty of basil, a bay leaf, oregano, some marjoram and/or rosemary
Salt and freshly ground pepper to taste

2 cups thinly sliced or diced cabbage

2 cups shredded greens such as kale, beet, Swiss chard, or one 10-ounce package frozen chopped spinach

1 cup minced fresh parsley

Pasta such as rotelle, rotini, shells, or elbows, cooked al dente
Freshly grated Parmesan or other hard grating cheese

Rinse and pick over the beans. Place them in a large pot, add enough water to more than cover, and let sit overnight. Or bring the beans to a boil and simmer gently for 10 minutes. Cover, turn off the heat, and let the beans sit for 1 hour. Whichever process you choose, from this point on make sure the beans are covered with water and continue simmering them until they are just about tender.

In a wok or sauté pan sauté the onion, carrots, and celery in the oil or rendered prosciutto or bacon fat until the onion is tender, adding the minced garlic during the last minute or two. Add the vegetables to the pot of beans along with the tomatoes, stock, herbs, and salt and pepper. Bring to a boil. Add the cabbage and greens and simmer for about 30 minutes, or until the vegetables and beans are tender. Stir in the parsley and simmer a few minutes more. Thin the soup to the desired consistency with additional stock or water. Taste for seasoning.

To serve, place cooked pasta in soup bowls and ladle on hot soup. Sprinkle generously with grated Parmesan and pass additional grated cheese.

*Italian markets often sell the rind and fat from a trimmed prosciutto ham for a nominal amount. Cut up, then rendered, and used in place of oil, this will give your soup a subtle smoky flavor. You can also add a small smoked hock or ham bone to the soup.

**I prefer whole imported tomatoes with basil; a 28-ounce can of crushed tomatoes is fine also.

LEMON LENTIL SOUP *yields 2¹/2-3 quarts*

This is the lentil soup for people who don't like lentil soup, wonderfully herbed and faintly lemony. Serve it sprinkled with Parmesan, and with al dente pasta and cubes of Cheddar or other cheese mixed in for a heartier meal.

It, too, is a superb vegetarian sauce for long pastas. Allow 1-1¹/2 cups of thick soup for each 4-ounce serving of spaghetti, linguini, or fettucini. Pour over the al dente pasta and sprinkle with cubed cheese and plenty of grated Parmesan.

    1 cup (or more) diced onion
    1 cup diced carrot
    1 cup diced celery
    4 Tablespoons olive oil
    4 large cloves (or more) garlic, minced
      One 28-ounce can crushed tomatoes
  5-6 cups liquid (I suggest half chicken stock,
      half water)
    2 cups lentils, rinsed
  ¹/4 cup lemon juice (juice of 1 large lemon)
      Grated rind of 1 lemon
    2 Tablespoons dry sherry
  1-2 Tablespoons soy sauce or tamari
  2-3 teaspoons basil
    2 teaspoons oregano
    2 teaspoons thyme
³/4-1 teaspoon sage
      Salt and freshly ground pepper to taste
      A few dashes Tabasco sauce, or to taste
      Garlic powder to taste
      One 10-ounce package frozen chopped
      spinach, or 2 large bunches fresh parsley,
      minced

In a large soup pot or casserole sauté the onion, carrot, and celery in olive oil, adding the garlic during the last few minutes of sauté time. Add the tomatoes, stock and water, lentils, lemon juice and lemon rind, sherry, soy sauce or tamari, basil, oregano, thyme, and sage. Bring to a boil, reduce the heat, and simmer until the lentils are tender (2-2¹/2 hours), adding more liquid as needed.

Season with salt and pepper and Tabasco sauce to taste, adding a dash or more of garlic powder if needed. Add the spinach or parsley and cook 10-15 minutes more. Thin to the desired consistency.

FAVORITE SPLIT PEA SOUP *yields 2-3 quarts*

My favorite way to serve this soup is to place some cooked pasta and cubes of Cheddar cheese in each bowl then ladle on the steaming hot soup. Pasta adds a wonderful extra chew and the cheese softens and melts slightly, giving additional subtle flavor as well as tiny intense mouthfuls of pure cheese smoothness. And, if you have any leftover cooked meats, you can add them to this already satisfying meal in a bowl.

1 1/2-2 cups diced onion or white of leek
   1/2 cup diced carrot
   1/2 cup diced celery

3-4 Tablespoons olive oil or rendered prosciutto or bacon fat*
  1 pound split peas, rinsed
  6 cups liquid (I suggest half chicken stock, half water)
  1 Tablespoon soy sauce or tamari, or to taste
 1/2 teaspoon marjoram, or to taste
 1/4 teaspoon allspice, or to taste
 1/4 teaspoon sage
    Salt and freshly ground pepper to taste

garnish

Pasta cooked al dente or cooked spaetzle
Cheddar cheese, cubed
Sliced cooked sausage or diced leftover chicken, turkey, or pork, etc.

In a soup pot or large casserole sauté the onion, carrot, and celery in olive oil or rendered prosciutto or bacon fat until the onion is translucent and tender. Add the split peas, stock and water, soy sauce or tamari, marjoram, allspice, and sage. Bring to a boil and simmer until the split peas are soft. If you want a very smooth soup, puree in a blender or put through a food mill. Thin to the desired consistency and season with salt and pepper to taste.

To serve, put cooked pasta or spaetzle, cheese, and meat in soup bowls and ladle on hot soup.

VEGETARIAN SPLIT PEA SOUP

Omit the prosciutto or bacon fat and the ham bone and add 1 clove garlic and a few drops of liquid smoke.

*You can use olive oil and simmer a ham bone in the soup for a traditional smoky flavor.

GINGERED CARROT
AND PEAR BISQUE *yields 7-8 cups*

The flavors of this soup are exquisite. When you taste it you *know* that ginger, carrot, and pear were meant to be together.

  1 cup (or more) diced onion
  2 Tablespoons (1/4 stick) butter
  1 Tablespoon chopped fresh gingerroot
  2 cups chicken stock (see p. 50)
  1 pound carrots, peeled and cut into chunks
  2 large, ripe pears (Bosc, if possible), unpeeled, stems and cores removed, flesh chopped coarse (you will have about 2 cups)
1/2 cup cooked white or brown rice
  1 bay leaf
1 1/2-2 cups cream or half milk/half cream
    Salt and freshly ground pepper to taste
    Generous pinch of sugar

garnish
  2-3 strips finely julienned carrot

Sauté the onion in butter until it is translucent and tender, adding the ginger during the last minute or two of sautéing. Add the chicken stock, carrots, pears, rice, and bay leaf and simmer, partially covered, until the carrots are tender. Remove the bay leaf. Puree the mixture in a blender, adding cream or milk and cream to thin to the desired consistency. Season with salt and pepper and the pinch of sugar. Serve hot or chilled, garnished with julienned carrot.

CREAM OF
BROCCOLI STALK SOUP *yields about 4 1/2 cups*

Here's a delicious solution for what to do with those broccoli stalks left over after you've cut off the flowerets for stir-fry or other dishes. Reserve some cooked flowerets if you can, and garnish each bowl of soup with a tiny sprig.

  1 cup (or more) diced onion
  1 small clove garlic, minced
  2 Tablespoons (1/4 stick) butter
    Stalks from 1 large bunch broccoli (2 1/2-3 cups, cut up)
1/2 cup pasta, cooked al dente
    About 1 1/2 cups chicken stock (see p. 50)
    About 1 cup cream or half milk/half cream
    Salt and freshly ground pepper to taste
    Several gratings of fresh nutmeg

Sauté the onion and garlic in butter until the onion is translucent and tender. Remove the tough ends of the broccoli stalks and cut the stalks into small chunks. Add these to the sautéed onion along with the pasta and chicken stock. Simmer, partially covered, until the broccoli is tender, about 10 minutes. (Do not overcook to the point where the broccoli is mushy and has lost its greenness.)

Transfer the mixture to a blender and puree until smooth, adding enough cream or milk and cream to thin to the desired consistency. Season with salt and pepper and grated nutmeg.

CREAM OF BROCCOLI STALK SOUP II

Substitute fish stock (see p. 51) or clam juice for the chicken stock. Use 1-2 cut-up potatoes instead of the pasta and add cooked fish or seafood if you have it.

CURRIED
BUTTERNUT BISQUE *yields about 6 cups*

Butternut squash gives a creamy, buttery texture and rich taste, deepened and sweetened by cinnamon and aromatic curry.

1½ cups diced onion or white of leek
 ½ cup diced celery
  2 Tablespoons (¼ stick) butter
  1 clove garlic, minced
  1 teaspoon (or less) curry powder
  2 cups chicken stock (see p. 50)
1½ pounds butternut squash, peeled and cubed
  1 bay leaf
  1 small stick cinnamon
 ¾ teaspoon salt
    Dash cayenne pepper
    About ¾-1 cup cream or
    half milk/half cream

garnish
    Paprika, cayenne pepper, or
    ground cinnamon

Sauté the onion or leek and celery in butter until softened. Add the garlic and curry powder and sauté briefly. Add the chicken stock, butternut squash, bay leaf, cinnamon stick, salt, and cayenne. Cover and cook until the squash is tender. Remove the bay leaf and cinnamon stick.

Puree the mixture in a blender, adding enough cream or milk and cream to thin to the desired consistency. Taste for seasoning. Reheat and serve garnished with a dash of paprika, cayenne, or cinnamon.

CREAM OF
CAULIFLOWER AND
CHEDDAR CHEESE SOUP *yields 6-7 cups*

A pleasant soup—hot, light, and cheesy. Scallions will give it a pale green color. You can prepare the soup without cheese as well and serve it, hot or cold, as a cream of cauliflower bisque. In either version, add ½-1 Tablespoon finely minced capers for a lovely flavor expansion.

  2 cups chopped green of scallion or
    diced onion
  4 Tablespoons (½ stick) butter
  1 head cauliflower, broken up
    (about 1¾ pounds)
  2 cups chicken stock (see p. 50)
1-1½ cups cream or half milk/half cream
    About 4 ounces Cheddar cheese, grated
    Salt and freshly ground pepper to taste

garnish
    Cayenne pepper and/or minced
    fresh chives

Sauté the scallion or onion in butter until tender. Add the cauliflower and stock and cook, partially covered, until the cauliflower is tender.

Puree the mixture in a blender or food processor until it is smooth, adding enough cream or milk and cream to thin to the desired consistency. Return to the saucepan and add the Cheddar cheese. Cook over low heat, stirring, until the cheese is melted. Season with salt and pepper to taste.

To serve, garnish with a dash of cayenne pepper and a light sprinkling of minced fresh chives if you have them.

SPINACH
WALNUT BISQUE *yields 4 1/2 cups*

Rich, and best appreciated in moderate portions, this easy-to-prepare soup is also delicious served cold.

    One 10-ounce package frozen spinach
  2 cups chicken stock (see p. 50)
  8 ounces cream cheese
 1/2 cup walnuts
 1/4 cup freshly grated Parmesan cheese
    Salt and freshly ground pepper to taste

garnish
    Grated Parmesan cheese or finely chopped
    walnuts

Cook the spinach in the stock until it is fully defrosted and lightly simmering in the stock. Place the cream cheese, broken up, in the jar of a blender. Add the walnuts and grated Parmesan then pour in the hot spinach and stock mixture.

  Blend at high speed until the mixture is well pureed and evenly green. Season with salt and pepper to taste. Serve hot garnished with a light sprinkling of grated Parmesan or finely chopped walnuts. If serving chilled, thin with milk or cream to the desired consistency.

NANTUCKET
SCALLOP CHOWDER *yields 11 cups*

Serve with Fruited Soda Bread with Nuts and Caraway for a hearty but elegant meal.

  4 Tablespoons (1/2 stick) butter
 1/4 pound bacon, minced*
  2 Tablespoons minced shallot, or more to taste
 1/2 cup all-purpose flour
  4 cups fish stock (see p. 51) or clam juice
  2 cups cream or half milk/half cream
 1 1/2 pounds (about 3 good-sized) potatoes, peeled,
    diced, and cooked until tender
    One 10-ounce package frozen asparagus,
    defrosted and cut into 1-inch lengths**
  1 pound scallops (quartered if scallops are large)
    A dash Tabasco sauce
    Salt and freshly ground pepper to taste

Melt the butter in an enamel or stainless steel saucepan. Add the minced bacon and shallot and sauté until bacon is done but not crisp. Add the flour and cook over medium heat for several minutes, whisking and being careful that the "roux" doesn't darken and lose its golden color. If the roux gets too thick, add a little more butter. Add the fish stock or clam juice and cook over medium-high heat, whisking occasionally, until the mixture begins to thicken. Add the cream, whisking until the mixture thickens. Add the cooked potatoes, asparagus, and scallops and simmer over medium heat until the scallops are just cooked through. Add the Tabasco sauce and salt and pepper.

*If you would like a milder bacon flavor, decrease the amount of bacon by 1-2 ounces and increase the butter by 1-2 Tablespoons.
**You can substitute freshly cooked asparagus or other fresh or thawed frozen green vegetables.

A SIMPLE AND SIMPLY BEAUTIFUL FISH SOUP *yields about 2 quarts*

There is a lovely clarity and delicacy to this soup with its pieces of fish and pasta, herbs and bits of leek floating atop an aromatic tomato-flecked broth. Use chunks of fish left over from stock making for an inexpensive but still elegant soup. Or purchase a variety of fish and seafood to create a glorious and filling bouillabaisse dinner. You can substitute diced cooked potatoes or chick-peas for the pasta. And you can add vegetables: diced or sliced zucchini, or diced cabbage, or short lengths of green beans, cooked to tender crispness in the broth before adding the fish. You can also add more herbs, thyme especially, plus generous pinches of basil and oregano for a deeper Mediterranean or Italian emphasis.

Whether presented in its most simple or ornate versions, accompany with homemade bread and follow with a tossed salad, for a light, satisfying meal.

1-2 cloves garlic, minced
  1 cup chopped white of leek, or a combination of minced scallion and diced onion
  1 large carrot, sliced thin
  2 Tablespoons olive oil
  4 cups fish stock (see p. 51)*
    One 1-pound can tomatoes
  1 bay leaf
    Pinch of saffron
    Salt and freshly ground pepper to taste
  1 cup (or more) small or medium pasta shells or other pasta form, partially cooked

* You can use part clam juice. If you do not have any fish stock, use 2 cups clam juice, double the amount of tomatoes called for, and add a little dry white wine.

1/2-1 pound fish or mixed fish and seafood, diced or cut into chunks*
  2 Tablespoons (or more) minced fresh parsley

In an enamel or stainless steel saucepan sauté the garlic, leek, and sliced carrot in olive oil until the leek is tender. Be careful not to let the vegetables brown. Add the fish stock, tomatoes, bay leaf, saffron, and salt and pepper. Simmer for 15-20 minutes to blend the flavors. Add the pasta, fish and/or seafood, and parsley and simmer briefly until the fish is cooked and the pasta is tenderly al dente.

* Half a pound to a pound of fish will give you a soup with fish or seafood in it. As you increase the amounts you will be creating more and more of a bouillabaisse or seafood stew.

HOT BEET SOUP WITH DILLED MEATBALLS *yields about 4 1/2 quarts*

This soup is also good in a meatless version. If you eliminate the meatballs, consider preparing your spaetzle with dill.

8 medium-size beets
4 cups liquid (combination rich chicken or beef stock and water)
2 cups diced cabbage
2 cups finely diced onion
  One 28-ounce can crushed tomatoes
  About 1/4 cup brown sugar (packed) or honey, or to taste
  Juice of 1/2 large lemon, or to taste
  Salt and freshly ground pepper to taste
  Dilled Meatballs (following recipe)

garnish
  Cooked spaetzle or steamed potatoes
  Minced scallion

Peel and halve the beets. Place them in a stainless steel or enamel saucepan and add the 4 cups stock and water, cabbage, and onion. Bring to a boil, partially cover, and simmer until the beets are tender but slightly underdone (25–30 minutes).

Remove the beets and grate them by hand or food processor then return the beets to the pot. Add the tomatoes, a 28-ounce can's measure of water, and enough brown sugar or honey and lemon juice to give a light sweet-and-sour flavor. Season with salt and pepper. Bring the mixture to a simmer.

Gently drop in the Dilled Meatballs, return to the simmer, and cook for 20–30 minutes, or until the meatballs are done. Taste and adjust seasoning.

Ladle hot soup into bowls. Add spaetzle or steamed potatoes and garnish with minced scallions.

DILLED MEATBALLS *yields 16–20*

    1 pound lean ground beef
  1/2 cup bread crumbs
    1 egg
    1 rounded Tablespoon sour cream (optional)
  1/4 cup minced scallion
  1/4 cup minced fresh dill, or 1 Tablespoon (or more) dried
  1–2 Tablespoons minced fresh parsley
    About 1 1/2 teaspoons salt
    Freshly ground pepper to taste

Combine the ingredients, mixing well. Form into walnut-size balls.

SCOTCH BROTH *yields 3 quarts*

stock
2-3 pounds stewing lamb (neck, shoulder, breast), cut up
       Stock vegetables (onion, carrot, celery, parsley—these need not be peeled)
       Water to cover (better yet: part beef stock)
       Beef bouillon cube (optional)

soup
  1/2 cup barley, rinsed
  1/4 cup split peas, rinsed
1 1/2 cups diced onion
    1 cup carrots, peeled and cut into 1/4-3/8-inch slices
    1 cup yellow turnip (rutabaga), peeled and cut into 3/4-inch dice
    1 cup potatoes, peeled and cut into 3/4-inch dice
  1/2 pound mushrooms, sliced
       Additional water or stock
       Salt and freshly ground pepper to taste

Place the lamb, stock vegetables, water and stock, and optional bouillon cube in a soup pot. Bring to a boil, lower the heat, and simmer until the lamb is tender. Remove the lamb and separate the meat from the bones. Set the meat aside. Strain the broth, discarding the vegetables, and refrigerate the broth overnight. Remove most of the fat that has solidified on top of the broth, leaving a little for flavor.*

Return about 6 cups of the stock to the pot. Add the barley and split peas and simmer for 20-30 minutes. Add the onion, carrots, turnip, potatoes, mushrooms, and additional water or stock as needed. Simmer until the barley and vegetables are tender, about 35-40 minutes. Add the cooked lamb. Season to taste with salt and pepper and serve.

*If you have very lean lamb, you can eliminate the overnight refrigera-

WON TON SOUP

       Chicken stock (see p. 50) (1-2 cups per person)
       Shrimp and Tofu Won Tons (p. 61) (3-4 per person)*
       Dark sesame oil
       Tamari or soy sauce
       Shredded fresh spinach, stems removed
       Minced scallion

garnish
       Minced scallion

Bring to a simmer enough chicken stock for the number of people you are serving. Add Shrimp and Tofu Won Tons and simmer for 5-8 minutes, depending on the size of the won tons and whether they are fresh or frozen. For the last few minutes of cooking add a few drops each per serving of sesame oil and tamari, then stir in some shredded spinach and minced scallion. Serve when the spinach is wilted. Garnish with additional minced scallion, if desired.

*You can use dumplings or won tons formed in the classic dumpling or won ton shapes or just place some filling in the center of the wrapper (square or round), put water on the dough around the filling and bring the edges of the dough up around the filling, pinching or squeezing it together to seal.

tion, but this is really the best and easiest method for removing fat from a stock. Another way is to move the stockpot off the center of the heating element, turning the heat up to the highest setting. Part of the soup will boil, and the fat will migrate to the nonbubbling surface where you can skim it off more easily.

AUNT CLARA'S
FRUIT SOUP *yields about 4 cups*

This is a very simple and very delicious soup. Pitting the cherries can be a little time consuming, particularly if you want to make this soup in quantity; so just settle into a relaxing and juicy hands-on task.

1 pound fresh cherries
2 large ripe peaches
2 ripe plums
   Honey or sugar to taste

garnish
   Sour cream, or a combination of sour cream and unflavored yogurt

Remove the stems and pits from the cherries. Cut the cherries in half and dig out the pits over the pot you'll be cooking in (a stainless steel or enamel pot is best) so you catch all the juice, then drop the pitted fruit right into the pot. Blanch the peaches and plums in boiling water for a minute or two and peel off the skin. Cut up the pulp and add it to the pot along with the pits. (Clara says the peach and plum pits add flavor to the soup.) Add water just barely to cover the fruit. Bring to a boil, then simmer, uncovered, for 20–30 minutes. Add honey or sugar to taste—a small amount is all that is needed to sweeten slightly and heighten the flavors of the fruit.

At this point Clara beats the soup with a hand eggbeater to break up the pulp. I blend it briefly in the blender, being careful not to puree it. Sometimes I add sour cream at this point, sometimes I choose to keep the deep red color of the soup unchanged. Chill the soup and serve it cold with a dollop of sour cream or a combination of sour cream and yogurt.

SUMMER
BLUEBERRY GRAPE SOUP *yields 7 1/2 cups*

A light, refreshing, sweet-tart soup. For a little extra sophistication add 1/4–1/2 cup dry vermouth. The fruity Boissière dry vermouth is my choice.

1 pint blueberries, rinsed and picked over
1 pound seedless red grapes, rinsed and removed from the stem
1 pound seedless green grapes, rinsed and removed from the stem
1 quart unflavored yogurt
2–3 Tablespoons honey
1/8 teaspoon vanilla extract

In a blender or food processor puree the blueberries, red and green grapes, 2 cups of the yogurt, 2 Tablespoons of the honey, and the vanilla. Stir in the remaining yogurt and taste; add additional honey, if desired. Turn into a pitcher or glass bowl and serve. Or chill for an hour or two before serving. The blueberries on the surface of the soup will discolor slightly—just stir them down into the soup.

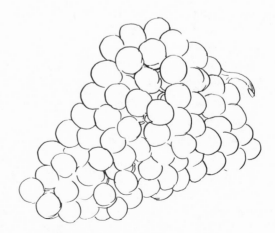

CHILLED
FRESH BEET BORSCHT *yields about 4 cups*

Served with Kasha and Potato Pie, this soup contributes to an earthy and soul-satisfying summer meal. For an elegant soup course or light lunch, accompany the soup with regular or oversize Seafood Mousse Turnovers filled with fresh salmon and dill or sole with minced smoked salmon and dill.

4 medium-large beets
2 cups water
1 cup chicken or beef stock
(see pp. 50–51), or additional water
1/2 cup diced onion or white of leek
3 Tablespoons honey, or to taste
Juice of 1/2 small lemon
2 teaspoons salt, or to taste

garnish
Sour cream
Minced scallion

Peel and halve the beets. Place in an enamel or stainless steel saucepan with the water, stock, and diced onion or leek. Simmer until the beets are tender. Grate the beets in the food processor, or by hand directly into the pot. Add honey, lemon juice, and salt to taste, remembering that flavors will be muted by chilling.
   Serve the soup cold with a dollop of sour cream and a sprinkling of minced scallion.

QUICK BEET
AND ORANGE SOUP *yields 8 cups*

Two 1-pound cans shoestring beets
1 can measure of orange juice
1 can measure of unflavored yogurt or sour cream

garnish
Sour cream (optional)
Finely minced chives or scallion and/or orange rind cut in very fine julienne

Empty 1 can of the beets into a bowl. Pour the other can of beets into a blender. Use one of the empty cans as a measure and add a can measure of orange juice and a can measure of yogurt to the blender with the beets. Blend the mixture until liquefied then stir into the unblended beets. Chill and serve with a dollop of sour cream, if desired. Garnish with a sprinkling of chives or scallion and/or a few julienne strips of orange rind.

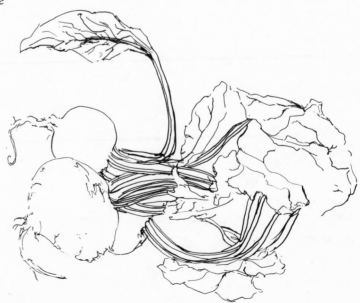

FRESH
TOMATO BORSCHT *yields 4-5 cups*

Your borscht will only be as good as your tomatoes, so it's important to use deep red, full-flavored in-season tomatoes. If you pass a farm stand or farmer's market offering baskets of burstingly ripe red fruit at a fantastic price and wishfully wonder, "How can I use all that?"—think borscht!

3-4 pounds (or more) ripe summer tomatoes
    Basil to taste
    Sugar to taste
    Salt and freshly ground pepper to taste

garnish
    Sour cream

Blanch the tomatoes in boiling water for 1-2 minutes then peel. Cut up the tomatoes and place them in a stainless steel or enamel saucepan with enough water just barely to cover. Season with a little basil and a very light sprinkling of sugar. Simmer for 20-30 minutes, breaking up the tomatoes even more with the back of a spoon. Season with salt and pepper, remembering that flavors will be muted when the soup is chilled. Refrigerate the borscht and serve it cold with a dollop of sour cream.

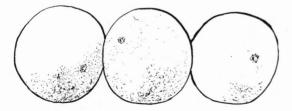

SUMMER CHILLED
DILLED GREEN SOUP

This is an improvisational soup, fun to prepare when you've come home from a farmer's market or a friend's garden (or in from your own) laden with green stuff. Amounts and types of vegetables are variable. Just be sure to use zucchini and peas, since they give the soup body—and dill. Its refreshing light flavor seems to unify all the diverse vegetable elements.

1-2 large zucchini
  1 cup (or more) shelled fresh peas
  1 large handful green beans
3-4 (or more) scallions
1-2 stalks celery
    A handful chopped lettuce
    Fresh dill (be very generous)
    Fresh parsley
    Chicken stock (see p. 50)
    Cream or half milk/half cream
    Salt and freshly ground pepper to taste
    (I prefer this soup on the peppery side)

garnish
    Fresh dill sprigs or thin slices radish or lemon

Chop the vegetables and herbs coarse and put them in a saucepan with enough rich chicken stock just barely to cover. Simmer until the vegetables are tender. Puree the mixture in a blender, adding the cream or milk and cream to thin the soup to the desired consistency. Season with salt and pepper to taste, remembering that flavors will be muted when the soup is cold.

    Serve chilled garnished with sprigs of fresh dill or thin slices of radish or lemon.

STOCKS
AND STOCK MAKING

A good stock is a marvelous thing. It is the basis for soups, sauces, and flavorful grain dishes. Yet, what is it but water transformed in long, slow cooking with flavors given up to it by all the ingredients in the pot? Strained, skimmed, and reduced in volume, it is the search for heightened flavor realized in a single brew. And what creates such magic? Onions, carrots, celery, parsley, the so-called aromatic vegetables that are the staples of our vegetable bins. Salt and pepper and sometimes simple herbs. And bones! Bones with scraps of chicken, meat, or fish on them. Shrimp shells. Roasted turkey carcasses. The weeds in somebody else's garden, someone else's discards. But not mine.

This is a wonderful joke that bubbles up in me like a gently simmering stock—that something so fine and important, a veritable flavor essence, can be so easy, accessible, and inexpensive to prepare. In the past, the very word "stock" would conjure up in me intimidating images of French chefs and huge copper pots in professional kitchens. But, really, it's just clear soup. And I know how to make that!

It's this I've realized: stock making is more of an attitude and a general method than any special recipe or technique; and it can be done with the left hand; fitted without fuss into the ongoing processes of cooking. You can do as much or as little stock making as fits your eating habits and cooking needs, putting an occasional pot on to simmer when chickens or beef bones are on sale or a turkey or beef roast has been polished off, leaving those inviting bones. Or you may be like me, unquenchable maker and user of stocks, ever on the lookout for raw materials . . . the guest who leaves with the wrapped-up remains of the party turkey nestled in her arms, on its way to becoming a bubbling pot of stock.

CHICKEN STOCK

Chicken stock is the one I prepare and use most often. Once you are comfortable with preparing this, you can prepare meat and fish stocks with slight variations in ingredients and method. I begin my stock with either a broken-up chicken carcass and/or several pounds of rinsed and cut-up chicken parts. I place the chicken in a pot large enough to hold it comfortably and with room for a large onion, halved or quartered; 2 or 3 carrots, scrubbed and broken in half; 1 or 2 stalks of celery; and a handful of fresh parsley. Amounts are informal, depending on how much chicken there is, how large the carcass is, even how much of that bunch of parsley in the fridge is still fresh and usable. I add water to cover, sprinkle on salt and freshly ground pepper or whole peppercorns, bring the pot to a boil over high heat then immediately lower the heat. I let the stock simmer for several hours, replacing water as needed, until all the ingredients have sacrificed their flavors to the stock.

Traditionally one of the major ingredients in fine stock making is time, lots of it—hours of slow simmering that fill a kitchen, a whole house or apartment really, with the richest of aromas. I'm flexible about time, though. If I'm preparing stock from chicken parts and have the double motive of also arriving at cooked chicken for salad, I'll remove the chicken when it is done—before it has given all its flavor to the pot. Sometimes I'll remove the meat and return the bones to the pot to continue simmering. If I don't, this particular stock is done when the chicken is removed. I also often use a pressure cooker to prepare stock. In a mere 30–45 minutes it seems as if every bit of flavor and nutritional essence is urged into the stock.

Whatever timing or method you choose, the next step is to strain the stock and refrigerate it overnight. The fat congeals at the top and is easily scraped off and discarded. Ideally what you will have left is a deeply flavored, thickly jelled stock. If your result falls short of the ideal, no matter. It needs only to be boiled down, "reduced" in volume, to arrive at an appropriate intensification of flavor.

Boiling down and reducing stock is a handy technique with a dual benefit. First, and most important, it is a way to intensify the flavor of a stock and thereby intensify exquisitely the flavors of the dish in which it is playing a contributing role. Stock can be reduced a little or a lot, even down to a syrupy essence that can be frozen and added in small amounts to heighten the very fish-ness or chicken-ness or meat-ness of a dish. It takes a lot of stock to produce a very small amount of syrup; but you have a choice as to where in the range from soup to syrup you want your stock to end up.

Therein lies a second benefit in reducing: you can control the finished volume of your stock for easy refrigerator or freezer storage. Use the however-richly-reduced stock as is, or reconstitute it with water as appropriate for the recipe you are preparing.

At this point stock can be refrigerated for several days or frozen for longer. Reduced stock frozen in ice cube trays or small round containers (then popped out once frozen and stored in a plastic bag so you have the use of the container) takes up less freezer space and makes stock available in handy amounts. I like to freeze 1/2 cupfuls of chicken stock in small square plastic containers. When the stock is a thin solid sheet it can be removed and stored in a plastic sandwich bag, 3–4 sheets to a bag. When I need a small amount of stock, for stir-frying for example, I just remove 1 of the stock sheets and warm it back to liquid consistency.

BEEF STOCK

The method for preparing beef stock is similar to that for chicken stock. Substitute meaty beef bones or a combination of bones and soup meat for the chicken. Roasting the bones and vegetables in a hot oven until the bones are browned is a technique that deepens the flavor of the stock. Since beef is a heartier stock than chicken, it benefits from the addition of herbs—thyme and bay leaf, 1 or 2 cloves pressed into the onion used with the other aromatic vegetables—even a few cloves of unpeeled garlic.

FISH STOCK

There are important unique features in preparing fish stock. Put a broken-up fish frame (head and bones) or a combination of bones and chowder fish in an enamel or stainless steel pot. Cover with water and a generous small proportion of dry white wine or vermouth. The stock will simmer for only 30 minutes, since longer cooking creates a bitter taste. So, slice your vegetables thinly so that they will be able to impart their flavors to the stock in this briefer amount of time. Add parsley, a bay leaf, some thyme, salt and pepper, and a few thin slices of lemon.

Clam juice is an excellent and easily available substitute for fish stock. It can be simmered with stock vegetables, herbs, and white wine for an even finer result. Sometimes I use clam juice as part of the liquid in a fish stock. If I have shrimp or even lobster shells (cajoled from my fish market) I'll add them to the pot. All of these things enrich the flavor of the stock. Commercial beef and chicken stocks are less satisfactory substitutes for homemade, but these, too, can be improved on by simmering with stock vegetables and reducing the volume.

CHINESE HORS D'OEUVRES	Emmy's Spring Rolls
	Spring Rolls II
	Homemade Dumpling Dough
	Chinese Steamed Dumplings (Jao-Tze)
	Shrimp, Scallop, or Fish Dumplings with Spinach
	Chinese Dipping Sauce
	Chinese Mustard
	Shrimp and Tofu Won Tons
PASTRY HORS D'OEUVRES	Turnover Pastry
	Sour Cream Pastry for Turnovers
	Seafood Mousse Turnovers
	Mushroom Marsala Turnovers
	Mushroom Pecan Turnovers
	Mexican Cheese Bean Turnovers
	Empanadas (Mexican Meat Turnovers)
	Empanada Tarts
	Kasha Knishes
	Kasha and Potato Tarts
CHEESES IN PASTRY AND BRIOCHE	En Croûte Pastry
	Brie en Croûte
	Miniature Brie or Camembert en Croûte
	Cheese in Brioche
OTHER OPENING DELIGHTS	Hummus
	Guacamole
	Party Guacamole
	Tortilla Crisps
	Eggplant Walnut Pesto
	Eggplant Tuna Parmesan

For appetizers using phyllo, see pages 99-100.

With hors d'oeuvres and appetizers I offer my guests a very special welcome. A few mouthfuls of exquisite flavors, a glass of wine, the gentle laughter while sharing news and catching up, or getting to know someone better—these create a very special feeling and suggest the pleasures of food and friendship to come.

As with conversations and people, I appreciate variety in these small tastes. I might bring out golden pastry turnovers with mouth-watering mushroom fillings, or spicy-smooth cheese, chilis, and beans. Or serve finely layered phyllo filled with an unusual raisiny spanokopita or dill-flecked seafood mousse. One or two of any of these buttery pastries will awaken hunger even as they begin to satisfy it. (See p. 90-92 for recipes for preparing phyllo hors d'oeuvres and main course strudel.)

I prepare these hors d'oeuvres ahead, when I have the time and wish to play and create with dough. They all freeze beautifully, separated by waxed paper and wrapped in heavy-duty foil. Whether I am entertaining 1 friend or 20, I can simply open my freezer and take out what I need.

Whatever hors d'oeuvres I choose, I feel I am subtly orchestrating a special event, striving for a balance of flavors and textures, both within my choices and in relation to the dinner to come. I am careful, too, about how much I serve, for I want my guests to feel full of anticipation, not food, when they sit down to the table.

There are many ways to begin. Larger parties suggest an elegant Cheese in Brioche or Brioche Lattice Loaf or a magnificent Brie en Croûte. Any occasion is enhanced by delicately crunchy won tons or spring rolls or juicy steamed Chinese dumplings. Cold tortellini or won tons in intensely flavored dressing (see the chapter on salads) are wonderful tastes on a toothpick, as are crisp fried oysters or Hoi Sin Spicy Chicken or Beef on a Skewer (see the chapter on poultry, meat, and seafood). Several of these can serve as a generous prelude to a delicious stir-fry dinner. Or try Chatham Clam Crêpes (p. 116) or Sausage Crêpe Rolls (p. 117), especially good to use for a brunch.

Still another truly memorable way to serve these beginnings is not really as a beginning at all, but as an hors d'oeuvre party of continuous tastes that goes on all evening long. Until it's time for sweet restitution for the evening's end in the form of fantastic desserts.

CHINESE HORS D'OEUVRES

You don't have to go to a Chinese restaurant to experience incredible tastes and share them with friends. You can prepare your own tender dumplings filled with pork or seafood and steamed to moist, pearly translucence. You can create won tons stuffed with shrimp paste then boiled and tossed in a flagrantly spicy and gingery vinaigrette or fried crisp and golden for dipping in sweet or fiery sauces. You can prepare your own crisp spring rolls easily. And serve flavorful bites of meat on a skewer or succulent spicy-sweet mouthfuls of chicken or duck on the bone, or ribs, or deep-fried walnut chicken crisps.

An Oriental market is the ideal place to stock up on ingredients called for in these recipes: dark aromatic sesame oil, soy sauce or tamari, "dark" soy sauce (a deeper-flavored soy with molasses added), and sweet hoi sin. With the current emphasis on eclectic and healthful cooking styles, Oriental produce, sauces, and oils are now also available in health-food and specialty stores and can often be found in the produce and gourmet sections of supermarkets. The produce section of my supermarket stocks bulk bean sprouts (buy only very white, fresh ones) as well as packaged egg roll and won ton skins made from noodle dough.

If you have never before prepared Chinese dishes, these beginnings are a good place to start. Read ahead in the stir-fry chapter for more information on ingredients and stir-fry technique. And be sure to utilize the Oriental-style recipes in the chapter on meat as part of your repertoire. Use this group of recipes when you want to serve more filling hors d'oeuvres or create the kind of "hors d'oeuvre dinner" we all secretly adore.

I am indebted to old Brooklyn neighbors Emmy and Kuo Wei, who first introduced me to Chinese home cooking. One Sunday afternoon I was invited over for a Chinese brunch of dumplings. Watching Kuo Wei roll out the homemade dough and cut it into rounds then stuff and pleat it, I assumed all I could do was watch. Thankfully I was to learn how easy these dumplings are to make, especially with commercially made wrappers.

Here are 2 recipes for spring rolls. Use them as is, or as springboards for your own combinations and experimentation. In truth, I never make them exactly the same way twice. Any combination of these ingredients stirred up tender-crunchy with a tiny amount of thickened, very flavorful sauce tastes wonderful inside the crispy wrapping dipped in mustard and duck sauce.

If you are able to purchase only conventional egg roll noodle dough wrappers, you will still have a delicious, albeit different, result. You will need about twice the amount of filling for a single egg roll as you would use for a spring roll—and so will have half the number of rolls. Allow about 2 spring rolls and 1 egg roll per person.

Spring rolls can be formed several hours ahead and refrigerated until you are ready to fry them. Even spring rolls left over and fried the next day turn out delicious, although juices from the filling tend to ooze into the wrapper and soften it. A little of this oozing doesn't seem to matter very much, but to cut down on it, make sure your filling is not a wet one. It is also easier, I find, to work with a cool or cold filling. A warm one tends to soften the wrapper.

EMMY'S SPRING ROLLS *yields 20 spring rolls*

1/4 pound raw shrimp, diced
 1 teaspoon sherry
 1 teaspoon cornstarch
1/2 pound ground pork
 1 Tablespoon tamari or soy sauce
 1 Tablespoon cornstarch
   Scant 1 Tablespoon brandy
 1 teaspoon dark soy sauce
 1 teaspoon sugar
 4 Tablespoons oil
 2 slices fresh gingerroot
2-3 carrots, grated (not too fine)
 1 bunch scallions, cut into 1 1/2-inch lengths
1/2 head Chinese cabbage, bottom half only,
   shredded
6-8 dried Chinese mushrooms, soaked, squeezed,
   and shredded
2-3 cups bean sprouts
1/2 teaspoon salt, or to taste
 1 Tablespoon cornstarch mixed with 1/4 cup
   stock or mushroom water
20 spring roll wrappers (2 packages)
 1 egg white, beaten until foamy

Combine the shrimp with the sherry and the tea-spoon of cornstarch. Set aside. Combine the pork with the tamari, Tablespoon of cornstarch, brandy, dark soy sauce, and sugar. Set aside.

Heat a wok until very hot. Add 2 Tablespoons of the oil. When it is shimmering (very hot), add the ginger, stir-fry until it is golden then remove it. Add carrots and stir-fry for 20-30 seconds. Add scallions and stir-fry until they begin to wilt. Add cabbage and mushrooms and stir-fry until the cabbage soft-ens slightly. Add the bean sprouts and salt and stir-fry until the sprouts are crisp-tender. Remove the vegetables to a bowl.

Heat the wok again until very hot. Add the remaining 2 Tablespoons of the oil. When the oil is shimmering, add the shrimp and stir-fry until they are pink and cooked through. Remove with a slot-ted spoon to the bowl with the vegetables. Add the pork and its marinade to the wok and cook, both mashing and breaking up the pork with the back of spoon or stir-fry utensil until the pork is thoroughly cooked. Add the cornstarch and stock mixture. When the liquid has thickened, return the vege-tables and shrimp to the wok and toss to mix ingredients and coat with sauce. Set aside to cool.

Separate the spring roll wrappers carefully. (The package has good directions for this. Wrappers are often sold frozen, and if the ones you get are, they will need to be defrosted.) Place 1 generous Table-spoon of filling along 1 corner, spreading it out to a thin line. Fold the corner of the dough up over the filling. Brush the remaining dough with beaten egg white. Bring the 2 side corners in over the filling, envelope style. Continue rolling up and brushing the last corner with egg white, as needed, to seal. Repeat with remaining 19 wrappers.

Line up on a baking sheet or tray lined with waxed paper and refrigerate until you are ready to fry.

Fry spring rolls in about 1/2 inch hot oil, or enough to come halfway up the side of the roll. Spring rolls fry up *very* quickly. Have your heat high enough so that the oil crisps but does not soak into the rolls (the oil should respond with sounds and bubbling when the roll is put in it) yet not be so hot that the spring roll cooks unevenly or burns. Drain on paper towels. Cut rolls in half if you are using them as "finger food." Serve with small bowls filled with duck sauce and Chinese Mustard.

SPRING ROLLS II *yields 16–20 spring rolls or about 8 egg rolls*

1 Tablespoon tamari or soy sauce (you may use half dark soy sauce)
1 Tablespoon Gingered Sherry (p. 258)
1/2 teaspoon salt
1/2 teaspoon sugar
1/2 teaspoon cornstarch
2 Tablespoons oil
2 Tablespoons dark sesame oil
About 1 cup diced raw shrimp or shredded chicken (optional)
2 cups shredded cabbage
2 carrots, grated (not too fine)
1/2 pound bean sprouts
1 bunch scallions, minced, or 1/2 cup (or more) chopped Chinese chives
16–20 spring roll wrappers (2 packages) or about 8 egg roll wrappers
1 egg white, beaten until foamy

Combine the tamari, sherry, salt, sugar, and cornstarch and set aside.

Heat the wok until it is very hot; add the oils. When the oils are very hot and shimmering, add the shrimp or chicken, if you are using them, and stir-fry until the shrimp has changed color and the chicken crisps slightly. Remove with a slotted spoon and set aside. When the oil is shimmering again, add the cabbage and carrots and stir-fry until the cabbage wilts slightly. Add the sprouts and scallions or Chinese chives and continue stir-frying until the sprouts are wilted but still somewhat crisp. Push the vegetables to the side. Stir the tamari sauce well to mix up the cornstarch then add the sauce to the wok. When the liquid begins to thicken, add the shrimp or chicken and toss with the vegetables to coat. Let cool.

Follow the directions for Emmy's Spring Rolls (preceding recipe) for forming and frying the rolls. (You will need more oil if using egg rolls—the oil should come halfway up the side of the egg roll or spring roll.) Serve the rolls cut in half, with Chinese Mustard (p. 60) and duck sauce.

I love Chinese dumplings and often have them on hand in my freezer. I like to steam them for a quick yet special lunch or use them as an impromptu addition to a simple stir-fry dinner. Dumplings are really quite easy to make, especially if you are using commercial wrappers. Early in my dumpling career I preferred to make my own dumpling dough, liking the slight extra-soft doughiness. Now I choose commercial wrappers for their delicate pearly texture and their convenience. Each has something to recommend it.

Dumplings can be either steamed or boiled. I tend to prefer steaming them and boiling won tons. They can be served immediately or sautéed in a small amount of oil to brown and crisp them slightly. Accompany them with Chinese Dipping Sauce (p. 60).

HOMEMADE DUMPLING
DOUGH *yields 40 round dumpling skins*

2 cups all-purpose flour
3/4 cup hot water

Place the flour in the work bowl of a food processor. Add the hot water through the feed tube with the processor running and process until the dough forms a smooth ball, kneading a few extra seconds until a smooth, nonsticky dough is formed. (Add a small amount of water or flour if necessary.) The dough can also be mixed and kneaded by hand. Place the kneaded dough in a bowl, cover, and let sit for at least 30 minutes.

Divide the dough in half. On a lightly floured surface roll one half of the dough into a sausage shape. Divide into 20 equal pieces. Cover the dough and pieces you are not working with to prevent the dough from drying. Roll each piece into a circle about 3–3½ inches in diameter, rolling the dough a little thinner toward the edges than in the middle. Fill with a generous teaspoonful of filling and seal as you would using commercial wrappers (see following recipe), pleating and pressing the edges together. Place on a lightly floured sheet of waxed paper (flour is necessary, as this dough is softer and stickier than commercial noodle dough). Repeat with the other 19 pieces and the other half of the dough.

Steam or freeze as in the directions for commercial wrappers (see following recipe).

CHINESE STEAMED
DUMPLINGS (JAO-TZE) *yields 65–75 dumplings*

1 pound ground pork
½ pound ground or finely chopped shrimp
2 cups cooked, well-squeezed, and chopped cabbage
1½ cups finely chopped scallion
2 Tablespoon dark sesame oil
2 Tablespoons dark soy sauce
2 Tablespoons Gingered Sherry (p. 258)
2 Tablespoons chicken (p. 50) or mushroom stock
1 Tablespoon plus 1 teaspoon cornstarch
1 teaspoon salt
1 pound round dumpling skins (about 80)*

Combine the pork, shrimp, cabbage, scallion, sesame oil, dark soy sauce, sherry, stock, cornstarch, and salt. Place a generous teaspoon of this filling in the center of a dumpling skin, elongating the filling slightly. Wet the edges of the skin with a finger dipped in water. Bring the opposite edges of skin together, but before you press them together to seal, form pleats with the side of skin facing you, pressing the opposite side of the dough against the pleated side as you pleat. Place the finished dumpling on a baking sheet lined with waxed paper. At this point you can either proceed with steaming or place the entire baking sheet of dumplings in the freezer. When the dumplings are frozen, remove them to plastic bags and seal. Keep frozen until you are ready to steam.

Steam the dumplings, covered, for 15 minutes in a bamboo or other steamer. Or you can create a makeshift steamer using a rack positioned over boiling water in a large covered pot (this works very well). If the dumplings are frozen, add an additional 5 minutes' steaming time.

*If only square won ton or dumpling skins are available, cut out rounds with a 3½-inch cutter.

SHRIMP, SCALLOP, OR FISH DUMPLINGS WITH SPINACH *yields about 40 dumplings*

If you prefer a meatless dumpling, you will find these light and flavorful. Sometimes I alter the amount of spinach in the recipe, particularly when using all scallops. I find that a little more scallop and a little less spinach allows more of the delicate sweet scallop flavor to come through.

Substituting 1/4 pound ground pork for part of the seafood will add to the taste and succulence of these dumplings. If you prepare a double recipe, consider using half pork and half seafood, reducing the sesame oil by half. Remember, too, if you add the pork, increase the steaming time by 5 minutes.

- 3/4 pound raw shrimp, scallops, or sole, or a combination
- 1 egg white
  One 10-ounce package frozen chopped spinach, cooked and well squeezed
- 3/4 cup minced scallion
- 4–6 Chinese mushrooms, soaked, squeezed, and minced fine

- 2 Tablespoons dark sesame oil
- 1 Tablespoon Gingered Sherry (p. 258)
- 1 Tablespoon tamari or soy sauce
- 1/2 Tablespoon oyster sauce
- 1/2 Tablespoon cornstarch
- 1/2 teaspoon salt
- 1–2 Tablespoons reduced mushroom water or rich chicken stock (omit if using all scallops)
- 1/2 pound round dumpling skins (p. 59) (about 40)

Process the shrimp, scallops, and/or fish in a food processor with the egg white. Or grind the seafood and add lightly beaten egg white, mixing together well. Add the remaining ingredients except the dumpling skins and mix well.

Form and cook the dumplings according to the directions for Chinese Steamed Dumplings (preceding recipe), reducing the cooking time by 5 minutes. Serve with Chinese Dipping Sauce (following recipe).

CHINESE DIPPING SAUCE *yields 1/3 cup*

- 1/4 cup red wine vinegar
- 1 Tablespoon tamari or soy sauce
- 1 Tablespoon sesame oil
- 1/2 teaspoon chili paste with garlic
  Minced scallion

Combine the ingredients, increasing proportions as needed. Use as a dipping sauce for steamed dumplings. (About a Tablespoon of leftover sauce can be added to stir-fry dishes for extra zip.)

CHINESE MUSTARD

Dry mustard, such as Colman's
Water

Place 3–4 Tablespoons dry mustard in a bowl (or more depending on the amount you need). Add a small amount of water, stirring to make a smooth paste. Continue adding small amounts of water and stirring until the desired consistency is reached.

SHRIMP AND TOFU WON TONS *yields 100–110 won tons*

These won tons are in their glory served cold, tossed in Szechuan Vinaigrette (see Cold Shrimp Won Tons with Broccoli in Szechuan Vinaigrette, p. 235). They are also spectacular boiled and drained then quickly fried in 1/2 inch or so of hot oil—until all sides are beautifully crisped and browned. Serve these fried won tons with 2 dipping sauces—a sweet duck sauce and Chinese Dipping Sauce (p. 60). Halve the recipe if you wish. Remember, however, that uncooked won tons can be frozen—and be forewarned that a lot is rarely too much!

1 1/4 pounds (or more) raw shrimp with shells on, enough to yield 1 pound shelled*
1 egg
1/2 pound firm-style tofu, broken up (you can also use soft)
1 Tablespoon dark sesame oil
1 Tablespoon soy sauce or tamari
1 teaspoon salt
1/2 cup finely minced scallion
2 pounds square won ton wrappers (110–120)

Place the shrimp in the work bowl of a food processor and process until the shrimp are ground up. Add the egg and tofu and process until the mixture is the consistency of a smooth paste, scraping down with a rubber spatula as needed. Add the sesame oil, soy sauce, salt, and scallion and process until the ingredients are well blended.

Place a short stack of won ton wrappers in front of you with points top and bottom, left and right. Using a regular teaspoon, place a generous 1/2

*Buy the smaller, inexpensive size, since the shrimp will be ground up. And don't forget to make stock from the shells, using water or clam juice or a combination. Drain, reduce, and freeze.

teaspoonful of filling in the middle of the wrapper. Dip your finger in water and wet the top half edge (or upper triangle part) of the wrapper. Bring the bottom triangle up to exactly cover the top triangle. Press along the edges very firmly to seal them. Next, with a finger dipped in water wet the bottom of the right point of the triangle you now have. Pick up the triangle. Grasp the left point with your right thumb and forefinger and pull it under the center of the won ton (or the bottom of the triangle) and curve it around to the right point so you can stick the top of the right point to the top of the left point. ("Top" is the front part of the triangle that has been facing you.) Line up the completed won tons on a baking sheet covered with waxed paper.

At this point you can either boil the won tons or freeze them for future boiling. If you are going to freeze them, place the whole tray or trays in the freezer until the won tons are frozen or at least quite firm. (If freezer space is at a premium, you can have several layers of won ton on one 10 by 15-inch baking pan with the layers of won ton separated by waxed paper.) When the won tons are firm, place them in a double plastic bag or bags and remove as needed. If you are going to cook them immediately, bring a large pot of water to a boil. Cook the won tons in batches in gently boiling water for 3–5 minutes, or until a won ton tests done. Remove the won tons with a slotted spoon to a strainer to drain them then place them in a bowl. Drizzle on a little bit of dark sesame oil and toss the won tons. This will prevent them from sticking together. Refrigerate the won tons until ready to use or serve them immediately with Chinese Dipping Sauce (p. 60). If you are cooking won tons that are frozen, add 1–2 minutes to the cooking time.

PASTRY
HORS D'OEUVRES

Not only are these mouthfuls savory pleasures, but to increase the pleasure still more, all these beginnings can be made ahead and kept frozen until they are needed.

See pages 75–77 for instructions and support on working with pastry, as well as on creating different and complementary pastry doughs.

TURNOVER PASTRY

1½ cups all-purpose flour
10 Tablespoons (1¼ sticks) butter
½ teaspoon salt
2 Tablespoons cream plus 1 Tablespoon wine *or* 1 egg plus 1 Tablespoon wine
Fresh or dried herbs (optional)

SOUR CREAM PASTRY
FOR TURNOVERS

1½ cups all-purpose flour
10 Tablespoons (1¼ sticks) butter
½ teaspoon salt
3 Tablespoons sour cream plus 1 Tablespoon wine *or* ¼ cup sour cream *or* 1 egg plus 2 Tablespoons sour cream

SEAFOOD MOUSSE
TURNOVERS *yields 24–26 turnovers*

The pairing of mousse with flaky, buttery pastry makes a truly elegant hors d'oeuvre. Use the mousse flavorings suggested or let your own imagination guide you. Create very special turnovers entirely of shrimp, or fold fresh crab meat into the mousse mixture, or substitute fresh salmon for the fish or seafood, adding flecks of minced smoked salmon to heighten color and flavor. Serve with cold soup or borscht for an elegant lunch or light supper.

1 recipe Turnover Pastry or Sour Cream Pastry for Turnovers (p. 62)
1 recipe Seafood Mousse I (p. 249)
Egg wash (1 egg beaten with 1 Tablespoon milk or water)

On a lightly floured surface roll out the dough about ⅛–¼ inch thick. Cut out 3-inch rounds, rerolling scraps to use all the dough. Place about 1 rounded measuring teaspoonful (or a regular generous ½ teaspoonful) of mousse in the center of each round. Brush the edge of half the pastry round with egg wash, fold the dough in half to enclose the filling, and press the edges gently but firmly to seal. Press again lightly with the back of the tines of a fork. Prick the tops of the turnovers once or twice with the fork and refrigerate or freeze until ready to bake.

Preheat the oven to 400°F. Bake for 20 minutes, or until the pastry is lightly golden. Bake slightly longer if the turnovers have been frozen.

MUSHROOM MARSALA TURNOVERS *yields 36-38 small turnovers*

Mushroom Marsala Filling is densely mushroomy, subtle with the flavors of wine and cheese. If you would like a larger turnover, use a 3-inch round cutter and slightly more filling.

1 recipe Turnover Pastry (p. 62)
3/4 cup Mushroom Marsala Filling (p. 251)
    Egg wash (1 egg beaten with 1 Tablespoon milk or water)

On a lightly floured surface roll out the dough about 1/4 inch thick, or a little less. Cut out rounds with a 2 1/2-inch cutter, rerolling scraps to use all the dough. Place a scant 1/2 teaspoon of filling on each round. Brush half the edge with a little egg wash, fold to enclose the filling, and press the edges firmly but gently to seal. Press again lightly with the back of the tines of a fork. Prick the tops of the turnovers once or twice with the fork and refrigerate or freeze until you are ready to bake.

Preheat the oven to 400°F. Brush the turnovers with egg wash if you would like a glazed surface. Bake for 20 minutes, or until the turnovers are

lightly golden. Bake slightly longer if the turnovers have been frozen.

MUSHROOM PECAN TURNOVERS

Follow the directions for forming and baking Mushroom Marsala Turnovers, substituting Mushroom Pecan Filling (p. 251).

MEXICAN CHEESE BEAN TURNOVERS *yields 26-28 turnovers*

Spicy, mouth-watering pastries—beany, cheesy, and smooth. Prepare larger turnovers to serve with soup for a light, satisfying meal.

1 recipe Cornmeal Tart and Turnover Pastry (p. 77)
1 recipe Cheese Bean Filling (p. 253)*
    Egg wash (1 egg beaten with 1 Tablespoon milk or water)

On a lightly floured surface roll out the dough about 1/8-1/4 inch thick. Cut circles with a 3-inch round or fluted cutter. Place a scant teaspoon of filling in the center of each round and brush the edges of half the round lightly with egg wash. Press the edges together to form a turnover. Crimp them lightly with the back of the tines of a fork then press the points of the fork once into the top of the

*You will need only about 1 cup of filling. Refrigerate or freeze leftover filling to prepare turnovers another time, or use for making tostadas.

turnover. Place the finished turnovers on an un-greased baking sheet (they can be quite close together so long as they aren't touching). If you want to make these in quantity and store some, line the pan with waxed paper first. This facilitates their removal at a later date. Then the turnovers are ready to refrigerate (or freeze) until you are ready to bake. When they are all formed, refrigerate (or freeze) until ready to bake.

Preheat the oven to 375°F. Brush the turnovers with egg wash if you would like a more finished, shiny crust. Bake for 15–20 minutes, or until lightly browned. Bake slightly longer if the turnovers have been frozen.

EMPANADAS (MEXICAN MEAT TURNOVERS) *yields 26–28 turnovers*

1 recipe Cornmeal Tart and Turnover Pastry (p. 77)
    About 1 cup Picadillo (p. 254)
    Egg wash (1 egg beaten with 1 Tablespoon milk or water)

Prepare according to the directions for Mexican Cheese Bean Turnovers (preceding recipe).

EMPANADA TARTS *yields 24 tarts*

Another Picadillo and cornmeal pastry variation, these tarts take more time to prepare than the turn-overs, but make a particularly charming presentation.

1 recipe Cornmeal Tart and Turnover Pastry (p. 77)
1 recipe Picadillo (p. 254) (you will use about 2 cups)*
    Grated Cheddar cheese
    Minced fresh parsley

Preheat the oven to 400°F.

On a lightly floured surface roll out the dough and cut 2¼-inch rounds with a pastry cutter, pref-erably fluted. Fit the rounds into lightly buttered mini-muffin pans. Fill each round almost to the top with Picadillo and bake for 15–18 minutes. Then lower the heat to 350°F, sprinkle the tarts with grated cheese and a little minced parsley, and return to the oven for 4–5 more minutes.

KASHA KNISHES *yields about 24 knishes*

These have the warming quality of Jewish soul food.

1 recipe Kasha with Herbs (p. 254)**
½ pound potatoes
2 Tablespoons (¼ stick) butter
2 Tablespoons milk
¼–⅓ cup freshly grated Parmesan cheese
1 egg yolk
    Salt and freshly ground pepper to taste
1½ recipes Cottage Cheese Pastry (p. 77)

*For this dish, substitute red bell peppers, if available, for green peppers and dried currants for raisins in the Picadillo recipe.
**Follow the recipe but use ⅔ cup medium buckwheat groats and ¾ cup stock. Add a little more stock if you wish, but keep this mixture on the dry side.

Egg wash (1 egg beaten with 1 Tablespoon milk or water)

Prepare Kasha with Herbs. Wash the potatoes well. (I leave the skins on; if you prefer, you can peel the potatoes.) Chop the potatoes roughly and place them in a small saucepan with just enough water to cover. Cook until the potatoes are tender. Boil or drain off any excess water. (If you drain the water, save it for use in yeast bread making.)

Add the butter, milk, and cheese and beat or mash until creamy and smooth. Let cool.

Combine the kasha mixture, the potato mixture, and the egg yolk. Beat with an electric mixer, mash by hand, or use a food processor. The processor will give the smoothest texture, which is my choice, but be careful not to make it too smooth. Add salt and pepper to taste. You will have about 3¼ cups of filling.

Prepare Cottage Cheese Pastry. You can form the pastry and filling any way you like, including using a turnover form, but here is a suggestion for a thin strudel roll that is baked then cut into individual miniature "knishes." Feel free to change the dimensions of the roll to make it thicker, if you prefer it that way.

Roll out the dough to form a rectangle about 12 by 14 inches. Cut the dough into 3 strips measuring 4 by 14 inches each. Form 3 long rounded sausage-shaped lines of the kasha mixture down the center of each dough strip, leaving a 1-inch border at each of the short ends. Bring the left side of each strip over the kasha, stretching the dough slightly. Brush the right side of the dough with egg wash. Roll the left or filled part of the dough onto the egg-washed dough, pressing or stretching gently

so there is some overlap. Smooth the seam with a finger to seal further.

Preheat the oven to 400°F. Place the kasha rolls seam side down on a buttered baking sheet. Prick the tops with a fork and brush with egg wash. Bake for 20-25 minutes, or until the rolls are lightly golden. Cool slightly and slice. If the rolls were frozen, extend the baking time by 5-10 minutes.

KASHA AND POTATO TARTS *yields 32-34 tarts*

1 recipe Cottage Cheese Pastry (p. 77)
½ recipe filling for Kasha Knishes (see preceding recipe)*
 About ½ cup sour cream
 Finely minced fresh parsley
 Freshly grated Parmesan cheese

Preheat the oven to 400°F.

On a lightly floured surface roll out the dough about ⅛ inch thick. Cut out rounds with a 2¼-inch pastry cutter, preferably fluted. Fit the rounds into very lightly buttered mini-muffin pans. Fill almost to the top with Kasha Knishes filling. Spread about ½ teaspoon of the sour cream over the top of each tart, sprinkle with parsley, and a scant ¼ teaspoon grated Parmesan. Bake for 15-18 minutes. Let cool slightly in the pan before removing.

*Prepare filling for Kasha Knishes but use 1 cup stock when preparing the kasha and use 1 whole egg when mixing the ingredients together.

CHEESES IN PASTRY AND BRIOCHE

An entire wheel of Brie, warmed and meltingly soft, enclosed in golden, flaky pastry is an elegant treat, perfect for a large party of 40-60 and more. Visually impressive, half the fun is in creating a personal pastry design with an entire pastry surface as your palette. Cut long pastry leaves and stems, with tendrils and tiny leaves, and arrange them as a plant that almost flows off the round. Create flowers, abstract designs, initials—as simple or elaborate as your own style, imagination, and the pastry allow. The Brie is rich, small slices go very far—how far will depend on what else is being served. For a smaller party of 20-40 a Brie en Croûte can be made with half-size wheels of Brie or herbed Brie weighing about 2½ pounds instead of 5-6 pounds. And for a cocktail hors d'oeuvre for 4-6 you can create a lovely Miniature Brie or Camembert en Croûte using an 8-ounce wheel.

Cheese in Brioche is another impressive way to present cheese for a party or special occasion. Softly melting cheese (with Mushroom Duxelles, or sautéed onions and herbs) in a large, high round of rich brioche, ready to be sliced into mouth-watering wedges, is my favorite for a party hors d'oeuvre table—guests will devour it—and beautiful, too, as an elegant bread at a table of cold salads and savory meats for either a small or large dinner party. It can be prepared with grated cheese (a great way to use leftover cheese) or half or whole wheels of cheese—choose whichever method suits your budget, supplies, and tastes. And it freezes beautifully—just allow plenty of time for defrosting and reheating to perfect cheese-melting warmth.

EN CROÛTE PASTRY

    4 cups all-purpose flour
   12 Tablespoons (1½ sticks) butter
   ½ cup vegetable shortening
    1 teaspoon salt
    1 egg
   ½ cup cold water, or 1-2 Tablespoons kirsch plus
        enough water to measure ½ cup

If you are using a food processor this is best prepared in 2 batches processing half the recipe for each batch.

BRIE EN CROÛTE

    One 5-pound wheel of ripe Brie*
   1½ recipes En Croûte Pastry (preceding recipe)
        Egg wash (1 egg beaten with 1 Tablespoon
        milk or water)

Remove the paper from the Brie. Reserve most of the ½ recipe of pastry for your design and set aside. Divide the remaining pastry in half. Roll the first half to a round large enough to come up just over the sides of the Brie. Place the Brie in the

*To prepare a half-size wheel of Brie weighing about 2½ pounds, prepare 1 recipe En Croûte Pastry (you will have some left over) and follow the directions for forming and baking the larger wheel.

center of the dough. Brush the side pieces of dough around the cheese with egg wash and press them up onto the sides of the cheese and slightly over the top. Roll out the second piece of dough the same way. Turn the Brie over onto this second round of dough with the pastry side up. Trim the pastry if needed. Brush the sides of the dough around the cheese with egg wash and bring the bottom pastry up, pressing it gently into the sides of the first layer of pastry around the cheese to seal well. Turn the Brie package over again carefully so that the second round of dough you have rolled is on top and tuck it under the sides so that a smooth surface of pastry is all that you see.

Place the Brie on a pizza pan or baking sheet large enough to hold it. Most ideal is to bake the Brie in a pan that can also be used as a serving dish. Roll out the reserved dough and use it to create a design for the top. Brush the decorative pieces of dough with egg wash to help them adhere to the pastry surface. Make several steam holes in the pastry using a chopstick or the handle of a wooden spoon.

The Brie can be refrigerated at this point for several hours or overnight. (It can also be frozen.) Remove it from the refrigerator *at least* 1 hour before baking.

Preheat the oven to 375°F. Brush the entire surface of the Brie with egg wash, covering the sides particularly well. Bake the Brie for 35–45 minutes, or until it is beautifully and lightly golden. Let cool for at least 30 minutes before serving.

Note: There are rare times when the Brie bursts through the pastry and oozes all over the baking pan (and your oven as well). To avoid this, make sure that you don't roll out your dough too thin and that there are no holes or perforations in the dough, especially along the sides and bottom of the Brie. Also, overlap your dough well, especially the second round of dough. And, when you brush with egg wash before baking, brush the sides of the dough heavily where it meets the pan. This seems to provide an extra barrier and strengthening of the side dough wall.

MINIATURE BRIE OR CAMEMBERT EN CROÛTE *serves 4–6*

Miniature Brie or Camembert en Croûte make lovely holiday or house gifts.

One 8-ounce wheel of Brie or Camembert or Camembert with herbs
1 recipe Herbed Pastry with Wine (I recommend dill and Marsala) (p. 76)
Egg wash (1 egg beaten with 1 Tablespoon milk or water)

Follow the directions for forming Brie en Croûte (preceding recipe), simply working on a smaller scale. Preheat the oven to 375°F. Brush the cheese with egg wash and bake for about 30 minutes, or until the pastry is golden. Let cool slightly and cut into 6 wedges. Serve on small plates as an hors d'oeuvre.

CHEESE IN BRIOCHE *serves at least 10-12*

There are two different ways that I prepare a Cheese in Brioche, both using 2 pounds of cheese to create a buttery, light, egg-rich dough centered with a thick layer of meltingly soft cheese. In the first I use grated cheese, often a mixture of ends of cheese that I have stored in my freezer. I use predominantly creamy but solid cheeses like Havarti, sometimes adding some grated Cheddar and a small amount of a smoked cheese like Bruder Basil. I might also choose simply to use 2 pounds of a single cheese like dilled Havarti. The second way I am particularly partial to if I am making two Cheeses in Brioche at one time. I buy a 4-pound wheel of a semisoft cheese such as a Port Salut or St. Paulin, remove the waxy rind, cut the wheel in half horizontally, fitting each solid wheel of cheese into the waiting Brioche. A small whole 2 1/2-pound wheel of Brie can be used in the same way. With either technique I can also spread a thin layer of Mushroom Duxelles or sautéed onion or onion and herbs over the top of the cheese before the brioche is pleated over it.

There are two more methods provided in this book for combining cheese with brioche. One, Brioche with Savory Cheese Filling, appears in the bread chapter (see page 9). It uses less cheese (1 1/2 pounds), combined with sautéed onions and eggs. The result is a light, high round of bread with cheese layered through it—a bread I'm most likely to choose as a flashy accompaniment to a dinner. Stuffed Brioche Lattice Loaf (see page 214) combines cheese with other flavorful fillings for an elegant and cheese-rich calzone. It works equally well as an unusual dinner loaf or a substantial buffet hors d'oeuvre.

1 recipe Easy Processor Brioche (p. 7)
2 pounds cheese (see above)
 Egg wash (1 egg beaten with 1 Tablespoon water, milk, or cream)
 Poppy, caraway, or lightly toasted sesame seeds

When the brioche dough has risen fully, punch it down, kneading very lightly, then let the dough rest for 5 minutes or so. On a very lightly floured surface roll the dough out to an 18–20-inch circle. Fold the dough in quarters and fit it into a well-buttered 9-inch springform pan then open the dough up and let the excess hang over the sides. Put the cheese (either grated cheese or a solid round) in the center of the dough, then stretch the dough gently so that it comes to the edge of the pan or where the pan meets the counter. (This stretching may not be necessary if the dough is rolled out to a large enough circle.) Bring the dough up over the cheese, beginning at one point and slowly moving around the pan so that the dough forms neat folds or pleats as it comes over the cheese. Take the wad of dough in the center in your thumb and fingers, pinch it together and twist, causing the folds to swirl slightly.

While the brioche is rising in a warm place for 20 minutes (it will not expand much), preheat the oven to 350°F. Brush the top of the dough generously with egg wash and sprinkle generously with seeds. Place the pan on a baking sheet and release the spring, fully expanding the pan. Place the sheet in the oven and bake for 55–60 minutes, or until the brioche is golden.

Remove the bread to a rack to cool. Serve slightly warm. Or cool completely and refrigerate or freeze. Defrost and reheat until the cheese is warm and soft.

OTHER OPENING DELIGHTS

Here are more tastes to add to your hors d'oeuvre repertoire. See pages 116–117 for two crêpe recipes that also work well as hors d'oeuvres, particularly for brunch—though they are by no means limited to this type of entertaining.

HUMMUS *yields about 3 cups*

This is a flavorful and wholesome dip; it's great, too, as a sandwich filling. Stuff half a fresh, soft pita with hummus and add crisp fresh alfalfa sprouts and an accent of Best Pickled Vegetables. Delicious.

- 2 cloves garlic
  Two 1-pound cans chick-peas, drained
- 2/3 cup sesame tahini (or more)
- 1 cup fresh or frozen lemon juice
- 1 1/2 teaspoons salt, or to taste
- 1/2 teaspoon cumin seed or ground cumin*
  Garlic powder to taste (optional)
  Dash Tabasco sauce (optional)

Chop the garlic in a food processor. Add the drained chick-peas and process until ground up. Add the remaining ingredients, processing until smooth. Taste for seasoning. Add additional salt and garlic powder, if desired. (Hummus should have a pleasantly assertive garlic flavor.)

*Cumin adds a very special Middle Eastern flavor accent.

GUACAMOLE *yields 1 1/2–2 cups*

This guacamole is also used as a stuffing for cold pasta shells in the salad on page 226.

- 2 avocados (weighing a combined total of 1 pound or more)
- 1/2 cup finely minced tomato, seeds and juice discarded
  One 4-ounce can green chilis, drained and chopped
- 1 Tablespoon lemon juice
- 2 teaspoons (or more) finely minced onion
- 1/2 teaspoon garlic powder
  Several drops Tabasco sauce
  Salt to taste

Mash the avocado with a fork, leaving tiny chunks for texture. Mix in the tomato, green chilis, lemon juice, onion, garlic powder, Tabasco sauce, and salt. Serve with Tortilla Crisps (see p. 70).

PARTY GUACAMOLE

This creamy guacamole with attractive flecks of green and red is perfect for a large party. Serve it unmolded as a ring, or in a 10–12-cup-capacity glass or pottery bowl, or in two smaller bowls set in large baskets and surrounded by Tortilla Crisps (following recipe) or commercial tortilla chips.

  3 envelopes unflavored gelatin
  ¾ cup liquid*
  6 cups avocado puree (from 8–10 ripe
      avocados, preferably Haas)**
  12 ounces cream cheese, softened
  ⅔ cup lemon juice
  1 bunch scallions, minced fine
      Two 4-ounce cans whole peeled green chilis,
      drained and chopped
  1 medium-large tomato, juice squeezed out and
      chopped fine
  ¼ cup finely minced onion, or to taste
  2–3 teaspoons salt, or to taste
  1–2 teaspoons garlic powder, or to taste
      Tabasco sauce to taste

Lightly oil a 10-cup ring mold and set aside, or have ready a deep glass or earthenware bowl. Sprinkle gelatin over the ¾ cup liquid and let soften. Place cup or container with softened gelatin in simmering water and heat until gelatin is melted and mixture is completely clear.

In a food processor, process enough avocado pulp to yield 6 cups of puree. If you have a small-capacity food processor you will need to do the processing in 2 or more batches. Process cream cheese until it is soft and smooth. Add avocado puree and lemon juice and process until mixture is well combined. With processor running, add the gelatin in a thin stream. Add the minced scallions, chopped green chilis, chopped tomato, minced onion, salt, garlic powder, and Tabasco sauce. Process briefly but combine well. Taste for seasoning and make any necessary corrections.

Pour the guacamole into the lightly oiled mold, cover with plastic wrap, and refrigerate overnight. Unmold when ready to serve. Fill center of ring with parsley, watercress, or a large tuft of alfalfa sprouts—a single 4-ounce package. Serve with homemade Tortilla Crisps, using 4–6 packages of tortillas.

This amount of guacamole will serve 30–50 or more, depending on how much other food is available.

TORTILLA CRISPS

Slice corn tortillas into triangles, 6 for each tortilla. Fry the triangles in hot oil (about ½ inch deep) until crisp and golden. Drain on paper towels.

*Drain the liquid from the 2 cans chopped green chilis called for in the recipe and add enough water to measure ¾ cup.
**A pinch or two of sugar will improve the taste of a less than full-flavored avocado.

Here are 2 unusual dips that use Seasoned Eggplant Puree as their base. Eggplant imparts a smooth creamy texture and a subtle nutty flavor that is pleasing and distinctive. If you already have packets of Seasoned Eggplant Puree prepared and stored in your freezer, these dips are easy to whip up. They are delicious with crackers or raw vegetables, and also become sauces for cold pasta salads.

EGGPLANT WALNUT PESTO *yields 1 1/3 cups*

I love basil pesto, but it's very rich and fresh basil isn't always available. Eggplant Walnut Pesto is a pleasing alternative.

 1 cup Seasoned Eggplant Puree (p. 257)
 1/4 cup finely chopped walnuts
 1 small clove garlic, minced fine
 1-2 Tablespoons finely minced fresh basil, or
    1 teaspoon dried
 2-4 Tablespoons mayonnaise, preferably
    homemade or Hellman's
1/2-3/4 teaspoon salt
    Freshly ground pepper to taste

Combine the ingredients. Serve with crackers, raw vegetables, or as a sauce for cold pasta (see Eggplant Walnut Pasta Salad, p. 225).

EGGPLANT TUNA PARMESAN *yields 1 3/4 cups*

 1 cup Seasoned Eggplant Puree (p. 257)
    One 6 1/2-ounce can chunk light tuna (drain
    oil for dip, include for pasta sauce)
 1/4 cup mayonnaise, preferably homemade
 1/4 cup freshly grated Parmesan or Asiago cheese
 1 clove garlic, minced fine
 1-2 Tablespoons minced fresh basil,
    or 3/4-1 teaspoon dried
3/4-1 teaspoon oregano
 1/2 teaspoon salt, or to taste
    Freshly ground pepper to taste
    Minced fresh parsley or diced pimento

Combine all the ingredients, mashing tuna well with a fork. Serve with crackers or raw vegetables, or use as a sauce for hot or cold pasta (see Eggplant Tuna Pasta Salad, p. 225).

SAVORY PIES,
QUICHES,
AND TARTS

PASTRY CRUSTS	Herbed Pastry with Wine
	Pat-In Yogurt and Mayonnaise Pastry
	Cornmeal Pastry
	Cornmeal Tart and Turnover Pastry
	Ricotta Pastry
	Cottage Cheese Pastry
SAVORY PIES, QUICHES, AND TARTS	Elegant Artichoke Quiche
	Salmon Quenelle Quiche
	Spinach and Avocado Torte
	Carrot and Dill Quiche
	Broccoli and Blue Cheese Quiche
	Eggplant Mushroom Quiche
	Spinach and Tofu Tart
	Dilled Mushroom Tofu Tart
	Ricotta Basil Pie
	Zucchini and Basil Tart
	Torta Rustica
	Tostada Pie
	Kasha and Potato Pie
OTHER PASTRY DELIGHTS	Sole or Seafood and Spinach Pastry Lattice Loaf
	Lattice Loaf Pastry
	Seafood Mousse Strudel Slices with Crab Meat Velouté
	Seafood Mousse Pockets with Crab Meat Velouté
	Spanokopita Turnovers
	Potato and Cheese Turnovers
	Parsnip and Spinach Turnovers
	Carrot and Almond Bisteeya
	Spanokopita Pie
	Individual Potato Strudels
	Mushroom Marsala or Mushroom Pecan Phyllo Strudels
	Seafood Mousse in Phyllo
	Carrot Almond Bisteeya Hors d'Oeuvre Pastries
	Phyllo Nests
	Eggs Jacobson
	Golden Huevos Rancheros
	Picadillo Pinwheel Tarts
	Mexican Cheese Bean Pinwheel Tarts

I love these delectable tastes in a crust, the pairing of flavorful good-for-you fillings with thin, rich flaky pastry or phyllo. I love the bake-ahead, reheat-for-serving reliability that even the most delicate of these pastries offers. And I love, too, the many forms they can take, from familiar quiches to oversized tortes and loaves or individual strudels, turnovers, and tarts. Steamy with goodness, a wedge or slice on a plate demands a fork. And then a mouthful— creamy and melting (sometimes crunchy, too), subtle with herbs, cheese, vegetables, beans, or fish, and, best of all, the pastry, dissolving in every bite.

If you are using pastry dough for your savory pie or tart, here are some suggestions to assist you. Pastry making is basically a simple process.

Butter is cut into flour, a little salt added (and perhaps herbs for a savory pastry or sugar for a sweet one), until the mixture achieves the consistency of fine meal. This can be done by hand with a pastry blender, or with a food processor. Next a small amount of liquid is added, just enough to bind the ingredients and form a soft but unsticky dough, then, a few gentle kneadings on a lightly floured surface to integrate into a smooth round ball and the pastry is ready to be rolled and formed.

A great mystique and even fear often surround pastry making, but actually there are a variety of approaches for producing successful pastry. Some cooks chill *everything*. Butter is the only thing that comes out of my fridge. Some cooks refrigerate their dough before rolling; I prefer to work with a freshly made, soft, responsive dough. Experiment and find the ways that yield the best results for you. You will find you have more choice in technique than you might have thought.

In general, just avoid overhandling, especially overprocessing your dough. Too much working increases the gluten, which is great for bread making but makes pastry tough. When adding liquid in the food processor, add through the feed tube with the motor running and process just until the dough begins to cohere. In rolling and forming, handle your dough with a quick, light touch—and a sense of humor. Often a soft dough that tears and falls apart a bit in the rolling, one you're sure is going to be a mess and a failure, will turn out to be your most flaky crust. Patch where necessary and go on.

A wide range of ingredients is available to you for pastry making. Butter is always my choice for shortening, although vegetable shortening, margarine, and lard are available as alternatives, used alone or in combination.

Choosing liquids is where I especially like to play. I use beaten egg when I need a pastry that will hold up particularly well to forming—as for turnovers or Brie en Croûte. Wines and liqueurs, even reduced clam juice, add subtle flavor essences; mustard, a gentle zip. Heavy cream or sour cream yields a rich and tender pastry, cottage cheese and ricotta a pastry high in protein and tenderly crisp. Yogurt and mayonnaise used together create a pat-in crust that is superbly flaky and easy to make. Combining flavors and textures to create a special complement of filling to crust adds to the challenge of pastry making—and to the pleasures of pastry eating.

Whether you are using these pastry recipes, your own inventions, or even store-bought pastry, it is essential that the pastry be partially baked before the filling is added. Unless you prebake, your finished pie will have a crust that is soft and undistinguished, and you will lose that counterpoint of light, flaky texture to soft filling that makes a pie exciting. Pre-baking is simple. After lining your pie pan, fluting the edge of the dough, and pricking the dough lightly all over with a fork, refrigerate the dough for a short time to firm it. While it is chilling, preheat your oven to 400°F. Then line the slightly chilled pastry with a good-size sheet large enough to hang over the edges—and fill the foil almost to the rim with uncooked rice or beans. This weight will keep the crust from shrinking and losing its shape as it bakes. Bake for 10 minutes to set the pastry then remove the foil and weights carefully and return the pastry to the oven for 10 minutes more, longer if you want a fully baked shell. Now you are ready to add your filling. When your rice or beans have cooled, transfer them to a plastic bag and save for other prebakings.

One final note: for recipes that call for a 9-inch pie pan, a slope-sided traditional pie pan and a removable-bottom quiche pan can be used inter-changeably. Your choices will depend on your visual preferences and the equipment you have. Many of the recipes call for a particular pastry to be used with a particular filling. I hope you enjoy the combi-nations suggested here, but also feel free to create your own.

HERBED PASTRY
WITH WINE *yields 9-inch crust*

    1 cup all-purpose flour
    6 Tablespoons (3/4 stick) butter
    1 teaspoon dried herbs or herb of choice
      (optional)
    1/2 teaspoon salt
    1 egg yolk
    1 Tablespoon wine such as Marsala, sherry,
      Madeira, or white wine

PAT–IN YOGURT AND
MAYONNAISE PASTRY *yields 9-inch crust*

This soft pastry is not rolled out. It is simply patted onto the bottom and sides of a pie or quiche pan.

    1 cup all-purpose flour
    6 Tablespoons (3/4 stick) butter
    1/2 teaspoon salt
      Generous 1 Tablespoon yogurt
      Generous 1 Tablespoon mayonnaise
    1 teaspoon (or more) Dijon or grainy mustard

CORNMEAL PASTRY *yields 9-inch crust*

A little oil makes this flavorful, grainy crust more on the crisp than the flaky side. The small amount of sugar brings out the natural sweetness in the cornmeal but does not make a sweet crust.

3/4 cup all-purpose flour
1/2 cup cornmeal, preferably stone ground
4 Tablespoons (1/2 stick) butter
1 teaspoon sugar
1/2 teaspoon oregano
1/2 teaspoon salt
1 egg
2 Tablespoons oil
1 Tablespoon milk

CORNMEAL TART AND TURNOVER PASTRY

1 1/2 cups all-purpose flour
1/2 cup cornmeal, preferably stone ground
1 teaspoon sugar
1 teaspoon salt
1 teaspoon oregano
1/2 teaspoon baking powder
12 Tablespoons (1 1/2 sticks) butter
1 egg
2 Tablespoons milk
1 Tablespoon Dijon mustard

RICOTTA PASTRY *yields 9-inch springform crust*

1 1/2 cups flour (use 1/4 cup whole wheat flour if you like)
8 Tablespoons (1 stick) butter
1/2 teaspoon salt
3/4 cup ricotta cheese
1 Tablespoon Marsala

COTTAGE CHEESE PASTRY *yields 9-inch crust*

1 cup flour (use 1/4 cup whole wheat flour if you like that taste)
6 Tablespoons (3/4 stick) butter
1/2 teaspoon salt
1/2-2/3 cup small-curd cottage cheese, or enough to form a smooth dough

ELEGANT ARTICHOKE QUICHE *yields 9-inch quiche*

This is an extremely elegant quiche, pale green and smooth, subtly evocative of artichoke.

For an even more deluxe tart, distribute 8 ounces fresh crab meat over the grated Swiss cheese on the crust before adding the artichoke filling.

    1 prebaked 9-inch Herbed Pastry with Wine
       (use Marsala) or Pat-In Yogurt and
       Mayonnaise Pastry crust (p. 76)

  ½ cup minced green of scallion
  ½ teaspoon minced garlic
    2 Tablespoons (¼ stick) butter
       One 9-ounce package frozen artichoke hearts
    2 Tablespoons lemon juice
    2 Tablespoons water
    1 cup light cream or milk
    3 eggs
1 ½ teaspoons salt
       Freshly ground pepper to taste
  ½ teaspoon sugar
    4 ounces mild Swiss cheese, grated
    2 Tablespoons freshly grated Parmesan cheese
    2 Tablespoons minced fresh parsley

Preheat the oven to 375°F. Have the crust ready.

Sauté the minced scallion and garlic in butter in a medium-size saucepan. Add the artichoke hearts, lemon juice, and water, cover and cook until the artichokes are tender. Remove the cover and reduce the liquid over high heat until it has evaporated. Be careful not to let the artichokes burn.

Let cool slightly, then combine the cream or milk, eggs, salt, pepper, and sugar in the container of a blender or food processor. Add the cooled artichoke mixture and puree well.

Distribute the grated Swiss cheese over the bottom of the pastry crust. Pour in the artichoke mixture (pour through a sieve for a smoother pie) and sprinkle with the Parmesan cheese and parsley. Bake for 30–35 minutes, or until a knife inserted into the center of the pie comes out clean.

SALMON QUENELLE QUICHE *yields 9-inch quiche*

A wonderfully classy quiche, beautiful to look at with its salmon-colored mounds in a soft yellow custard. It's an excellent way to use salmon—a little goes a long way—and very easy to prepare, using the processor.

1 prebaked 9-inch Pat-In Yogurt and Mayonnaise Pastry crust (p. 76)

mousse

8 ounces skinned and boned fresh salmon, cut up
1 egg white
1/2 cup heavy cream
1/2 teaspoon salt
3-4 drops Tabasco sauce
2-3 drops (or more) lemon juice
1-1 1/4 ounces smoked salmon or lox, minced

custard

1 1/4 cups light cream
2 eggs plus 1 yolk
1 teaspoon salt, or to taste
2 drops Tabasco sauce
Pinch of dry mustard, or to taste

8 ounces dilled Havarti, grated
Minced fresh dill, or dried dill and minced fresh parsley

Preheat the oven to 400°F. Have the crust ready.

Prepare the salmon mousse. Place the salmon in the work bowl of a food processor and process to a smooth paste. Add the egg white and process until well combined. With the machine running, gradually pour the heavy cream through the feed tube, scraping down the sides once or twice. Add the salt, Tabasco, and lemon juice and process to mix. Add the minced smoked salmon and process again to mix, being careful not to overprocess and lose the flecks of darker pink. Taste the mousse mixture for seasoning.

Sprinkle half the grated dilled Havarti over the bottom of the prebaked crust. Drop the mousse mixture by generous rounded teaspoonfuls (you will have about 16 small quenelles) over the cheese then sprinkle on the remaining cheese.

Beat together the custard ingredients, then pour in enough of this mixture to cover the quenelles. Sprinkle with the minced fresh dill or dried dill and minced fresh parsley. Bake for 20-30 minutes, or until the quiche is puffed and golden.

SPINACH AND AVOCADO TORTE *yields 8-12 wedges or more*

This torte is beautiful with its pastry and two layers —one deep green with bright flecks of sweet red pepper, and one pale jade.

 1 recipe Herbed Pastry with Wine using sherry and basil or herb of choice or Pat-In Yogurt and Mayonnaise Pastry (p. 76)
 2 Tablespoons (¼ stick) butter
 1 medium to large onion, sliced
 1 medium red bell pepper, diced*
 1 clove garlic, minced fine
 1 teaspoon dried basil, or minced fresh basil or herb of choice
   Two 10-ounce packages frozen spinach, defrosted and squeezed to remove all excess liquid
 ½ cup freshly grated Parmesan cheese
   Salt and freshly ground pepper to taste
 3 large avocados (preferably Haas) or 4 regular-size, pureed (you want approximately 2½ cups pureed avocado pulp)
 4 ounces cream cheese, softened
 4 eggs
 ⅓ cup freshly grated Parmesan cheese
 3 Tablespoons lemon juice
 1 Tablespoon sherry
1-1½ teaspoons salt, or to taste
   Few drops Tabasco sauce
 ¼ teaspoon sugar (recommended especially if using a dry sherry)
 2 Tablespoons freshly grated Parmesan cheese for topping

Preheat the oven to 425°F. Lightly butter a 9-inch springform pan. Prepare pastry and pat it into the bottom of the springform pan. Prick with a fork and bake 10 minutes. Remove from the oven and lower oven temperature to 375°F.

While pastry is baking sauté the onion, red pepper, and garlic in butter until the onion is softened. Add the basil or other herb and stir. Add spinach and ½ cup Parmesan cheese and stir well to combine all ingredients. Season with salt and pepper to taste. Spread this mixture evenly over the prebaked pastry.

Prepare the avocado topping. Using a food processor or an electric mixer puree the avocado. Process or beat the cream cheese until it is smooth. Add the avocado puree, eggs, ⅓ cup Parmesan cheese, lemon juice, sherry, salt, Tabasco sauce, and sugar and beat or process until mixture is well combined, light, and fluffy. Taste for seasoning and correct if necessary. Turn mixture into the springform pan over the spinach, smoothing the top with a spatula. Sprinkle with approximately 2 Tablespoons Parmesan cheese and bake until the torte is puffed and golden and a knife inserted into the center comes out clean—about 55-60 minutes. Serve hot or at room temperature.

*If you cannot get red bell pepper, add diced pimento to the combined spinach and Parmesan cheese. Stir gently so as not to break up the pimento too much. The red color is important to the overall impact of this dish, and you don't want to eliminate it.

CARROT AND DILL QUICHE *yields 9-inch quiche*

1 prebaked 9-inch Herbed Pastry with Wine or
 Pat-In Yogurt and Mayonnaise Pastry crust,
 adding dried or fresh dill (p. 76)

8 ounces carrots, peeled and grated
1/4 cup sherry, preferably cream or medium-dry
1 cup milk
3 eggs
4 ounces cream cheese, softened
1 teaspoon salt
 Freshly ground pepper to taste
 A few gratings of fresh nutmeg
4 ounces Cheddar cheese, grated
2 Tablespoons freshly grated Parmesan cheese
2 Tablespoons minced fresh dill, or 2 teaspoons
 dried plus minced fresh parsley

Preheat the oven to 375°F. Have the crust ready.

Steam the carrots and sherry in a small covered saucepan for several minutes to cook the carrots lightly. In a blender or food processor combine the milk, eggs, cream cheese, salt, pepper, and nutmeg and blend until the mixture is smooth. Sprinkle the crust with the grated Cheddar cheese, then arrange the carrots over it. Pour in the custard gently, sprinkle with the grated Parmesan, then with the minced dill or dill and parsley. Bake for 30–35 minutes, or until the filling is puffed and golden and a knife inserted into the center comes out clean.

BROCCOLI AND BLUE CHEESE QUICHE *yields 9-inch quiche*

1 prebaked 9-inch Pat-In Yogurt and
 Mayonnaise Pastry crust (p. 76)

2 cups coarsely chopped cooked broccoli
4 ounces mozzarella or other mild white cheese,
 cubed
2 ounces blue cheese, crumbled
1 1/2 cups milk or light cream
3 eggs
1 teaspoon salt
 Freshly ground pepper to taste
 A few gratings of fresh nutmeg
1/4 cup coarsely chopped walnuts

Preheat the oven to 375°F. Have the crust ready.

Distribute the broccoli over the bottom of the crust. Top with the mozzarella and blue cheese. Beat the milk or cream together with the eggs, salt, pepper, and nutmeg then pour this mixture slowly into the pie shell. Top with the walnuts. Bake for 45–50 minutes, or until a knife inserted into the center of the pie comes out clean.

EGGPLANT MUSHROOM QUICHE *yields 9-inch quiche*

Eggplant puree gives this quiche a subtle nutlike flavor and a rich yet delicate texture.

1 prebaked 9-inch Herbed Pastry with Wine
  (use Marsala) crust (p. 76)

  1 small onion, chopped
  4 ounces mushrooms, chopped coarse
  1 clove garlic, minced
  2 Tablespoons (¼ stick) butter
  1 teaspoon basil
  1 teaspoon oregano
  3 eggs
¾ cup milk or light cream
  1 cup Seasoned Eggplant Puree (p. 257)
¼ cup freshly grated Parmesan cheese
  2 Tablespoons tomato paste
  1 teaspoon salt
    Freshly ground pepper to taste
    A grating of fresh nutmeg
    About ¼ cup Basic Tomato Sauce (p. 241) or
    commercial tomato sauce
    Grated cheese (hard such as Parmesan or
    medium-soft such as mozzarella)

Preheat the oven to 375°F. Have the crust ready.

Sauté the onion, mushrooms, and garlic in butter. Add the basil and oregano and sauté a few minutes more. Let cool slightly.

Place this in a blender or food processor along with the eggs, milk or cream, Seasoned Eggplant Puree, grated Parmesan, tomato paste, salt, pepper, and nutmeg. Puree then pour this mixture into the prebaked crust and bake for 40 minutes, or until a knife inserted into the center of the pie comes out clean.

Spread a thin layer of Basic Tomato Sauce over the surface of the pie, sprinkle with grated cheese, and return to the oven for 5 minutes to allow the cheese to melt.

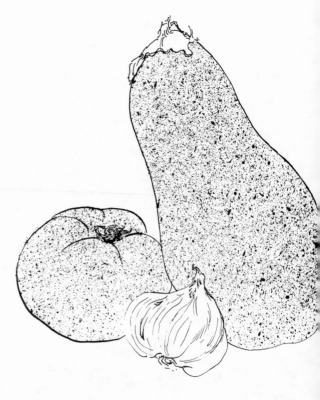

SPINACH AND TOFU TART *yields 9-inch tart*

This high-protein, low-fat tart will surprise and please you with its light texture and appealing taste. Feta cheese lends a mild, refreshing tang, tahini and sesame seeds give richness and flavor balance. And a whole wheat crust with sesame seeds adds just the right delicate graininess. This is a good place to begin experimenting with different uses for tofu.

1 prebaked 9-inch Herbed Pastry
  with Wine crust (p. 76)*

1 clove garlic, minced fine
1 cup minced scallion
1/2 cup minced fresh parsley
2 Tablespoons (1/4 stick) butter or oil
1 Tablespoon dried dill, or
  2–3 Tablespoons minced fresh

*Use 1/4 cup whole wheat flour with 2 Tablespoons sesame seeds and 1 Tablespoon dried chives or dill. Use white wine as the liquid.

1 pound tofu
3 eggs
8 ounces feta cheese, well crumbled
  One 10-ounce package frozen spinach,
  cooked and well squeezed
2 Tablespoons tahini
1 Tablespoon soy sauce or tamari
1 Tablespoon lemon juice
  Freshly ground pepper to taste
  Sesame seeds
  Freshly grated Parmesan cheese
  Butter

Preheat the oven to 375°F. Have the crust ready.

Sauté the garlic, scallion, and parsley in butter or oil until they soften. Add the dill and stir it through. Set aside.

Process or beat the tofu and eggs together until they are smooth and creamy. Add the crumbled feta and process or beat until they are well combined. Add the spinach, tahini, soy sauce or tamari, lemon juice, and pepper. Process or beat until the ingredients are combined then turn them into the crust. Sprinkle with sesame seeds and grated Parmesan and dot with butter. Bake for 30–35 minutes.

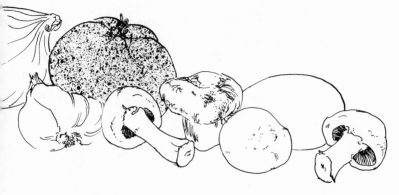

DILLED MUSHROOM TOFU TART *yields 9-inch tart*

This tart is deceptively rich-tasting, like a mushroom cheesecake with a mild nuttiness and faint underlay of dill.

- 1 prebaked 9-inch Pat-In Yogurt and Mayonnaise Pastry crust, using half whole wheat flour (p. 76)

- 1 pound tofu
- 8 ounces feta cheese, crumbled fine
- 3 eggs
  Generous 2 Tablespoons peanut butter (unsweetened, natural style)
- 1 Tablespoon dill
- 1 Tablespoon lemon juice
- 1 Tablespoon Madeira or cream sherry (optional)
  Freshly ground pepper to taste
- 1 recipe Mushroom Duxelles (p. 250)

- 2–3 Tablespoons finely chopped roasted peanuts (dry or regular roast)
- 1 Tablespoon freshly grated Parmesan cheese
- 1/2–1 Tablespoon dill
- 1 Tablespoon butter

Preheat the oven to 375°F. Have the crust ready.

Process or beat together the tofu, feta cheese, and eggs until they are smooth and creamy. Add the peanut butter, the 1 Tablespoon dill, the lemon juice, Madeira or sherry, and pepper and beat or process until they are well combined. Add the Mushroom Duxelles and beat or process just until they are mixed through. Turn the mushroom and tofu mixture into the crust and sprinkle with chopped peanuts, Parmesan cheese, and the 1/2–1 Tablespoon dill then dot with bits of butter. Bake for 35 minutes, or until the filling is puffed and golden.

RICOTTA BASIL PIE *yields 9-inch tart*

A delightful, satisfying, basil-rich tart.

- 1 prebaked 9-inch Herbed Pastry with Wine (use Marsala) crust (p. 76)

- 1 pound ricotta cheese
- 3 eggs, beaten
- 1/4 cup freshly grated Parmesan cheese
- 1/4 cup all-purpose flour
- 3 Tablespoons butter, softened
- 1 small clove garlic, minced fine

- 1 teaspoon salt
  Freshly ground pepper to taste
  A few gratings of fresh nutmeg
- 1/2 cup well-packed finely minced basil leaves
- 2–3 Tablespoons finely grated or chopped pignolis or walnuts
- 2 Tablespoons freshly grated Parmesan cheese
- 1 Tablespoon butter

Preheat the oven to 375°F. Have the crust ready.

Beat together or process the ricotta cheese, eggs,

the 1/4 cup grated Parmesan, the flour, butter, garlic, salt, pepper, and nutmeg. Add the minced basil leaves and mix or process to combine well. (If using the processor, be careful not to overprocess and cause a uniform green color.)

Smooth this mixture into the crust. Sprinkle with nuts and the 2 Tablespoons Parmesan and dot with butter. Bake for 30–35 minutes, or until the top is beginning to puff and color slightly and a knife inserted into the center comes out clean.

ZUCCHINI AND BASIL TART *yields 9-inch tart*

A nice way to use fresh basil, zucchini, and vine-ripened tomatoes when they are all at their peak. Use as much fresh basil as you like!

1 prebaked 9-inch Herbed Pastry with Wine (use Marsala) or Pat-In Yogurt and Mayonnaise Pastry crust (p. 76)

1 cup chopped scallion
1 clove garlic, minced
3 Tablespoons olive oil or butter, or a combination
2 cups thinly sliced zucchini
1 cup chopped tomato pulp (fresh, or canned plum tomatoes)
1 teaspoon dried basil, or 2 Tablespoons (or more) minced fresh
1 teaspoon salt
Freshly ground pepper to taste
1/4 cup freshly grated Parmesan cheese

6 ounces mozzarella or other mild white cheese, grated or diced, or half mozzarella and half provolone
2 Tablespoons minced fresh parsley
3 eggs, beaten

Preheat the oven to 350°F. Have the crust ready.

Sauté the scallion and garlic in the olive oil and/or butter. Add the zucchini and sauté over medium-high heat until the zucchini begins to soften. (A wok is a good pan to use for this.) Add the tomato pulp, basil, salt, and pepper and toss over the heat for a minute or two. Add the Parmesan and toss to distribute the cheese.

Transfer this mixture to the crust, juices and all, top with the grated or diced cheese, sprinkle with minced fresh parsley then pour the beaten eggs over everything. Bake for about 40 minutes.

TORTA RUSTICA *serves 6-8*

This is a glorious, abundant, oversized "pie," with layers of flavor and colorful ratatouille peeking through a golden lattice topping.

1 recipe Ricotta Pastry (p. 77)
2 pounds ricotta cheese (use 3/4 cup of this for the pastry)
2 eggs
1/3 cup freshly grated Parmesan or other hard grating cheese
1/4-1/2 cup minced fresh basil leaves, or 1 Frozen Pesto Cube (p. 247), or 1-2 teaspoons dried basil plus 1/4 cup minced fresh parsley
2 Tablespoons all-purpose flour
2 Tablespoons minced fresh parsley
1 teaspoon salt
Freshly ground pepper to taste
A few gratings of fresh nutmeg
1 pound cooked Italian sausage, sliced 3/8 inch thick (optional)
1 pound mozzarella or other mild white cheese, cubed or grated
1 cup Ratatouille Sauce (p. 244), or a tomato sauce with plenty of sautéed small whole mushrooms
Additional freshly grated Parmesan cheese
Additional minced fresh parsley

Preheat the oven to 400°F.

Roll out two thirds of the Ricotta Pastry and fit it into a 9-inch springform pan. Set aside the remaining third to make a lattice. The sides of the dough should be at least 2 inches high. Prick the dough with a fork, cover with 2 sheets of aluminum foil, and fill the foil with rice or beans. Place the springform pan on a jelly-roll pan or baking sheet and bake for 10 minutes. Remove the foil and beans and with the back of the tines of a fork gently press back up the pastry that has shrunk down on the sides of the pan. Replace the foil and beans and bake for an additional 10 minutes to set the pastry. Remove the foil and beans again and bake for 10 minutes more—a total of 30 minutes altogether. Take the crust out of the oven and let it cool slightly. Reduce the oven temperature to 375°F.

Mix the remaining ricotta, eggs, the 1/3 cup grated Parmesan, the basil, flour, parsley, salt, pepper, and nutmeg. Turn into the cooled crust. Arrange the sausage rounds, if desired, over the ricotta mixture, pressing them in slightly. Distribute the mozzarella over the sausage and cover with the Ratatouille Sauce.

Roll out the remaining one third of the dough and cut it into strips for a lattice topping. Form a lattice, pressing the edges of the uncooked dough onto the edge of the baked crust gently with the back of the tines of a fork. Bake the torta on a baking sheet for 35 minutes at 375°F. Sprinkle with additional grated Parmesan and minced fresh parsley and bake for 10-15 minutes more, or until the pastry lattice is golden.

TOSTADA PIE *yields 9-inch pie*

This pie oozes with cheesy goodness, spicy bite, and plenty of whole-grain and vegetable crunch.

1	prebaked 9-inch Cornmeal Pastry crust (p. 77)
1	cup chopped onion
1-2	cloves garlic, minced
2	Tablespoons oil*
6	cups packed chopped fresh kale leaves (1 good-size bunch)
	A few Tablespoons water
	Salt and freshly ground pepper to taste
1½-2	cups Seasoned Bean Puree (p. 252)
½-¾	cup Mexican Tomato Sauce (p. 241), or canned tomatoes with green chilis, reduced and thickened
4-6	ounces Cheddar cheese, or a combination of Cheddar and Jack, grated
	Freshly grated Parmesan cheese
	Tabasco sauce (optional)

*Unrefined corn oil is particularly nice to use, but if you don't have it, olive or vegetable oil will work just fine.

Preheat the oven to 350°F. Have the crust ready.

Sauté the onion and garlic in oil until tender. Add the kale and sauté a few minutes longer. Add the water, cover and steam until the kale is tender but not soggy. Season to taste with salt and pepper and raise the heat to boil off any excess liquid. Spread the Seasoned Bean Puree over the bottom of the crust. Spoon Mexican Tomato Sauce over the beans and distribute the Cheddar cheese over the sauce. Top with the kale and onion mixture, sprinkle lightly with grated Parmesan and, if you like it hot, with a few shakes of Tabasco sauce. If you have a little tomato sauce left over, you can also drizzle this lightly over the kale. Bake for 30-40 minutes.

KASHA AND POTATO PIE *yields 9-inch pie*

Earthy and satisfying, this is one of my favorite pies, in either its vegetarian or sausage-topped version. Delightful when served with cold beet borscht. It has the impact of a delicious and doughy knish.

1 prebaked 9-inch Cottage Cheese Pastry crust (p. 77)

3/4 pound potatoes
3 Tablespoons butter
1/2 cup freshly grated Parmesan cheese
1/3 cup milk
3 eggs
1 teaspoon salt, or to taste
Freshly ground pepper to taste
1 recipe Kasha with Herbs (p. 254)
1/2 pound cooked small-link sausage, sliced thin lengthwise (optional)
2-3 Tablespoons freshly grated Parmesan cheese
Minced fresh parsley
Butter (if you don't use sausage)

Preheat the oven to 375°F. Have the crust ready.

Boil the potatoes until tender, then either boil off all the excess water or drain the potatoes and use the potato water in bread making. Add the 3 Table-spoons butter, the 1/2 cup grated Parmesan (or to taste), and the milk and mash or beat until smooth. Let cool slightly then add the eggs and salt and pepper to taste. Add the Kasha with Herbs and combine the mixtures well. Taste for seasoning.

Turn the kasha and potato mixture into the crust. Arrange the sausage slices, if you are using them, on top of the pie in a sunburst pattern, pressing them into the filling slightly. Sprinkle with the 2-3 Tablespoons grated Parmesan and the minced parsley. (Dot with butter if you are not using sausage.)

Bake for 30 minutes then raise the oven tempera-ture to 425°F and bake for an additional 5-10 minutes to brown and crisp the pie's surface. (If the pastry edges are browning too much, cover them with strips of aluminum foil.)

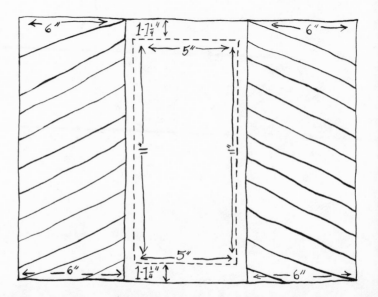

SOLE OR SEAFOOD AND SPINACH PASTRY LATTICE LOAF *serves 5-6*

Deep green spinach peeks through golden pastry, and bright orange yolks melt their silken sauce with every slice. The loaf makes a breathtaking presentation surrounded by sprigs of parsley or leaves of kale and cherry tomato accents and is an excellent choice for either supper or brunch. I like to serve it, particularly for brunch, with sautéed apples and raisins. Homemade bread—Nutted Soda Bread with Herbs (with pecans and dill)—rounds out the meal.

1   recipe Lattice Loaf Pastry (following recipe)
1   recipe Spinach Mornay (p. 256), adding
    1 teaspoon Dijon mustard
12   ounces fillet of sole, sautéed lightly in butter;
    or 8 ounces fillet of sole, sautéed, plus
    4–6 ounces fresh crab meat; or 12 ounces
    scallops, small or cut into quarters or thirds
    and sautéed lightly in butter
3/4   recipe Mushroom Duxelles (p. 250)
5   egg yolks from extra-large eggs
    Salt and freshly ground pepper to taste
2   ounces (1/2 cup) Gruyère or Swiss cheese,
    grated
1–2   Tablespoons freshly grated Parmesan cheese
    Egg wash (1 egg beaten with 1 Tablespoon
    milk or cream)

Preheat the oven to 375°F.

Roll out the pastry to form a rectangle about 13 by 18 inches, with one of the long sides nearest you. Being careful not to cut through the pastry, score lightly with the edge of a knife an inner rectangle measuring 5 by 11 inches with a 6 1/2-inch border of pastry on the long sides and a 1 1/4-inch border on the short sides. Mark off 6 inches on both wide borders and cut slightly angled strips about 1 inch thick. Cut these all the way through. (See the diagram on p. 88.)

Spread a little less than half the spinach mixture evenly over the inner 5 by 11-inch rectangle. Arrange the fish or seafood down the center of the rectangle. (If you are using crab meat, arrange it on top of the sole.) Mound the remaining spinach on top of the fish or seafood. Form a deep trough down the center of the spinach, leaving a small edge of spinach at both ends. Spoon the Mushroom Duxelles down the center of this trough and top with 5 unbroken egg yolks. Season the yolks lightly with salt and pepper and sprinkle with grated Gruyère and Parmesan.

Next form the lattice. Beginning at the top end, farthest from you, fold the 1 1/4-inch pastry border up over the spinach and at the same time curve the left top lattice strip around so that it partially covers and overlaps it. Repeat with the right top lattice strip, crossing it over the first strip. Continue crossing over alternate lattice strips, angling the strips over toward the opposite side and slightly downward. When you get to the bottom, bring up the bottom border and overlap 1 or 2 of the bottom lattice strips over it. There will be very narrow openings between the strips.

Extremely carefully, using 2 large spatulas, lift the lattice loaf onto a baking pan, preferably one attractive enough to serve it from.* (At this point the lattice loaf can be refrigerated for several hours before baking.) Bake for 35 minutes, or until the

---

*You can also form the loaf on 2 sheets of heavy-duty aluminum foil and use this as a sling to transfer the loaf to a baking dish and then to a serving dish. Before serving, cut away the excess foil with a sharp knife.

LATTICE LOAF PASTRY

2 cups all-purpose flour
14 Tablespoons (1¾ sticks) butter*
1 teaspoon dried herbs (optional)
1 teaspoon salt
2 Tablespoons milk, cream, or liquid of choice
1 egg
1 Tablespoon Dijon mustard

pastry is golden and the filling is hot. If the loaf has been refrigerated, bake initially at 425°F for 10 minutes then continue for the 35 minutes' baking time at 375°F. The lattice loaf will expand during baking. Rolling up sheets of aluminum foil and placing them around the loaf will help it keep its shape.

PHYLLO

Phyllo is a fragile, paper-thin, commercially pre-pared dough with which you can create exquisitely layered, rave-producing hors d'oeuvre pastries and main course strudels, turnovers, and tarts. Each has a delicacy that totally belies phyllo's make-ahead and freeze-ahead flexibility, and phyllo is amazingly easy to work with once you know how.

Phyllo is available fresh in Armenian and Middle Eastern markets, and frozen in most supermarkets. It comes in 1-pound packages with about 20–24 sheets to the package. When you are ready to use your phyllo, unroll it carefully, remove half the layers, or the number of sheets you will need, and return the remainder to the plastic bag in which it came so that these layers will not dry out. Have plenty of melted butter ready (I generally use salted butter) and unflavored store-bought bread crumbs. Bread crumbs can be omitted, but they increase the separation and flakiness between the layers and will absorb any excess moisture from your filling. Cover your work surface with 2–3 large sheets of

waxed paper before you begin (you will find it much easier to throw away the waxed paper than to clean up a buttery counter). Using a 2–2½-inch-wide brush (which you can purchase at a hardware store and wash) brush the phyllo with butter in light sweeping strokes. Don't worry about covering every inch of surface. You can also dip your brush in butter and sprinkle the butter generously and evenly over the phyllo. After buttering, sprinkle each layer with crumbs.

Phyllo can be shaped into a great variety of forms. One of my favorites is a strudel roll which I use when preparing hors d'oeuvres or main course strudel slices in quantity. You can use the roll form, however, for either large or small amounts. The hors d'oeuvre roll is approximately 12 inches long and 1½–2 inches wide. It is baked until crisp and golden, then cut into 8 or 9 individual slices. The main course strudel is two to three times the diame-

*You can substitute up to 4 Tablespoons vegetable shortening without affecting the taste.

ter of the hors d'oeuvre roll and yields 6–8 slices. Seafood and fish mousse in any variation, spanoko-pita and mushroom Marsala and pecan fillings make exquisite hors d'oeuvre slices. Seafood mousse and spanokopita create very special main course and first course strudel slices. Small individual finger-shaped "cigars" are another favorite choice when I have more time and want an especially elegant appearance.

Here are instructions for forming and baking rolls and cigars. Instructions for pockets, turnovers, and tarts, as well as for individual shells and nests, appear with related recipes.

To form rolls: You will need 5 sheets of phyllo for each hors d'oeuvre–size roll and about 2/3 cup filling. (This can be a generously rounded 1/2 cup of filling or more.) For the larger main course strudel roll use 6 sheets of phyllo and approximately 1 1/2 cups of filling, slightly more if you want a larger slice. Place a sheet of phyllo in front of you on the waxed paper with one of the long sides nearest you. Butter it, sprinkle lightly with crumbs, and cover with another sheet. Repeat until you have a stack of 5 (or 6) sheets, with the top sheet buttered and sprinkled lightly with crumbs. Form a line of filling 1 inch in from the edge nearest you and centered at least 1 inch in from either side. Fold the edge near you up over the filling, brush the side borders with butter and fold them in over the filling, then roll up the strudel forming a fairly firm roll. Brush the top of the roll with butter and place it seam side down on a pan lined with waxed paper. Continue forming strudels until you have the number of rolls that you want. Refrigerate them until the butter is firm, or overnight. When the butter is firm

you can transfer the rolls to a jelly-roll pan and bake them, or freeze them wrapped either individually or together in one large piece of foil.

When you are ready to bake, preheat the oven to 375°F. Place the rolls seam side down on a jelly-roll pan with at least 1 inch of space between them. (The rolls will exude butter as they bake, so make certain to use a jelly-roll pan with sides, not a cookie sheet.) Bake the rolls for about 15 to 20 minutes. When the rolls are beginning to feel crisp and firm to the touch, turn them so that the underside is on the top. Continue baking the rolls another 15 to 20 minutes until the strudel is deep golden and crisp. (The strudels do not have to be turned, but this helps ensure even browning.) Main course and frozen strudel will require a longer baking time.

Let the finished rolls cool slightly, then slice with a sharp, serrated knife into 1–1 1/2-inch straight lengths (for hors d'oeuvres) or thicker diagonal slices (for main courses servings). Rolls can be baked several hours before serving, cooled, sliced, then placed cut side up on a baking sheet to be warmed before they are served. If the filling is seafood mousse, brush the cut side lightly with melted butter. If the filling is spanokopita, it may give somewhat when sliced, especially if your knife is not a really sharp one. If this happens, re-form the slice with a gentle squeeze. Serve the slices with the cut side showing.

To form cigars: Each sheet of phyllo forms 2 cigars, so you will need half as many sheets as the number of cigars you wish to make. Two cups of filling will give you 18–20 cigars. Make a stack of the number of sheets of phyllo you plan to use and place them on the waxed paper with the short side nearest you.

Brush the top sheet with melted butter and sprinkle lightly with crumbs. Fold this sheet of phyllo in half top to bottom, that is, by folding the top half over the bottom half. If your phyllo measures 13 by 15 inches, your working sheet will now measure 7½ by 13 inches. With kitchen scissors make a vertical cut down the center of this double sheet, dividing it into 2 pieces measuring 6½ by 7½ inches. Brush both halves with melted butter and sprinkle lightly with crumbs. Fill a ¼ cup measure with filling and level it off. Divide the filling in half and use each half to form a line 4 inches long 1 inch in from the base of each half sheet. Leave a 1½-inch border on each side. (This is a suggested way to measure your filling. You can also use a rounded Table-spoonful of filling for each cylinder or—my preference—fill a pastry bag fitted with a large plain tip and pipe a 4-inch strip of filling quickly and neatly across each phyllo rectangle.) Bring the bottom

border up over the filling and roll 1 turn. Butter the sides and fold them in then continue to roll up the phyllo firmly and evenly, but not so tightly that there is no room for the filling to expand. Brush with butter wherever the phyllo is dry. Repeat with the remaining sheets of phyllo.

As each cigar or individual strudel is complete, brush the top with butter and place them seam side down on a baking sheet lined with waxed paper. Refrigerate until the butter is firm, or overnight. Cigars can be baked or wrapped for freezing as soon as the butter has hardened. When you are ready to bake, preheat the oven to 375°F. Place the strudels on a baking sheet so that there is *at least* 1 inch of space between them. Bake for 20–25 minutes, or until the strudels are crisp and golden. Turn the cigars if necessary for even browning. Cigars can be baked an hour or so ahead of time and warmed gently before serving.

SEAFOOD MOUSSE STRUDEL SLICES WITH CRAB MEAT VELOUTÉ

Here is an elegant yet easy-to-prepare main course strudel—seafood mousse formed into a large strudel roll, baked, sliced, and served with Crab Meat Velouté.

Prepare Seafood Mousse IV (p. 249) using 2 eggs. This will give you about 5 cups of mousse. Follow instructions for forming and baking main course strudel rolls (see p. 90). You will need 18 sheets of phyllo for 3 rolls, about 3 sticks of melted butter, and will be using a generous 1½ cups of filling in each roll.

Strudels can be prepared ahead and frozen before baking. They can also be baked several hours ahead of time, sliced, and laid out on a baking pan, tops brushed with butter. To reheat, place in a 375°F oven until mousse is warmed through and phyllo is gently crisped.

Slice the rolls on the diagonal after baking. You will get 7–8 slices per roll, unless you prefer thicker slices. Allow 2 slices for a main course serving, 1 slice for a first course. Serve with Crab Meat Velouté (p. 246). You can also serve this with hollandaise sauce.

SEAFOOD MOUSSE POCKETS WITH CRAB MEAT VELOUTÉ *yields 12-14 strudels*

These individual strudels with their filling of Seafood Mousse, buttery Spinach Mornay, and Mushroom Duxelles are to be reserved for very special occasions—not times when one is dieting or hungry for whole grains. Although the strudels may appear complex to prepare, when mousse, spinach, and duxelles are prepared the day before and pockets assembled early on the day they will be baked, they are a low-effort choice relative to the pleasure and appreciation they bring. I like to serve them with shredded carrots sautéed in butter to which I've added minced fresh gingerroot and a little honey. A crisp salad and Velvet Pumpkin Bread or Buttery Brioche Twists round out this enchanting dinner.

12-14 sheets phyllo
  3-4 sticks (3/4-1 pound) butter, melted
       Toasted bread crumbs
    1 recipe Seafood Mousse IV (p. 249)
  1/2 recipe Mushroom Duxelles (p. 250)
    1 recipe Spinach Mornay (p. 256)
    1 recipe Crab Meat Velouté (p. 246)

Lay the sheets of phyllo in a stack on your work surface with one of the short sides nearest you. Brush the sheet with butter and sprinkle it lightly with bread crumbs. Place a heaping Tablespoon (or scant 1/3 cup) of Seafood Mousse in the middle of the short side near you 3-31/2 inches from the edge. With a teaspoon create a small indentation in the mound of mousse and place about a generous teaspoon of Mushroom Duxelles in the indentation. Top with a Tablespoon of Spinach Mornay.

Fold the 3-inch border near you up over the mousse, mushroom, and spinach mound, pressing slightly, and roll it over one more time so that what was once the border is now on the bottom and the mousse mixture is just under the top layer. Butter the phyllo that is exposed to you over the mound of mousse. Fold the left side over the mousse mound, then the right side, envelope style. Do not enclose the mousse very tightly in the phyllo as it will expand during baking. (Even if the filling breaks through the phyllo, it will keep its shape and the strudel will look and taste wonderful.) Repeat the roll up two more times, buttering any unbuttered parts and the top of the strudel.

As the strudels are completed, place them on a baking pan, leaving a 11/2-2-inch space between each strudel. Refrigerate until the butter is cold and firm. This can be several hours ahead and even overnight, if you wish to prepare them that far in advance. (Cold, unbaked strudels can be frozen.)

When you are ready to bake, preheat the oven to 375°F. Bake the strudels for 35-40 minutes, or until they are puffed and deeply golden. If the strudels are browning too much, lower the oven temperature, although strudels can be baked at a higher temperature for a shorter period of time. If you cannot serve them immediately, keep the strudels warm in a 250°-275°F oven for 15-20 minutes. Serve each strudel with 1-2 Tablespoons of the Crab Meat Velouté napped over the center of it, but not covering it.

Allow 1 strudel for a main course serving.

Use this next group of recipes to create elegant and delicious vegetable turnovers, individual strudels, and pies. These are mouth-watering accompaniments to holiday turkeys and roasts as well as to simple broiled seafoods and meats—perfect for those times when you want something special and are willing to spend a little extra time and calories for the effect.

These vegetables in phyllo also make fabulous brunch offerings. Imagine even simple scrambled eggs served (glorified, really) with buttery, flaky potato strudels or turnovers. Imagine, too, a brunch, lunch, or dinner buffet with an assortment of tastes, among them spanokopita turnovers or a carrot almond pie. All of these can be prepared in advance and even frozen, then baked to golden crispness just before serving.

SPANOKOPITA TURNOVERS *yields 10 turnovers*

People say this is the best spanokopita they have ever tasted. It is a very special version of the spinach and phyllo classic, excellent in turnover, cigar, strudel roll,* or pie form. Golden raisins and a hint of cinnamon provide an exciting flavor contrast and highlight to the dilled and scalliony rich cheese base. The flavors resonate and the overall impact with the buttery phyllo is sublime.

filling

    4 ounces cream cheese, softened
    4 ounces feta cheese, crumbled
    1 small bunch scallions, chopped fine
        (1/2–1 cup)
    1 Tablespoon butter

1/2 Tablespoon dried dill, or 2 Tablespoons minced fresh
    1 egg, lightly beaten
1/4 teaspoon ground cinnamon
    A few gratings of fresh nutmeg
    Freshly ground pepper to taste
    One 10-ounce package frozen chopped spinach, cooked lightly and well squeezed
1/3 cup golden raisins (more if you like—up to 1/2 cup)

turnover

    10 sheets phyllo (1 for each turnover)
1 1/2–2 sticks (3/8–1/2 pound) butter, melted
    Bread crumbs

Process or beat together the cream cheese and feta until they are smooth. Sauté the scallions in the

*This recipe yields approximately 2–2 1/4 cups of filling. Use 15 sheets of phyllo to form 3 hors d'oeuvre strudel rolls or 10 sheets for 20 cigars. One recipe will give you more than enough filling for 1 main course strudel roll (6 sheets of phyllo). A double recipe will give you enough filling for 3 rolls.

butter until they are softened. Add the dill and stir it through, cooking briefly. Add this along with the egg, cinnamon, nutmeg, and pepper to the cheeses and process or beat well. Add the spinach and raisins and process or stir enough to mix the ingredients together evenly. You will have about 2 cups of filling.

You can form triangles immediately or, better, refrigerate the mixture for several hours or overnight and work with it when it is firmer. Either way, next place a stack of 10 sheets of phyllo in front of you with one of the long sides closest to you. Brush the top sheet with melted butter and sprinkle lightly with crumbs. Fold the sheet into thirds by folding the right third over the middle third then folding the left third over both of these. You will have a 3-layer strip about 5 inches by 12–13 inches, with a short side closest to you.

Butter this strip and sprinkle it lightly with more crumbs. Place ¼ cup of filling at the bottom right-hand corner of the strip. Using the flag-fold technique, bring the right bottom point up to the left side so that a perfect triangle is formed. Continue to fold this triangle 4 more times, maintaining the triangle shape and folding up the whole strip of dough. Brush the top of the triangle with butter and place on a baking sheet lined with waxed paper. Repeat with the new top sheet of phyllo, then the next until all the sheets are used up and all 10 triangles are formed. Refrigerate until the butter is firm, or overnight. (You can also freeze the triangles when the butter has firmed.)

When you are ready to bake, preheat the oven to 375°F. Place the triangles on an unbuttered baking sheet and bake for about 20–25 minutes, or until the turnovers are crisp and golden.

POTATO AND CHEESE TURNOVERS

For the filling, substitute 1 recipe Dilled Potato Cheese Filling II or Rich Potato Cheese Filling III (p. 255). If you like, sauté chopped onion in butter until golden and a little browned and place a small spoonful of onion in the center of the filling. You can also sprinkle a small amount of dehydrated onion flakes over the phyllo along with the bread crumbs.

PARSNIP AND SPINACH TURNOVERS

For the filling, substitute 1 recipe Parsnip and Spinach Filling (p. 256).

CARROT AND ALMOND BISTEEYA *serves 8-10*

Serve this vegetarian version of a Moroccan pigeon pie as a first course, main course, side dish, or as part of a party or potluck buffet. Although the phyllo loses some of its flakiness, the Bisteeya is good eaten cold the next day, when flavors have had a chance to blend, making it a wonderful picnic pie. Even with the optional dustings of sugar and cinnamon this is definitely not a dessert. See page 100 for Bisteeya prepared as an hors d'oeuvre.

    1/2 pound unblanched almonds
      2 Tablespoons granulated sugar
   1 1/4 teaspoons ground cinnamon
      1 pound carrots, peeled
    1/2 cup chicken stock (see p. 50)
      1 cup minced fresh parsley
    1/2 cup finely chopped onion
      2 Tablespoons (1/4 stick) butter
      1 Tablespoon lemon juice
         About 1/2 teaspoon minced fresh gingerroot,
         or 1/4 teaspoon powdered ginger
         Scant 3/4 teaspoon salt, or to taste
         A small pinch of saffron
         Pinch of freshly ground pepper
      5 eggs, beaten
     12 sheets phyllo
      8 Tablespoons (1 stick) (or more) butter, melted
         Bread crumbs
         Confectioners sugar (optional)
         Additional ground cinnamon (optional)

Process the almonds with the granulated sugar and cinnamon until the almonds are chopped moderately fine. Grate the carrots (not too fine) and set aside.

In a saucepan combine the chicken stock, parsley, onion, the 2 Tablespoons butter, lemon juice, ginger, salt, saffron, and pepper. Heat until the butter is almost melted. Add the carrots and cook over high heat, stirring frequently, until the carrots are softened and the liquid is almost entirely evaporated. Add the beaten eggs and stir until the eggs set. The mixture will be custardy, but not too loose. Add the carrot and egg mixture to the almonds and mix well.

Butter a 9- or 10-inch pie pan. Place 12 sheets of phyllo in a stack before you and brush the top sheet of phyllo with melted butter. Sprinkle it lightly with crumbs and fold it in half. Brush the top of the folded-over sheet with melted butter. Fit this double sheet into the pie pan with excess phyllo hanging over the plate rim. Repeat with a second sheet of phyllo and fit this double sheet into the pie pan so that the overhang is opposite the first sheet's and covers the remaining rim of the pan. Continue buttering, crumbing, folding, buttering, and fitting until you have used a total of 6 sheets of phyllo, arranging them so that the overlaps are distributed fairly evenly. Turn the carrot bisteeya filling into the pie pan and smooth it out evenly.

Continue to butter, crumb, fold in half and butter 4 more sheets of phyllo and arrange them over the filling so that the overlapping areas are again distributed evenly. Brush the last 2 sheets of phyllo with butter and lay them, unfolded, over the top of the pie. With a pair of scissors trim all the phyllo so that only a 1/2 inch or so extends beyond the rim. Brush the edges of phyllo with butter and tuck and fold the edges in and under to form a smooth edge to the pie. Butter the top. Refrigerate until the butter is firm, or overnight. With a sharp knife precut the top layer of phyllo into 8-10 wedges, almost but not quite down to the filling.

When you are ready to bake, preheat the oven to

350°F. Bake for 30 minutes then raise the heat to 450°F and bake for an additional 5-10 minutes, or until the crust is crisp and golden. If desired, dust confectioners sugar very lightly over the surface of the warm Bisteeya and follow with an accent of cinnamon. Serve in wedges directly from the pie pan or serve the whole Bisteeya from a platter.

SPANOKOPITA PIE *serves at least 6-8*

8 ounces cream cheese, softened
8 ounces feta cheese, crumbled
1 large or 2 small bunches scallions, chopped fine
2 Tablespoons (¼ stick) (or more) butter
1 Tablespoon dried dill, or 4 Tablespoons minced fresh
2 large eggs, lightly beaten
½ teaspoon ground cinnamon
  A few gratings of fresh nutmeg
  Freshly ground pepper to taste
  Two 10-ounce packages frozen chopped spinach, cooked lightly and well squeezed
⅔ cup golden raisins
12 sheets phyllo
8 Tablespoons (1 stick) butter, melted
  Bread crumbs

Process or beat together the cream cheese and feta until they are smooth. Sauté the scallions in the 2 Tablespoons butter until they are softened. Add the dill and stir it through, cooking briefly. Add this along with the eggs, cinnamon, nutmeg, and pepper to the cheeses and process or beat well. Add the spinach and raisins and process or stir enough to mix the ingredients together evenly.

Using the phyllo, melted butter, and bread crumbs, form, fill, and bake the pie according to the directions for Carrot and Almond Bisteeya (see preceding recipe).

INDIVIDUAL POTATO STRUDELS *yields 15-16 strudels*

These strudels are a treat whether served with an omelette or roast beef.

  8 sheets phyllo
    About 12 Tablespoons (1½ sticks) butter, melted
    Bread crumbs
    Instant minced onion (optional)
½ recipe Dilled Potato Cheese Filling II or Rich Potato Cheese Filling III (p. 255)

Place the 8 sheets of phyllo in a stack with a short side nearest you. Brush the top sheet with melted butter, sprinkle lightly with crumbs and a generous pinch of minced onion. Fold this sheet of phyllo in half by bringing the top of the sheet to the bottom. If your phyllo measures 13 by 15 inches, your working sheet will now measure 7½ by 13 inches. With a pair of scissors cut down the center of this double sheet, dividing it into 2 pieces each measuring 6½ by 7½ inches. Brush both folded pieces with melted butter.

Pack a ¼ cup measure with potato filling and level it off. Using half of this measure form a strip of potato 4 inches long across the base of one of the sheets, leaving a 1-inch border of phyllo below it and a 1½-inch border on either side. Form the same strip with the remaining filling on the other doubled sheet of phyllo. (This is a suggested way to measure your filling. You can also use a rounded Tablespoon of filling or, most conveniently I think, fill a pastry bag with a large plain tip and pipe a 4 by 1-inch strip of filling quickly and neatly onto each phyllo rectangle.)

Bring the bottom border up over the potato and roll it over one more turn. Butter the sides around the potato and fold them in. Roll up the phyllo firmly and evenly but not so tightly that there is no room for the filling to expand.

Repeat with the second half piece of phyllo and continue with the remaining sheets. As the strudels are completed, brush the tops (away from the seam) with melted butter and place them seam side down on a baking sheet lined with waxed paper. Refrigerate until the butter is firm (for several hours or overnight). Strudels can be wrapped and frozen at this point.

When you are ready to bake, preheat the oven to 350–375°F. Place the strudels seam side down again on an unbuttered baking sheet so that there is at least 1 inch of space between each strudel. Bake for 15–25 minutes, slightly longer if they were frozen, or until the strudels are crisp and golden. Allow 2–3 strudels per person as an accompaniment.

Here are suggestions for some outrageously good hors d'oeuvres prepared with phyllo in strudel roll or cigar forms. Don't forget spanokopita (see p. 94 for filling recipe).

You can increase or decrease the amounts of filling depending on the number of strudels you wish to produce. Use the general instructions (see pp. 90-94) as a guideline for determining the ratio of filling to other ingredients and to yield. For the following recipe 1¾ cups Mushroom Marsala Filling will give 2-3 hors d'oeuvre rolls and about 14-16 cigars.

MUSHROOM MARSALA OR MUSHROOM PECAN PHYLLO STRUDELS

Both are delicious, though Mushroom Marsala Phyllo Strudel rolls and cigars are my favorite and seem to get the most intense rave reactions. Add a little grated Bruder Basil cheese for a rich smoky flavor.

1 recipe (1¾ cups) Mushroom Marsala Filling (p. 251)
            or
1 recipe (2½-3 cups) Mushroom Pecan Filling (p. 251)
   Phyllo
   Butter
   Bread crumbs

Form, fill, and bake strudel rolls or cigars according to the directions on page 91.

SEAFOOD MOUSSE IN PHYLLO *yields 2 rolls or 8-10 cigars*

These make handsome, delicious hors d'oeuvres. Prepare a mousse that strikes your fancy, one with bits of smoked salmon and minced fresh dill, or one with crab meat or a small amount of cooked chopped spinach for bright flecks of green.

1 recipe Seafood Mousse I (p. 249)*
10 sheets phyllo for 2 rolls or about 4-5 sheets phyllo for 8-10 cigars
1-1½ sticks (¼-3/8 pound) butter, melted
   Bread crumbs

Form, fill, and bake strudel rolls or cigars according to the directions on page 91.

*You can, of course, use other mousses, including salmon mousse. If you do, make sure to take into account the varying yields of these recipes and increase or decrease to coordinate the amounts of mousse and phyllo so you produce the number of strudels you want.

CARROT ALMOND
BISTEEYA HORS D'OEUVRE PASTRIES *yields 3 cups of filling, enough for 36 cigars or 6 rolls*

This vegetarian carrot version captures Bisteeya's complex, evocative flavors.

This is interesting to serve as an hors d'oeuvre if you are preparing Chicken Marrakech or Couscous with Turkey and Ported Prunes as a main course.

1/2 cup chicken stock (see p. 50)
1/2 small onion, grated
1/4 cup minced fresh parsley (packed)
 2 Tablespoons (1/4 stick) butter, cut up
 1 teaspoon lemon juice, or to taste
 1 small cinnamon stick
1/2 teaspoon powdered ginger
1/2 teaspoon salt
   A few grindings of pepper
   Pinch of saffron
1/2 pound carrots, grated not too fine
 3 eggs, well beaten
1/2 pound almonds, blanched and lightly toasted*
1/4 cup toasted, unflavored bread crumbs

1/4 cup confectioners sugar
 1 teaspoon ground cinnamon
   Confectioners sugar
   Ground cinnamon

Combine stock, onion, parsley, butter, lemon juice, cinnamon stick, ginger, salt, pepper, and saffron. Bring to a boil, add carrots, and simmer 1–2 minutes or until carrots soften slightly. Remove cinnamon stick. Stir in eggs over medium-high heat until eggs set. Mixture will be custardy but somewhat wet.

Process or grind almonds with crumbs, confectioners sugar, and cinnamon, being careful not to process almonds too finely. Add to the carrot and egg mixture and combine well.

Form and bake according to directions for rolls or cigars (p. 91). (The cigar is my favorite shape for Bisteeya.) Immediately after baking, sift confectioners sugar lightly over top of pastry, then sprinkle with a dash of cinnamon.

PHYLLO NESTS

You can also use phyllo to create freestanding nests for Eggs Jacobson and other recipes:

Place a stack of phyllo sheets on your work surface with one of the short sides facing you. How many sheets you will need will be determined by how many nests you wish to make. Brush the top sheet with butter and sprinkle lightly with bread crumbs. Beginning with the short side nearest you, fold the edge over 1 inch. Continue folding the sheet of phyllo, inch by inch, until you get to within 2 inches of the opposite edge. Now you are going to form a nest with this 2-inch flap overlapping itself and forming the base and the rolled part being the rim. Curve the phyllo tube into a circle, crimping the dough gently as you curve it. Join the two ends by rolling

*To blanch and toast almonds: Bring water to a boil. Add almonds and boil 1–2 minutes. Drain. Rinse under cold water briefly, then slip almonds out of their skin with a gentle pinching-pressing finger motion. Dry almonds in dish or on paper towels, place on baking sheet, and bake at 350°F until they begin to color slightly.

them together and folding them under, pinching or crimping them together gently. Roll the rest of the tube or circle inward slightly to form a neat round nest about 3–3½ inches in diameter. (The larger diameter works better for Eggs Jacobson.)

Place the nest on a baking sheet, brush the nest with butter, and bake in a preheated 375°F oven for 12–15 minutes or until lightly golden. Proceed with the recipe for Eggs Jacobson.

For a quick yet very special breakfast or brunch treat, crumble bacon into the prebaked nest, break an egg into each nest, sprinkle lightly with salt and pepper, and then with Parmesan. Bake in a preheated 375°F oven for 10–12 minutes or just until egg is set. Serve with Mornay Sauce (p. 245) or spoon some Mornay over the egg before baking. You can also bake the nests a little longer and fill them with a poached egg. Top with a dollop of sauce (Mornay, Crab Meat Velouté, or hollandaise) and broil or bake briefly in a hot oven until sauce is glazed and bubbly.

EGGS JACOBSON *yields 8–10 cups*

Eggs Benedict, move over. These are at their absolute best served with a small dollop of Mornay Sauce. If you would like to bake them an hour or so ahead and then reheat, just underbake them slightly the first time so that the egg doesn't overcook in reheating.

About 2–3 sticks (½–¾ pound) butter, melted
8–10 sheets phyllo
Instant minced onion
⅓ recipe Spinach Mornay (about ⅔ cup) (p. 256), well seasoned
8–10 extra-large eggs
Salt and freshly ground pepper to taste
About ¼ cup freshly grated Parmesan cheese
About ¼ cup heavy cream
1 recipe Mornay Sauce (p. 245) (optional)

Preheat the oven to 350°F.

Brush the inside of 8–10 muffin cups lightly with melted butter. Place a stack of 8–10 sheets of phyllo with a long side closest to you. Brush the top layer with more butter then sprinkle with a generous pinch of instant minced onion. Fold first the right third then the left over the middle third, forming a 3-layer strip 5 by 13 inches, the 5-inch side closest to you. Brush the folded strip again with butter and sprinkle with more onion. Rotate the strip so a long side is again facing you, then fold this strip into thirds the same way, forming a square roughly 5 by 5 inches. Butter this square then turn it over and butter the other side. Fit the square into a muffin cup and crimp the edges to form an even rim. Brush the edge with butter if needed.

Repeat with the remaining phyllo, forming 8–10 phyllo pastry cups, depending on how many Eggs

Jacobson you wish to have. Prick the bottoms of the phyllo with the tines of a fork and bake for 10-12 minutes. Remove the phyllo cups from the oven. Press phyllo that has puffed up back into place—it doesn't matter if it cracks and breaks.

Loosen the phyllo cups with a knife, making sure that none is sticking to the pan, then place a level Tablespoonful of Spinach Mornay in the bottom of each cup. Using a spoon or your fingers, smooth the spinach so that it lines the phyllo cup and comes up just about to the rim. Break an egg over a cup and, in the same manner that you would normally separate the egg white from the yolk, separate off some of the white and discard it or save for another use. Put the egg yolk with the remaining white into the spinach-lined cavity. Fill each of the phyllo cups in this manner. Season each egg with salt and pepper then sprinkle each with 1/2 teaspoon grated Parmesan then with 1/2 teaspoon heavy cream. Drizzle each with a little more melted butter. Return the muffin pans to the oven and bake the eggs for about 12 minutes, longer if you want a firmer egg. Serve with Mornay Sauce. Allow 1-2 eggs per person.

Here are still more individual-portion-size pastries. These use flaky, flavorful cornmeal pastry and subtle Mexican seasonings.

GOLDEN HUEVOS RANCHEROS *yields 6 pastries*

Golden pastry, spicy tastes, and creamy textures plus a softly running yolk make these a brunch, or anytime, treat.

1/2 recipe Cornmeal Tart and Turnover Pastry (p. 77)
  1 recipe Seasoned Bean Puree (p. 252)
1/4 cup freshly grated Parmesan cheese
  6 medium or large eggs
    About 1/2 cup Mexican Tomato Sauce (p. 241)
  4 ounces Cheddar cheese, grated
  2 ounces canned chopped green chilis
1/2 cup minced green of scallion

Preheat the oven to 400°F.

Divide the pastry into 6 equal parts and form each part into a ball. Roll each ball out to a 5 1/2-6-inch circle then press the edges up and in to form a slight lip around a circle of 4 1/2 inches diameter. Place the circles on a very lightly buttered baking sheet. Mix together the Seasoned Bean Puree and Parmesan and place a scant 1/4 cup of it in the center of each circle. With the back of a tablespoon make a good-size indentation in the puree, at the same time smoothing it almost but not quite to the edges of the circle. Break an egg into each indentation. Spoon about 1 Tablespoon of Mexican Tomato Sauce over each egg and sprinkle each with a generous Tablespoon of Cheddar. Distribute the chopped green chilis and minced scallion over each Huevo Ranchero and bake for 15-20 minutes, depending on how loose or firm you like your eggs.

PICADILLO PINWHEEL TARTS *yields 12 pinwheel tarts*

A tasty accompaniment to soups or salads for a light supper or hearty lunch.

1 recipe Cornmeal Tart and Turnover Pastry (p. 77)
1 recipe Picadillo (p. 254)
6 ounces Cheddar cheese, grated
   One 4-ounce can chopped green chilis, or minced scallion

Preheat the oven to 400°F.

Roll out the dough into a rectangle slightly larger than 12 by 16 inches then trim edges with a knife or pastry or pizza cutter so you have a clean 12 by 16-inch rectangle. Cut into twelve 4-inch squares.

Place paper baking cups in twelve 2½-inch muffin forms. Take the pastry squares and ease them into the cups, opening them up so that all 4 flaps or points are lying outside over the edges of the paper.

Fill each cup with a scant ¼ cup of Picadillo, mounding it slightly in the center. Sprinkle with grated cheese then with chopped green chilis or minced scallion. Bring the 4 points together at the center and pinch gently.

Bake for 30–35 minutes, or until the pastry is golden and crisp. Make sure the bottoms especially are not soft or soggy. Let cool slightly, remove from the pan, peel off the papers and serve.

When cool, the tarts can be wrapped in foil and frozen, then defrosted and reheated as needed.

MEXICAN CHEESE BEAN PINWHEEL TARTS *yields 12 pinwheel tarts*

These are also delicious at room temperature and even cold—great fare for picnics.

1 recipe Cornmeal Tart and Turnover Pastry (p. 77)
1 recipe Seasoned Bean Puree (p. 252)
¼ cup freshly grated Parmesan cheese
   About ½ cup Mexican Tomato Sauce (p. 241)
4 ounces Cheddar cheese, grated
2 ounces canned chopped green chilis
¼–½ cup minced scallion

Preheat the oven to 400°F.

Roll out the dough into a rectangle slightly larger than 12 by 16 inches, then with a knife or pastry or pizza cutter trim the edges so you have a clean 12 by 16-inch rectangle. Cut into twelve 4-inch squares. Place paper baking cups in twelve 2½-inch muffin forms. Take the pastry squares and ease them into the cups, opening them up so that all 4 flaps or points are lying outside over the edges of the paper.

Fill each cup with a rounded Tablespoon of Seasoned Bean Puree mixed with the grated Parmesan. Top each with a Tablespoon of Mexican Tomato Sauce and a Tablespoon of grated Cheddar. Sprinkle with some chopped green chilis and minced scallion then bring the 4 pastry points together at the center and pinch gently.

Bake for 30–35 minutes, or until the pastry—including the bottoms—is crisp and golden. Cool slightly, remove from pan, peel off papers and serve.

CRÊPES, BLINTZES,
PANCAKES
AND WAFFLES

CRÊPES

Basic Crêpe Batter
Buckwheat Crêpes
Cornmeal Crêpes
Mexican Cornmeal Crêpes
Sweet Cornmeal Crêpes
Broccoli Crêpes
Mushroom Crêpes
Herbed Crêpes
Sweet Crêpes
Chocolate Crêpes
Cheese and Apricot Corn Crêpes
Maple-buttered Buckwheat Triangles
Herbed Crêpes with Brie
Crêpes à la Mexicaine
Spinach and Mushroom Crêpes
Mushroom Pecan Crêpes
Ratatouille Crêpes
Eggplant Pockets
Elegant Seafood Mousse Stuffed Crêpes
Broccoli Crêpe Roll-ups with Cheddar Cheese and Bacon
Mushroom Crêpe Roll-ups with Cheddar Cheese and Bacon
Chatham Clam Crêpes
Sausage Crêpe Rolls
Hana's Palatchinken

BLINTZES

Basic Blintz Batter
Whole Wheat Blintz Batter
Joe Lazar's Strawberry Cheese Blintzes
Sweet Cheese Blintzes with Raisins
Savory Cheese Blintzes with Feta and Dill
Herbed Kasha and Potato Blintzes
Sweet Blintz Soufflé
Savory Kasha Blintz Soufflé

PANCAKES AND WAFFLES

Cottage Cheese Pancakes
Cottage Cheese Pancakes with Herbs
High-Protein Griddle Cakes
High-Protein Waffles

Delicate egg-rich pancakes rolled around sweet or savory fillings, dusted with sugar or sprinkled with cheese, or lightly napped with sauce . . . Crêpes are delicious for lunch or dinner, or as elements in a party buffet. But I think they are in their glory when served for brunch—crêpe brunches are one of my favorite ways to entertain.

There are 2 kinds of crêpe brunches I like to serve. One is a crêpe extravaganza with 2, 3, and even 4 different varieties of crêpes, usually 1 sweet and 1 or 2 nonsweet recipes so that people can savor crêpes in different flavors, colors, and forms. The combination might be Maple-buttered Buckwheat Triangles, Herbed Crêpes with Brie, and Elegant Seafood Mousse Stuffed Crêpes; plus a platter of sautéed apples or pears surrounded by sausages and a basket of Velvet Pumpkin Bread. Another brunch may feature 1 favorite crêpe, Cheese and Apricot Corn Crêpes, along with a round or lattice loaf of Picadillo- or cheese-stuffed brioche and Spinach and Avocado Torte. A lightly dressed green salad, a basket of homemade bread, and the suggestive smell of coffee brewing complete this marvelous meal.

The best thing about serving crêpes is that everything can be done the day before. The crêpes themselves can be made 2 days ahead, if need be, then filled the following day. The filled crêpes are arranged in their baking pans with all their sprinklings of sugar, gratings of cheese, or dots of butter, taken out of the fridge that morning, put into the oven 30-40 minutes before serving time, checked after 20 minutes—and just kept warm until ready to serve. It never ceases to amaze me how anything so tender and fragile as a finely made crêpe can be so durable a performer—yet it is. The finished crêpes are every bit as perfect and delicious as if they were assembled, baked, and eaten on the same day.

Here's how I prepare crêpes—and organize crêpe making to go as quickly and smoothly as possible.

I begin by laying out a large, clean bath towel on the kitchen counter where I want my freshly made crêpes to go. I get out my 2 trusty crêpe pans—inexpensive Teflon-coated frying pans about 6-6½ inches in diameter that I reserve for crêpe and blintz making alone. I melt butter in one of them, pour the butter into a bowl and set this in the center of my stove top along with a pastry brush. I place the crêpe batter nearby along with a plastic coffee measure on a small plate—setting up a traffic pattern that will accommodate the smooth, repetitive motions of crêpe making.

When all is arranged, I set my crêpe pans on a medium-high flame. When they are quite hot, I brush them with butter and pour a coffee measure of batter into each. (I have also used a ¼ cup measure filled one-half to three-quarters full.) I swirl the batter around to cover the bottom of the pan completely then return the pan to the flame. When the edges of the crêpe begin to darken, I pull back the farthest edge with my fingers, and if the bottom of the crêpe is golden and the edges well colored I flip the crêpe toward me, turning it over onto its other side. When it has cooked a bit on its second side, forming a few light specks of color, I turn the crêpe out onto the towel with its wrong or second cooked side facing up.

When the towel is covered with crêpes, I begin filling and folding the cool ones and arranging them in a baking pan or on a platter brushed with melted butter. If I am making a large quantity of crêpes, they will be arranged in double layers, with the appropriate sauce or topping on each layer. Then the crêpes are covered with plastic wrap or foil and put in the fridge until time for baking.

If you are a beginning crêpe maker, you may want to use only 1 pan. But once you have gotten into the special rhythm and ease of crêpe making, you will feel comfortable and efficient keeping 2 pans going at once. This is especially useful if you are producing crêpes in quantity.

Extra crepes can be stacked with a small piece of waxed paper in between them, then wrapped in foil and stored in the freezer ready for a leftover that suggests itself as a filling for an impromptu crêpe meal.

It's difficult to give suggested servings for crêpes because the number of crêpes people will eat depends on the particular crêpe being served, what is served along with it, and how hungry people are (*most* hungry at brunch, least hungry if there are lots of hors d'oeuvres). If you are serving a single type of crêpe as a main course, allow 3, possibly 4, crêpes per person. If you are serving several different kinds of crêpes, most people will help themselves to 2 of each kind. If you are serving crêpes plus other main courses, people will often serve themselves 2 crêpes, sometimes 1, and return for seconds. I always prepare more than I need because crêpes can be reheated and enjoyed days later.

BASIC CRÊPE BATTER *yields eighteen to twenty 6¹/2-inch crêpes or twenty-two to twenty-four 6-inch crêpes*

1½ cups milk
¼ cup water
3 extra-large eggs
1 cup all-purpose flour
½–¾ teaspoon salt
2 Tablespoons (¼ stick) butter, melted

Combine the ingredients in a blender jar. Blend at high speed, scraping down the sides as necessary, until the batter is well mixed. Pour the batter into a bowl and let sit for 1 hour before making crêpes. The batter can also be prepared the day before and kept overnight in the refrigerator.

If you want 6½-inch crêpes, use 3 Tablespoons batter; for 6-inch crêpes, use 2 Tablespoons (a coffee measure) of batter. See page 107 for crêpe-making techniques.

BUCKWHEAT CRÊPES *yields 24–30 crêpes*

3 cups milk*
4 extra-large eggs
3/4 cup all-purpose flour
1/2 cup buckwheat flour
1/4 cup cornmeal
2 Tablespoons sugar
2 Tablespoons sesame seeds (optional)
2 teaspoons salt
4 Tablespoons (1/2 stick) butter, melted
About 1/4 cup water, or as needed to thin to
desired consistency

*I use 2 cups regular milk and 1 cup skim or low fat.

Prepare according to the directions for Basic Crêpe Batter (p. 108). Stir the batter frequently when forming the crêpes as buckwheat flour and cornmeal both tend to separate out and sink to the bottom of the bowl.

The number of crêpes depends on their size and thickness.

CORNMEAL CRÊPES *yields twenty-one to twenty-two 6-inch crêpes*

1 1/2 cups milk
3 extra-large eggs
1/2 cup all-purpose flour
1/2 cup cornmeal, preferably stone ground
1/2–3/4 teaspoon salt
1/2–1 teaspoon sugar (optional)
2 Tablespoons (1/4 stick) butter, melted

Prepare according to the directions for Basic Crêpe Batter (preceding recipe). When making the crêpes, be sure to stir the batter regularly as cornmeal tends to sink to the bottom of the bowl.

MEXICAN CORNMEAL CRÊPES

Add 1 teaspoon oregano, 1/2 teaspoon chili powder (optional), and 1/2 teaspoon sugar.

SWEET CORNMEAL CRÊPES

Add 1 Tablespoon sugar and 1 Tablespoon Grand Marnier or liqueur of choice.

BROCCOLI CRÊPES *yields 17-18 crêpes*

2 Tablespoons finely minced shallot or onion
2 Tablespoons (¼ stick) butter
1½ cups milk
4 extra-large eggs
1 cup all-purpose flour
1 teaspoon salt
4 dashes Tabasco sauce
1 dash garlic powder
1½ cups bright green cooked chopped broccoli
flowerets, or one 10-ounce package frozen
chopped broccoli, cooked and well squeezed

Sauté the shallot or onion in butter until translucent and tender. Combine the milk, eggs, flour, salt, Tabasco sauce, and garlic powder in a blender jar. Add sautéed shallot or onion and blend until well mixed, scraping down the sides of the jar as needed. Add cooked chopped broccoli and blend until broccoli is minced and well distributed, but not pureed.
Use ¼ cup batter for each 6½-inch crêpe.

MUSHROOM CRÊPES
Instead of the broccoli, substitute Mushroom Duxelles (p. 250) prepared from ½-¾ pound mushrooms. Season the duxelles according to taste—fresh dill and/or chives are good choices.

HERBED CRÊPES *yields eighteen to twenty 6½-inch crêpes or twenty-two to twenty-four 6-inch crêpes*

1 recipe Basic Crêpe Batter (p. 108)

3-4 Tablespoons minced fresh herbs
(a combination of parsley, chives,
and/or dill)

Prepare according to the directions for Basic Crêpe Batter, adding minced herbs to taste.

SWEET CRÊPES *yields eighteen to twenty 6½-inch crêpes or twenty-two to twenty-four 6-inch crêpes*

1 recipe Basic Crêpe Batter (p. 108)

1 Tablespoon sugar
1 Tablespoon kirsch, brandy, rum, or other liqueur

Prepare according to the directions for Basic Crêpe Batter, adding sugar and liquor.

CHOCOLATE CRÊPES *yields eighteen to twenty 6½-inch crêpes or twenty-two to twenty-four 6-inch crêpes*

1 recipe Basic Crêpe Batter (p. 108)

2-3 Tablespoons unsweetened cocoa
1 Tablespoon sugar
1 Tablespoon kirsch, brandy, rum, or
other liqueur

Prepare according to the directions for Basic Crêpe Batter, adding cocoa, sugar, and liquor.

CHEESE AND APRICOT
CORN CRÊPES *yields forty-two to forty-four 6-inch crêpes*

These crêpes are seductively tender and creamy, gently fruity and sweet.

2 recipes Cornmeal Crêpes or
   Sweet Cornmeal Crêpes (p. 109)

16 ounces ricotta cheese
 8 ounces cream cheese, softened
18 ounces apricot preserves
   Butter
2-3 Tablespoons brandy
   Dried whole apricots (optional)

Preheat the oven to 375°F. Butter a large, shallow baking dish or ovenproof platter—2 pizza pans would work well.

Prepare the crêpes. Process or cream the ricotta and cream cheeses together. Spread a thin film of apricot preserves over half of each crêpe and spread about 1 Tablespoon of cheese filling over the other half. Fold the 2 halves together, then fold the crêpe in quarters to form a fan shape or triangle.

Arrange the crêpes points up and overlapping in the prepared pan or pans. (If you are using only 1 pan you will probably need to make a double layer.) Dot the crêpes with butter.

Warm about 1/4 cup of the preserves and thin with brandy. (I pour the brandy over the preserves, warm it, then ignite it to burn off the alcohol. Then mix the brandy and preserves together.) Drizzle this mixture lightly over the crêpes. If desired, scatter 5-6 dried whole apricots over the crêpes. Bake for 20-25 minutes, or until the crêpes are hot.

MAPLE–BUTTERED
BUCKWHEAT TRIANGLES *yields 24-30 crêpes*

I particularly love the delicate yet earthy flavor and subtle maple sweetness of these whole-grain crêpes. They are a tried and true favorite, wonderful with sausage and fresh strawberries or apples, or pears peeled, sliced, then sautéed in butter with a little sugar and lemon juice added.

1 recipe Buckwheat Crêpes (p. 109)

8 Tablespoons (1 stick) butter, softened
1/3-1/2 cup maple syrup

Preheat the oven to 375°F. Butter a shallow baking dish or ovenproof platter. Prepare the crêpes.

Beat the butter in an electric mixer or food processor. Add the maple syrup in a thin stream until the desired sweetness is achieved. Spread each crêpe lightly with the maple butter mixture. Fold the crêpe in half, spread with a little more maple butter, then fold again into quarters—into a fan or triangle shape.

Arrange the crêpes in an overlapping pattern on the prepared dish or platter. Brush with any remaining maple butter or with melted butter and bake until the crêpes are hot, but not crispy.

HERBED CRÊPES WITH BRIE *yields eighteen to twenty 6 1/2-inch crêpes or twenty-two to twenty-four 6-inch crêpes*

These crêpes are meltingly delicate, subtly flavored with herbs and Brie. For an interesting variation substitute a mushroom Brie-type cheese such as Bonchampi.

1 recipe Herbed Crêpes (p. 110)

1 recipe Thick Béchamel (p. 245)
1/2 pound (or more) Brie, rind removed
    Melted butter
    Freshly grated Parmesan cheese

Preheat the oven to 375°F. Butter a baking dish or ovenproof platter. Prepare the crêpes and the Béchamel. Add the Brie to the warm Béchamel, stirring until the cheese is melted and the sauce is smooth. Spread a little of this mixture (about 1 Tablespoon) over each crêpe and roll up into a thin cylinder.

Arrange the crêpes in the prepared dish or platter. Brush with melted butter and sprinkle lightly with grated Parmesan. Bake for 20 minutes, or until the crêpes are hot.

CRÊPES À LA MEXICAINE *yields twenty-one to twenty-two 6-inch crêpes*

Spicy Mexican seasonings, creamy cheese and beans, and tender grainy crêpes make these a delight of earthy and fine textures and intense yet subtle tastes.

1 recipe Mexican Cornmeal Crêpes (p. 109)

1 cup Seasoned Bean Puree (p. 252)
8 ounces cheese, grated (half Cheddar, half Jack)
2 rounded Tablespoons tomato paste
1 teaspoon chili powder
    Dash cayenne pepper
1 recipe Thick Béchamel (p. 245) to which you
    add one 14-ounce can drained green chilis
    Salt and Tabasco sauce to taste
1 recipe Mexican Tomato Sauce, reduced to quite
    thick consistency (p. 241)
    Additional grated Cheddar and/or Parmesan
    cheese for topping

Preheat the oven to 375°F. Butter a shallow baking dish or ovenproof platter. Prepare the crêpes.

Mix together the Seasoned Bean Puree, grated cheese, tomato paste, chili powder, and a dash of cayenne pepper. Add 1/4 cup Thick Béchamel with green chilis. Season with salt and Tabasco sauce to taste. Divide and spread the filling over the crêpes. Roll up the crêpes into thin cylinders and arrange them in the prepared baking dish or platter.

Thin the remaining Béchamel to a medium sauce consistency and nap the crêpes with the sauce, almost but not quite covering them. Spoon the thick Mexican Tomato Sauce down the center of the crêpes. Reserve any leftover sauce for another use or serve it in a sauceboat along with the crêpes.

Sprinkle the crêpes with grated cheese and bake for 20–25 minutes, or until the crêpes are hot and the sauce is bubbly.

SPINACH AND MUSHROOM CRÊPES *yields thirty-six to forty 6¹/2-inch crêpes or forty-four to forty-eight 6-inch crêpes*

2 recipes Basic Crêpe Batter (p. 108)

Two 10-ounce packages frozen spinach, cooked and well squeezed, or 2 pounds fresh spinach
1 recipe Mushroom Duxelles (p. 250)
6 hard-boiled eggs, grated coarse or chopped
2 recipes thick Mornay Sauce (p. 245)*
Dijon mustard to taste
Garlic powder to taste
Salt and freshly ground pepper to taste
Milk or cream
Grated Cheddar or longhorn cheese
Grated Parmesan cheese
Minced fresh parsley

Preheat the oven to 375°F. Butter a large, shallow ovenproof dish generously. Prepare the crêpes.

Combine the spinach, Mushroom Duxelles, hard-boiled eggs, and 2 cups of the thick Mornay Sauce. Season with a little Dijon mustard, garlic powder, and salt and pepper to taste. Spread each crêpe with a generous Tablespoon of the spinach and mushroom mixture. Roll up the crêpes and arrange in the prepared dish or platter.

Thin the Mornay Sauce with milk or cream to a pourable consistency and cover the first layer of crêpes thinly with some of this sauce and a sprinkling of grated cheeses. Arrange the second layer of crêpes, cover almost to the edges with the remaining sauce, sprinkle with grated cheeses, and garnish with minced parsley down the center of the crêpes.

Bake for 20–30 minutes, or until the crêpes are hot and the sauce is bubbly.

MUSHROOM PECAN CRÊPES *yields eighteen to twenty 6¹/2-inch crêpes or twenty-two to twenty-four 6-inch crêpes*

1 recipe Basic Crêpe Batter (p. 108)

2 recipes Mornay Sauce (p. 245)**
1 recipe Mushroom Pecan Filling (p. 251)
Grated Cheddar or longhorn cheese
Grated Parmesan cheese
Minced fresh parsley
Pecan halves

Preheat the oven to 375°F. Butter a shallow baking dish or ovenproof platter. Prepare the crêpes.

Add 1 cup of the Mornay Sauce to the Mushroom Pecan Filling. Spread a generous Tablespoon of this mixture over each crêpe. Roll up the crêpes and arrange them in the baking dish or on the platter.

Nap the crêpes with the remaining Mornay Sauce, leaving the edges uncovered. Sprinkle with grated Cheddar or longhorn and grated Parmesan, and sprinkle minced parsley down the center of the crêpes. Arrange pecan halves down the center of crêpes on top of the parsley. Bake for 20–25 minutes, or until the crêpes are hot and the sauce is bubbly.

*Prepare the sauce in a thick version, using 1 cup liquid to each 3 Tablespoons flour. For the cheese add 4 ounces cream cheese, 4 ounces Cheddar, and Parmesan to taste.
**Prepare the sauce with light cream and 4 ounces Cheddar cheese.

RATATOUILLE CRÊPES *yields eighteen to twenty 6 1/2-inch crêpes or twenty-two to twenty-four 6-inch crêpes*

1 recipe prepared Basic Crêpe Batter (p. 108)

2½-3 cups Ratatouille Sauce (p. 244)
 ½ pound mild white cheese, grated
   or diced fine
 ¼ cup freshly grated Parmesan or other hard
   grating cheese
 1 recipe Basil Béchamel (p. 246)
   Finely chopped fresh or canned tomato pulp
   Additional freshly grated Parmesan cheese

Preheat the oven to 375°F. Butter a shallow baking dish or ovenproof platter. Prepare the crêpes.

Combine the Ratatouille Sauce with grated or diced mild cheese and grated Parmesan. Divide and spread ratatouille mixture over the crêpes then roll them up and arrange in single or double layers in the prepared dish or platter.

Nap the crêpes with Basil Béchamel, not quite to the edges of the crêpes. (If you make 2 layers, cover the bottom crêpes with a light napping of Béchamel sauce and grated cheese.) Decorate with chopped tomato pulp down the center of the crêpes. Sprinkle with grated Parmesan. Bake for 20-25 minutes, or until the crêpes are hot and the sauce is bubbly.

EGGPLANT POCKETS *yields 12 pockets*

12 crêpes prepared with Basic Crêpe Batter
   (p. 108)

1 cup Seasoned Eggplant Puree (p. 257)
½ pound mozzarella, fontina, or part mozzarella/
   part provolone cheese, grated
¼ cup freshly grated Parmesan cheese
 1 recipe Basic Béchamel (p. 245) or
   Basil Béchamel (p. 246)
 1 recipe Basic Tomato Sauce, reduced to very
   thick consistency (p. 241)
   Additional freshly grated Parmesan cheese
   Minced fresh parsley or basil (optional)

Preheat the oven to 375°F.
 Combine Seasoned Eggplant Puree, grated mozzarella, grated Parmesan, and ¼ cup of the Bécha-

mel. Divide the filling among the crêpes: Place the filling in the center of each crêpe and fold the crêpe up envelope style to form a square pillow or pocket.

Spread the Basic Tomato Sauce over the bottom of a 9 by 13-inch baking dish. Arrange the Eggplant Pockets flap side down over the tomato sauce. Nap the top of each pocket with the remaining Béchamel and sprinkle generously with Parmesan. If you are using plain Béchamel, sprinkle the pockets with minced parsley or basil. Bake for 20-25 minutes, or until the crêpes are hot and the sauce is bubbly.

ELEGANT SEAFOOD
MOUSSE STUFFED CRÊPES *yields eighteen to twenty 6 1/2-inch crêpes or twenty-two to twenty-four 6-inch crêpes*

1 recipe Basic Crêpe Batter (p. 108)*

1 recipe Seafood Mousse II (p. 249)
1 recipe Seafood Velouté (p. 246)
   Freshly grated Parmesan cheese
   Minced fresh parsley

Preheat the oven to 375°F. Butter a shallow baking dish or ovenproof platter. Prepare the crêpes.

Spread each crêpe with 2-3 Tablespoons of mousse mixture, roll the crêpes into cylinders, and arrange in the prepared dish or platter.

Nap with velouté and sprinkle lightly with grated Parmesan and minced parsley. Bake for 25-30 minutes, or until the crêpes are hot and puffed and the sauce is bubbly. Brown briefly under the broiler.

BROCCOLI CRÊPE ROLL-UPS
WITH CHEDDAR CHEESE AND BACON *yields 17-18 crêpes*

Beautifully green broccoli crêpes are all the more savory with bacon and cheese. For variation use different cheeses. Or omit the bacon and spread the crêpes thinly with garlic and herb cheese, fold into triangles, brush with melted butter, and sprinkle with grated Parmesan.

1 recipe Broccoli Crêpes (p. 110)

8 ounces Cheddar cheese, grated
1 recipe Basic Béchamel (p. 245)
10-12 slices bacon, cooked and crumbled
   Melted butter
   Milk or cream

Preheat the oven to 375°F. Butter a shallow baking dish or ovenproof platter. Prepare the crêpes.

Set aside one quarter of the grated Cheddar.

*For a lovely taste and visual variation, substitute Broccoli or Mushroom Crêpes (p. 110) for the Basic Crêpes.

Spread about 1 Tablespoon of the Béchamel over each crêpe and distribute the bacon and remaining grated Cheddar over the sauce. Roll the crêpes up and arrange them in the prepared dish or platter.

Brush the crêpes with melted butter or, if you have enough sauce left over, thin it with milk or cream and brush or spoon this lightly over the crêpes. Sprinkle with the reserved Cheddar. Bake for 20-25 minutes, or until the crêpes are hot and the sauce is bubbly.

MUSHROOM CRÊPE ROLL-UPS WITH CHEDDAR CHEESE AND BACON

Substitute 1 recipe Mushroom Crêpes (p. 110) for the Broccoli Crêpes.

CHATHAM CLAM CRÊPES *yields forty-four to forty-six 2–2¹/₂-inch crêpes*

These tiny herbed clam pancakes are also wonderful hors d'oeuvres.

2 cups finely chopped onion
2 Tablespoons olive oil
2 cloves garlic, minced fine
1 anchovy, minced
1¹/₂ cups minced fresh parsley (1 large bunch)
Two 6¹/₂-ounce cans minced clams (packed in clam juice, not water)
¹/₂ teaspoon thyme
¹/₂ teaspoon oregano
¹/₂ teaspoon basil
¹/₄ teaspoon or generous pinch of sage
¹/₃ cup milk
¹/₃ cup all-purpose flour
2 eggs, beaten
¹/₂–³/₄ teaspoon salt
Several drops Tabasco sauce
Butter for frying
Lemon wedges

Sauté the onion in oil until it is tender. About midway through the sauté time add the minced garlic and anchovy. When the onions are transparent and softened, add the parsley and sauté until it is wilted. Strain the clam juice from the canned clams into the onion mixture then add the thyme, oregano, basil, and sage, raise the heat to high, and reduce until all the liquid is evaporated. Add the clams and continue cooking until the mixture is quite dry. Let cool.

Transfer the mixture to a bowl and add the milk, flour, and beaten eggs, stirring until the ingredients are well combined. Season with salt and Tabasco sauce to taste.

Drop the clam batter by Tablespoonfuls onto a hot, well-buttered griddle. Fry first on one side then the other until the crêpes are lightly golden. (Fry 1 clam crêpe to test for seasoning. You may want to add a little garlic powder or salt, etc.) Arrange these tiny crêpes, slightly overlapping in lines or concentric circles on a warm platter. Garnish with lemon wedges.

These can be fried in butter ahead of time, refrigerated, then reheated in a 350°F oven.

SAUSAGE CRÊPE ROLLS *yields eighteen to twenty 6 1/2-inch crêpes or twenty-two to twenty-four 6-inch crêpes*

These crêpes are fun to eat secured with toothpicks and served as a brunch hors d'oeuvre.

1 recipe Herbed Crêpes (p. 110)

Cooked small pork sausage links
Grated or sliced cheese such as Havarti or Swiss
Melted butter

Preheat the oven to 375°F. Butter a shallow baking dish or ovenproof platter. Prepare the crêpes.

Cook as many sausage links as you have prepared crêpes. Place 1 cooked sausage at the end of a crêpe and sprinkle some grated cheese over the sausage. (You can also use thin slices of cheese and just roll these around the sausages.) Roll up the crêpe with the sausage inside. Place in the baking dish or platter, brush lightly with melted butter, and bake for 15–20 minutes, or until the roll is warmed through.

HANA'S PALATCHINKEN

Hana served this dessert, and it was gobbled up despite already well-sated appetites. Prepare it with Chocolate Crêpes for an interesting variation.

12–14 Sweet Crêpes (p. 110)

filling
8 ounces cream cheese, softened
6 Tablespoons (¾ stick) butter, softened
1 egg yolk
¼ cup granulated sugar, or to taste
½ teaspoon vanilla extract

custard
1½ cups light cream, warmed
1 egg plus 1 yolk
½ cup confectioners sugar
½ teaspoon vanilla extract
1 Tablespoon rum, brandy, or kirsch
Additional confectioners sugar

Preheat the oven to 350°F. Have the prepared crêpes ready. Butter a 9- or 10-inch pie pan, preferably glass.

Process or cream together the cream cheese, butter, egg yolk, granulated sugar, and vanilla. Divide the filling and spread it evenly over the crêpes. Roll each up into a cylinder and cut it in half.

Arrange the crêpe rolls in 2 concentric circles in the prepared pie pan. Place in the oven until the crêpes are hot and slightly puffed, about 15 minutes.

Meanwhile blend or beat together the warmed cream, egg and egg yolk, confectioners sugar, vanilla, and rum, brandy, or kirsch. Pour this custard over the crêpes and bake for 35–45 minutes, or until the custard is set and a knife inserted into the center comes out clean. Serve warm, sprinkled generously with additional confectioners sugar.

BLINTZES

Blintzes will always have a very special place in my heart. My father, whom I adored, was the chief blintz maker in our family; and he would gather my younger brother and me together on an occasional Sunday afternoon to act as his lieutenant fillers and folders. I can still see him mixing and cooking his blintz batter, standing tall over the kitchen stove, an apron slung over his paunch and a cigar extending from his mouth. The ashes, he claimed, were the secret ingredient in his batter. Undoubtedly some ashes did find their way into the blintzes. However he achieved the result, these tender, fragile pancakes —enclosing sweet strawberry-flavored cheese, fried lightly golden in butter, and served with cool sour cream—were absolutely delicious.

Making blintzes is similar to making crêpes, but there are important differences. A blintz wrapper is slightly thinner than a crêpe and is cooked on only one side. When the batter (¼ cup) is poured into the lightly buttered hot 6-inch crêpe pan, the pan should be hot enough so that you hear a soft steamy sound and the batter lightly adheres, but not so hot that the batter begins to brown on contact. The goal is a very thin, tender, uncolored or only very slightly colored pancake. After the batter is poured into the pan, it is swirled around quickly, then the excess is poured back into the bowl, leaving a small flap on the side of the crêpe pan. If the batter does not adhere, raise the fire under the pan.

When the cooking pancake is beginning to look a little dry, but not yet coloring at the edges, turn the pan over on a bath towel laid out on the counter and rap it sharply. If the pancake doesn't come out, try loosening the flap with the tip of a knife or returning the pan to the heat for a few seconds more. When the pancakes are all cooked, or there is no more room on your towel for more, place a generous Tablespoon of filling on each cooled pancake, just above the flap. Shape the filling with the back of the spoon to form a square or a 1 by 3-inch rectangle, then turn the flap over to cover the filling, bring the 2 outsides together envelope fashion, then roll the blintzes over twice to seal and complete.

The assembled blintzes can be fried in butter immediately or stored in the refrigerator for a day or so covered lightly with waxed paper. Blintzes freeze well if you first refrigerate them on paper towels to absorb excess moisture. (I line them up in 2 layers on a jelly-roll pan.) To freeze, wrap the blintzes in aluminum foil in serving-size packages with waxed paper between the rows. Separate them while they are still frozen to prevent the fragile dough from sticking and tearing as it softens. Place them on paper towels for about an hour to defrost. When the blintzes are defrosted, fry them lightly in butter until they are golden, then enjoy as is or with a sauce or topping of choice.

Here are some favorite blintz recipes—minus the cigar ashes—for you to try.

BASIC BLINTZ BATTER *yields twenty-six to twenty-eight 6-inch blintz wrappers*

1 1/2 cups milk
1/4 cup water
3 extra-large eggs
1 cup all-purpose flour
2 Tablespoons (1/4 stick) butter, melted
3/4-1 teaspoon salt

Combine the milk, water, eggs, flour, melted butter, and salt in the jar of a blender. Blend, scraping down the sides of the jar as necessary, until the batter is well mixed. Pour the batter into a bowl and let stand for 30–60 minutes before cooking. See pages 107–108 for crêpe-making techniques.

WHOLE WHEAT BLINTZ BATTER

Substitute 1/2 cup whole wheat pastry flour (available at health-food stores) for 1/2 cup of the all-purpose flour. This yields a slightly heavier, less delicate blintz pancake that goes well with the Herbed Kasha and Potato Blintzes on page 121.

JOE LAZAR'S STRAWBERRY CHEESE BLINTZES

1 recipe Basic Blintz Batter (preceding recipe)

1 1/2 cups (12 ounces) strawberry preserves
6 ounces cream cheese, softened
1 egg plus 1 yolk*
1/2 teaspoon salt
24 ounces farmers cheese
Sour cream (optional)

Prepare the blintz wrappers.

Place the strawberry preserves, cream cheese, egg and egg yolk, and salt in the container of a blender or food processor. Blend until smooth. Pour into a bowl and add the farmers cheese. Beat with a hand electric mixer or a spoon until the ingredients are well combined. (If you like more pieces of the strawberry preserves in your blintzes you can simply beat all the ingredients together at once, eliminating the processing or blending stage.)

Follow directions for filling, folding, and cooking blintzes.

Serve plain or with sour cream.

*If you prefer a thicker filling, add only 1 egg or 2 egg yolks.

SWEET CHEESE BLINTZES WITH RAISINS

  1 recipe Basic Blintz Batter (p. 119)

  8 ounces cream cheese, softened
  3 eggs plus 2 yolks
4–5 Tablespoons sugar
 ½ teaspoon vanilla extract
      Pinch of salt
 28 ounces farmers cheese
 ⅓ cup raisins, plumped in boiling water and
      drained
      Sour cream and/or fresh fruit (optional)

Prepare the blintz wrappers.

Process or beat together the cream cheese, eggs and egg yolks, sugar, vanilla, and salt until smooth and creamy. Add the farmers cheese and beat or process until the ingredients are well mixed. Stir in the raisins.

Follow directions for filling, folding, and cooking blintzes.

Serve plain or with sour cream and/or fresh fruit.

SAVORY CHEESE BLINTZES WITH FETA AND DILL

  1 recipe Basic Blintz Batter (p. 119)

16 ounces cottage cheese
  1 cup feta cheese, well crumbled
  1 egg yolk
  1 cup minced scallion
  2 Tablespoons (¼ stick) butter
 ½ cup minced fresh dill
 ½ cup minced fresh parsley
      Plenty of freshly ground pepper
      Sour cream or grated Parmesan cheese
      (optional)

Prepare the blintz wrappers.

Combine the cottage cheese, feta cheese, and egg yolk. Sauté the scallion in the butter until it is softened then add the dill and parsley and sauté a few minutes more. When the scallion mixture has cooled slightly, add it to the cottage cheese mixture and season generously with freshly ground pepper.

Follow directions for filling, folding, and cooking blintzes but use slightly less than a generous Tablespoon of this filling for each blintz.

Serve these blintzes plain or with sour cream. Or, after the blintzes are sautéed in butter sprinkle them with grated Parmesan and heat in a hot oven or under the broiler briefly until the cheese begins to melt.

HERBED KASHA AND POTATO BLINTZES

1 recipe Basic Blintz Batter or Whole Wheat
   Blintz Batter (p. 119)

2 cups minced scallion, or a combination of
   scallion and onion
2 Tablespoons oil
2 Tablespoons (¼ stick) butter
¾ cup medium kasha (buckwheat groats)
2 teaspoons salt
1 teaspoon dill
½ teaspoon basil
½ teaspoon tarragon
   Freshly ground pepper to taste
1¼ cups chicken stock, heated (see
   p. 50)
¾ pound potatoes, boiled and drained
¼ cup freshly grated Parmesan cheese
2 Tablespoons milk
2 eggs, beaten

Sour cream mixed with fresh dill or
fresh scallions or chives (optional)

Prepare the blintz wrappers.

Sauté the scallion or scallion and onion in oil and butter until they are tender. Add the kasha and stir until the grains are separate and beginning to give off a slightly roasty aroma. Add salt, dill, basil, tarragon, and pepper, stirring them through the kasha. Add the hot chicken stock, cover and let cook over lowest heat for 10 minutes. Cool.

Mash the potatoes with the grated Parmesan and milk. Add them to the kasha. When the filling is cool, add the eggs and mix all the ingredients well. Taste for salt and pepper.

Follow directions for filling, folding, and cooking blintzes.

Serve plain or with sour cream that has been mixed with fresh dill or fresh scallions or chives.

SWEET BLINTZ SOUFFLÉ

A delicious way to serve blintzes at a large gathering or brunch. Prepare and bake as many pans as you need.

12 Sweet Cheese Blintzes with Raisins (p. 120)

2 cups sour cream
4 eggs
¼ cup sugar
4 Tablespoons (½ stick) butter, melted
1 teaspoon vanilla extract

Pinch of salt
Ground cinnamon or cinnamon sugar

Preheat the oven to 375°F. Butter a 9 by 13-inch baking pan generously and arrange the blintzes in 1 layer in the pan.

Blend together or process the sour cream, eggs, sugar, melted butter, vanilla, and salt and pour over the blintzes. Sprinkle the top lightly with cinnamon or cinnamon sugar and bake for 35–40 minutes.

SAVORY KASHA BLINTZ SOUFFLÉ

12 Herbed Kasha and Potato Blintzes (p. 121)

2 cups sour cream
4 eggs
4 Tablespoons (½ stick) butter, melted
   Pinch of salt
   Grated Cheddar and/or Parmesan cheese
   Minced fresh dill and/or parsley

Preheat the oven to 375°F. Butter a 9 by 13-inch baking pan generously and arrange the blintzes in the pan.

Blend together or process the sour cream, eggs, melted butter, and salt and pour over the blintzes. Top with grated cheese and minced fresh dill and/or parsley. Bake for 35–40 minutes.

COTTAGE CHEESE PANCAKES *yields nine 2½-inch pancakes*

These delicate pancakes are low in calories, high in protein, and easy to prepare. They make a lovely quick light lunch or breakfast, served with fresh strawberries or other fresh fruit. One recipe will serve 2 moderate eaters, so multiply accordingly.

¼ teaspoon salt
 2 eggs, separated
 2 Tablespoons sugar
⅓ cup cottage cheese
⅓ cup all-purpose flour
   Optional flavorings: dash vanilla extract, ground cinnamon, grated orange rind

Add salt to the egg whites and beat with an electric mixer until soft peaks form. Add the sugar gradually, beating until the whites are stiff but not dry. In a separate bowl, beat together the cottage cheese, flour, egg yolks, and any flavoring you might wish to add. Fold in the beaten egg whites.

Drop the batter by Tablespoonfuls onto a generously buttered hot griddle and cook over medium-high heat until the pancakes are golden. Turn and cook the other side.

COTTAGE CHEESE PANCAKES WITH HERBS *yields nine to ten 2¹/2-inch pancakes*

3 eggs, separated
1/2 teaspoon salt
1/3 cup cottage cheese
1/3 cup all-purpose flour
4 Tablespoons freshly grated Parmesan or other hard grating cheese
2 Tablespoons finely minced fresh parsley
2 Tablespoons finely minced green of scallion
2 Tablespoons finely minced fresh dill, or 1¹/2 teaspoons dried
  Dash garlic powder
  Freshly ground pepper to taste

Beat the egg whites and salt until the whites are stiff but not dry (an electric mixer is easiest for this). In a separate bowl beat together the cottage cheese, flour, egg yolks, grated cheese, parsley, scallion, dill, garlic powder, and pepper until the mixture is smooth. Stir in a little of the beaten egg white to lighten the mixture, then fold in the remaining egg whites.

Drop the batter by generous Tablespoonfuls onto a well-buttered hot griddle and cook over medium-high heat until the pancakes are golden. Turn and cook the other side.

HIGH-PROTEIN GRIDDLE CAKES *serves 4-6*

2/3 cup all-purpose flour
2/3 cup cornmeal, preferably stone ground
2/3 cup buckwheat flour or coarsely ground rolled oats
1/2 cup wheat germ
2 rounded Tablespoons dry milk (optional)
1-2 Tablespoons sesame seeds
4 teaspoons baking powder
1 teaspoon salt
4 eggs, plus enough milk to measure 2 cups
6 Tablespoons (3/4 stick) butter, melted, or oil
2 heaping Tablespoons unflavored yogurt

Combine the all-purpose flour; cornmeal; buckwheat or oat flour; wheat germ; dry milk, if you are using it; sesame seeds; baking powder; and salt. Beat together the eggs with milk, butter or oil, and yogurt and add to the flour mixture, stirring or beating with an electric mixer until the ingredients are well blended. Add additional milk if needed. Cook the pancakes on a well-buttered hot griddle and serve with maple syrup and butter.

HIGH-PROTEIN WAFFLES

Prepare batter as for High-Protein Griddle Cakes but separate the eggs and beat the whites until stiff then fold them into the batter just before you cook the waffles. Add enough milk to the yolks to measure 1³/4 cups (rather than 2 cups), although you may want to add additional milk to the batter. You may also want to add sunflower seeds or coarsely ground walnuts or pecans for flavor and crunch. Cook the waffles according to the instructions on your waffle iron and serve with maple syrup and butter. If the waffles are for a particularly festive occasion, you might also like to serve them with bowls of whipped cream, fresh fruit purees, and grated chocolate!

PASTA

LONG PASTAS

Ricotta and Walnut Sauce for Pasta
Basic Spaghetti and Eggs
Spaghetti and Eggs with Blue Cheese and Sunflower Seeds
Spaghetti and Eggs with Mushrooms
Spaghetti and Eggs with Asparagus and Mushrooms
Spaghetti and Eggs Pesto
Spaghetti with Favorite Meat Sauce
Spaghetti with Marinara Sauce
Vipasśtana
Spaghetti with Ratatouille Sauce
Pasta with Pesto
Fruits of the Sea Pasta
Linguini with Bluefish Sauce
Pasta with Squid, Squash, and Tomato Sauce
Chicken Fettucini
Vermicelli with Eggplant and Caper Sauce
Charlotte's Pasta

LASAGNA, CANNELLONI, AND MANICOTTI

Garden Lasagna
Ricotta Cheese Filling
Seafood Lasagna
Spring Celebration Lasagna
Garlic Béchamel
Mexican Lasagna with Chili and Beans
Meat and Sausage Lasagna with Eggplant
Eggplant Béchamel
Cannelloni Seafood Mousse
Manicotti Ratatouille
Manicotti Stuffed with Eggplant and Mushrooms

HOMEMADE PASTA DOUGHS

Homemade Egg Pasta
Food Processor Method
Hand Method
With a Pasta Machine
Carrot Pasta
Spinach Pasta
Tomato Pasta
Buckwheat Pasta
Herbed Pasta

PASTA ROLLS

Spinach and Ricotta Pasta Rolls
Seafood Mousse Pasta Rolls
Mexican Pasta and Bean Rolls

TORTELLINI, AGNOLOTTI, AND RAVIOLI

Seafood Tortellini
Bean Tortellini with Egg Sauce
Tortellini with Ricotta
Tortellini with Parsnip and Spinach Filling
Mushroom Pecan Tortellini
Mushroom Marsala Ricotta Tortellini

OTHER DOUGHY DELIGHTS

Pierogin
Spaetzle
Spaetzle with Mushrooms
Buckwheat or Whole Wheat Spaetzle
Herbed Spaetzle
Seeded Spaetzle
Cheese Spaetzle
Lemon Spaetzle
Potato Drop Gnocchi
Semolina Squares
Spanakugel

Pasta is one of the deeper passions in my life. Within moments of entering an Italian grocery I've gravitated to the shelves of commercial pastas, wondering how I can possibly add to my overflowing supply—and buying a box or two anyway. If there are bins of bulk pastas I can stare at them endlessly, luxuriating in the wheaty colors and lush forms, imagining them sauced and responding resiliently to my bite. Should they bring out a tray of fresh ravioli, my heart practically leaps at the sight of these perfect pillows of pasta. I used to joke that I must have been Italian, or a durum wheat plant, in a previous life. But I've given up trying to understand this fascination, acknowledging that I simply love pasta and that it touches and absorbs me in the most sensual and creative ways.

There are many worlds of pasta from which to choose. Each type and shape of pasta has its own characteristic way of holding a sauce and responding to the mouth and to the tongue. Whether to have the finest angel hair or broad thick lasagna, long pastas or short curves and tubes, commercial pasta or homemade depends on the particular pasta experience I wish to create. I'm especially partial to long pastas—spaghetti, linguini, vermicelli—anything that rolls around a fork in an exquisitely chewable lump. I tend to choose commercial dried pasta for lasagna, because I prefer a finished lasagna with more body and bite. I reserve homemade pastas for sauces that will enhance their subtle flavor and tender texture or for when I want the special delight of preparing and serving tortellini or other small stuffed pasta forms.

Good pasta, properly cooked, has a clarity of taste and texture and an exquisite receptivity to flavor. In choosing commercial pastas, it's important to find brands that don't have a floury, bland, or stale flavor, that hold up well under cooking and are not underdone one moment then limp the next. Generally the imported pastas purchased in Italian markets have a firmness and flavor not found in most supermarket brands. DeCecco and Menucci are my favorites, but I have also stocked up on the excellent Spigadoro on sale at my supermarket for half the price. There are fine American brands also—San Giorgio is one. Experiment with what is available in your area and find the ones that you like best.

Half the pleasure of eating pasta is in the bite, but when pasta is overcooked—for me at least—*all* the pleasure is gone. Pasta should be cooked al dente—to the tooth. It should have a firm, resilient, yet tender quality, not at all floury or brittle. The best way to tell when pasta is done is to test by tasting. Many nonimported brands suggest overly long cooking times, so begin testing several minutes before the time given on the package.

Cooking times vary with the shape and brand of pasta and, importantly, with the use to which it will be put. Fine angel hair (capelletti) needs to come out of the water still stiff, for it continues to cook in the heat of the sauce and will become soft and undistinguished on the plate. Lasagna, or any pasta that will be baked, needs to start off really extra al dente in order to maintain its character and appeal. Cooking times are different still for homemade noodles. These require only the barest of boilings, for they come to the pot in an already softly fragile and pliant state.

It saddens me that there was a long period in my life when I avoided pasta, believing that it was fattening. Paired with sauces that are all butter and cream, it is—and provides a pleasure that is fleeting at best. Pasta sauces using low-calorie herbs and stock reductions, vegetables or vegetable purees, nuggets of meat, chicken, or seafood, and moderate amounts of fats, cheeses, and beans can be brilliantly flavorful and nutritionally rich. Eaten in moderation, such well-sauced, well-stuffed pastas can satisfy body and spirit in the most generous and splendid ways.

A NOTE ON CHEESE

Most of the recipes in this chapter call for freshly grated Parmesan or other hard grating cheese. Treat "grated Parmesan" as a key flavor ingredient, one you choose and purchase with care, and you will be rewarded with better and deeper-flavored pasta dishes. Either grate your own (a food processor or hand grater works fine), or purchase small quantities of cheese freshly grated in an Italian market or cheese store. (If for convenience sake you need to purchase large quantities of grated cheese, it will keep better longer if stored in the freezer.) Parmesan that is freshly grated and sold in the cheese sections of some supermarkets can also be of good quality and is definitely superior to vacuum-packed grated cheese sold in cans and jars on supermarket shelves.

Different types of Parmesan, Romano, Asiago, and hard provolone all have subtle and wonderful flavor differences. Experiment with these cheeses, or a combination of cheeses in your recipes. Spaghetti and Eggs is even more wonderful with a really good-quality, well-aged Parmesan; with an excellent Parmesan mixed with a deep-flavored Asiago, it can be sublime.

In recipes where a mild white cheese is called for, such as in lasagna and cannelloni, I tend to choose a creamy cheese like Havarti or Muenster over mozzarella; or I might use a combination of mozzarella, Havarti, and a mildly smoky provolone. As with Parmesan, I enjoy modulating flavors by using different cheeses. Small amounts of unusual cheeses you have on hand can add to recipe experimentation and give surprisingly good results.

These recipes give proportions for using 1 pound of pasta but work equally well if halved.

LONG PASTAS

When I was growing up the word "spaghetti" *meant* spaghetti with a tomato and meat sauce. I had no idea of the variety of flavors and textures that could accompany a length of pasta. The pleasure has been in the finding out.

I want to introduce you to some of these beginning with a knockout ricotta and walnut sauce. So start twirling your forks—and pass the Parmesan.

RICOTTA AND WALNUT SAUCE FOR PASTA *serves 4-6*

This is one of my favorite pasta sauces and judging from the reactions of others I'm not alone. Don't let the blue cheese turn you away. It adds just the flavor balance needed with the sweetness of the currants, the richness of the nuts, and the tang of the grated cheese. Served with homemade Carrot Pasta, it is sublime.

        1   cup ricotta cheese
        1   cup light cream
 1¹/2–2   ounces mild blue cheese such as Danish
              blue
        1   large clove garlic, minced fine or crushed
   1–1¹/2   teaspoons salt
              Freshly ground pepper to taste
      ³/4   cup medium finely chopped walnuts
      ¹/4   cup currants
      ¹/4   cup freshly grated Parmesan or other hard
              grating cheese
        1   pound fettucini, or 2 recipes (equivalent of
              a 4-egg batch) Carrot Pasta (p. 149)
      ¹/4   cup (or more) pasta cooking water
        4   Tablespoons (¹/2 stick) butter, softened
      ¹/4   cup minced fresh parsley

Process or beat together the ricotta cheese, light cream, blue cheese, garlic, salt, and pepper until they are smooth and well blended. Stir in the walnuts, currants, and grated Parmesan until they are well distributed.

Cook and drain the pasta. Just before draining, add some boiling pasta water to the sauce to thin to the desired consistency.

Place the softened butter and minced parsley in a heated serving dish along with some salt and freshly ground pepper. Toss the drained pasta until it is evenly coated with parsley and butter.

Serve pasta with 2 generous Tablespoons of sauce on each plate. Sprinkle with additional currants, if desired, and pass additional grated cheese and the remainder of the sauce.

Spaghetti and Eggs. That's what "Daddy" called them. I watched this short, gruff Italian grandfather, whom everyone called "Daddy," beat together eggs, Parmesan cheese, and olive oil, toss it into a steaming pot of hot pasta, and create this sensual and immediate sauce. Years later I learned it was called "carbonara" and was traditionally prepared with bacon. But for me it will always be "spaghetti and eggs" the way Daddy makes them.

Spaghetti and Eggs is a wonderfully flexible recipe and lends itself readily to creative variations. It's also a favorite of mine to serve when friends drop by unexpectedly. Stay for dinner—why not? There are always eggs and Parmesan cheese in the fridge and, without a doubt, pasta in the cupboard. I can serve it as a main course or as an accompaniment-extender to any simple meat or fish main course I may have planned.

Preparing Spaghetti and Eggs is easy, but speed and coordination are of the essence. The heat of the pasta gently cooks the egg sauce and causes it to coat each steamy pasta strand. Too much heat (if your pot is on too high heat) and the sauce can scramble. Too little heat (if the pasta has cooled down) and the sauce will not thicken and coat. So have all your ingredients at the ready. Drain your pasta and immediately return it to the hot cooking pot (placed on a very low flame or none) and as soon as you have a free hand add the egg and cheese mixture and begin to toss. The cheese will melt, the eggs will thicken, and the sauce will happen before your eyes.

BASIC SPAGHETTI AND EGGS *serves 4 as a main, 6 as a first course*

The variations on this recipe begin to suggest the creative possibilities of Spaghetti and Eggs. Make your own variations with beans, tuna, or cooked sausage or pepperoni. Use fresh or dried herbs to taste. Add sautéed vegetables cut in thin julienne strips. Or just enjoy the original—the most delectable and sophisticated version of "macaroni and cheese" that I know.

        4 extra-large eggs
1¼–1½ cups freshly grated Parmesan or other
           hard grating cheese
       ⅔ cup milk
        4 Tablespoons olive oil
1½–2 teaspoons salt
           Plenty of freshly ground pepper
        1 pound spaghetti, linguini, or vermicelli
        4 Tablespoons (½ stick) butter, softened
           very thoroughly
           Minced fresh parsley or basil, or a
           combination (optional)
           Additional grated cheese

Beat together the eggs, grated cheese, milk, olive oil, salt, and pepper. Set aside.

Cook the pasta until it is perfectly al dente. Drain quickly then return the pasta immediately to the hot cooking pot along with the softened butter. Add the egg mixture and toss until thickened lightly. Taste for seasoning and add additional salt and pepper and grated cheese as needed. Add minced parsley and/or basil and toss or sprinkle on top of each serving.

Serve immediately on warmed plates, passing additional grated cheese.

SPAGHETTI AND EGGS WITH BLUE CHEESE AND SUNFLOWER SEEDS

Crumble 2–4 ounces blue cheese (domestic, Danish, or Gorgonzola) into the beaten egg mixture. Serve sprinkled generously with lightly toasted sunflower seeds and minced fresh parsley. Blue cheese adds a subtle extra zip and sunflower seeds just the right nutty crunch to this spirited variation.

SPAGHETTI AND EGGS WITH MUSHROOMS

Use only 2 Tablespoons (¼ stick) butter. Prepare Mushroom Duxelles (p. 250) using wine (Marsala suggested) and herbs of choice. Add Mushroom Duxelles (all or in amount desired) and toss to distribute. Serve sprinkled with minced fresh parsley.

SPAGHETTI AND EGGS
WITH ASPARAGUS AND MUSHROOMS *serves 4 generously as a main, 6 as a first course*

Superb. Fresh and asparagus-tasting, with the subtle nutty sweetness of Marsala.

    2   pounds fresh asparagus*
1 1/2   cups chopped onion
    4   Tablespoons (1/2 stick) butter
    4   large cloves garlic, minced fine
 1/2   pound mushrooms, sliced
    8   Tablespoons dry Marsala
        Salt and freshly ground pepper to taste
    4   extra-large eggs
1 1/2   cups freshly grated Parmesan cheese
 2/3   cup milk
    4   Tablespoons olive oil
    2   teaspoons salt
    1   pound spaghetti, linguini, or vermicelli
        Additional grated cheese

Trim off and discard tough nongreen bottoms of the asparagus stalks. (If the stalks have a good deal of this, you may want to start with a larger amount of asparagus.) Cut off the tips then cut the asparagus into 1/2-inch slices on a sharp diagonal. You should have about 5–6 cups of asparagus pieces. Set aside.

In a large wok or sauté pan sauté the onion in the butter until it is tender. Add the garlic, asparagus, and mushrooms and sauté over high heat until the asparagus slices are crisp-tender. Add the Marsala and continue cooking and stirring over high heat until the Marsala is completely absorbed and evaporated. Season lightly with salt and pepper then turn off heat.

*When asparagus is no longer in season, substitute broccoli, separated into fine flowerets. Blanch to precook slightly, then dry before sautéing.

Beat together the eggs, Parmesan, milk, olive oil, the 2 teaspoons salt, and pepper to taste. Set aside.

Cook the pasta until it is perfectly al dente. Before draining the pasta, though, turn the heat on under the asparagus mixture and make sure that it is very hot. Drain the pasta and add it immediately to the hot asparagus mixture. Turn off the heat or reduce it to low. Add the egg mixture and toss with the hot pasta and asparagus until the ingredients are well distributed and the pasta is coated with lightly thickened sauce. Taste for seasoning. Add additional cheese or salt and pepper if needed. Serve immediately on warmed plates, passing additional grated cheese.

SPAGHETTI AND EGGS PESTO *serves 4 or more*

This recipe captures some of the nutty richness of pesto and is a good high-protein "winter pesto." If you have Frozen Pesto Cubes in your freezer made at a time when basil was plentiful, substitute 2 cubes, or to taste, for the dried basil and reduce the olive oil to 2 Tablespoons.

      4 extra-large eggs
1 1/2 cups freshly grated Parmesan or other hard
         grating cheese
   2/3 cup milk
      4 Tablespoons olive oil
      2 Tablespoons basil
1 1/2 teaspoons salt
         Plenty of freshly ground pepper
      2 large cloves garlic, minced fine
      4 Tablespoons (1/2 stick) butter
      1 cup finely chopped (but not powdery) walnuts
      1 cup minced fresh parsley
      1 pound spaghetti, linguini, or vermicelli
         Additional minced fresh parsley
         Additional grated cheese

Beat together the eggs, grated cheese, milk, olive oil, basil, salt, and pepper. Set aside.

In a wok or large sauté pan sauté the garlic lightly in the butter. Add the walnuts and parsley, tossing for a few seconds, then turn the heat off until just before adding the pasta when you will turn it to high. Cook the pasta until it is perfectly al dente, drain quickly, then add the pasta to the hot walnut and parsley mixture. Toss briefly over high heat then turn the heat off or reduce it to very low. Add the beaten egg mixture and toss gently until the sauce thickens.

Serve sprinkled generously with more minced fresh parsley and pass additional grated cheese.

SPAGHETTI WITH FAVORITE MEAT SAUCE *serves 4 as a main, 6 as a first course*

Classic. The generic of spaghetti sauces. Meaty and rich tasting—a superb sauce for pasta.

      1 pound spaghetti, linguini, or long pasta of choice
      6 cups Favorite Meat Sauce (p. 243)
         Freshly grated Parmesan or other hard grating
         cheese

Cook the pasta until it is al dente. Drain and divide into 4 portions. Spoon Favorite Meat Sauce over the pasta and sprinkle with grated cheese. Pass additional cheese.

SPAGHETTI WITH MARINARA SAUCE *serves 4 as a main, 6 as a first course*

When I learned there was more than one way to sauce a pasta, this quickly cooked, sweet, and incredibly mellow tomato sauce was a revelation. If you like, you can add sautéed meatballs or sautéed sliced sausage during the last 15-20 minutes of simmering the sauce.

      1 pound spaghetti or linguini, or a 3-4-egg
         batch of Homemade Egg Pasta (p. 148)
   4-6 cups Marinara Sauce (p. 242)
         Freshly grated Parmesan or other hard
         grating cheese

Cook the pasta until it is al dente. Drain and divide into portions. Spoon Marinara Sauce over the pasta and sprinkle with grated cheese. Pass additional cheese.

VIPASŚTANA
(PASTA WITH BROCCOLI, TOMATOES, AND BLACK BEANS) *serves 4 or more*

Linguini sauced with broccoli and summer tomatoes was one of the delicious vegetarian dinners served at a weekend meditation retreat (Vipaśsana) at the Insight Meditation Society in Barre, Massachusetts. I've been making, eating, and loving it ever since—in my own herb-rich black bean variation. The beans add a marvelous taste and visual contrast and make this a high-protein meatless meal.

My friend and business partner, Norman Fine, who continually creates his own versions of this recipe, supplied the name, which is a play on the word "pasta" and the form of meditation practiced at the retreat. The sauce is delicious with either fresh tomatoes in season or canned when fresh are unavailable, and can be served cold, over pasta or by itself, for a deeply flavorful pasta or vegetable salad.

1 medium-large onion, chopped
3-4 Tablespoons olive oil
1 red bell pepper, cut into thin strips
6-7 cups small broccoli flowerets*

*Use flowerets from 1 large head broccoli plus enough thin slices of stem to give this volume.

4-5 large cloves garlic, minced
One 28-ounce can tomatoes
One 6-ounce can tomato paste
3 teaspoons basil
1 teaspoon oregano
1 teaspoon sage, or to taste
2 teaspoons salt
Freshly ground pepper to taste
4-6 drops Tabasco sauce
One 1-pound can black beans, drained
1 pound linguini
Toasted sunflower seeds
Freshly grated Parmesan cheese

In a large wok or sauté pan sauté the onion in olive oil until it is translucent, adding the red pepper strips toward the end of the sauté time. Add the broccoli and garlic and continue sautéing over medium-high heat for about 5 minutes. Add the tomatoes, tomato paste, and a tomato paste can (6 ounces) full of water. Add the basil, oregano, sage, salt, pepper, and Tabasco and simmer for 10 minutes. Add the drained black beans and simmer until the broccoli flowerets are tender but still a little crisp, 5–10 minutes more at the most.

Cook the linguini until it is al dente. Drain and toss the linguini with the broccoli mixture. Divide among 4 or more serving dishes. Sprinkle generously with toasted sunflower seeds and Parmesan cheese.

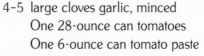

SPAGHETTI WITH RATATOUILLE SAUCE *serves 4*

This is so good. Sometimes I serve it with cubes of Italian fontina or Jack cheese or another mild white cheese. Sometimes I add kidney beans for added texture and protein. But it's sublimely simple and delicious just as it is. I prepare Ratatouille Sauce in large amounts and freeze it in 3-cup containers, so a healthy and delicious pasta meal is at my fingertips.

1 pound spaghetti, linguini, or long pasta of choice
6 cups Ratatouille Sauce (p. 244)
    Freshly grated Parmesan or other hard grating cheese

Cook the pasta until it is al dente. Divide into 4 portions and top each with well-spiced and simmering hot Ratatouille Sauce and plenty of freshly grated Parmesan.

PASTA WITH PESTO

serves 4 as a main, 6 as a first course

1 pound pasta of choice
2 Tablespoons (1/4 stick) butter
1 recipe Pesto Sauce (p. 247)
    Freshly grated Parmesan cheese

Cook the pasta until it is al dente; drain. Toss with the butter. Add the Pesto Sauce and toss, adding a little pasta water if needed to thin. Pass grated Parmesan.

FRUITS OF THE SEA PASTA *serves 4 as a main, 6 as a first course*

Seafood Marinara Sauce is simply one of the best pasta sauces I know. The addition of fresh sautéed seafood gives this pasta a sweet, garlicky, taste-of-the-sea elegance that is pure joy to eat.

2-3 large cloves garlic, minced
  4 Tablespoons (1/2 stick) butter
1 1/2 pounds scallops, shrimp, clams, or crab meat, or a combination, minced
  1/2 cup minced fresh parsley
  1 recipe Seafood Marinara Sauce (p. 242)
  1 pound angel hair or vermicelli, cooked al dente

Sauté the garlic lightly in the butter. Add the minced seafood and sauté until cooked through, adding parsley during the last few minutes of cooking. (If you are using crab meat, just toss lightly in the butter to heat through.) Toss the cooked pasta with just enough hot Seafood Marinara Sauce to coat each strand lightly. Divide the pasta among 4 dinner plates and spoon the seafood mixture over the pasta. Pass any additional sauce.

LINGUINI WITH BLUEFISH SAUCE *serves 4*

Fast and easy to prepare, this is a delicious variation on the traditional clam sauce for pasta. Rosemary and thyme add an earthy depth of flavor that
penetrates the pasta in its extra tossing and cooking in the sauce. If you prefer, you *can* prepare this
same sauce with canned clams or with minced
fresh clams.

- 4 large cloves garlic, minced fine
- 4 Tablespoons olive oil
- 4 Tablespoons (½ stick) butter
- 16 ounces (2 cups) clam juice or rich fish stock
  (see p. 51)
- 6 Tablespoons (or more) finely minced fresh
  parsley
- 2 teaspoons thyme
- 1–1½ teaspoons rosemary, crumbled
- ½–1 teaspoon oregano
  Salt and freshly ground pepper to taste
- 1½ pounds (or more) bluefish fillets
- 1 pound linguini

In a large wok or sauté pan sauté the minced garlic
lightly in the olive oil and butter. Add the clam juice
or rich fish stock, parsley, thyme, rosemary, oregano,
salt, and pepper. Bring the liquid to the simmer,
add the bluefish and poach in the liquid until just
cooked through. Remove the fish and flake into
pieces.

Cook the pasta until it is just short of al dente.
Drain the pasta and add it to the sauce. Toss the
pasta over medium heat until it is perfectly al dente
and most of the sauce has been absorbed. Add the
bluefish and toss to distribute. Serve immediately.

PASTA WITH SQUID, SQUASH, AND TOMATO SAUCE *serves 4*

I'm very fond of squid, and this is a flavorful,
aromatic, and nutritious way to serve it. In the
summer when zucchini is plentiful and I may not
feel much like cooking, this easily becomes a quick
but satisfying one-dish meal. If you don't want to
use squid, you can prepare this recipe with almost
any firm-fleshed fish or seafood, which will need
less simmering time than the squid.

- 1 cup chopped onion or white of leek
- 3 Tablespoons butter
- 3 Tablespoons olive oil
- 4–6 large cloves garlic, minced
- 2–4 anchovy fillets, minced
- 1 pound (or more) cleaned squid, diced
- 4 cups roughly chopped tomato pulp, preferably
  fresh
- 8 ounces (1 cup) clam juice or rich fish stock
  (see p. 51)
- ¼ cup minced fresh parsley
- 2 Tablespoons minced fresh basil, or
  2 teaspoons dried
- 2 teaspoons oregano
- 2 teaspoons thyme
- 2–3 teaspoons salt
- ½ teaspoon sugar or a generous pinch of saffron

6–8 drops Tabasco sauce
   Generous grindings of pepper
4 cups zucchini, cut into 1/2-inch dice
1 pound spaghetti, linguini, or vermicelli, cooked
   al dente

Sauté the onion or leek in the butter and olive oil until it is translucent. Add the garlic, anchovy fillets, and squid and sauté until the squid becomes opaque. Add the remaining ingredients except for the zucchini and pasta and simmer until the squid is tender. Add the zucchini and simmer until the zucchini is cooked through and tender but not soft.

Divide the cooked pasta into 4 portions and spoon the sauce over them.

CHICKEN FETTUCINI *serves 4 as a main, 6 as a first course*

Rich, but the servings are a little smaller to compensate. This is not the pasta for everyday eating—save it for a special treat. It's very easy to prepare. Shredded raw spinach can also be added to the chicken and mushroom sauté for additional lovely green color.

4 Tablespoons (1/2 stick) butter
1 pound skinned and boned chicken breasts,
   cut into small (1/2-inch) cubes
4 ounces (or more) mushrooms, sliced
1/2 cup minced scallion
1/2 cup minced fresh parsley
1 cup heavy cream
   One 4-ounce package herb cheese with
   garlic, such as Rondelé or Boursin
1/4–1/2 cup freshly grated Parmesan cheese
   Salt and freshly ground pepper to taste
12 ounces green fettucini, or a 3-egg batch of
   Homemade Egg Pasta (p. 148), or an
   equivalent amount of Carrot or Spinach
   Pasta (p. 149)
   Additional grated cheese

Melt the butter in a wok or large sauté pan. Sauté the chicken cubes and mushrooms over medium-high heat until the chicken loses its raw color, adding the scallion and parsley during the last minute or so of sauté time. Lower the heat, pour in the cream, crumble in the garlic-herb cheese, and add the Parmesan. Stir until the cheese is melted. Season with salt and pepper to taste and add additional Parmesan, if desired.

Cook the pasta until it is al dente, drain and add to the hot sauce. Toss and serve with additional grated cheese.

VERMICELLI WITH EGGPLANT AND CAPER SAUCE *serves 4*

A light, herb-flecked sauce, creamy with eggplant, piquant from capers and cheese.

1 medium onion, diced
1 red bell pepper, diced
1 green bell pepper, diced
4 large cloves garlic, minced
4 Tablespoons (1/2 stick) butter
3 cups chopped tomato pulp, fresh or canned
1 cup chicken stock (see p. 50)
2 Tablespoons (or more) minced fresh parsley
2 Tablespoons minced fresh basil, or
  2 teaspoons dried
2 cups Seasoned Eggplant Puree (p. 257)
3-4 Tablespoons capers
1 1/2 teaspoons salt, or to taste
  Freshly ground pepper to taste
1 pound vermicelli or long pasta of choice
  Freshly grated Parmesan or other hard
  grating cheese

Sauté the onion, diced peppers, and garlic in the butter, adding the garlic as the onion begins to soften and become translucent. Add the tomato pulp, chicken stock, parsley, and basil and cook over medium-high heat for about 10 minutes, so the tomato pulp can cook down a bit and the liquid reduce. Add the Seasoned Eggplant Puree, capers, salt, and pepper and heat through.

Cook the pasta until it is al dente. Divide it into 5 portions and spoon the sauce over them. Sprinkle with grated cheese and pass additional cheese.

CHARLOTTE'S PASTA *serves 2*

My friend Charlotte Layman serves this healthy, simple-to-prepare pasta primavera. She uses cauliflowerets and yellow squash, adding diced pimento and sliced black olives with the butter. Use your imagination and the suggestions of your refrigerator and market to create pastas of great simplicity and taste. I especially love the addition of sunflower seeds for texture and protein. Try pine nuts, if you like them. I sometimes add minced fresh herbs, especially basil, as well.

6 ounces (1/2 box) spinach fettucini, or 1/2 recipe
  homemade Tomato or Spinach Pasta (p. 149)*
4 cups vegetables, cut up:
  1 small yellow squash, halved lengthwise and
  sliced
  small broccoli flowerets
  small cauliflowerets
  1 small red bell pepper, diced
2 Tablespoons (1/4 stick) butter, softened
  Freshly ground pepper to taste
  Parmesan cheese to taste
  Sunflower seeds to taste (optional)

Cook spinach fettucini, if using, approximately 5 minutes in boiling salted water. Add the vegetables and cook 1 1/2-2 minutes more or until pasta is just al dente. Drain. Toss with butter and a few grinds of pepper. Serve sprinkled generously with Parmesan cheese and, if you like, sunflower seeds.

*If you are using homemade pasta, add vegetables and pasta to the boiling water at the same time since each needs only a minute or two to cook to proper tenderness.

LASAGNA, CANNELLONI, AND MANICOTTI

These pastas are among my favorites for entertaining. They can be prepared the morning of the day I am going to serve them, or even the night before. Warmed homemade bread or rounds of crisp, hot garlic toast and a perfectly dressed salad are all that are needed to complete this beautiful and satisfying meal.

I take the lasagna, cannelloni, or manicotti out of the refrigerator a couple of hours before serving time and give it a little extra time when baking to come to a hot and bubbly state. Then I let it stay in a warm oven until I am ready to serve. It's so simple, easy, and neat. With this kind of dinner my kitchen is clean, and I feel relaxed and freed of any complicated cooking tasks when friends arrive.

The main thing to be aware of when preparing these pastas in advance is to make doubly sure the pasta is extra al dente, for both contact with wet sauces and baking soften pasta considerably. It's hard to err on the side of too al dente. If pasta is just flexible enough to work with or to stuff, you can be sure it will be delicious when baked and served.

My oven-to-table lasagna pan measures 8 by 13 inches and will accommodate four layers of lasagna noodles with four strips of pasta in each layer. (There are sixteen strips in a 1-pound box.) If you are using a pan that measures 9 by 13 inches, you can either make just three layers of pasta with five strips in each layer (and divide the filling accordingly) or take four additional noodles from another box to give you enough for four layers of five strips each.

GARDEN LASAGNA *serves 8*

This is one of my favorite lasagne, full of health, gorgeous color, and great textures and tastes.

3 cups Ratatouille Sauce, well seasoned and tomato-y (p. 244)
  One 10-ounce package frozen chopped spinach, cooked and well squeezed, or 10 ounces fresh spinach, cooked, squeezed, and chopped
  One 1-pound can kidney beans, drained
1/2 cup freshly grated Parmesan or other hard grating cheese
1 recipe Ricotta Cheese Filling (following recipe)
  Dried or minced fresh basil to taste

1 pound lasagna noodles, cooked *extra* al dente
1 pound creamy mild white cheese, such as Muenster, Havarti, mozzarella, or a combination, grated or cubed

Preheat the oven to 375°F. Butter a lasagna pan generously.

Combine the Ratatouille Sauce, half the cooked spinach, the kidney beans, and the grated Parmesan; set aside. Combine the Ricotta Cheese Filling, the remaining cooked spinach, and dried or fresh basil to taste; set aside. Cover the bottom of the prepared pan with the noodles. Spread one half of the ricotta mixture over the noodles and sprinkle with one quarter of the grated or cubed white cheese. Cover with noodles and spread on one half of the ratatouille mixture, then top that with another one quarter of the grated or cubed cheese. Repeat these 2 layers one more time, ending with the ratatouille then the cheese as the topmost layer. Bake for 35-45 minutes, or until hot and bubbly. Let cool slightly before serving.

RICOTTA CHEESE FILLING *yields about 4 cups*

1½ pounds ricotta cheese
  2 eggs
½ cup freshly grated Parmesan or other hard grating cheese
    Salt, pepper, and freshly grated nutmeg to taste
    Minced fresh parsley or basil (optional)

Combine all the ingredients.

SEAFOOD LASAGNA *serves 8 or more*

This is an extraordinary lasagna, one that I save for very special occasions. Crab meat, shrimp, and scallops make it an expensive dish to prepare, but the flavors are exquisite, well worth the expense.

  3 cups Seafood Marinara Sauce (p. 242)
  1 pound (or more) any combination of scallops, shrimp, diced monkfish, minced fresh clams, or other fish or seafood, sautéed in butter
½ pound fresh or frozen crab meat
  1 pound lasagna noodles, cooked *extra* al dente
  1 recipe Basic Béchamel (p. 245)*
  1 pound mild white cheese, such as mozzarella, Muenster, Havarti, or a combination, grated or sliced thin
¾ cup freshly grated Parmesan or other hard grating cheese

*There will be beautifully flavored juices after sautéing the seafood. Drain these and use as part of the liquid in your Béchamel. I often prepare the Béchamel with part cream and part clam juice—more like a seafood velouté—for even more rich seafood flavor.

  2 Tablespoons minced fresh parsley
  1 teaspoon oregano or thyme, or a combination

Preheat the oven to 375°F. Butter a lasagna pan.
    Reserve 1 cup of the Seafood Marinara Sauce for topping. Mix the sautéed fish or seafood and the crab meat with the remaining sauce. Place 1-2 Tablespoons of the reserved sauce on the bottom of the prepared pan and cover with noodles. Spread one third of the seafood and sauce mixture over the noodles. Dot with Béchamel and distribute over this one quarter of the mild white cheese and the Parmesan. Repeat with 2 more layers. Cover with the last layer of noodles, spread with the reserved sauce and remaining cheeses. Sprinkle with minced parsley and oregano or thyme. Bake for 35-45 minutes, or until hot and bubbly. Let cool slightly before serving.

SPRING CELEBRATION LASAGNA *serves 8 or more*

The fresh, crisp flavor and jewel-green color of asparagus make this lasagna a delicious affirmation of spring. Smooth and cheesy, with juicy bites of mushroom, the subtle, smoky hint of prosciutto, and the elegant taste of crab meat—what better way is there to celebrate the end of winter?

  3 pounds asparagus, preferably thin stalks
1½ cups chicken stock (see p. 50)
  2 Tablespoons olive oil
  1 pound mushrooms, large if possible
  4 ounces (or more) prosciutto, sliced paper thin*
  1 recipe Garlic Béchamel (following recipe)
  1 pound lasagna noodles, cooked *extra* al dente
  1 pound fresh crab meat

¾ pound mild white cheese, such as Muenster, Jack, Havarti, grated
¾ cup freshly grated Parmesan or other hard grating cheese
2–3 ounces longhorn cheese for topping (optional, for color)

Preheat the oven to 375°F. Butter a lasagna pan.

Cut off the top 2 inches or so of asparagus tips and cook them in the chicken stock until they are just tender. Remove them with a slotted spoon and set aside for the top of the lasagna. Cut the remaining asparagus into 1-inch lengths, discarding the tough bottoms, and cook these in the chicken stock until they are crisp-tender. Remove them with a slotted spoon and set aside. Reduce the chicken stock over high heat to 1 cup. (This can be used as part of the liquid in the Garlic Béchamel.)

Heat the olive oil in a wok or large sauté pan. If the mushrooms are large, cut them in somewhat thick slices; if small, leave whole or cut in halves. Sauté the mushrooms over high heat until they begin to lose their raw look. Slice the prosciutto slices into thin strips and add these to the mushrooms, tossing and stirring until the mushrooms are cooked but not soft. (The mushroom juices can be used as part of the liquid in the Garlic Béchamel.)

Next assemble the lasagna. Spread a few Tablespoonfuls of Garlic Béchamel over the bottom of the prepared pan and cover with a layer of noodles. Distribute one third of the mushrooms, one third of the asparagus pieces, one third of the crab meat, and one quarter of the grated white cheese and the Parmesan over the noodles. Spoon about one quarter of the Garlic Béchamel over all. Repeat with 2 more layers. Top with a fourth layer of noodles and spread the remaining Béchamel over the noodles so they are lightly covered. Sprinkle with the remaining white cheese. Arrange the asparagus tips in rows over the top of the lasagna and sprinkle the remaining grated Parmesan down the center of the asparagus tips. If you have any Béchamel left over, thin it slightly and dribble this also down the center of the tips. Finish with a sprinkling of orange longhorn cheese, if desired. Bake the lasagna for 35–45 minutes, or until hot and cooked through. Let cool slightly before serving.

*If you would like a vegetarian lasagna, eliminate the prosciutto and use smoked mozzarella or Bruder Basil for part of the cheese.

GARLIC BÉCHAMEL

6 Tablespoons (¾ stick) butter
1 small onion, minced fine
1-2 large cloves garlic, minced fine
6 Tablespoons all-purpose flour
3-3¼ cups liquid:
    1 cup reduced chicken-asparagus stock (see preceding recipe)
    2 cups milk or light cream
    Liquid exuded from mushroom-prosciutto cooking (see preceding recipe)
    Salt and freshly ground pepper to taste
4-6 drops Tabasco sauce

Melt the butter in a medium-size saucepan. Sauté the onion until it is tender, adding the garlic toward the end of the sauté time. Add the flour and stir with a wire whisk, cooking this "roux" over medium heat for several minutes, being careful that it doesn't burn and lose its golden color. Add the liquid to the butter and flour mixture, whisking constantly. Cook over medium heat until thickened, whisking regularly. Season with salt, pepper, and Tabasco sauce.

MEXICAN LASAGNA WITH CHILI AND BEANS *serves 8-12*

Mexican Lasagna? Wait till you taste this wonderful combination of spicy, creamy, beany, chewy, and smooth. Begin with an assertively flavored chili, for the cheeses, pasta, and sour cream tame the spice and heat considerably.

5 cups Jack's Famous Chili and Beans (p. 211), well spiced, or 4 cups Jack's Chili with 1 cup Mexican Tomato Sauce (p. 241) for topping
1 pound lasagna noodles, cooked *extra* al dente
6 ounces Monterey Jack cheese, grated
6 ounces Cheddar cheese, grated
    About ¾ cup freshly grated Parmesan cheese
1 cup sour cream
    One 4-ounce can (or more) green chilis, chopped or cut into thin strips

Preheat the oven to 375°F. Butter a lasagna pan lightly.

Spread a little Jack's Famous Chili or Mexican Tomato Sauce on the bottom of the prepared pan and cover with noodles. Reserve 1 cup of chili or 1 cup of tomato sauce for topping. Spread the noodles with one third of the remaining chili, one quarter of the cheeses, and dot with little teaspoons of sour cream. Repeat with 2 more layers. Cover with the last layer of noodles, the reserved chili or tomato sauce, and the remaining cheese. Make a lattice pattern over the top of the lasagna with the thin strips of green chili and place a dab of sour cream in the center of each lattice opening. Or just chop the chilis and sprinkle over the top of the lasagna. (If you like, you can chop additional green chilis and add to the inner layers.) Bake the lasagna for 35-45 minutes, or until hot and bubbly. Let cool slightly before serving.

MEAT AND SAUSAGE LASAGNA WITH EGGPLANT *serves 8-12*

Eggplant Béchamel gives this classic lasagna an exquisitely smooth quality and a subtle nutlike taste.

4 cups (or more) Favorite Meat Sauce (p. 243)
1 pound lasagna noodles, cooked *extra* al dente
1 pound mild white cheese, such as Muenster, Havarti, mozzarella, or a combination, plus a small amount of provolone if you like it, grated
1 cup freshly grated Parmesan or other hard grating cheese
1 recipe Eggplant Béchamel (following recipe)
   Minced fresh parsley
   Basil or oregano

Preheat the oven to 375°F. Butter a lasagna pan.

Reserve 1 cup Favorite Meat Sauce for topping. Spread a little sauce in the bottom of the prepared pan and cover with noodles. Spread the noodles with one third of the remaining meat sauce, one quarter of the cheeses, and one third of the Eggplant Béchamel. Repeat with 2 more layers. Cover with the last layer of noodles, the reserved sauce, and the remaining cheese. Sprinkle with minced parsley and basil or oregano. Bake for 35–45 minutes, or until hot and bubbly. Allow to cool slightly before serving.

EGGPLANT BÉCHAMEL

2 Tablespoons (¼ stick) butter
2 Tablespoons all-purpose flour
2 cups Seasoned Eggplant Puree (p. 257)
   A few gratings of fresh nutmeg
   Salt and freshly ground pepper to taste

Melt the butter in a small saucepan, preferably one with a stainless steel or enamel surface. Add the

flour and whisk the gently bubbling mixture over medium heat for a minute or two, being careful not to let this "roux" burn or lose its golden color. Add the Seasoned Eggplant Puree and whisk until the mixture has thickened. Season to taste with nutmeg, salt, and pepper.

I've always baked and served cannelloni and manicotti in a way that maintains their individual form, with each person receiving 1 or 2 cylinders. My friend Michael Keane showed me another way. Preparing Cannelloni Seafood Mousse for a large dinner party, he layered filled cannelloni, sauce, and cheese up to the top of an earthenware casserole, baked then served it in large lasagnalike spoonfuls. The recipes reflect my penchant for single layering. Thanks to Michael I can invite you to try the cannelloni and manicotti assembled another way.

CANNELLONI SEAFOOD MOUSSE *serves 4-6*

Utterly delicious. This can be enriched with a thin layer of Seafood Velouté (p. 246) spooned over each cannelloni before napping on the tomato sauce.

12 commercial manicotti tubes, or a 2-egg batch of Homemade Egg Pasta (p. 148), or an equivalent amount of Spinach Pasta (p. 149)
1 recipe Seafood Mousse III (p. 249)
1 recipe Seafood Marinara or Seafood Tomato Sauce (p. 242)
1/2 pound mild white cheese, such as Havarti, Muenster, or mozzarella, grated or sliced
   Minced fresh parsley

Preheat the oven to 375°F.

If you are using commercial pasta, boil the tubes until they are just pliable, drain, and rinse in cool .

water. If using homemade pasta, roll out by hand or machine (#4 setting) and cut into 3½ by 5-inch pieces. Let dry for 20-30 minutes. Drop the pasta into boiling water for 20-30 *seconds,* rinse in cool water, and lay on kitchen towels to absorb excess moisture.

Stuff manicotti tubes with the mousse mixture using a pastry bag or a small spoon. Or place a line of mousse mixture down the center (the short way) of the pasta squares and fold each of the long sides over the mousse. Spread several Tablespoons of sauce in the bottom of a large ovenproof baking dish. Lay out the cannelloni in a single layer. Top with the remaining sauce and place a thin slice or a grating of cheese over each cannelloni. Sprinkle with parsley. Bake for 30-40 minutes, or until puffed and bubbly.

MANICOTTI RATATOUILLE *serves 5-6*

These manicotti are fresh and delicious with vegetables. Sometimes I add cooked kidney beans to the ratatouille filling.

 2 cups thick Ratatouille Sauce (p. 244), cooled
1/2 pound mild white cheese, such as mozzarella or Muenster, grated or diced fine
1/4 cup freshly grated Parmesan or other hard grating cheese
12 manicotti tubes, cooked *extra* al dente
 1 recipe Basil Béchamel (p. 246)
1/2 cup finely chopped tomato pulp, from fresh tomatoes or canned plum tomatoes

Preheat the oven to 375°F. Butter lightly a baking dish large enough to hold the manicotti in a single layer.

Combine the Ratatouille Sauce, grated or diced white cheese, and grated Parmesan. Stuff the manicotti tubes with this mixture. Spread 1/2 cup of the Basil Béchamel on the bottom of the prepared baking dish and arrange the manicotti over it. Nap with the remaining Béchamel. Arrange chopped tomato pulp down the center of the dish. Bake for 30-40 minutes, or until hot and bubbly.

MANICOTTI STUFFED WITH EGGPLANT AND MUSHROOMS *serves 4-6*

1 medium eggplant (about ¾ pound)*
½ cup chopped onion
2 large cloves garlic
2 Tablespoons olive oil
4 ounces mushrooms, halved if small, quartered if large
2 teaspoons dried basil, or 2 Tablespoons minced fresh
1 teaspoon oregano
Salt and freshly ground pepper to taste
½ cup freshly grated Parmesan cheese
1 recipe Basic Béchamel (p. 245)
One 10-ounce package frozen chopped spinach, cooked and well squeezed**
8 ounces mozzarella or other mild white cheese (some provolone lends a nice flavor), grated or diced fine
12 manicotti tubes, cooked *extra* al dente
1 recipe Basic Tomato Sauce (p. 241)

Peel the eggplant and cut into ½-inch slices. Salt generously and let sit on paper towels for 30 minutes. Blot dry then cut into ½-inch cubes. In a wok or large frying pan sauté the onion and garlic in olive oil. Add the eggplant cubes and mushrooms and sauté over medium-high heat until the eggplant begins to brown a little. Add the herbs, toss and cook a bit, but before the eggplant begins to burn, cover the pan tightly, lower heat slightly, and sauté/steam over low heat until the eggplant is tender. Season with salt and pepper to taste. Let

cool. (The eggplant can be prepared up to this point and refrigerated or frozen.)

Preheat the oven to 375°F. Add the grated Parmesan to the Basic Béchamel. Combine the cooled eggplant with the cooked spinach, grated or diced cheese, and ¼ cup of the Béchamel. Stuff the manicotti tubes with this mixture. Spread a few Tablespoons of Basic Tomato Sauce in the bottom of a baking dish large enough to hold the manicotti in a single layer. Arrange the manicotti over it. Nap the remaining Béchamel down the center of the manicotti then cover the manicotti almost to the edges with the remaining Basic Tomato Sauce. If desired, you can sprinkle on additional grated Parmesan or other hard grating cheese. Bake for 35 minutes, or until hot and bubbly.

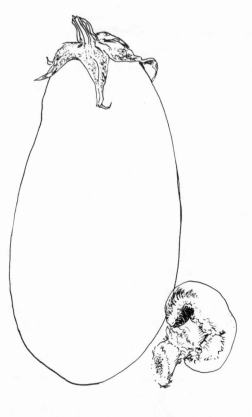

*There is nothing more frustrating than ruining a delicious dish with the addition of a bitter eggplant. Salting helps remove excess, and potentially bitter, juices. The best insurance, though, is to peel a small portion of the eggplant then touch it with your tongue. If it tastes obviously bitter, replace it with another eggplant.
**You can omit the spinach and substitute minced fresh parsley.

Cannelloni
and
Manicotti

HOMEMADE PASTA DOUGHS

It certainly isn't necessary to make your own pasta. You could be content to eat only pasta that is commercially made—it tastes so good and takes so many different forms. Yet you would never have the thrill of seeing your own noodles tossed and drying on a counter or hanging elegantly from wooden dowels; nor would you swell with pride as you form your own tortellini and watch them line up on a pan. You can order tortellini and other stuffed homemade pastas at a restaurant or buy them at an Italian market and even a supermarket. Yet you will never find them so varied or filled so imaginatively as you can do it yourself—with seafood mousse; beans and herbs; parsnips; or mushrooms, nuts, and cheese. You could actually have quite extraordinary pasta-eating experiences without *ever* making your own—of this I am quite sure. Yet you would miss the experience of creating golden carrot pasta tossed with glorious ricotta walnut sauce or egg pasta swirled around bright spinach filling, sliced into beautiful contrasting pinwheeling rounds.

The world of homemade pasta is a creative and gratifying place in which to cook and play, yet I approached it with enormous trepidation, procrastinating and rationalizing for the longest time. It would make such a mess in the kitchen! You had to have a pasta machine, and an Italian relative at *least!* Then one day I was visiting a friend and watched her unceremoniously throw together a batch of noodles in her simple, unsophisticated kitchen. I realized unquestionably that this long-wished-about and far-out process of making your own pasta was something I could, and would, do.

She mixed flour and fine granular semolina together in a bowl with eggs and a little water, kneaded them briefly, then completed the kneading and cutting in her pasta machine. I didn't own a pasta machine then and wasn't sure I wanted to invest in one but knew I wanted to try pasta making. I found that my food processor kneaded small batches of dough neatly, quickly, perfectly. I had only to let the dough rest, roll it out on my counter to a fine noodle thinness, flour it, let it dry slightly so it wouldn't stick to itself, then roll it up and cut it into thick or thin noodle widths. These I would toss to unfurl, then let dry on a floured pan or waxed paper for an hour or more until it was time to boil and serve.

Allowing myself to experiment with pasta, I discovered the ways that worked best for me. A certain ratio of flour to semolina made the best pasta. Noodles made without semolina (pasta flour milled from durum wheat and available in Italian, Middle Eastern, and specialty markets) lack a certain resilient tenderness. Too much semolina and the dough is fragile and difficult to work.

I learned the importance of having a really soft and supple dough. It's easier to roll out and more responsive when shaping and stuffing pasta forms. I improved my rolling technique—getting used to a rolling pin without handles and learning to press down and forward on the pin at the same time to both thin and extend the elastic dough. Still, the dough was usually thinner around the edges, so I cut rounds for tortellini from the perimeter—then just rolled a new perimeter! With time and experience I learned to gauge the correct thinness for the dough—not so thin that it tore easily and lacked character, not so thick that it was heavy or doughy tasting when cooked.

It was only a matter of time before I began experimenting with different flours, herbs, and vegetable purees in my pasta dough, then only a little more time until I felt adventurous enough to attempt ravioli then tortellini. It was helpful to watch a brief segment on TV where a housewife who was saving money was shown speedily forming her own free-form ravioli. Roll, roll, plop, plop, cover, cut. They weren't all the same size or shape and looked appealingly homemade. I knew that whatever I did would turn out just fine.

Teaching myself to form tortellini, however, was an adventure of the spirit and the will. No matter how many different sets of instructions I read, I couldn't get that special lip that graces the tortellini's outer curve. Sometimes in frustration I would make simpler half-moon-shaped agnolotti as a vacation from tortellini learning. Then one day the hands found the way. It helped, too, to decide to make large-size tortellini using 4-inch rounds cut using empty coffee cans as cutters. These were easier and less time-consuming to form. And 6 mega-tortellini, lightly napped with sauce, look magnificent on a dinner plate.

Purchasing a pasta machine came next. But I hesitated. Would I feel committed to making my own pasta *all* the time? And give up my beloved boxes of linguini, spaghetti, vermicelli . . . ? I was doing fine without a machine; did I really need to spend the money? Finally I just went ahead and bought it, along with a collapsible wooden clothes dryer on which to hang my uncut and cut pasta. As suggested, I first ran a simple flour and water dough through the rollers and cutters to clean them. The machine sits ready in its box, needing only a quick dusting off of excess flour or dried pasta crumbs for maintenance. I take it out whenever I make homemade noodles and want the spe-

cial ease of pasta making it offers. I love cranking out the velvety-smooth dough, catching the supple strands of perfectly cut noodles on my forearm, and transferring them to wooden dowels to dry.

Three 1-egg batches yield 4 *generous* main course servings of long pasta or 6 generous first course servings. Decide how many batches you will need and, if you are using a processor, prepare a 1-egg batch at a time. If you have a large-capacity processor you can prepare 2-egg batches. And if you are using the hand method you can mix together as many egg batches as you need—you are limited only by your own muscle power.

Homemade pasta freezes beautifully. So if you are making noodles for a particular recipe, prepare a double amount and freeze half for another time.

I make my own pasta whenever I want the special pleasures (of process and product) that only home-made pasta can provide. I urge you to try pasta making if you haven't already.

HOMEMADE EGG PASTA

1/2 cup semolina
1/4 cup all-purpose flour
1/4 teaspoon salt
 1 extra-large egg
 1 teaspoon olive oil
 1 teaspoon water*

FOOD PROCESSOR METHOD

Put the semolina, flour, and salt in the processor work bowl. Beat the egg, olive oil, and water together and pour through the feed tube with the processor running. The dough will cohere into a ball. Continue processing and kneading the dough for 20–30 seconds more, then remove it from the processor and knead once or twice on a very lightly floured counter or work surface. The dough should be supple, but not sticky, approximating the feel of an earlobe. Rub the dough lightly with olive oil, cover it with plastic wrap, and let it rest for 30–60 minutes.

HAND METHOD

Beat the egg, olive oil, and water together in a bowl. Add the semolina, flour, and salt and mix together with a fork until the dough coheres into a ball. Knead the dough on a very lightly floured surface, being careful not to add too much flour, which can create too stiff a dough. Knead until you have a smooth, supple, nonsticky dough if you are rolling out the dough by hand. If you are using a pasta machine, a brief kneading will suffice, for kneading will continue as you put the dough through the different roller settings. Rub the dough lightly

with olive oil, cover it with plastic wrap, and let it rest for 30–60 minutes.

IF YOU ARE ROLLING OUT THE DOUGH WITH A PASTA MACHINE

Set the rollers on the widest setting. Lightly flour a fist-size lump of dough and put it through the rollers. Fold the dough in half, flour it lightly, and put it through this setting again or continue on to the next roller setting, depending on how smooth and cohesive your dough seems. If you move on to a narrower setting but find the dough is not moving through smoothly or is not holding together well, fold it up again and go back and repeat the previous roller setting. Continue putting the dough through successively narrower roller settings until you reach the thickness you want. Let the sheets of dough dry slightly (20–60 minutes) so that they are firmer but still pliant. Put the dough through the noodle cutters or hand cut into cannelloni squares, etc. Continue drying. If you are making ravioli or any other pasta for which the dough needs to be supple and have a good self-sticking capacity, eliminate the drying stage, working with the dough as soon as it is rolled out. If you are working with several batches of pasta, roll out a 1-egg batch (about the size of a tennis ball or a small fist) at a time and keep the remaining dough covered with plastic wrap so it doesn't dry out.

*Substitute Marsala if this complements your sauce.

CARROT PASTA

This is my favorite pasta. Carrot puree produces an extra-tenderly resilient pasta with a beautiful golden color. This recipe makes the equivalent amount of a 2-egg batch of regular pasta, plus.

  1 large, thick carrot or 2 regular-size carrots
     (3–4 ounces)
3/4 cup semolina
1/2–3/4 cup (or more) all-purpose flour
  1/2 teaspoon salt
    1 egg
    1 teaspoon olive oil

Peel and cut up the carrots. Cook them in a small amount of water until they are tender. Then raise the heat and reduce the cooking water to about 1 Tablespoon and puree the mixture. Let cool.

Combine the semolina, flour, and salt in a processor work bowl or mixing bowl. Beat together the carrot puree, egg, and olive oil and add to the flour mixture, mixing and kneading by processor or hand method.

SPINACH PASTA

This recipe makes the equivalent amount of a 2-egg batch of regular pasta. If you are not using a food processor, puree your spinach before mixing the ingredients together.

  1 extra-large egg
1/2 a 10-ounce package frozen chopped spinach,
    cooked and well squeezed, or 1/4 pound
    (or more) fresh spinach, cooked, drained,
    squeezed, and chopped
  1 teaspoon olive oil
1/2 teaspoon salt
3/4 cup semolina
1/2 cup (or more) all-purpose flour

Place the egg, spinach, olive oil, and salt in the processor work bowl. Process until the spinach is pureed. Add the semolina and flour and process until the mixture coheres then process-knead a little longer, adding a small amount of additional flour if necessary.

TOMATO PASTA

This recipe makes an amount equivalent to a 2-egg batch of pasta, and gives you a pasta with a lovely deep rosy color.

  1 cup semolina
    Scant 1 cup all-purpose flour
1/2 teaspoon salt
  2 eggs
    One 6-ounce can tomato paste
  1 Tablespoon water
  2 teaspoons olive oil
    Additional all-purpose flour as needed

Follow the method for Homemade Egg Pasta (p. 148).

BUCKWHEAT PASTA

Speckled brown buckwheat pasta is more earthy tasting and wheaty looking than egg pasta. I love eating it tossed with butter and fresh dill—or with fresh dill mixed into the dough. It is also delicious tossed with sautéed shredded cabbage and onions, herbed with tarragon and dill then finished with a light sprinkling of freshly grated Parmesan.

1/4 cup semolina
1/4 cup all-purpose flour
 2 Tablespoons buckwheat flour
1/4 teaspoon salt
 1 extra-large egg
 1 teaspoon oil
 1 teaspoon water

Prepare according to the directions for Homemade Egg Pasta (p. 148).

HERBED PASTA

Depending on whether you use dried or fresh herbs and how much you process your dough, you may have a pasta dough with a flecked appearance or a faint greenish tint. If you want a more prominent herb flavor, increase the amount of herb or herbs that you use. Herbs can be added to any of the pasta recipes. Remember, if adding herbs, that the Spinach and Carrot Pasta recipes yield an amount the equivalent of 2-egg batches.

   1-egg batch of Homemade Egg Pasta (p. 148)
1-2 Tablespoons minced fresh herbs, such as basil, dill, or chives, or 1-2 teaspoons dried herbs

Prepare according to the directions for Homemade Egg Pasta, adding the herbs to the beaten egg mixture.

PASTA ROLLS

A pasta roll is an easy, exciting, and incredibly gratifying place to begin creating with homemade pasta. It's as easy as rolling pasta dough out on your counter. The pasta is spread with a filling, rolled up jelly-roll style into a cylinder that is tied in muslin or cloth then poached and cut into rounds of pinwheeling filling and dough. Brushed with butter and warmed atop a brilliant red sauce, these swirling rounds are a magnificent visual and taste experience.

Pasta rolls can be prepared ahead in a number of different ways. The rolls can be poached, left in their cloth, placed in a plastic bag so they won't dry out, and refrigerated for several hours, even overnight. They are then sliced and placed atop sauce and given a little extra time in the oven. The rolls can also be arranged on top of the sauce and refrigerated in this state until baking time. I have also frozen the roll, wrapped securely in plastic wrap, before poaching and just added an additional 20–30 minutes or so to the poaching time. All methods work out well.

SPINACH AND RICOTTA PASTA ROLLS *yields 16–20 slices from 2 rolls*

I sometimes add minced dried tomatoes (the kind that are sold in jars, preserved in olive oil) to the spinach filling. These are expensive. A little goes a long way, adding bits of flavor and bright red color.

Three 10-ounce packages frozen chopped
  spinach, cooked and well squeezed, or
½ pound (or more) fresh spinach, cooked,
  drained, and well squeezed*
½ pound ricotta cheese
2 eggs
½ cup freshly grated Parmesan cheese
1 teaspoon salt
  Freshly ground pepper to taste
  A few gratings of fresh nutmeg
  2-egg batch of Homemade Egg Pasta (p. 148)
  Melted butter
1 recipe Marinara Sauce (p. 242)
  Additional freshly grated Parmesan cheese

Mix together the spinach, ricotta cheese, eggs, grated Parmesan, salt, pepper, and nutmeg. Set aside.

Bring water to a simmer in a pot large enough to hold the rolls and deep enough for the rolls to be completely submerged. A large Dutch oven or a deep, oversize baking pan works well. Salt the water lightly.

Roll out half the pasta (a 1-egg batch) into a rectangle measuring 10 by 15 inches. Spread one half of the spinach and ricotta filling (about 1½ cups) over the pasta, leaving a 1-inch border at one of the short sides. Beginning at the opposite short

side, roll up the dough and filling jelly-roll style. When you have finished, wet the border of dough lightly to seal the roll. You will have a roll 10 inches long and about 1½ inches in diameter. Roll the pasta cylinder up in a piece of muslin or light cloth or several thicknesses of cheesecloth. Tie it at the ends, securing the cylinder in its sausagelike shape. Form a second roll with the remaining pasta and filling and tie that roll up too.

Now you are ready to poach the rolls. Place them in the simmering salted water and simmer them for 90 minutes, turning them 3 or 4 times during the cooking time. Add additional hot water to the pot or pan as needed to maintain the water level. After 90 minutes, remove the rolls from the water and from their cloth casing. Trim off the ends and cut each roll into eight to ten 1-inch or larger slices.

Preheat the oven to 350°F. Pour enough Marinara Sauce (mixed with a little grated Parmesan cheese) into a baking pan to cover the bottom completely and come about one-third to one-half up the side of the rolls. Arrange the rolls on top of the sauce, side by side, making sure that the bright red sauce shows up between the rows of rolls. Brush the rolls with melted butter and sprinkle lightly with additional grated Parmesan.

Bake for 15–20 minutes, or until the sauce is hot and gently bubbling. Allow at least 4 slices for a main course, at least 2 for an accompaniment—but be aware that these are gobbled up. Serve additional sauce on the side.

*Cook the spinach briefly, being careful it doesn't lose its bright green color.

SEAFOOD MOUSSE
PASTA ROLLS *yields 18-20 slices from 2 rolls*

Unbelievably wonderful to look at and to taste.

1 recipe Spinach Pasta (p. 149)
1 recipe Seafood Mousse IV (p. 249)
    (Use 1-1 1/4 cups
    cream instead of 1 1/2 cups)
    Mildly garlic-flavored melted butter*
1 recipe Seafood Marinara Sauce (p. 242)**

Prepare according to the directions for Spinach and Ricotta Pasta Rolls (preceding recipe), using Seafood Mousse as the filling. You will have about 2 cups of filling for each roll, so the rolls will be slightly larger in diameter than the spinach and ricotta rolls.

Allow 3 slices per serving. With 18-20 slices you can serve 6 with possibly some extra.

*Just sprinkle a little garlic powder into your melted butter or sauté a whole clove for a minute or so. You want only a suggestion of garlic.
**For a truly fabulous sauce, simmer shrimp shells from the shrimp used in the filling in about 8 ounces clam juice plus the juice from a can of minced clams. Strain and use this to prepare the Seafood Marinara Sauce, adding the minced clams to the finished sauce. Or strain and reduce the seafood stock to about 1/4 cup and add this reduction to an excellent prepared commercial meatless marinara sauce, warming the sauce at the end with the minced clams. Even a good commercial sauce is transformed through this method, creating an easy yet excellent sauce for this magnificent dish.

MEXICAN PASTA
AND BEAN ROLLS *yields 20-24 slices from 2 rolls*

If you love Mexican flavors (and pasta!) these rolls will be a favorite.

    2-egg batch of Homemade Egg Pasta (p. 148)
2-3 cups Bean Filling or Cheese Bean Filling
    (p. 253)*
1 recipe Mexican Tomato Sauce (p. 241)
    Freshly grated Parmesan cheese
    Melted butter

Prepare according to the directions for Spinach and Ricotta Pasta Rolls (p. 151), using Bean Filling inside the rolls. Place the Mexican Tomato Sauce in a baking dish to a depth of about 1/2 inch. Sprinkle the sauce lightly with grated Parmesan. Slice the pasta rolls (sometimes I get 12 of these from each roll) and arrange the slices on top of the sauce. Brush them with melted butter and sprinkle them very lightly with grated Parmesan, being careful not to obscure the pattern of filling and pasta.

Allow 4 slices per serving. With 20-24 slices you can serve 5-6.

*I add an extra egg yolk and a little extra grated Parmesan cheese (1/2 cup) to the Bean Filling. I use black beans for color contrast and spread the pasta with about 1 generous cup of filling. The smaller amount of dark filling gives a very fine pinwheel pattern that is quite attractive. I also use the slightly more cheesy and textured Cheese Bean Filling—about 1 1/2 cups per roll—with 2 egg yolks added to a 3-cup batch of filling. I use kidney beans for this filling and it, too, is delicious, though a little less dramatic looking. You can play with black or red beans for either filling. If you use a larger amount of filling (1 1/2 cups), the rolls are easier to slice if they have been refrigerated after poaching. Cover them with plastic wrap while refrigerating so the pasta does not dry out.

TORTELLINI, AGNOLOTTI, AND RAVIOLI

Making, serving, and eating your own tortellini is an experience not to be missed. True, they require more skill, time, and patience than other home-made pasta preparations. Ravioli, even agnolotti, are faster and easier to form. Yet there is something wondrous about creating these eloquent curves of filled pasta (did I *really* do that?).

One of the bonuses with all of these small home-made stuffed pastas is that they can be prepared well in advance and frozen. Often I serve them as a special yet simple main course pasta preceded by a varied and complex antipasto platter. While we are polishing off the antipasto, talking and eating, a large pot of water is coming to a boil; a sauce is warming on a low flame. All I need do is take the tortellini (or agnolotti or ravioli) from my freezer, boil and sauce them, then serve them to an appreciative group.

Recipes are given for tortellini, but are applicable to ravioli and agnolotti as well.

Because of the individual nature of hand pasta making, you may sometimes find you have a little more or less filling than needed. The size and type of pasta and your adeptness at filling and forming them will all affect the ratio of filling to pasta. Flexibility reigns. Sometimes I deliberately prepare extra pasta dough for the few extra tortellini I could form if filling is left over. I can always turn this extra pasta into noodles for the evening's meal—or for the freezer. A quick batch of pastry mixed in the processor and rolled out on an already floury counter turns some extra filling into pastry turnovers—and an impromptu hors d'oeuvre for future entertaining.

FORMING AGNOLOTTI AND TORTELLINI

Prepare a 2-egg batch of Homemade Egg Pasta (p. 148). On a lightly floured surface roll out a 1-egg batch of pasta, covering the remaining dough with plastic wrap so it doesn't dry out. Roll the pasta sheet quite thin (you want to be able to see light through it) but not so thin that it tears easily. Using an empty 1-pound coffee can (or a 4-inch round cutter) cut out circles as close to each other as possible. (Save the scraps in between the circles and use them for noodles.) If you would like smaller tortellini or agnolotti use smaller cutters.

Working with 4–5 circles at a time, brush the edge of half the circle lightly with water. Place a scant teaspoon of filling in the center and bring the 2 edges together to form a half circle. Press to seal. These are agnolotti. If you wish to go on to form tortellini, hold the half circle or half moon of dough in the fingers of both hands, with the curved part facing away from you. Your fingers are cradling the underside of the curve lightly, while your thumbs are resting lightly on the straighter filled portion where the dough was folded. Bring your fingers around slowly, toward the 2 points or tips, folding and curving the rounded edge gently as you do so. Dab 1 of the 2 points lightly with water, bring the 2 points together, and pinch gently to seal.

Have ready trays covered with lightly floured waxed paper and place the completed tortellini (or agnolotti) on them. Continue forming agnolotti or tortellini until all the circles are filled then repeat with the second batch of dough. Let the tortellini dry for 45–60 minutes (or longer in the refrigerator) then boil until tender and gently al dente (7–12 minutes). The amount of time will depend on how thick your dough is, how dry, and whether it is fresh or frozen.

To freeze tortellini, place the trays or baking pans with the tortellini in the freezer until they are quite firm or frozen. Transfer to plastic bags and store in the freezer until ready to use.

FORMING RAVIOLI

Ravioli can be made using either hand- or machine-rolled pasta dough. Whichever method you choose, you want to work with 2 thinly rolled about equal-size sheets of dough. On 1 (the slightly smaller if there is one) sheet of pasta place heaping teaspoons of filling at regular intervals over the dough, leaving a

space the width of a finger around each mound of filling. Brush all uncovered areas of dough lightly with water and lay the second sheet of pasta over the first. With your fingers, press the pasta together to seal at all points around the mounds of filling. Cut between the mounds with a ravioli cutter or, if you don't have one, a knife. Have ready trays covered with lightly floured waxed paper and place the ravioli on them. Let the ravioli dry for 45–60 minutes (or longer in the refrigerator) or freeze on trays then store in plastic bags.

Boil fresh or frozen ravioli for 10–15 minutes, or until tender (longer if frozen). Drain and serve with a complementary sauce. Or layer boiled al dente ravioli with sauce and cheese in a casserole and bake until the cheese is melted and the sauce bubbly.

Any of the following recipes can be modified for ravioli or agnolotti. Just form the dough into the desired shape. The recipes will yield about 24–26 tortellini using 4-inch rounds of dough and about 28–30 using 2½–3-inch rounds of dough. This will serve 4 as a main course and 6 as a first course.

SEAFOOD TORTELLINI *yields 24–26 tortellini*

These are my favorite tortellini. Very elegant. Very special. Garnish with whole small shrimp sautéed in garlic butter for an extra-fine touch.

    2-egg batch of Homemade Egg Pasta (p. 248)
1 recipe Seafood Mousse II (p. 249)
1 recipe Seafood Marinara Sauce (p. 242)
    Minced fresh parsley

Form tortellini according to the directions on page 153, using 4-inch rounds of pasta dough and generous teaspoons of Seafood Mousse. Boil the tortellini for 7–12 minutes, or until the pasta is tenderly al dente and the filling is cooked through. (Cooking time will depend on the thickness of the pasta and whether the tortellini were fresh or frozen.) Remove the tortellini with a slotted spoon and dry gently on a clean kitchen towel to remove excess moisture. Divide the tortellini among 4 warm dinner plates. Nap lightly with simmering hot Seafood Marinara Sauce, covering the tortellini only partially so that the shape shows through. Sprinkle with minced parsley. Pass additional sauce.

Allow 6 tortellini per serving. With 24-26 tortellini you can serve 4 with some extra.

BEAN TORTELLINI
WITH EGG SAUCE *yields 28-32 tortellini, to serve 4 as a main course or 6 as a first course*

The velvety carbonaralike sauce lightly graces these earthy, herby bean tortellini. They are also delicious baked with a napping of tomato sauce and grated mild cheese.

> 2-egg batch of Homemade Egg Pasta (p. 148), or equivalent amount of pasta of choice
> 1 recipe Bean Filling (p. 253)

egg sauce
> 4 eggs
> 1½ cups freshly grated Parmesan cheese
> ⅔ cup milk or cream
> 2 Tablespoons olive oil*
> 2 teaspoons salt
> Freshly ground pepper to taste
> Minced fresh parsley

Form small tortellini according to the directions on page 153, using 2½-3-inch rounds of pasta dough and moderate teaspoons of filling.

*If you have it, a deep-flavored virgin olive oil adds a special extra touch.

To make the sauce, beat together the eggs, grated Parmesan, milk or cream, olive oil, salt, and pepper. Set aside.

Boil the tortellini for 7-12 minutes, or until the pasta is tenderly al dente and the filling is cooked through. (Cooking time will depend on the thickness of the pasta and whether the tortellini were fresh or frozen.) Drain the tortellini in a colander then immediately return them to the hot cooking pot placed over a very low flame. Add the egg mixture and stir and toss gently until it begins to thicken. Be careful that your mixture does not scramble. Place the tortellini on warm plates and spoon on excess egg sauce. Sprinkle with minced parsley and serve with additional grated Parmesan.

Tortellini, Agnolotti, Ravioli

TORTELLINI WITH RICOTTA *yields 24-26 tortellini*

Try these tossed with Pesto Sauce too.

   2-egg batch of Homemade Egg Pasta (p. 148)
1 recipe Ricotta Cheese Filling (p. 140)
1 recipe Marinara Sauce (p. 242) or Basic Tomato
   Sauce (p. 241)
   Freshly grated Parmesan cheese
   Minced fresh parsley

Form tortellini according to the directions on page 153, using 4-inch rounds of pasta dough and generous teaspoons of filling. Boil the tortellini for 7-12 minutes, or until the pasta is tenderly al dente and the filling is cooked through. (Cooking time will depend on the thickness of the pasta and whether the tortellini were fresh or frozen.) Remove the tortellini with a slotted spoon and dry gently on a clean kitchen towel to remove excess moisture. Divide among 4 warm dinner plates. Nap lightly with simmering hot sauce, covering the tortellini only partially so that the shape shows through. Sprinkle with grated Parmesan and minced parsley. Pass additional sauce and grated Parmesan.

Allow 6 tortellini per serving. With 24-26 tortellini you can serve 4 with some extra.

TORTELLINI WITH PARSNIP AND SPINACH FILLING *yields 28-32 tortellini, to serve 6 as a side dish or first course*

Parsnips plus grated cheese lend these tortellini an indescribable sweet-savory zing. They are an elegant and tasty accompaniment to any simple broiled or grilled meat/fish dinner. I love to serve them with bluefish brochettes marinated in Mayonnaise Marinade for Fish, broiled until juicy and crisp.

   2-egg batch of Homemade Egg Pasta (p. 148)
1 recipe Parsnip and Spinach Filling (p. 256)
   Softened butter
   Salt and freshly ground pepper to taste
   Freshly grated Parmesan cheese
   Minced scallion

Form small tortellini according to the directions on page 153, using 2½-3-inch rounds of pasta dough and moderate to scant teaspoons of filling. Boil the tortellini for 7-12 minutes, or until the pasta is tenderly al dente and the filling is cooked through. (Cooking time will depend on the thickness of your pasta and whether the tortellini were fresh or frozen.) Drain the tortellini and return them immediately to the hot cooking pot. Toss with softened butter and season lightly with salt and pepper and grated Parmesan. Turn onto a warmed serving platter or individual warmed plates and sprinkle generously with minced scallion. (If you prefer, you can also cook the scallion lightly in the butter before tossing with the tortellini.) Pass additional grated Parmesan.

MUSHROOM PECAN TORTELLINI *yields 28-32 tortellini, to serve 4 as a main course or 6 as a first course*

Intensely mushroomy.

2-egg batch of Homemade Egg Pasta (p. 148),
  or equivalent amount of pasta of choice
1 recipe Mushroom Pecan Filling (p. 251)
  Egg Sauce (p. 155)
  Minced fresh parsley
  Freshly grated Parmesan cheese

Form small tortellini according to the directions on page 153, using 2½-3-inch rounds of pasta dough and moderate teaspoons of filling. These work best with the Egg Sauce. Boil the tortellini and prepare with the Egg Sauce according to the directions for Bean Tortellini with Egg Sauce (p. 155). Serve sprinkled with minced fresh parsley and pass grated Parmesan.

MUSHROOM MARSALA RICOTTA TORTELLINI *yields 28-32 tortellini, to serve 4 as a main course or 6 as a first course*

Gently mushroomy.

1 recipe Spinach Pasta (p. 149)
½ recipe Mushroom Marsala and Ricotta
  Filling (p. 252)
1 recipe Basic Tomato Sauce (p. 241) or
  Marinara Sauce (p. 242)
  Freshly grated Parmesan cheese

Form tortellini according to the directions on page 153, using 4-inch rounds of pasta dough and generous teaspoons of filling. Boil the tortellini for 7-12 minutes, or until the pasta is tenderly al dente and the filling is cooked through. (Cooking time will depend on the thickness of the pasta and whether the tortellini were fresh or frozen.) Remove the tortellini with a slotted spoon and dry gently on a clean kitchen towel to remove excess moisture. Nap lightly with simmering hot sauce, covering the tortellini only partially so that the shape shows through. Sprinkle with grated Parmesan. Pass additional sauce.

OTHER
DOUGHY DELIGHTS

Here are homemade pasta and noodle doughs in still other wonderful forms. In keeping with the true essence of a pasta they are elemental mouthfuls and just plain good chews—food that goes satisfyingly "chomp" in the mouth.

PIEROGIN

One bite of my first pierogin, a tenderly resilient dumpling dough filled with potatoes and cheese then smothered with golden onions, and I knew I had to have them as a regular part of my menus. I was introduced to pierogin (sadly late in life) at the home of a friend whose visiting mom was ministering to his Pierogin Hunger by turning them out all afternoon in his kitchen. I worked out a recipe based on her explanation and kept a steady supply in my freezer that entire winter. One of my enduring memories from that time is of coming home at night feeling drained from a very difficult day, boiling up some frozen pierogin, sautéing them with cabbage and onions, then sitting down to the most mouth-filling, heart-soothing meal.

Making pierogin, like eating them, is a soul-satisfying experience that connects me with an age-old cooking craft and a wholesome, earthy style of eating. Because I make several batches at one time, it becomes a roll-up-my-sleeve-and-clear-the-counter afternoon project, which I like to simplify by making the filling the day before. The pierogin freeze beautifully, so the fruits of my labor (and fun) are readily available for those times when I need quickly the sustenance that only pierogin can offer.

Great pierogin require a great filling—one that is a creamy and rich-*tasting* complement to their toothsome outer covering. The 3 fillings I suggest succeed admirably at this and are high in protein and reasonable in calories. One must, after all, be able to dig in to pierogin with some abandon—something I could never do if I knew I was going to weigh 2 pounds more the next morning.

All pierogin are enhanced by a light sautéing, with onions, in a moderate amount of butter. I love to eat the potato-cheese pierogin as a main course with herbed cabbage and onions. Parsnip pierogin are an evocative accompaniment to broiled bluefish or roasted chicken, turkey, or meats. And bean pierogin are a marvelous meal in themselves (virtually vegetarian pierogin steaks!), sprinkled lightly with grated Parmesan and served with a plain or buttered steamed vegetable. However you choose to eat them, you are in for a treat.

PIEROGIN *yields 14–18 pierogin*

2 cups all-purpose flour
1 egg, beaten
1/2 cup water
1/4 teaspoon salt
21/2–3 cups Potato Cheese Filling I (p. 255),
  Parsnip Filling (p. 256), or Bean Filling
  (p. 253)

Combine the flour, egg, water, and salt in a food processor and knead well. (This can also be done by hand, but beat the water and egg together before adding to the flour.) The dough should be soft, but not sticky. Let the dough rest in a bowl, covered with plastic wrap, for at least 1 hour before using.

On a floured surface roll out the dough to a thickness of about 3/16–1/4 inch. Cut out rounds with a 4-inch cutter (an empty 1-pound coffee can works well). If you prefer a small pierogin, use a smaller cutter.

Place a very generous rounded teaspoon of filling about 1 inch from one edge of each dough round. Lift up the round, wet the edges with a fingertip dipped in water, then fold the half of the dough without the filling over the filling half, stretching and pinching the dough gently to bring the edges together.* Press the edges of the dough firmly between your thumb and forefinger to form a sealed lip about 1/4–1/2 inch wide. Continue forming pierogin, re-rolling scraps until all the dough is used.

Have ready a large pot of boiling water. Add a little salt. Stir the water well then slip 4–5 formed pierogin gently into the swirling water. Cook for 5 minutes then transfer the pierogin with a slotted spoon onto a rack placed over a jelly-roll pan. Continue until all the pierogin are boiled. The number you have will depend on their size, the thickness of the dough, and the ratio of filling to dough.

When the pierogin that are draining on the rack begin to feel dry to the touch, lay them on a baking sheet lined with waxed paper and place in the freezer. When the pierogin are quite firm, transfer them to plastic bags and store in the freezer. When you are ready to use them, boil from the frozen state for 5 minutes. Drain and proceed.

To serve, sauté onions in butter until golden. The more onions the better! Add pierogin to the sauté pan and continue sautéing until the pierogin take on a little golden coloring on both sides.

For a heartier dish serve as a main course (my favorite way to eat potato-cheese pierogin) by sautéing onions then slicing cabbage in butter, adding tarragon and basil (or herbs of choice) to taste. Season with salt and pepper, cover and steam until the cabbage is tender but not too soft. Add the pierogin, pushing the vegetables aside around them, and sauté the pierogin briefly, adding a little more butter if necessary. Three to 4 pierogin are an ample main course portion per person; 2 pierogin do nicely when served as an accompaniment.

*The dough is very soft and elastic so this is easy to do. (Also, because of its elasticity, the dough shrinks a little when you cut out the round.) If the dough breaks or does not go around the filling, you may be rolling the dough too thin or using too much filling. Adjust your method or ratio accordingly. I personally prefer a slightly thick dough, chock-full of filling, with the edges just eased over the filling and pinched thin so as not to have too thick and doughy an edge.

SPAETZLE

Spaetzle are tender little nuggets of dough, halfway between a noodle and a dumpling. They are as individual as snowflakes in their bumps and curves, which are perfect for capturing a light glistening of butter. Spaetzle can be prepared ahead of time, refrigerated, then reheated by tossing with butter—especially useful if you are preparing them for a party or company dinner. To add to their versatility, spaetzle also freeze beautifully. Leftovers can be frozen for another dinner, tossed with a cooked grain (especially good with herbed kasha), or used as a hearty and nourishing addition to a bowl or a potful of soup.

Finally, spaetzle couldn't be easier to make. The best spaetzle maker I know of is an inexpensive flat metal grater with metal wire strung across its 6 by 9-inch frame creating 1/2-inch square openings. Push the thick batter along the crisscrossing wires. This will form individual dumplings that will fall into the boiling water. An alternative spaetzle maker is a frying basket with similarly spaced openings. Little homemade noodle-dumplings are yours for the stirring. You may never purchase noodles again.

SPAETZLE *yields 4 1/2–5 cups, to serve at least 4*

1 cup milk
2 eggs
1 teaspoon salt
    A few gratings of fresh nutmeg
2 1/3 cups all-purpose flour
2–4 Tablespoons (1/4–1/2 stick) butter, softened
    Salt and freshly ground pepper to taste

Combine the milk, eggs, salt, and nutmeg. Add the flour and stir with a wire whisk or electric hand mixer until the batter is smooth. (It will be quite thick.) Have ready a large pot of boiling water. Add a little salt. Lay a flat wire grater across the pot of water. Spoon the batter onto the grater in batches, pressing each batch across and through the wires with a spoon or rubber spatula. Continue until all the batter is used. Stir the spaetzle and cook for 2–3 minutes, or until they all have risen to the surface and taste done when tested. Drain then toss the spaetzle with the butter and season with salt and pepper to taste.

SPAETZLE WITH MUSHROOMS

Prepare 1/2 recipe Mushroom Duxelles (p. 250). Just before serving, toss hot spaetzle with the Mushroom Duxelles. Mushrooms sautéed in butter with onions can also be used.

BUCKWHEAT OR WHOLE WHEAT SPAETZLE

Substitute 1/4 cup buckwheat or whole wheat flour for the all-purpose flour.

HERBED SPAETZLE

Add 1 Tablespoon dried dill, or to taste, or 2–3 teaspoons dried herbs of choice. If using fresh herbs, mince and add to taste. Or herbs can be sprinkled over the prepared spaetzle.

SEEDED SPAETZLE

Add 2-4 Tablespoons poppy or sesame seeds. Or seeds can be sprinkled over the prepared spaetzle.

CHEESE SPAETZLE

Add 1/4 cup freshly grated Parmesan cheese. Or cheese can be sprinkled over the prepared spaetzle.

LEMON SPAETZLE

Add the grated rind of 1 small lemon.

GNOCCHI

Potato gnocchi are Italian potato dumplings that manage to be light as a feather and at the same time have substance and bite. Sound impossible? For me it was. Try as I might, I couldn't duplicate the unforgettable gnocchi I had once had in an Italian restaurant. However, in surrender lay success. Throwing up my hands in despair, exhausted at the thought of rolling still another sticky potato mess on my counter, I just began dropping the gnocchi dough by spoonfuls into the waiting boiling water.

The results were not quite as refined as the rolled and cut version but light and delicate nonetheless. And easy. Now, sometimes, I take my spoonful of dough and roll it lightly in my floured hands, press my finger into the middle of the ball, then roll the ball once gently on the counter. This creates a smooth, elongated gnocchi shape with an attractive ridge down the center. Either way you will have a delightful eating experience, somehow more like a pasta than a potato, or some heavenly place in between.

POTATO DROP GNOCCHI *serves 4-6 as a side dish or first course*

Try these topped with a tomato sauce (Marinara Sauce, Basic Tomato Sauce, Favorite Meat Sauce) and plenty of freshly grated Parmesan cheese. Or melted butter, grated Parmesan, and minced fresh parsley or basil.

1 pound potatoes
1/2-3/4 cup all-purpose flour, as needed
1 egg yolk
1/2 teaspoon salt

Preheat the oven to 400°F. Butter a baking dish.

Wash the potatoes well then steam them until tender. Peel the potatoes and put them through a ricer or mash with an electric hand mixer. Let cool slightly. Add the flour, beginning with 1/2 cup, the egg yolk, and salt. Mix or knead the mixture in a bowl with your hand just until it is blended. Add additional flour only as necessary to get a relatively unsticky mass.

Drop the dough by teaspoonfuls into boiling, well-salted water and simmer the gnocchi for 5–8 minutes, or until they are cooked through. Test your first gnocchi for appropriateness of flour proportions. Potatoes will differ in the amount of starch they have and the amount of flour needed to produce a fine gnocchi. You want a gnocchi that is firm but still soft. Too much flour will give you a hard, starchy-tasting dumpling. Remove the gnocchi from the water with a slotted spoon. Drain well on clean kitchen towels. Transfer to the prepared baking dish.

Top with what suits your fancy and bake for 15–20 minutes, or until hot and bubbly.

SEMOLINA SQUARES
(GNOCCHI WITH SEMOLINA, EGGS, AND CHEESE) *yields 16–18 squares*

Golden and chewy on the outside, soft and melting in the center, these cheesy semolina squares are a little like a transcendent macaroni and cheese. The dish is very easy and can be prepared ahead, refrigerated, then baked (and even reheated) just before serving time. A wonderful accompaniment to fish or chicken or simple grilled meats.

    4 cups milk, or 3 cups milk and 1 cup
       heavy cream
    2 teaspoons salt
  2–3 gratings of fresh nutmeg
       Freshly ground pepper to taste
    1 cup plus 2 Tablespoons semolina
    2 extra-large eggs plus 1 yolk
    1 cup freshly grated Parmesan or other hard
       grating cheese
       Melted butter

Additional grated cheese
Paprika

Butter very well a 9 by 13-inch pan (or an 8 by 12-inch pan for slightly thicker gnocchi).

Stir the milk or milk and cream with the salt, nutmeg, and pepper and bring to a boil in a large enamel or stainless steel pot. As it begins to bubble, whisk in the semolina gradually. Continue to whisk and cook the mixture until it is very thick and the whisk can almost stand upright in it. Remove from the heat.

Beat together the eggs and egg yolk and the grated cheese. Add this mixture to the semolina, mixing quickly to distribute before the heat sets the eggs. Pour into the prepared pan. Pat down the top of the mixture with a spatula to smooth and even out the surface. Dip the spatula in hot water occasionally if necessary to prevent sticking. Brush the top with melted butter and sprinkle lightly with grated cheese.

Refrigerate until cold and solid then cut into 16 or 18 squares.

Arrange the squares butter side down and over-lapping in a 9 by 13-inch baking dish. Brush or spoon on melted butter and sprinkle generously with grated cheese. Sprinkle paprika down the center of each row of gnocchi. Bake gnocchi in a 400°F oven for 30–35 minutes, or until they are crispy and golden. Allow 2 gnocchi per person as a side dish.

SPANAKUGEL *serves 10-12*

A cross between a Jewish noodle pudding or kugel and a Greek spanokopita, this easy-to-prepare and delicious "spanakugel" is a delicious dinner accompaniment as well as an interesting potluck dish.

- 1 large bunch scallions, chopped (about 1½ cups)
- 8 Tablespoons (1 stick) butter
  About 4 Tablespoons chopped fresh dill, or 1 Tablespoon dried
- 8 ounces cream cheese, softened
- 8 ounces feta cheese, crumbled
- 1 pint (16 ounces) sour cream
- 4 eggs
- 1½ teaspoons ground cinnamon
  Several gratings of fresh nutmeg
  Freshly ground pepper to taste
  Two 10-ounce packages frozen spinach, defrosted and well squeezed
- 1½ cups golden raisins
- 12 ounces orzo (rice-shaped pasta) (about 1⅔ cups), cooked 10 minutes and drained
  Cinnamon sugar
  Bread crumbs or cornflake crumbs

Preheat the oven to 350°F. Butter a 9 by 13-inch baking pan.

Sauté chopped scallions in 6 Tablespoons of the butter until scallions are soft. Add dill, stir until wilted, then remove from heat. Process or cream together the cream cheese and feta. Add the sour cream, eggs, cinnamon, nutmeg, pepper, and scallion mixture and process or beat until smooth. Add the spinach, raisins, and orzo and stir until completely mixed. Turn into the prepared pan and smooth top. Sprinkle lightly with cinnamon sugar and crumbs and dot with the remaining 2 Tablespoons of butter. Bake for 45–50 minutes or until a knife inserted in the center comes out clean.

STIR-FRY Mixed Vegetables with Tofu or Chicken in Oyster Sauce

Stir-Fry Cabbage, Tofu, and Ground Pork in Oyster Sauce

Stir-Fry Cabbage and Tofu in Oyster Sauce

Number 97 (Stir-Fry Tofu and Broccoli)

Number 97 Noodles

Double-Cooked Pork

Double-Cooked Chicken

Double-Cooked Tofu

Sweet-and-Sour Fish or Seafood with Vegetables

Chicken with Peaches and Peanuts

Mu Shu Pork My Way

Mu Shu Chicken

Chinese Pancakes

Asparagus Stir-Fry

Stir-Fry Asparagus with Ground Beef

Spicy Lamb with Zucchini and Onions

A Basic Sauce for Vegetables

NOODLE DISHES The Best Lo Mein Outside Chinatown

Rice Sticks with Scallops and Vegetables

Rice Sticks with Crab Meat (or Tofu), Pork, and Vegetables

Noodles with Beef and Asparagus (or Broccoli)

Spicy Noodles with Sesame, Scallions, and Chicken or Beef

Do you ever think to yourself, "If I *had* to choose only one style of cooking, which would it be?" Whenever I do this, I always pick Chinese or stir-fry cooking. Then almost immediately my heart sinks into grief at the thought of giving up pierogin, pasta with sauces, tostadas, blintzes . . . "Oh, I can't!" I say to myself, then gratefully, laughingly, realize— I don't have to choose.

And yet I do choose to prepare stir-fry dishes often. They lend themselves to an incredibly vibrant cuisine, one that is balanced, colorful, sensual, and healthy. Each ingredient retains its uniqueness and individuality while contributing to an exciting and delicious whole. Vegetables quick-cooked over high heat have intense color and a wonderfully tender crispness. The easily prepared, almost translucent sauces coat each morsel of food lightly with a glistening, deeply flavorful glaze. And I can merely change 1 or 2 sauce ingredients, my choice of vegetable or protein (or even add noodles), and create an entirely different result.

I also love the very act of stir-frying, of standing and tossing ingredients as they hiss and crackle in the shimmering hot wok. Stir-frying is of the moment. Everything comes together just at the point of presentation. There is an immediacy here that is very exciting—and can also be, without supportive planning, incredibly chaotic for the cook.

Stir-frying is not the method of choice for either beginners or hosts who want to linger over wine and conversation with guests then accompany them to the table in a leisurely manner. However, it *is* a lot of fun to prepare a Chinese meal for a group. What works for me is to make sure I am doing no more than 2 stir-fry dishes for dinner, and 1 is ideal. To accomplish this, my menu will include marvelous hors d'oeuvres so that the dinner itself

needn't be too filling and extensive. I'll serve Chinese Steamed Dumplings or Cold Shrimp Won Tons with Broccoli in Szechuan Vinaigrette, and Hoi Sin Spicy Beef or Turkey on a Skewer and perhaps crisp spring rolls to go with them. For the dinner, I'll be sure to have a large platter of chicken or pork that can be baked ahead and kept warm in the oven (Norman's Chinese Chicken or Hoi Sin Spicy Chicken or Pork). And I may stir-fry a vegetable and noodle dish before guests arrive, allowing it to come to room-temperature mellowness while we socialize.

Whether stir-frying for 2 or many, organization and advance preparation are the key. Let me explain how I divide a stir-fry recipe into 3 parts, each with its characteristic procedures that can be done ahead.

THE VEGETABLES

The first thing I do is prepare the vegetables. Although each recipe specifies how a vegetable might be cut, this is really a matter of personal choice. You can change the whole character of a dish just by cutting the ingredients a particular way— for example, into julienne strips or a small even dice instead of large chunks. If you are preparing 2 dishes using the same vegetable, you can increase the textural richness of the meal just by cutting that vegetable differently for each dish. Feel free also to substitute vegetables that you particularly like but that may not appear in the recipe. Snow peas, for example, are not specified because they are so expensive. They add an elegant splash of green and a unique flavor and crunch whenever they are used. And rutabaga, cut in strips, is wonderful.

When I prepare the vegetables, I first line a bowl with a double layer of paper towels. I then place on the towels the last vegetable ingredient or ingredients in the recipe to be added to the wok. I cover this with another double layer of towels, the next layer of vegetables, towels, vegetables, etc., until all the vegetables to be used are cut and arranged in layers, ending with the first vegetables I'll be adding to the wok. I can do this several hours ahead and refrigerate the bowl until about 30 minutes before stir-frying. The advantage of this method is that all the vegetables are contained in 1 neat space with those for different dishes separated into different bowls. The paper towels dry and crisp the vegetables so that their contact with the oil has the maximum searing effect and causes the minimum of steaming or spattering. The vegetables are conveniently ready to be lifted up in layers and added in turn to the sizzling hot wok.

When it comes time to stir-fry, you will be adding vegetables to the wok in reverse order to the amount of time it takes them to cook; ones that require more cooking are added first and cook longest. How long to stir-fry each batch of vegetables is something you learn to gauge with practice. Trust yourself, and make whatever adjustments you feel are necessary when next you stir-fry.

It's also very important when stir-frying to be careful not to add too many vegetables to the wok at one time. Crowded, they will just steam each other rather than crackle into intense color and crisp tenderness. If your wok is small, or the amount of vegetables large, it is better to divide the vegetables into 2 entirely different wok journeys, removing 1 batch, and allowing the wok to come back up to a smoking hot temperature before adding more oil and stir-frying the next batch.

THE PROTEIN

After the vegetables are cut I prepare the protein. This consists of either 1) seafood, fish, or chunks of chicken breast coated lightly with cornstarch and deep fried; 2) tofu, cut into cubes or slices then sautéed or deep fried to golden crispness; or 3) ground beef, pork, or lamb marinated in a small amount of soy sauce and other flavorings.

If I am using tofu, I sometimes press soft-style tofu, which I purchase in 1/2-pound pads. Pressing means that the tofu is pu. between folded kitchen towels or several thicknesses of paper towels, topped with a board or plate, and then weighted with a heavy can for an hour or two. This removes excess liquid and produces tender tofu with firmness and compactness. Firm-style tofu can be purchased in vacuum-sealed 1-pound pads in supermarkets and health-food stores. Whichever style or firmness of tofu I am using, I cut it as desired then pat it dry with paper towels and either sauté it over high heat in the wok in several Tablespoons of oil or deep fry it in several cups of oil until it is golden. Drained on paper toweling, the tofu can sit and wait until the time for it to be added to the bubbling hot sauce.

Marinated ground meat is the easiest preparation. Thirty minutes or more before stir-frying a few special seasonings are mixed into the meat to penetrate and flavor every tiny particle.

When a recipe calls for deep frying I sometimes do this step well in advance then drain the food on paper towels and refrigerate it until 30 minutes before stir-frying. When I deep fry I coat the food to be fried lightly with cornstarch. Usually I shake the chicken, seafood, or fish in a plastic bag with a small amount of cornstarch then empty this into a strainer over my kitchen sink or waxed paper. Shaking the strainer removes any excess coating nicely. I deep fry foods in just enough oil to cover them (about 3-4 cups) and at a temperature (350°-375°F) hot enough to seal and crisp without letting the food absorb any excess oil. When the oil is cooled it can be strained through several layers of cheesecloth and returned to the bottle for deep-frying reuse.

Sometimes I use a simpler alternative method to deep frying, particularly for strips of turkey or chicken breast, whole scallops or shrimp, or sliced beef or pork. I place the seafood, chicken, or meat in a bowl and drizzle a few teaspoons of sesame oil over it, toss to coat all surfaces with oil, then let sit for about 30 minutes. After the vegetables in the recipe have been stir-fried I push them to the sides of the wok (or remove them if that works better for you) and add the protein and stir-fry quickly. Then I pour the sauce and stir until it has thickened and all the ingredients are combined.

THE SAUCE

Just before stir-frying, or up to an hour ahead of time if that fits into my schedule better, I combine my sauce ingredients in a small bowl or measuring cup. Sauces of great subtlety and impact can be created with a moderately stocked pantry of Oriental ingredients.

Chicken stock is the base for most Chinese sauces. Whenever I prepare a batch of stock (see p. 50) I strain it then reduce it for a fuller flavor. I freeze 1/2 cupfuls in square plastic containers, remove the frozen squares, then store 3 or 4 of them in plastic sandwich bags. When I need stock for Chinese sauces I remove a square and let it melt in a saucepan or bowl. Simple.

A wonderful addition to (or vegetarian substitute for) chicken stock is the reduced soaking liquid from reconstituting Chinese mushrooms. It is hauntingly flavorful, and my heart aches when I think of how many times in the past I unthinkingly threw it away. Never again.

A basic sauce is typically made up of well-flavored chicken stock (1/2 cup) and a Tablespoon each of soy sauce, sherry, and cornstarch for thickener. From this point on, fine tuning can begin. Substitute dark soy sauce for regular or use it in addition. Add oyster sauce or hoi sin. Consider a pinch or more of sugar, minced gingerroot, or a small dollop of chili paste with garlic. You can use one or several; each will modify the sauce in gentle but definite ways.

And who says a sauce needs to be traditional? Hoi sin sauce, sherry, and chili paste with garlic make a tantalizing sauce for Double-Cooked Pork (as well as for chicken and tofu). Reduced mushroom liquid is the simple and superb sauce for an already deeply flavored Mu Shu Pork. A Tablespoon each of dark or regular soy sauce, sherry, and oyster sauce mixed with a little cornstarch, sugar, and salt is all that is needed to make exquisite a simple stir-fry of bean sprouts with scallions and bind up the excess liquids in the wok.

Now, with all the parts of the stir-fry dish or dishes ready, you can approach your wok with the poise of a conductor approaching the podium before an orchestra whose sections are ready to play. The most important thing for you to do next is to make sure your wok is very, very hot. Turn the heat source to its highest setting and let the wok heat up until you see it almost shimmering. Then, and only then, add your Tablespoons of oil around the top perimeter of the wok. And when this oil is very, very hot, again at the point of smoking and shimmering, then and only then add your first batch of vegetables. Now, you're off and conducting—and on your way to producing a great stir-fry symphony of color, textures, and tastes.

Here are ingredients it would be useful to have in your Chinese or stir-fry pantry:

Chicken stock—Most often used as a base for Chinese sauces, a full-flavored stock will yield the best results. When mixing a sauce, be sure to use cold stock because cornstarch, the thickening agent, will not dissolve in a hot liquid.

Chili paste with garlic—A fiery mixture of chili peppers, salt, soybean oil, and garlic, 1/4 teaspoon to a teaspoon or more added to any dish will give you a range of effects from a subtle resonance of flavor to a clarifying heat. It can be used in place of garlic in a dish, though additional garlic flavor can be obtained by frying a clove or two in the hot oil before adding the vegetables. Different varieties of chili paste are available (with radish, with black beans, etc.) and it is fun to experiment with these.

Cornstarch—The thickening agent for Chinese sauces, it is dissolved into cold liquid then thickens when heated, producing a light, semitranslucent sauce. If a sauce seems a little too thick, additional stock or water can be added; if too thin, the sauce can be boiled down or a teaspoon or so more of cornstarch may be dissolved in a Tablespoon of dry sherry then stirred into the cooking sauce. Cornstarch is also used in deep frying, as it produces a light, fine, crisp coating.

Dried black fungus—A form of fungus, like mushrooms, but without their deep flavor, it comes in several sizes, known as tree ears, wood ears, and cloud ears. Several of the smaller sizes left whole are attractive in a dish such as Stir-Fry Cabbage and Tofu in Oyster Sauce. The larger sizes are easily cut into julienne strips and add a dramatic accent to noodle dishes. They are reconstituted by soaking in boiling water for 20-30 minutes then squeezed to remove excess water. (The water can be discarded as it has no special flavor.) These add a pleasant crisp texture and take on the flavor of the sauce they are in.

Dried black mushrooms—Sold in plastic bags in various sizes, these are quite expensive, but a little goes a long way. To reconstitute, pour boiling water over the mushrooms and let stand, covered, for 20-30 minutes. Squeeze the mushrooms to extract excess water and remove stems before using. Mushrooms can be added to stir-fry dishes whole or cut in julienne strips. The flavorful soaking liquid can be reduced and used as part or all of the stock in Chinese sauces.

Fermented black beans—Also known as salted black beans, these lend a pleasant preserved, salty flavor and attractive speckled appearance to a dish. In a glass jar, they keep almost indefinitely in the refrigerator.

Hoi sin sauce—A rich-flavored, sophisticated Chinese "ketchup" or barbecue sauce, this sauce made of sugar, soybeans, flour, and sesame oil brings a special flavor and sweet accent to any dish. Different brands have slightly different flavors; you may want to experiment. It requires refrigeration after opening, but keeps well.

Oil—For stir-frying use a vegetable oil with a high smoking point, such as safflower, sunflower, peanut, corn, or soy oil, or a combination. Do not use olive oil.

Oyster sauce—An extract of oysters with water, salt, and starch added, it has a deep but modulated saltiness and the light sweetness of oysters. It does not add a fishlike flavor to a dish, but lends a special depth, intensity, and tempered saltiness that no other ingredient approximates.

Scallions—Not a Chinese ingredient per se, scallions are used in many Chinese dishes for their mild oniony flavor and attractive color. They can be minced and sprinkled over a dish raw as well as stir-fried along with the other ingredients.

Sesame oil (referred to also as dark sesame oil)— The least refined of sesame oils, this has a dark amber color and deep sesame flavor and aroma. Because of its low smoking point it is traditionally used as a flavoring rather than a frying agent. I have found, however, that sesame oil works beautifully in stir-frying when used in combination with regular cooking oil, and this eliminates the need to add additional oil.

Soy sauce or tamari—A dark, salty liquid, one of the products of the fermentation of soybeans. It is sold as "tamari" in Japanese and health-food markets. Dark, black, or double black soy sauce, which is soy sauce with molasses added, has a somewhat deeper flavor and adds additional accent to a dish. Be sure to avoid using so-called soy sauce sold in the supermarket, which is nothing more than water and salt with caramel added for color. An exception is Kikkoman, widely sold in supermarkets and Oriental markets, which is a good choice.

Sugar—Like scallions, sugar is also not a Chinese ingredient. I mention it here because it is used in small amounts to great advantage in Chinese sauces (even those not considered "sweet") to enhance and deepen flavor. It tends also to serve as a balance for more intensely salty flavorings.

AN EXTENDED WORD ON TOFU

I don't know where you are in your tofu development—whether it's a staple in your household or a new and only faintly familiar word. Tofu is a unique soybean product that is inexpensive and very high in protein. In the past, "pads" of tofu could be purchased only in Oriental markets or health-food stores with a serious macrobiotic bent. But a current growth in its use has brought tofu into the supermarkets in convenient specially sealed and dated containers that hold a single 1-pound pad.

In the past I found tofu unappealing in both taste (tasteless!) and texture (too soft and mushy). When I ate a particularly wonderful tofu presentation in a Chinese restaurant, it became clear to me that pressing and frying lent tofu just the character change it needed (for me to enjoy it). I also saw how tofu's blandness was part of its charm—the very thing that makes it a superb participant in a full-bodied Oriental sauce. Developing Stir-Fry Cabbage and Tofu in Oyster Sauce changed tofu from being a stranger in my refrigerator to a regular on my shopping list, and I've gone on to use it in non-stir-fry contexts as well (see Spinach and Tofu Tart and Dilled Mushroom Tofu Tart).

I generally purchase bulk tofu sold in 1/2-pound pads and keep it refrigerated in a container filled with water. Ideally the water should be poured off and replaced each day. Cared for in this way, tofu will keep easily a week and longer. (Tofu that is turning will lose some of its bounciness of texture and simple clarity of flavor.) I sometimes weight and press soft-style tofu before I use it (see instructions on p. 168). This reduces its water content and gives it a firmer, more compact texture. I also buy firm-style tofu in the supermarket. I always sauté or deep fry tofu, since otherwise it tends to disintegrate in stir-fry dishes and I prefer the crisper, chewier result.

Each recipe (if it is the only main course in the meal) serves 2 people generously. The noodle dishes are exceptions and will serve 3–4. In Chinese cooking, if you are serving more people you always add more dishes rather than increasing the proportions of the original dish.

A WORD ON WOKS

You can prepare stir-fry dishes even if you don't own a wok. But, oh, the wok is half the fun. Besides being an important part of the ambience of stir-fry cooking, the wok is, pure and simple, my most valued cooking pot. Its versatility is unsurpassed. It performs superbly as a steamer, deep fryer, sauté pan, and saucepan and, of course, stir-fry vessel without peer. The slope-sided design offers a large, full cooking surface and encourages a small amount of oil to go a very long way. The wok I own is large and deep (4 inches high and 14 inches across at the top). Produced by Taylor and Ng, it has a long wooden handle and, importantly, a flat bottom and so needs no stabilizing ring. This means it will sit directly on any heat source and reach the really hot temperatures needed to achieve the best stir-fry results. It is constructed of heavy material, which conducts and holds the heat well.

I begin with 2 recipes that utilize the same basic "oyster sauce" and yet are quite different in appearance and taste. Together they demonstrate the versatility of stir-fry cooking, the wide flexibility you have in your choice of ingredients, and the creativity with which you can change a single dish by your choice of protein, the particular vegetables you have on hand or wish to eat, and even whether or not you add that extra pinch of sugar or splash of soy.

Mixed Vegetables with Tofu or Chicken in Oyster Sauce with its flowers of deep green broccoli, chunks of red pepper, and bright orange carrot sticks is colorful and festive in appearance. When I have them on hand, I sprinkle hickory-smoked almonds over the finished dish.

Stir-Fry Cabbage, Tofu, and Ground Pork in Oyster Sauce is elegant in its simplicity and almost pristine in its appearance. Stir-fried cabbage is a special treat—sweet in a way that raw cabbage never even hints at, and moist and crunchy under the flavorful brown sauce. This dish can be elaborated on with the addition of ground pork, which permeates the sauce with its flavor and flecks the tofu and cabbage delicately. If you wish, you can also add Chinese mushrooms or whole small tree ears (fungus) for a dark accent and special texture.

MIXED VEGETABLES
WITH TOFU OR CHICKEN IN OYSTER SAUCE *serves 2 generously*

sauce

- 3/4 cup chicken stock (see p. 50), or 1/2 cup stock and 1/4 cup reduced mushroom liquid from soaking dried Chinese mushrooms
- 1 Tablespoon oyster sauce
- 1 Tablespoon Gingered Sherry (p. 258)
- 1 Tablespoon dark soy sauce
- 1 Tablespoon cornstarch
- 1/2 teaspoon salt
- 1/2 teaspoon sugar
- 1/4–1/2 teaspoon chili paste with garlic (optional)

  Oil for frying
- 1 pound soft-style tofu that has been pressed (see p. 171) or firm-style tofu, cut into 1/2–3/4-inch cubes, or 1/2 pound (or more) skinned and boned chicken breast, cut into cubes*
  Cornstarch
- 3 Tablespoons oil (up to 1 1/2 Tablespoons dark sesame oil)
  Flowerets from 1 head broccoli, blanched, drained, and patted dry
- 1 large or 2 medium carrots, peeled, halved horizontally then cut into julienne strips
- 1 sweet red pepper, cut into cubes about 1 inch square
- 1 medium onion, quartered and separated

- 4 dried Chinese mushrooms, soaked, squeezed, stems removed (optional)
  Chopped scallion
  Hickory-smoked almonds (optional)

Combine the ingredients for the sauce. Set aside.

Heat the wok. Add oil (can be part sesame oil) to the hot wok. If you are using tofu, pat it dry on paper towels. For tofu, use 4 Tablespoons oil; when the oil is very hot add the cubes of tofu and sauté until they are lightly golden on all sides. Remove with a slotted spoon to paper towels to drain. If you are using chicken, dust the cubes of chicken with cornstarch. (Technique is not crucial here—you can either sprinkle cornstarch over the chicken pieces and pat evenly around or shake the chicken in a plastic bag with cornstarch then turn the contents of the bag out into a colander and toss so the excess cornstarch is shaken off.) Heat 3–4 cups oil in the wok until hot. Add the chicken and fry briefly until only slightly pink in the center. Remove with a slotted spoon to paper towels to drain. (Chicken can be fried ahead of time and refrigerated.) Strain the oil through cheesecloth into another bowl and when cooled pour into a bottle and save for deep-frying reuse.

Heat the wok until it is very hot. Add 3 Tablespoons fresh oil, using up to half dark sesame oil if you like. When the oil is hot and shimmering, add the broccoli flowerets and stir-fry for several minutes, or until the broccoli begins to brown at the edges. Add the carrots and stir-fry for another minute or so. Add the red pepper, onion, and optional mushrooms and stir-fry until the vegetables are crisp-tender, adding chopped scallion for the last few tosses and stirs.

*If I have some of Norman's Chinese Chicken (p. 195) left over, I cut the larger chunks in half with a cleaver or heavy knife and simply add them to the thickening sauce instead of the fried boneless chicken or tofu. These tender bits of chicken on a bone lend an earthy home-style quality, and the deep marinated flavor (like barbecued chicken you might find at a Chinese grocery) further enhances this dish.

Remove the vegetables to a serving platter and return the wok to the heat. Stir up the sauce ingredients to dissolve the cornstarch and add the sauce to the hot wok. Add the tofu or chicken and stir gently a few times as the sauce thickens. Return the vegetables to the wok and toss until the ingredients are well mixed and coated lightly with sauce. Turn onto the platter and sprinkle with hickory-smoked almonds, if desired. Serve with rice.

STIR–FRY CABBAGE, TOFU, AND GROUND PORK IN OYSTER SAUCE *serves 2 generously*

½ pound ground pork
½ Tablespoon dark soy sauce
½ Tablespoon dark sesame oil (optional)
½ teaspoon sugar
½ teaspoon cornstarch
1 recipe Stir-Fry Cabbage and Tofu in Oyster Sauce (following recipe)

Combine the pork, soy sauce, optional oil, sugar, and cornstarch. Prepare Stir-Fry Cabbage and Tofu in Oyster Sauce. When the vegetables are cooked, remove to a serving platter, return the wok to the heat, and add the ground pork mixture. Press the pork flat against the hot wok and cook, pressing and chopping with the stir-fry spatula until the pork has lost its pink color and is well broken up. Stir the sauce mixture to dissolve the cornstarch then add the sauce to the meat mixture. Add the tofu and cook until the sauce thickens, stirring occasionally as needed. Add the cabbage mixture to the wok and toss until all the ingredients are coated with sauce. Taste for seasoning.

STIR–FRY CABBAGE AND TOFU IN OYSTER SAUCE *serves 2 generously*

sauce

- 3/4 cup chicken stock (see p. 50), or a combination of stock and reduced mushroom water*
- 1 Tablespoon dark soy sauce
- 1 Tablespoon Gingered Sherry (p. 258)
- 1 Tablespoon oyster sauce
- 1 Tablespoon cornstarch
- 1/2 teaspoon chili paste with garlic, or to taste (optional)
- 1/2 teaspoon salt
  Tamari or light soy sauce to taste

- 1 pound firm-style tofu or soft-style tofu that has been pressed (see p. 171)
- 5-7 Tablespoons cooking oil, or a combination of cooking oil and dark sesame oil
- 6 cups (or more) green cabbage, cut into 2-inch squares**
- 1 bunch scallions, cut into 1-2-inch lengths
- 3-4 dried Chinese mushrooms, soaked, squeezed, stems removed (optional)
  Generous handful shredded fresh spinach

Combine the ingredients for the sauce and set aside.

Cut the tofu into 1/2-inch-thick slices. Cut each slice in half if they are large and then cut into smaller rectangles or triangles and place on paper towels to dry. (Tofu will spatter less and fry more easily if you do this—or even just pat the surface of the tofu well with a paper towel.)

*For a strictly vegetarian stock, use only mushroom water left from reconstituting dried Chinese mushrooms and reduce to 3/4 cup.

**I usually just slice a hunk or two off a large head of cabbage, cut this into chunks, then separate the chunks into slices. The amount of cabbage is really up to you.

Heat a wok until it is very hot. Add 3-4 Tablespoons oil. When the oil is very hot and shimmering, add the tofu slices and sauté on either side until they are lightly golden. (You can decide where on the crisp/soft continuum you like your tofu.) Remove the tofu with a slotted spoon to a paper towel to drain.

Wipe the excess oil out of the wok if there are tofu crumbs. If not, just add enough oil so you have 2-3 Tablespoons. Reheat the wok until it is very hot and the oil is shimmering. Add the cabbage and stir-fry until the pieces begin to appear seared and brown in spots. (The cabbage will still be fairly crisp.) Add the scallions and mushrooms, if you are using them, and stir-fry until the scallions are limp. Add the spinach and stir-fry until the spinach softens—a relatively brief time. Remove the cabbage mixture to the serving platter you will be using and return the wok to the heat.

Stir up the sauce mixture to dissolve the cornstarch then add the sauce to the hot wok. Add the tofu and cook until the sauce thickens, stirring gently as needed. Return the cabbage mixture to the wok and stir and toss until all ingredients are coated lightly with sauce. Taste a piece of cabbage and add tamari (about 1 Tablespoon) if you think this is needed. Turn the mixture out onto the platter and serve immediately with rice.

NUMBER 97 (STIR–FRY TOFU AND BROCCOLI) *serves 2 generously*

Number 97 is my favorite stir-fry dish at an excellent local Chinese restaurant. The chef's Szechuan sauce is spicy, subtly sweet, and totally irresistible. If I haven't figured it out exactly, I've certainly come close.

sauce
- 1/2 cup chicken stock (see p. 50)
- 1 Tablespoon tamari or light soy sauce
- 1 Tablespoon dark soy sauce
- 1 Tablespoon Gingered Sherry (p. 258)
- 1 Tablespoon oyster sauce
- 1 Tablespoon sugar
- 1 Tablespoon cornstarch
- 1 teaspoon finely minced fresh gingerroot
- 1/2-1 teaspoon chili paste with garlic
- 1/2 teaspoon salt

- 3-4 cups oil for deep frying
- 1 pound firm-style tofu or soft-style tofu that has been pressed slightly (see p. 171)
- 2-3 Tablespoons oil (1-1 1/2 Tablespoons sesame oil)
  Flowerets from 1 small head broccoli, blanched, drained, and patted dry

Combine the ingredients for the sauce. Set aside.

Heat 3-4 cups oil in the wok for deep frying. Cut the tofu into cubes or thick slices then into squares or triangles. Blot dry with paper towels. When the oil is very hot, deep fry the tofu in 2 batches until it is puffed and golden. Remove the tofu from the oil with a slotted spoon to paper towels to drain. Return the oil to a container for reuse. Add 2-3 Tablespoons oil (half sesame) to the hot wok, and when the oil is smoking add the broccoli and stir-fry until it is crisp-tender. Push the broccoli to the side of the wok.

Stir up the sauce mixture and pour it into the wok. When the sauce begins to thicken, add the tofu and stir, tossing the broccoli and tofu together until all the ingredients are coated with the thickened sauce. If the sauce is too thick, add 1-2 Tablespoons additional stock or water.

NUMBER 97 NOODLES

Increase the stock to 3/4 cup. Stir-fry carrot strips, 8 ounces bean sprouts, and 1 bunch scallions along with the broccoli flowerets, cut into very small flowers. Toss with 1/2 pound linguini, cooked until it is al dente.

DOUBLE-COOKED PORK *serves 2 generously*

The combination of succulent pork and crunchy nuts and vegetables in a spicy-sweet sauce is wonderful.

1/2 pound boneless pork sirloin cutlet

sauce
1/3 cup hoi sin sauce
1/4 cup Gingered Sherry (p. 258)
1/2 teaspoon chili paste with garlic, or to taste
1/2 teaspoon salt

3-4 Tablespoons oil
   1 sweet red pepper, cut into 3/4-inch chunks
   1 green pepper, cut into 3/4-inch chunks
   1 carrot, cut on a diagonal into 1/4-inch slices
   1 medium onion, quartered and separated
      About 1 cup cabbage, cut or torn into 1-inch pieces or squares
2-4 scallions, cut into 1-inch lengths
1/3 cup dry roasted peanuts or cashews*

Simmer the pork cutlet in water to cover for about 5 minutes. The amount of time will depend on the thickness of the pork—it should be deep pink in the center. Let the meat cool then cut into slices about 1/4 inch thick. Set aside.

Combine the ingredients for the sauce. Set aside.

Heat the wok until it is very hot. Add 2-3 Tablespoons of the oil; when the oil is very hot and shimmering add the peppers, carrot, and slightly later the onion pieces. Stir-fry until the edges of the vegetables begin to brown slightly and the surface of the peppers begins to blister. Add the cabbage and scallions and stir-fry until the vegetables are crisp-tender. Remove the vegetables to a serving platter.

Reheat the wok until it is very hot. Add the remaining 1 Tablespoon of the oil. When the oil is very hot and shimmering add the pork slices and stir-fry quickly *just* until the pork loses its pink color. (Overcooking will toughen the pork.) Add the hoi sin mixture and boil for about 30 seconds to blend the flavors and reduce the liquid slightly. Return the vegetables to the wok along with the peanuts and toss until the ingredients are well mixed. Serve with rice.

DOUBLE-COOKED CHICKEN

Substitute for the pork 1/2 pound chicken breast, cut into chunks, coated lightly with cornstarch, then deep fried until crisped lightly.

DOUBLE-COOKED TOFU

Substitute for the pork 1/2 pound pressed soft-style or firm tofu. Slice, cut into triangles or small rectangles, and sauté or deep fry.

---

*In the past I would use blanched raw peanuts (or cashews) that I deep fried in 2-3 cups oil then drained on paper towels. Dry roasted nuts are easier and the results are good.

SWEET–AND–SOUR
FISH OR SEAFOOD WITH VEGETABLES *serves 2 generously*

Unlike the sticky sweet-and-sour Chinese dishes of my childhood, this recipe has the subtly intense sweetness of pleasure grown up. If you want to prepare this dish with fish, monkfish (also known as lotte or anglerfish) is the best choice. It is firm fleshed and stands up well under stir-frying where other fish tend to flake apart. When seafood is your preference, scallops are a sweet and juicy choice, shrimp crisp and full flavored, oysters unbelievably sensuous.

1/2–3/4 pound monkfish, scallops, shrimp,
     or oysters
     Cornstarch
     Oil for deep frying

sauce
   1/2 cup water (use oyster liquor for part of the liquid if using oysters)
    2 Tablespoons white vinegar
    2 Tablespoons sugar
    1 Tablespoon dark soy sauce
    1 Tablespoon cornstarch
    1 teaspoon light soy sauce or tamari
   1/2 teaspoon salt
   1/4 teaspoon chili paste with garlic (optional)
     Minced fresh gingerroot (optional)*

  2–3 Tablespoons oil
    1 good-size carrot, cut on a diagonal into 1/4-inch slices

    1 green pepper, cut into 1-inch chunks
    1 sweet red pepper, cut into 1-inch chunks
    1 medium onion, quartered and separated
  2–4 scallions, cut into 1-inch pieces

If using monkfish, partially freeze it then cut, on a slight angle, into about 3/8-inch-thick slices or bite-size cubes. If using scallops that are very large, cut them in half. Dust the fish or seafood lightly with cornstarch.

Heat several inches of oil in a wok or sauté pan until quite hot. Add the fish or seafood and fry until crisped lightly. Remove with a slotted spoon to paper towels to drain. (When cooled somewhat, the oil can be strained through cheesecloth to remove food particles, returned to bottle and reused for other deep frying.)

Combine the ingredients for the sauce. Set aside.

Heat the wok until it is very hot. Add 2–3 Tablespoons oil; when the oil is very hot and shimmering add the carrot slices. Toss the carrots a few times in the hot oil then add the peppers and onion and stir-fry until the vegetables are crisp-tender. (Don't worry if the carrots brown a little.) Add the scallions and stir-fry briefly until they soften. Either remove vegetables to a platter or push to one side of the wok. Stir the sauce up well to dissolve the cornstarch and add to the hot wok; add the fish or seafood to the sauce. Stir gently a few times until the sauce thickens. Stir in the vegetables and stir and toss gently just until all the ingredients are coated lightly with sauce. Turn out onto a platter and serve with rice.

*When I use minced ginger in this recipe, I remove a piece of ginger that has been soaking in sherry (see Gingered Sherry, p. 258), slice off a tiny edge, mince it fine, and add it to the sauce. Because of the soaking, the ginger flavor is very mild and adds a touch of sherry to the sauce as well.

CHICKEN WITH PEACHES AND PEANUTS *serves 2 generously*

Peaches add brilliant color and silky sweetness, peanuts a perfect crunch. This is a good choice to serve along with Stir-Fry Cabbage and Tofu in Oyster Sauce, in either its vegetarian or pork variations. Originally I prepared this dish with fresh peaches, peeled and sectioned, with chicken stock as the liquid, adding additional sugar for flavor balance. When peach season passed I tried canned peaches and found I even preferred them for their ease, appearance, and consistency of flavor.

> One 1-pound can "light" sliced peaches (not in heavy syrup), drained, with 3/4 cup juice reserved for sauce
> 2 Tablespoons vinegar
> 1 Tablespoon soy sauce or tamari
> 1 Tablespoon sugar
> 1 Tablespoon cornstarch
> 1/2 teaspoon salt
> 1/2–3/4 pound skinned and boned chicken breast, cut into 3/4-inch cubes
> Cornstarch
> 3–4 cups oil for deep frying
> 2 Tablespoons oil
> 2 large cloves garlic, flattened slightly with blade of knife
> 1 large green pepper, cut into 3/4-inch pieces
> 1 large carrot, cut on a diagonal into 1/4-inch slices
> 1 medium onion, quartered and separated
> 4 scallions, cut into 1-inch lengths
> 1/3 cup dry roasted peanuts

Combine the reserved liquid from the peaches, the vinegar, soy sauce or tamari, sugar, cornstarch, and salt. Set aside. Dust the chicken with cornstarch. Fry in hot oil (350°F) until the coating is crisped lightly but not browned, about 1–1 1/2 minutes. Remove with a slotted spoon to paper towels to drain. (Strain the oil and reserve for future deep-fry use.)

Heat the wok until it is very hot. Add 2 Tablespoons oil and the garlic cloves. Stir until the cloves turn golden, but remove them before they burn. Add the green pepper, carrot, and onion to the wok and stir-fry until they are almost crisp-tender. Add the scallions and stir-fry until they are wilted. Remove the vegetables to a serving platter.

Stir up the sauce ingredients well to dissolve the cornstarch and add to the hot wok. When the sauce begins to thicken, add peach slices, chicken, and dry roasted peanuts. Stir several times as the sauce continues to thicken. Return the vegetables to the wok and stir again to mix and coat with sauce. Turn onto the serving platter and accompany with rice.

MU SHU PORK MY WAY *serves 2 generously*

Although not a "traditional" mu shu (or mu shi) recipe, this dish has the wonderful smoky-sweet flavor characteristic of the best mu shu I've ever eaten and has more commonly available ingredients.

8 ounces ground pork
2 Tablespoons hoi sin sauce
3/4 Tablespoon light soy sauce or tamari
3/4 Tablespoon dark soy sauce
1 teaspoon cornstarch
3/4 teaspoon sugar
3 eggs
1 teaspoon sesame oil
1/2 teaspoon sugar
1/2 teaspoon salt
3 Tablespoons oil
5-6 cups shredded cabbage
6-8 dried Chinese mushrooms, soaked, squeezed, stems removed, and cut into julienne strips (reduce and reserve the liquid for sauce; see below)
1 bunch scallions, cut into 1-inch lengths
1 teaspoon salt
1/4-1/2 cup reduced mushroom liquid
Additional hoi sin sauce to taste
8-10 steamed Chinese Pancakes (following recipe)

About 2 hours ahead of time, combine the pork with the hoi sin sauce and refrigerate. Thirty minutes before cooking time, mix in the light soy sauce or tamari, dark soy sauce, cornstarch, and the 3/4 teaspoon sugar and set aside.

Beat together the eggs, sesame oil, the 1/2 teaspoon sugar, and the 1/2 teaspoon salt. Heat the wok and add 1 Tablespoon of the oil. Pour the beaten eggs into the hot oil and scramble gently until they are set but not too dry.* Remove from the wok and set aside. Wipe or clean out the wok.

Reheat the wok until it is very hot. Add the remaining 2 Tablespoons of oil; when it is hot and shimmering add the cabbage and stir-fry until it begins to brown slightly and reduce in volume. Add the mushrooms, scallions, and the 1 teaspoon salt, continuing to stir-fry until the scallions are softened and the cabbage is delightfully crisp-tender. Remove to a serving platter.

Heat the wok again until it is quite hot, then add the marinated pork mixture. Flatten it against the hot wok and cook, pressing and chopping with your spatula, until it has lost its raw color totally and is browned and well broken up. Return the cabbage mixture to the wok and toss the ingredients. Add the eggs and reserved mushroom liquid and toss to distribute the ingredients well. Taste and add up to 1 Tablespoon additional hoi sin sauce if you like a little more sweetness. Turn into a bowl or platter and serve with steamed Chinese Pancakes.

MU SHU CHICKEN

Substitute 8 ounces shredded chicken breast for the pork. (It is easier to cut into shreds when partially frozen.) Add 1-2 Tablespoons oil to the wok at the stir-fry stage, since chicken does not have as much fat as pork.

*I used to fry the eggs in thin pancakelike sheets, then stack and roll the sheets and cut the egg into thin strips. But scrambling the eggs works equally well and is quicker and easier, so for me the choice of techniques is clear. However, if you'd like to experiment, heat a 10-inch fry pan until it is fairly hot, brush generously with oil, and pour in one third of the beaten egg mixture. Swirl the egg around to form a thin but not too fragile pancake and cook over medium heat until the eggs are dry, being careful not to let the egg brown. Loosen the egg with a spatula and turn it out onto a work surface. Don't worry if the egg tears—you'll be slicing it up anyway. The second sheet will be easier!

CHINESE PANCAKES *yields 16 pancakes*

Chinese pancakes are fun and easy to make—once you get the hang of it. If it's a first-time endeavor, allow yourself an extra batch of dough to experiment with. (If they all come out perfectly, just wrap them in meal-size packages and freeze for future mu shu dinners.) The only really tricky part to making these pancakes is in getting the dough rolled to the right thinness—not *so* thin that you can't ease the 2 pancakes apart without tearing them, but not so thick that you sacrifice delicacy and tenderness. When your pancakes are steamed and your mu shu filling is prepared, place a warm, soft pancake on your plate. Place a generous spoonful of filling down the center of the pancake, roll the pancake up, lift it to your mouth, and bite into one of the juiciest, crunchiest, doughiest multimedia mouthfuls you can create!

2 cups unbleached all-purpose flour
3/4 cup boiling water
Dark sesame oil

Combine the flour and water in a bowl or food processor. If using the processor, run the machine until the dough coheres and then a little longer to knead. If mixing by hand, knead for about 5 minutes on a smooth surface. You should have a soft but unsticky dough. Rub the dough very lightly with sesame oil, place in a bowl, cover, and let rest for 1 hour.

Knead the dough once or twice then form into a long sausagelike roll about 1½ inches in diameter. Divide into 16 equal pieces. Have a griddle or sauté pan heating on a medium flame (I use 2 pans).

Have nearby a small bowl with sesame oil in it. Take 2 pieces of dough, flatten each slightly, then dip the flat side of 1 piece into the sesame oil. Place this piece oil side down on top of the other piece of dough so the oil is sandwiched between them. Flatten them together on a counter with the palm of your hand then roll them out, the one on top of the other, into a circle about 6 inches in diameter. Roll as evenly as possible, from the center out to the perimeter, all around, without moving the round of dough. (Don't worry if you don't come up with a perfect circle—this is part of the charm of the pancake.)

Place the round of dough on the hot griddle, brushed lightly with sesame oil, and cook until the top side begins to appear a little dry. Do not let the bottom color—turn the heat down if this is happening. Turn the pancake and cook the other side. Remove the pancake from the griddle, let it cool slightly, then carefully pull the 2 pancakes apart. Stack the finished pancakes on a sheet of aluminum foil and wrap them up when you have the number of pancakes you need (2-3 per person are usually sufficient). At this point you can either refrigerate or freeze the pancakes or proceed to cook them.

Steam them in the foil packet for 25-30 minutes before serving with Mu Shu Pork My Way (preceding recipe).

ASPARAGUS STIR-FRY *serves 2 generously*

A simple and delicious stir-fry, naturally sweet and full flavored.

1 1/2 pounds (or more) medium-size asparagus
   2 Tablespoons oil
   1 medium-large onion, sliced thin
   1 Tablespoon sesame seeds (optional)
   2 Tablespoons soy sauce or tamari
   1 Tablespoon oyster sauce
1-2 dashes Tabasco sauce

Roll-cut the asparagus into 1-1 1/2-inch lengths by cutting the asparagus tips off at an angle, rolling the asparagus slightly then making another angled cut. Do not use tough, nongreen bottoms. You should have approximately 4 cups of cut asparagus.

Heat the wok until it is very hot. Add the oil; when the oil is hot and shimmering add the asparagus. Stir-fry for about 3 minutes then add the onion slices. Stir-fry for an additional 2-3 minutes until the onion begins to brown then add the sesame seeds and toss for a minute or less. Add the soy sauce or tamari, oyster sauce, and Tabasco and cook briefly until the sauce is reduced and the asparagus is tender.

STIR-FRY ASPARAGUS WITH GROUND BEEF *serves 2 generously*

A delightful way to use asparagus when it is in season. When it is not in season, substitute the flowerets of 1 small head of broccoli.

   8 ounces ground beef
   1 Tablespoon hoi sin sauce
   1 Tablespoon dark soy sauce, or light soy
      or tamari
   1 teaspoon cornstarch
 1/2 teaspoon sugar
 1-2 Tablespoons oil
   1 clove garlic
1/2-1 pound thin asparagus spears, roll-cut into
      1 1/2-inch lengths*
 1/4 cup minced scallion

* To achieve the most attractive pieces of asparagus, hold the knife at a sharp angle to the cutting surface when you cut and roll the spear of asparagus a quarter turn before making the next cut.

   1 Tablespoon Gingered Sherry (p. 258)
      Additional hoi sin sauce

Combine the ground beef, hoi sin sauce, soy sauce, cornstarch, and sugar. Set aside.

Heat the wok until very hot. Add the oil; when it is hot add the garlic and asparagus and stir-fry until the asparagus begins to brown slightly. Remove the garlic. Add a few Tablespoons water, cover, and steam until the asparagus is crisp-tender.

Remove the asparagus or push to one side of the wok. Add the beef mixture to the hot wok, pressing it flat then chopping it with the spatula until the meat loses its raw color and is well broken up. Add the minced scallion and Gingered Sherry and mix. Add the asparagus and stir-fry until the ingredients are well mixed. Taste. If you would like the dish sweeter, add more hoi sin sauce. Serve with rice.

SPICY LAMB WITH ZUCCHINI AND ONIONS *serves 2 generously*

A simple and succulent lamb stir-fry that can be varied by substituting ground or sliced beef for the lamb and adding 1 Tablespoon sugar and 1/2–1 teaspoon minced fresh gingerroot to the sauce.

8 ounces lean ground lamb
1 Tablespoon dark soy sauce
1 teaspoon cornstarch
1/2 cup chicken stock (see p. 50)
1 Tablespoon light soy sauce or tamari
1 Tablespoon freshly squeezed lemon juice
1 Tablespoon cornstarch
1/2 teaspoon salt, or to taste
1/2 teaspoon chili paste with garlic, or to taste
3 Tablespoons oil (1 1/2 Tablespoons dark sesame oil)
2 large cloves garlic, peeled and bruised lightly with a knife blade
2 pounds zucchini (3 medium-large zucchini)*
1 medium onion, sliced thin
1 bunch scallions, cut into 2-inch lengths

*Cut the zucchini in half lengthwise (after removing stem ends). Slice off the skin about 1/4 inch or a little thicker and cut these slices into julienne strips. Discard the inner pulp or reserve for another use.

Reconstituted mushrooms or black fungus, cut into julienne strips

Mix together the lamb, dark soy sauce, and the 1 teaspoon cornstarch and set aside. Combine the chicken stock, soy sauce, lemon juice, the 1 Tablespoon cornstarch, salt, and chili paste with garlic. Set aside.

Heat the wok until it is very hot. Add the oil and sauté the garlic cloves until they are golden then remove and discard them. When the oil is very hot and shimmering add the zucchini and onion. Stir-fry until the vegetables begin to brown at the edges. Add the scallions and mushrooms or fungus and stir-fry until the scallions are wilted. Either push the vegetables aside or remove them from the wok. Add the lamb mixture to the hot wok and cook, pressing and chopping with your stir-fry spatula until the meat is browned and well broken up.

Stir up the sauce to dissolve the cornstarch and pour into the wok. Cook, stirring, until the sauce begins to thicken. Add in the vegetables and stir and toss until all ingredients are well coated with sauce. Serve with rice.

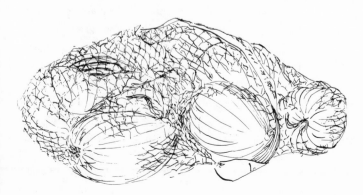

A BASIC SAUCE FOR VEGETABLES *yields ³/₄ cup*

Use this sauce for any vegetables-only dish. For variation add a small amount of minced gingerroot or garlic or a Tablespoon of oyster sauce (delicious with broccoli) or fermented black beans (attractive with green beans), or spike it with chili paste with garlic. Make your choices to emphasize differences between the dishes on your menu.

½ cup chicken stock (see p. 50), or part stock
    and part mushroom liquid
1 Tablespoon soy sauce or tamari
1 Tablespoon Gingered Sherry (p. 258)
1 Tablespoon cornstarch
½ teaspoon sugar
½ teaspoon salt

Combine the ingredients and set aside. Stir-fry your choice of vegetable(s) in a very hot wok. When the vegetables are crisp-tender, push them aside, stir up the sauce ingredients to make sure the cornstarch is dissolved, and pour into the hot wok. As the sauce begins to thicken, toss it with the vegetables until the desired consistency is reached and all ingredients are coated with sauce.

NOODLE DISHES

Being the lover of pasta and noodles that I am, it's surprising to me that I came to an appreciation of Chinese noodle dishes so late. I grew up noticing that noodles were always the last and cheapest item on a Chinese menu and mistakenly assumed they were what you ordered only when you couldn't afford something else. Also, my association of pasta with Italian cuisine was just too strong and blinding —it delayed the realization that here was yet another wonderful way to enjoy noodles and discover pastas of a whole different sort.

My attitude toward Chinese noodle dishes began to change when years ago a Brooklyn neighbor shared his passion for cold spicy Szechuan noodle with me. He would bring it home and we would eat greedily, unceremoniously, from the carton. These were long-stranded noodles coated lightly with a fiery peanut-based sauce and a mysteriously tasty crunch that seemed like a combination of minced pickled vegetables and crushed peanuts. It was heaven.

I remember equally vividly the first noodle dish I ever ordered at a Chinese restaurant. It was a pork and shrimp lo mein, eaten years later in one of the unadorned downstairs restaurants in Boston's China-town. The pork was barbecued and deep flavored, the noodles thin and tender. Bean sprouts added subtle crunch and volume, and everything had that marvelous smoky-seared flavor of fast, high-heat cooking.

I began to experiment at home, first with bean thread, an almost transparent, extremely fine, and incredibly resilient noodle. Bean thread comes in 2-ounce packages. They are soaked in boiling water to cover for just a few minutes until softened, drained, and added to a dish where they immediately begin to absorb the flavor of the surrounding sauce. As I moved on to other kinds of noodles, I evolved a favorite way to enjoy them. It's an Oriental pasta primavera—a combination of bite-tender noodles, crisp stir-fried vegetables, and bits of scallop, shrimp, pork, or beef with a small amount of intensely flavored Chinese sauce bringing it all together. A mere 1/2 pound of noodles becomes transformed into a healthful, bountiful feast for the eyes and palate.

Different kinds of noodles change the character of recipes slightly. Use fresh noodles purchased at an Oriental grocery, or imported Italian pastas (linguini, spaghetti, vermicelli, etc.), which are always on hand and cook up marvelously al dente. My favorite noodle is rice sticks—pearly white rice flour noodles that come in different widths (the widest are

the most dramatic in a dish) and cook in minutes to a beautifully tender but elastic consistency. Vary any of the ingredients or the types of noodle, and you'll see how easy it is to create satisfying and healthful noodle dishes.

Still another advantage of these dishes is that, unlike most stir-fry dishes, they are almost at their best eaten at room temperature. (They are also delicious eaten straight from the wok or refrigerator.) If you are preparing several stir-fry dishes at one meal, a noodle dish is the one to prepare first and have out of the way. A noodle dish is also a good choice for a potluck dinner, a picnic, or any kind of al fresco eating. Even prepared a day ahead, refrig-erated, then allowed to come to room temperature or reheated gently, a noodle dish is consistently pleasing.

As you prepare noodle dishes you will become more and more adept in your timing, having per-fectly al dente noodles ready to be added to the just-bubbling sauce. If the noodles are not ready, no matter. Just turn down the heat under the sauce. If the noodles are done ahead of time, drain them under cold water to stop the cooking and toss with a little sesame oil to prevent their sticking together.

Remember—noodle dishes have more volume than stir-fry dishes and will serve 3–4, especially if served with other foods.

THE BEST LO MEIN OUTSIDE CHINATOWN *serves 3–4*

This was my original "prototype" noodle dish and my pleasure in the results shows in the grandiosity of its title.

6 ounces linguini or vermicelli or thin fresh noodles
1 Tablespoon sesame oil

sauce
1/2 cup reduced mushroom liquid from soaking dried Chinese mushrooms (see below)
1 Tablespoon oyster sauce
1 Tablespoon dark soy sauce
1 Tablespoon Gingered Sherry (p. 258)
2 teaspoons cornstarch
1/2 teaspoon sugar
1/2 teaspoon salt

2 Tablespoons oil
1 sweet red pepper, cut into thin julienne strips
1 carrot, cut into thin julienne strips
1 cup shredded cabbage
3–4 dried Chinese mushrooms, soaked in boiling water, squeezed, stems removed, and cut into thin strips
4–5 scallions, cut into 2-inch lengths
1 cup bean sprouts
1 Tablespoon oil
1/2 pound Chinese barbecued pork,* leftover cooked chicken, or small raw shrimp or scallops

Cook the noodles until they are al dente; drain. Rinse quickly with cold water, drain well, and toss with sesame oil in the serving bowl or platter you will be using.

Combine the ingredients for the sauce. Set aside.

Heat the wok until it is very hot. Add the 2 Tablespoons oil; when the oil is very hot and shimmering add the pepper and carrot strips. Toss and stir-fry until the peppers begin to blister and the carrots brown a little at the edges. Add the cabbage, mushrooms, and scallions, stir-frying until the cabbage begins to soften. Add the bean sprouts. Stir-fry until the bean sprouts begin to reduce in volume and the vegetables are pretty uniformly crisp-tender. Add the vegetables to the noodles and toss to distribute them evenly.

Reheat the wok until it is very hot. Add the 1 Tablespoon oil; when the oil is very hot and shimmering add the pork, chicken, shrimp, or scallops. Stir-fry quickly until the raw seafood is cooked through or until the cooked meats have crisped slightly around the edges. Stir up the sauce to dissolve the cornstarch. Add the sauce to the hot wok and stir occasionally as it begins to thicken. Return the noodle and vegetable mixture to the wok and toss until the ingredients are well mixed and coated evenly with sauce. Turn into the serving platter or bowl. Serve immediately or closer to room temperature.

*Most Oriental markets carry barbecued pork. To prepare your own barbecued pork, marinate pork sirloin cutlet overnight in hoi sin sauce flavored with a little soy sauce and Gingered Sherry (p. 258). Bake at 350°F until cooked through, being careful not to overbake and dry out.

RICE STICKS WITH SCALLOPS AND VEGETABLES *serves 3–4*

This is my special-occasion noodle dish. The colors are lovely and the flavors rich and satisfying, with the subtle sweetness of scallops coming through.

sauce

3/4 cup chicken stock (see p. 50), or 1/2 cup chicken stock and 1/4 cup reduced mushroom liquid from soaking dried Chinese mushrooms (see below)

2 Tablespoons hoi sin sauce

1 Tablespoon dark soy sauce

1 Tablespoon Gingered Sherry (p. 258)

1 Tablespoon cornstarch

1/2 teaspoon chili paste with garlic, or to taste

1/2 teaspoon sugar

1/2 teaspoon salt

1/2 pound tiny scallops, or large scallops cut in thirds or quarters
Cornstarch

3–4 cups oil for deep frying

1 yellow squash

3–4 Tablespoons oil (part dark sesame oil)

1 large carrot, cut into julienne strips

1 sweet red pepper, cut into julienne strips

1 cup shredded cabbage

4–6 scallions, cut into 1–11/2-inch lengths

3–4 dried Chinese mushrooms, soaked in boiling water, squeezed, stems removed, and cut into thin julienne strips

3–4 large wood ears, soaked, squeezed, and cut into thin julienne strips

1/2 pound bean sprouts
Generous handful fresh spinach, cut into shreds

1/2 pound rice sticks, or noodle of choice

Combine the ingredients for the sauce. Set aside.

Shake the scallops in a plastic bag with cornstarch then shake in a strainer to remove excess starch. Deep fry the scallops in the 3–4 cups hot oil (350°F) until crisped lightly but not colored. Remove the scallops with a slotted spoon to paper towels to drain. Strain the oil and return to a bottle for deep-fry reuse.

Cut off the yellow squash's outer peel with some white part and cut this peel into julienne strips. Discard the rest of the squash or save for another use. Heat the wok until it is very hot. Add 3 Tablespoons oil (part dark sesame); when the oil is very hot and shimmering add the carrot, red pepper, and squash. Stir-fry briefly until the vegetables begin to brown slightly at the edges then add the cabbage, scallions, mushrooms, and wood ears. Stir-fry until the cabbage begins to soften and reduces in volume. Add the bean sprouts and stir-fry until they begin to reduce in volume. Add the spinach. Stir-fry until the spinach is wilted and the vegetables are crisptender. Remove to a serving platter.

Have ready a large pot of boiling water. Add the rice sticks and stir. Return the wok to the heat. Stir the sauce ingredients up to dissolve the cornstarch and add them to the wok, stirring once or twice. Add the scallops to the thickening sauce and stir. Add the noodles when the sauce has thickened and toss until the noodles are well coated with sauce. Return the vegetables to the wok and toss until all ingredients are evenly distributed. Taste for seasoning. Turn onto the platter and serve immediately or let cool to room temperature.

RICE STICKS
WITH CRAB MEAT (OR TOFU), PORK, AND VEGETABLES *serves 3–4*

Here's another noodle dish for a very special occasion. You can also prepare it in a more proletarian (but still delicious) tofu version.

sauce
- 1/2 cup chicken stock (see p. 50)
- 1/4 cup reduced mushroom liquid from soaking wood ears and/or dried Chinese mushrooms (see below)
- 1 Tablespoon soy sauce
- 1 Tablespoon oyster sauce
- 1 Tablespoon Gingered Sherry (p. 258)
- 1 Tablespoon hoi sin sauce, or to taste
- 1 Tablespoon cornstarch
- 1/2 teaspoon salt
- 1/2 teaspoon chili paste with garlic (optional)

- 1/2 pound ground pork
- 1 Tablespoon dark soy sauce
- 1/2 Tablespoon hoi sin sauce
- 1 teaspoon cornstarch
- 1/2 teaspoon sugar
- 2–3 Tablespoons oil (half dark sesame oil)
- 1 sweet red pepper, cut into thin julienne strips
- 1 large carrot, cut into thin julienne strips
- 1 cup shredded cabbage
- 1 bunch scallions, cut into 1–1 1/2-inch lengths
  Wood ears and/or dried Chinese mushrooms, soaked in boiling water, squeezed, stems removed, and cut into thin julienne strips
- 8 ounces bean sprouts
  Generous handful fresh spinach, cut into shreds
- 1/2 pound fresh crab meat, or 1/4–1/2 pound tofu, cut into cubes and sautéed until golden
- 1/2 pound rice sticks, or noodles of choice, cooked al dente and drained

Combine the ingredients for the sauce. Set aside.

Mix together the ground pork, dark soy sauce, hoi sin sauce, cornstarch, and sugar. Set this aside too.

Heat the wok until it is very hot. Add the oil; when the oil is very hot and shimmering add the red pepper and carrot and toss briefly. Add the cabbage, scallions, wood ears, and mushrooms and stir-fry until the cabbage is reduced in volume and almost crisp-tender. Add the bean sprouts and stir-fry until they are reduced in volume and tender. Add the spinach and stir-fry just until it is wilted. Remove the vegetables from the wok to a serving bowl or platter.

Reheat the wok until it is very hot. Add the ground pork mixture and cook, pressing and chopping with a stir-fry spatula until the pork is browned and well broken up. Add the crab meat (or tofu) and stir-fry lightly. Stir the sauce ingredients up to dissolve the cornstarch then add to the wok. Cook, stirring occasionally, until the sauce thickens. Add the cooked and drained noodles and toss until the noodles are well coated with sauce. Return the vegetables to the wok and toss until all ingredients are well distributed. Taste for seasoning. Serve immediately or let come to room temperature.

NOODLES WITH BEEF AND ASPARAGUS (OR BROCCOLI) *serves 3-4*

sauce

- 3/4 cup chicken stock (see p. 50), or 1/2 cup stock and 1/4 cup reduced mushroom liquid from soaking dried Chinese mushrooms and/or wood ears (see below)
- 1 Tablespoon dark soy sauce
- 1 Tablespoon Gingered Sherry (p. 258)
- 1 Tablespoon hoi sin sauce
- 1 Tablespoon cornstarch
- 1 teaspoon sugar
- 1/2 teaspoon salt
- 1/2 teaspoon chili paste with garlic, or to taste
  Dried Chinese mushrooms and/or wood ears, soaked in boiling water, squeezed, then cut into thin julienne strips*

- 1/2 pound ground beef
- 1 Tablespoon dark or light soy sauce
- 1 Tablespoon hoi sin sauce
- 1 teaspoon sugar
- 1 teaspoon cornstarch
- 2-3 Tablespoons oil (part dark sesame oil)
  About 3/4 pound thin asparagus spears, roll-cut into 1 1/2-inch lengths, or flowerets from 1 head broccoli (reserve stalk for other uses)**
- 1/2 pound bean sprouts
- 4-6 scallions, cut into 1 1/2-inch lengths
- 1/2 pound rice sticks, or other noodle of choice
  Additional hoi sin sauce to taste (optional)

Combine the ingredients for the sauce. Set aside.

Mix together the ground beef, dark or light soy sauce, hoi sin sauce, sugar, and cornstarch. Set aside.

Heat the wok until it is very hot. Add the oil (part dark sesame); when the oil is very hot and shimmering add the asparagus (or broccoli) and stir-fry until almost crisp-tender. Add the bean sprouts and scallions and continue to stir-fry until the sprouts reduce in volume and all the vegetables are pleasingly crisp-tender. Remove the vegetables to a serving platter.

Cook your noodles until they are al dente. While the noodles are boiling, add the meat mixture to the hot wok and cook, pressing and chopping with a stir-fry spatula until the meat is browned and well separated. Stir up the sauce ingredients to dissolve the cornstarch, add to the meat mixture, and stir once or twice as the sauce begins to thicken. When thickened, drain the noodles and add them to the sauce, tossing and stirring to coat evenly. Add the reserved vegetable mixture and toss to distribute the vegetables evenly. Taste for seasoning and serve hot or at room temperature.

---

*Traditionally mushrooms and wood ears are added during the stir-fry process. Because wood ears have little flavor of their own and the mushrooms have given most of their flavor to the soaking liquid, I often add them to the sauce, which serves as a flavor-imparting "marinade."

**Peel the broccoli stalk, slice thin, stir-fry with mushrooms and scallions, and serve with A Basic Sauce for Vegetables (p. 184).

SPICY NOODLES
WITH SESAME, SCALLIONS, AND CHICKEN OR BEEF *serves 3-4*

sauce
- 1/2 cup chicken stock (see p. 50)
- 3 Tablespoons soy sauce or tamari
- 1 Tablespoon sherry or Gingered Sherry (p. 258)
- 1 Tablespoon hoi sin sauce
- 1 Tablespoon sugar
- 1 Tablespoon cornstarch
- 1/2 Tablespoon chili paste with garlic, or to taste
- 1 teaspoon minced fresh gingerroot
- 1/2 teaspoon salt

- 2 Tablespoons oil
- 1 Tablespoon dark sesame oil
- 1/2 pound chicken (or turkey) breast or beef, sliced into thin strips
- 2 bunches scallions, sliced into 1-inch lengths
- 1/2 pound bean sprouts
- 2-3 Tablespoons lightly toasted sesame seeds
- 1/2 pound linguini, or noodles of choice, cooked al dente and drained
  Additional toasted sesame seeds

Combine the ingredients for the sauce. Set aside.

Heat the wok until it is very hot. Add both oils. When the oil is very hot and shimmering add the chicken or beef and stir-fry until it begins to lose its raw color. Add the scallions, bean sprouts, and toasted sesame seeds and stir-fry until the bean sprouts become a little limp.

Stir up the sauce ingredients to dissolve the cornstarch and pour into the wok. When the sauce thickens, add the noodles and toss until all ingredients are well blended. Turn into a serving bowl or platter and sprinkle with additional sesame seeds.

POULTRY, MEAT, FISH AND SEAFOOD

**POULTRY,
MEAT,
FISH
AND
SEAFOOD**

Hoi Sin Spicy Chicken (or Turkey) on a Skewer

Hoi Sin Spicy Beef on a Skewer

Hoi Sin Spicy Kebobs

Hoi Sin Spicy Chicken

Hoi Sin Spicy Pork, Beef, or Lamb

Norman's Chinese Chicken

Gentle Hoi Sin Duck

Gentle Hoi Sin Chicken

Chinese (Not So Spare) Ribs (Gentle Hoi Sin Pork)

Sesame Szechuan Chicken

Sesame Szechuan Beef, Lamb, or Pork Kebobs

Sweet Szechuan Seafood

Sesame Szechuan Seafood or Fish

Sweet-and-Sour Walnut Chicken Crisps

Crispy Fried Fish Bites

Favorite Fish Brochettes

Gravlaks

Dilled Mayonnaise

Here are some of the ways I like to prepare chicken, fish, and meat when it is served alone, as a "main course." My goal is an exquisitely flavorful food that will be satisfying in small amounts—a kind of sensuous accompaniment to any side dish, whether it be a richly textured pasta or pasta salad, a stir-fry, a mouth-filling pierogin, or a simple steamed vegetable and baked potato.

Many of these recipes also make excellent hors d'oeuvres. Crisp fried oysters or scallops served with toothpicks, 2–3 per person, are among my favorite things to serve with drinks. Hoi Sin Spicy Chicken, Turkey, or Beef on a Skewer is a great beginning for a stir-fry meal. Gravlaks has a fresh, elegant clarity whether served as an hors d'oeuvre, a light lunch, or as part of a brunch or party buffet.

The first series of recipes (Hoi Sin Spicy) marinates poultry or meat for 24 hours in tenderizing, flavor-infusing sweet hoi sin sauce then bakes, broils, or grills the meat, brushed with Special Szechuan Marinade.

If you prefer something less spicy try Gentle Hoi Sin Duck (or Chicken or Ribs). This method also marinates meat or poultry for 24 hours in hoi sin sauce, but then coats and bakes it instead in a sweeter, milder duck sauce–based mixture.

Norman's Chinese Chicken, one of my favorites, marinates small cut-up chicken pieces (also on the bone) in a beautifully balanced soy-sherry marinade, redolent of garlic, onions, and sweet hoi sin—and just enough chili paste with garlic to keep things really moving. Like the other recipes, it shines, too, when other meats are substituted, especially pork.

There are general instructions for using Szechuan Vinaigrette and Special Szechuan Marinade as an impromptu marinade to give new and different tastes to about-to-be-cooked poultry and meats, seafood and fish.

Next are 2 recipes for deep-fried foods—crisp, succulent, and juicy. My attitude toward deep frying is this: when it is done properly (in oil heated to correct deep-frying temperature), juices, flavors, and nutrients are marvelously sealed into foods—excess oil is sealed out. Deep-fried foods are a treat we need not deny ourselves. Both recipes create equally wonderful hors d'oeuvres and main course dishes. Either is an excellent adjunct to a stir-fry meal. Then there are fish brochettes, broiled flavorful and juicy in an herby mustardy mayonnaise coating.

And last is a recipe for refreshing, velvety Gravlaks—the best thing I know of to occupy the space between the pleasures of cooked and raw.

This is not a long or extensive chapter because meat and other animal protein as a main event accompanied by a less important vegetable and starch is not a large part of my cooking and eating style. Although I love meat and value its nutritional and aesthetic contribution to my cooking and my table, focusing on it constricts for me the number of wonderful ways I can combine and create with food. Whatever *your* style of using meat and other animal protein, I'm sure you will find these recipes easy to prepare and delicious. They work; they please and satisfy whether used as an hors d'oeuvre, a special accompaniment, or even as the most important food on the plate.

HOI SIN SPICY CHICKEN (OR TURKEY) ON A SKEWER *yields 12-25 pieces*

This is a very popular hors d'oeuvre, enticingly sweet and spicy. One pound of breast meat will give you anywhere from 12 to 25 hors d'oeuvre pieces, depending on how you slice them and whether or not you want a small taste or a medium mouthful on each skewer. I often substitute turkey breast for the chicken, finding the finished hors d'oeuvre even more full-bodied and flavorful.

1 pound skinned and boned chicken breast
1/3 cup hoi sin sauce
    Sixteen–twenty-five 6-inch wooden skewers, soaked in water for 24 hours
1 recipe Special Szechuan Marinade (p. 257)
    Lightly toasted sesame seeds

Cut the chicken at a slight angle into strips about 4 inches long, 1 1/4 inches wide, and 1/4 inch thick. (All these dimensions are approximate.) Place the chicken in a bowl or plastic bag and add enough hoi sin to coat all the pieces lightly. Refrigerate for 24 hours.

Preheat the oven to 375°F. Thread the chicken pieces onto the tip or upper third of the skewer. Arrange on a baking pan so that the chicken pieces do not overlap. Brush with Special Szechuan Marinade and sprinkle lightly with sesame seeds. Bake for 10–12 minutes, or until the chicken is cooked but still juicy. If you would like the chicken to be spicier, brush once more with the marinade before the cooking is complete. The chicken can also be grilled or broiled.

HOI SIN SPICY BEEF ON A SKEWER

Substitute tenderloin tips or a similar tender and flavorful cut of meat for the chicken breast. A butcher will often do this cutting for you, either by hand or using a slicing machine. It is best that the beef be sliced very thin and furled up around the skewer. Omit sesame seeds with the beef.

HOI SIN SPICY KEBOBS

Cut boneless beef, pork, turkey, or lamb into cubes. Use tender cuts of meat, appropriate for broiling or grilling. Follow the directions for Hoi Sin Spicy Chicken (preceding recipe) for marinating the meat in hoi sin sauce for 24 hours. Thread cubes of meat onto wooden skewers that have been soaked in water for several hours, preferably overnight. Brush the meat with Special Szechuan Marinade (p. 257) and grill or broil, turning and brushing once again, until the meat is cooked the way you like it.

HOI SIN SPICY CHICKEN *serves 4-6*

This is a deeply flavored chicken, gingery and hot. I think it is at its best when the chicken is cut into bite-size pieces. Buy whole chickens or leg quarters (leg, thigh, and back) and cut with a cleaver into 4-5 pieces, discarding the tip of the leg bone. You can ask your butcher to do this. You can also use regular cut-up chicken pieces, although they will require a longer baking time and more vigilance to prevent burning. This is a wonderful dish to bake a little ahead of time and serve as part of a stir-fry feast. And it is delicious served with non-Oriental dishes as well.

3-4 pounds chicken on the bone, cut up into small pieces
1/2-3/4 cup hoi sin sauce
1 recipe Special Szechuan Marinade (p. 257)

Mix the chicken with enough hoi sin sauce to coat each piece. Marinate in a large bowl in the refrigerator for at least 24 hours, stirring the chicken once or twice.

When you are ready to bake the chicken, preheat the oven to 350°F. Remove the chicken to a baking pan and mix the ingredients for Special Szechuan Marinade in the bowl. If you wish, you can use the hoi sin sauce that is left there as the hoi sin called for in the recipe. Dip both sides of each piece of chicken in the marinade and place the chicken on the baking pan skin side up. Bake for 60-70 minutes, or until the chicken is done, being careful that it does not burn. Serve warm or at room temperature.

HOI SIN SPICY PORK, BEEF, OR LAMB

Substitute small country-style ribs, spareribs, or lamb breast cut into individual riblets or beef back ribs. Bake as appropriate for each cut of meat.

NORMAN'S CHINESE CHICKEN *serves 4-5*

Norman Fine created this aromatic chicken, subtly redolent of garlic and spicy-sweet tastes. Try it with pork, too. Both chicken and pork marinated in this manner are excellent barbecued.

3-4 pounds chicken, cut up into small pieces
1 recipe Norman Fine's Chinese Marinade (p. 257)
1/2-2/3 cup honey water (half honey, half water)
Lightly toasted sesame seeds or finely chopped peanuts

Marinate the chicken in the marinade for 24 hours or longer.

Preheat the oven to 350°F. Place the chicken pieces in baking pans and bake for 65-75 minutes, brushing with honey water twice during baking. Brush lightly with honey water and sprinkle with sesame seeds or chopped peanuts. Serve chicken warm or at room temperature.

GENTLE HOI SIN DUCK *yields 28-30 pieces*

Mahogany-hued Gentle Hoi Sin Duck is a particularly nice beginning, or accompaniment, to a Chinese dinner, particularly when you are stir-frying, as too much last-minute cooking can simply wear out the cook. It is delicious cold and a superb choice for a picnic—a delightful change from the more usual flavor of tomato-based barbecued chicken.

One 4 1/2-5-pound duck
1 cup hoi sin sauce
1 cup commercial duck sauce, such as
  Saucy Susan
1 Tablespoon Gingered Sherry (p. 258)
1 Tablespoon soy sauce or tamari
  Chinese Mustard (p. 60) to taste

Have the butcher cut fresh or frozen duck into 28-30 pieces. This is done on a band saw-type machine and can be accomplished with either a fresh or a frozen bird. Ask the butcher to make 2 equidistant lengthwise cuts down the body of the duck and 4 crosswise cuts. (Supermarket butchers have been very nice about doing this.)

Defrost the duck if frozen and separate the pieces, cutting up any extra-large pieces with a cleaver or sharp, heavy knife. Trim any excess fat and place the duck pieces skin side up on a rack on a 10 by 15-inch pan. Prick the duck skin all over and broil on the lowest oven rack until it is crispy and brown, about 20 minutes. Turn the pieces and broil an additional 10 minutes.

Let the pieces cool slightly and brush or coat generously with hoi sin. (I often put the duck in a bowl or plastic bag, add hoi sin, and toss to coat.) Let marinate for at least 24 hours, or freeze in the plastic bag until ready to use. (Freezing in the marinade produces a wonderful flavor—and I do this especially when I buy fresh ducks or roasting chickens on sale but have no immediate use for them.) If you are marinating in the refrigerator, turn the pieces occasionally.

Preheat the oven to 350°F. Combine the duck sauce, Gingered Sherry, soy sauce or tamari, and the Chinese Mustard. Place the duck pieces on a rack over a 10 by 15-inch pan again and brush with this basting sauce or dip the pieces of duck into the sauce. Pour some boiling water into the pan and bake the duck for 1 hour. Turn off the oven and let the duck sit in it for 20-30 minutes. Serve warm with Chinese Mustard.

GENTLE HOI SIN CHICKEN

Substitute a 5-6-pound roasting chicken and cut it up as for the Hoi Sin Duck. You can also use 4-6 pounds cut-up chicken parts. Eliminate the broiling step and extend the baking time slightly.

CHINESE (NOT SO SPARE) RIBS (GENTLE HOI SIN PORK) *serves 6-10*

You can vary the basting sauce by adding honey, additional soy sauce and Gingered Sherry, minced garlic, ginger and scallions, etc.

3-5 pounds small country-style ribs, sliced thin with a minimum of bone and fat
1 cup hoi sin sauce
  About 1 cup commercial duck sauce, such as Saucy Susan
1 Tablespoon soy sauce or tamari
1 Tablespoon Gingered Sherry (p. 258)
  Chinese Mustard (p. 60) to taste

Coat the ribs generously with hoi sin sauce and let them marinate in the refrigerator for 24 hours or longer.

Several hours before baking time combine the duck sauce with the soy sauce or tamari and Gingered Sherry. Add a little Chinese Mustard for spark.

Preheat the oven to 350°F. Place the ribs on a rack on a 10 by 15-inch pan and brush the ribs generously with the mixture. Pour boiling water into the pan and bake the ribs for 90 minutes or more, depending on the thickness of the ribs, or until they are cooked through and beautifully browned. Serve with Chinese Mustard and duck sauce.

Szechuan Vinaigrette used as a marinade for chicken, fish, seafood, and meat imparts a subtle Oriental spiciness and juicy succulence. Special Szechuan Marinade has a sweeter, more fiery impact.

SESAME SZECHUAN CHICKEN *serves about 4*

Chicken prepared with this marinade is unbelievably juicy, with a hint of ginger and Szechuan punch.

3 pounds (or more) chicken, cut up
1 recipe Szechuan Vinaigrette (p. 235)
  Minced scallion
  Sesame seeds

Marinate the chicken in the Szechuan Vinaigrette with minced scallion mixed in for at least 24 hours, stirring 2-3 times.

Preheat the oven to 350°F. Sprinkle the chicken generously with sesame seeds (or roll the chicken in seeds to coat) and bake for 1-1½ hours, or until the chicken is done. Baking time will depend on the size of the pieces. The chicken can also be cooked on an outdoor grill, brushing occasionally with the marinade. If you barbecue outside, omit the sesame seeds.

SESAME SZECHUAN
BEEF, LAMB, OR PORK KEBOBS *serves 6*

3 pounds boneless beef, lamb, or pork,
   cut into cubes
1 recipe Szechuan Vinaigrette (p. 235)
   Minced scallion
   Sesame seeds

Marinate the beef, lamb, or pork in Szechuan Vinaigrette (to which you have added minced scallion) several hours or overnight, turning 2–3 times.

   Broil or grill the meat on skewers. Sprinkle with sesame seeds.

SWEET
SZECHUAN SEAFOOD *serves 2-4*

Special Szechuan Marinade gives fish or seafood a delightful, fiery, spicy-sweet flavor. Broil scallops, shrimp, or cubed fish on skewers for brochettes or an elegant, tasty hors d'oeuvre. If using fish, choose a firm-fleshed fish such as halibut or monkfish. Bluefish with its assertive flavors makes an interesting choice.

   1 recipe Special Szechuan Marinade (p. 257)
1-1½ pounds scallops or shrimp or fish, filleted
      or in cubes for skewers

Pour the marinade over the seafood or fish. Let stand for 20–30 minutes or refrigerate for a longer marinade. Broil or grill until the fish or seafood is done.

SESAME SZECHUAN
SEAFOOD OR FISH *serves 4-6*

½ recipe Szechuan Vinaigrette (p. 235)
2-3 pounds scallops or shrimp or fillet of fish,
     whole or cubed
     Minced scallion
     Sesame seeds

Marinate the fish or seafood in the refrigerator for about 1 hour in the vinaigrette to which you've added minced scallion. If you would like, put the scallops or shrimp or cubes of fish on skewers for brochettes. Sprinkle lightly with sesame seeds and broil (or bake for fillets) until the fish or seafood is done.

SWEET–AND–SOUR
WALNUT CHICKEN CRISPS *serves 4–8 as an hors d'oeuvre or as a main course with other dishes*

This dish can be served as either an hors d'oeuvre or a main course Chinese dish. If you are using this as an hors d'oeuvre, serve with toothpicks. Firm monkfish, cut into chunks, can be substituted for chicken.

3/4–1 pound skinned and boned chicken breast
 1/2 cup pineapple juice
 1/3 cup brown sugar (packed)
 1/3 cup white vinegar
 2 Tablespoons finely minced scallion
 1 Tablespoon soy sauce
 1 small clove garlic, minced fine
 2 drops Tabasco sauce
 2 cups moderately finely chopped walnuts
 1/4 cup cornstarch
 1 egg, beaten
3–4 cups oil for deep frying
 1/4 cup water
 1 Tablespoon cornstarch
 Chinese Mustard (p. 60)

Cut the chicken into 1/2-inch-thick slices. Combine the pineapple juice, brown sugar, vinegar, scallion, soy sauce, garlic, and Tabasco sauce and marinate the chicken in this mixture for 30 minutes at room temperature or several hours in the refrigerator, turning the chicken occasionally. Strain, reserving the marinade for the sweet-and-sour dipping sauce.

Combine the walnuts and the 1/4 cup cornstarch. Dip the chicken strips in beaten egg, then coat with the walnut mixture. Refrigerate the strips on a plate or waxed paper for at least 30 minutes to allow the coating to set. Deep fry in hot oil (350°F) for 3–4 minutes, or until the coating is golden and the chicken is just cooked through.

To prepare the dipping sauce, combine the water with the 1 Tablespoon cornstarch, add to reserved marinade, and heat in a saucepan until the mixture is bubbly and thickened.

Serve the chicken crisps with hot Chinese Mustard and sweet-and-sour dipping sauce or pour the sauce over the chicken.

CRISPY FRIED FISH
BITES *serves 2 as a main course or at least 4 as an hors d'oeuvre*

I love succulent fish or seafood with a light, crisp, golden coating. Served with toothpicks, this makes a wonderful hors d'oeuvre. Oysters or scallops are my favorite choices for it.

3-4 cups oil for deep frying
1 pound fish, cut into chunks, or scallops, shrimp, squid (cleaned and cut into rings), oysters, etc.
1 egg, beaten
2/3 cup all-purpose flour
1/3 cup cornmeal
1 teaspoon salt
1/2 teaspoon sugar
Freshly ground pepper to taste
2 Tablespoons (or more) sesame seeds (optional)
Freshly squeezed lemon juice
Lemon wedges

Place the oil in a wok or saucepan and heat to 350–375°F. Stir the fish or other seafood choices around in the beaten egg so that all the pieces are coated. Place the flour, cornmeal, salt, sugar, pepper, and optional sesame seeds in a plastic bag and shake to mix the ingredients. Remove the fish or other seafood from the egg mixture, drain off excess egg, and place the pieces of fish in the plastic bag.

Shake fish until it is coated with the flour mixture. Remove in batches to a strainer and shake off the excess coating. Fry each batch until the fish is crisp and golden and just cooked through. Remove with a slotted spoon to paper towels to drain. Sprinkle lightly with the lemon juice. Serve with lemon wedges and, if you like, Dilled Mayonnaise (p. 202).

FAVORITE
FISH BROCHETTES *serves 2-4*

Brochettes are a delightful way to prepare and serve fish. Ends, or chunks, of expensive fish like swordfish are usually sold at bargain prices at the fish market—perfect for brochettes. If you prefer to use the whole fillet, simply smooth a light coating of marinade on both sides of the fish and refrigerate for an hour or more then broil as with the brochettes. Thinner fillets can be broiled on 1 side only. Try dill or tarragon in the marinade with salmon or swordfish, rosemary or tarragon with swordfish, bluefish, or shark.

Crisply broiled bluefish brochettes and savory sweet parsnip pierogin (or potato pierogin) are a good combination.

1 pound (or more) salmon, swordfish, bluefish, shark, or other nonwhite fish, cut into about 1-inch cubes
1 recipe Mayonnaise Marinade for Fish (p. 258)
6-inch wooden skewers, soaked for several hours, or longer, in water
Lemon wedges

Toss the fish in the marinade and refrigerate for at least 1 hour. Divide the fish among 4 or 6 wooden skewers, arranging them so that the cubes touch and are compact.

Preheat the broiler for 5-10 minutes until it is very hot. Place the brochettes on a broiling pan or baking sheet and broil closest to the elements until the fish begins to crisp and brown. Turn the brochettes and broil on the other side until it too is crisp and brown. Be careful not to overcook. Serve with lemon wedges.

GRAVLAKS

To make Gravlaks, a full-flavored fish such as salmon or bluefish is cured in a simple marination process using splashes of Cognac, plenty of fresh dill, and sprinklings of coarse salt and sugar. The 4–6-day curing period produces a velvety textured, opalescent delicacy. The process is so gentle that it is the fresh sweet flavor of the fish you taste and not the cure—and yet, the fish is magically transformed.

Most recipes for gravlaks begin: "Fillet a whole salmon . . ." While I'm generally one to follow my food passions to their limit, this instruction always freezes my hand in my pocketbook. I've found, however, that I can use the number of smaller fillets of salmon that fit my serving and budget requirements —or I use bluefish, which, in fact, if it were twice instead of half the price might still be my first choice.

TO PREPARE GRAVLAKS

Buy 2 impeccably fresh fillets of salmon or bluefish that are matching in size and thickness. Lay the fillets fleshy side up and sprinkle them lightly with Cognac—about 3/4 Tablespoonful per pound. Next sprinkle about 1 teaspoon coarse salt and 1/2 teaspoon sugar (also per pound) over the fillets. Place a generous amount of fresh dill over 1 fillet and place the other fillet on top so that the 2 fleshy sides are facing with the dill sandwiched in between.

Place some dill in the bottom of a porcelain or glass dish large enough to hold the fish. Lay the fillet sandwich on top of the dill. Place more dill on top of the fish sandwich and seal the dish with plastic wrap. Lay a board or a plate and then a 3–5-pound weight on top of the fish. Refrigerate.

Every day for 3 or 4 days, separate the pieces of fish, push aside the dill, and sprinkle the 2 fleshy sides lightly with more sugar and salt. Replace the dill, resandwich the fish, and turn it over, basting with the juices that have gathered in the plate. Turn the fish a second time during the course of each day, but this second time don't salt or sugar.

After 3 or 4 days, cut a small slice off the fish and taste. If it is tender, silky textured, and sweet tasting, stop adding salt and sugar and either eat it on the spot or control yourself and serve it some time within the next week or so. While it is waiting in the refrigerator, continue to turn and baste the fish in its own juices. If you think it needs more curing (likely if you are using thicker fillets), continue salting and sugaring, checking in with a nibble every now and then over the next few days.

TO SERVE GRAVLAKS

Clean off the dill and slice the fillets into thin pieces, holding your knife at a 45-degree angle to the fish. Arrange the slices decoratively on a platter with Dilled Mayonnaise (following recipe) in the center and plenty of fresh dill for garnish.

You can also accompany your Gravlaks with fresh raw vegetables, such as radishes with their greens, sprays of scallion, cucumber spears, or cherry tomatoes. Serve with plenty of sliced dark pumpernickel or rye (Braided Rye, p. 16, is excellent) and butter, and a crisp white wine or other beverage.

If you would like to serve Gravlaks as individual hors d'oeuvres, remove the crusts from slices of pumpernickel, cut the slices into triangles, and place a small sliver of Gravlaks on each piece. Top with a small dollop of Dilled Mayonnaise and pass to guests. If you use Braided Rye, cut the slices in half to make an appropriate hors d'oeuvre-size piece.

This is a traditional recipe for gravlaks. For a less traditional (but equally delicious) version, Cognac may be replaced by vodka, sake, or various other wines or liquors and dill may be replaced or supplemented by other fresh (or dried) herbs to your taste.

DILLED MAYONNAISE

Also good as a dip for smoked seafood or Crispy Fried Fish Bites.

  1 cup mayonnaise, preferably homemade
 1/4 cup (or more) sour cream or unflavored yogurt
  1 Tablespoon Dijon mustard, or to taste
  1 teaspoon sugar
    Plenty of minced fresh dill
    Salt and freshly ground pepper to taste

Combine the mayonnaise, sour cream or yogurt, Dijon mustard, sugar, and dill, adding enough dill so that the mayonnaise is well flecked with green. Add salt and pepper to taste.

WITH–MEAT COOKING: CO–STARRING VEGETABLES, GRAINS, DAIRY, AND LEGUMES

**VEGETABLES,
GRAINS,
DAIRY,
AND
LEGUMES**

Chicken Marrakech

Lamb Marrakech

Couscous with Turkey and Ported Prunes

Vinegar Chicken with Broccoli and Kielbasa

Seafood, Salmon, and Spinach Mousse Loaf

Chicken 'Chiladas

Chicken (and Vegetarian) Tostadas

Taco Picadillo

Jack's Famous Chili and Beans

Enchiladas with Chili and Beans

Picadillo and Brioche Loaf

Torta Picadillo

Stuffed Brioche Lattice Loaf

Sweet-and-Sour Meatballs with Bulgur

Bulgur and Zucchini Casserole with Meat

Lamb Shanks with Barley and Turnips

Country-style Ribs with Figs and White Sweets

Maple Beans

Maple Beans and Corn Bread

WITH–MEAT COOKING: CO–STARRING VEGETABLES, GRAINS, DAIRY, AND LEGUMES

This chapter explores what I like to call with-meat or low-meat cooking. Although over the years I have tended to eat more and more in a vegetarian mode, I enjoy eating poultry, fish, and meat in small quantities. They have a place in my diet and in my cooking and add a very special aesthetic and nutritional dimension to grain, bean, and vegetable dishes.

There are many recipes in this cookbook that are prepared *with* meat, few that are *for* meat, fish, or poultry alone. Those that do appear are especially piquant preparations that can be served as hors d'oeuvres as well as moderate portions on plates balanced with grain, vegetable, or pasta salads; stir-fry combinations; or other good tastes. When I do eat meat, or animal protein, this is how I prefer to have it—in a small but important supporting role.

The recipes in this section vary greatly in style and form, but almost all use meat, or animal protein, in an important supporting role in conjunction with beans, vegetables, dairy products, and/or grains and grain products. From both a financial and health perspective, this is an economical way to use animal protein. Best of all, it is a way to use meat, poultry, and seafood that is rich in earthy and elegant tastes and inventive possibilities.

The first 2 recipes are special favorites and epitomize the art of elegantly combining meat with grain and beans. Couscous (tiny grains of semolina sold in boxes or bulk in health-food, ethnic, and specialty food stores) is a delicate and sensuous grain that absorbs and reflects the flavors of meat, fruit, herbs, wine, and stock in the most subtle and complete way. Other quick-cooking grains, such as bulgur and buckwheat, can be substituted for interesting and delicious results.

CHICKEN MARRAKECH *serves 4–5*

This dish is a visual treat, with its bright orange apricots, black olives, and deep green parsley nestled among golden grains. Chicken Marrakech can be prepared ahead and reheated, dotted with butter, if you like, for extra flavor and richness—and doubled or tripled in quantity for large dinner parties. Marrakech variations can also be prepared using bulgur or lightly pan-toasted buckwheat.

1 cup dry sherry
2 Tablespoons brown sugar
1 Tablespoon salt
1 teaspoon oregano
3/4 teaspoon ground cinnamon
1/4 teaspoon powdered ginger
6 drops Tabasco sauce
　Freshly ground pepper to taste
3 pounds chicken parts, preferably all dark meat
　or all breast meat, cut up
2 Tablespoons oil
2 Tablespoons (1/4 stick) butter
2 cups chopped onion or white of leek
2 large cloves garlic, minced
1 cup cooked chick-peas
3/4 cup dried apricots (packed), or 3/4–1 cup
　dried prunes
1/2 cup pitted black olives, water packed, not oil
　cured (omit if using prunes)
1 1/2 cups couscous
2 1/2 cups well-flavored chicken stock, boiling
　(see p. 50)
1/2 cup minced fresh parsley

In a large bowl mix together the sherry, brown sugar, salt, oregano, cinnamon, ginger, Tabasco sauce, and a little freshly ground pepper. Marinate the chicken in this mixture, turning occasionally, for 4–6 hours at least, but preferably overnight.

Preheat the oven to 350°F. Drain the chicken in a colander, reserving the marinade, and pat it dry with paper towels. In a large frying pan (or an ovenproof casserole large enough to hold the chicken in a single layer) sauté the chicken in oil and butter until it is well browned, about 10–15 minutes over medium-high heat. (If you are using all breast meat, sauté for a shorter period of time.) During the last few minutes, add the onion or leek and garlic and sauté until softened. Add the reserved marinade and cook over high heat, turning the pieces once or twice, until the marinade is reduced to a syrupy residue. Remove the chicken and the syrup to a 9 by 13-inch baking dish or lasagna pan. Distribute half the chick-peas, apricots or prunes, and olives, if you are using them, around the chicken. Distribute the couscous over the chicken and fruit, then the remaining chick-peas, dried fruit, and olives. Pour the boiling chicken stock gently over the chicken and couscous, making sure the couscous are covered with liquid, sprinkle with parsley, and cover well with aluminum foil. Bake for 30 minutes, remove the aluminum foil, and bake for an additional 5–15 minutes.

LAMB MARRAKECH

Substitute 3–4 pounds shoulder lamb stew meat or 2 pounds boneless lamb, cut up, for the chicken.

COUSCOUS WITH TURKEY AND PORTED PRUNES *serves 6*

Delicious, tantalizingly aromatic, subtly sweet from prunes and port.

8 ounces pitted prunes
1 cup port*
1½–2 pounds turkey breast or boned and skinned chicken breast, cut into 1-inch cubes
Flour
Salt and freshly ground pepper to taste
4 Tablespoons oil
4 Tablespoons (½ stick) butter
2 cups chopped onion
2 large cloves garlic, minced
2 teaspoons thyme
1 large bay leaf
2 teaspoons salt
½ teaspoon ground cinnamon
Freshly ground pepper to taste
1–1½ cups cooked chick-peas
1½ cups couscous
2½ cups chicken stock (p. 50), heated
Minced fresh parsley

Preheat the oven to 350°F.

Combine the prunes and port and set aside. Shake the turkey or chicken cubes in a small amount of flour seasoned with salt and pepper. In a wok or large sauté pan sauté the turkey in hot oil over medium-high heat until the cubes are golden. Remove them with a slotted spoon and set aside. Add the butter to the sauté pan and sauté the onion until it is tender, adding the garlic during the last

few minutes of cooking time. Add the thyme, bay leaf, the 2 teaspoons salt, cinnamon, and pepper and the port and prune mixture. Reduce over high heat until very thick and syrupy—almost evaporated. Add the chick-peas, turkey cubes, and couscous and toss to mix the ingredients.

Turn into a 9 by 13-inch baking pan or ovenproof casserole and pour on the hot stock. Cover with aluminum foil or the casserole lid and bake for 25–30 minutes. Sprinkle with parsley and serve.

Couscous

*An inexpensive port, such as Pastene or Taylor, works fine. A dry sherry can also be used, with the addition of 2 Tablespoons brown sugar.

VINEGAR CHICKEN WITH BROCCOLI AND KIELBASA *serves 3-4*

This richly flavored one-dish meal is quick and easy to prepare. Increase ingredients to fit your serving requirements.

3-4 pounds chicken parts, cut up*
  6 Tablespoons tamari or light soy sauce
  3 Tablespoons vinegar
  3 Tablespoons water
1/2 teaspoon chili paste with garlic (optional)
1-2 slices fresh gingerroot
1/2-1 pound kielbasa, sliced
  1 large head broccoli, broken into flowerets, with stems cut into 1/2-inch-thick slices

Place chicken pieces in a heavy sauté pan, skin side down, and begin to sauté over medium heat with no or very little oil. As the chicken renders some of its own fat, raise the heat and continue to sauté for 10-15 minutes, turning the pieces until they are nicely browned. Add the tamari, vinegar, water, optional chili paste with garlic, and gingerroot. Boil this mixture down over high or medium-high heat (lower heat for larger pieces) until the liquid is almost evaporated, turning the pieces occasionally. Add the kielbasa and broccoli, stir, cover, and cook until broccoli is just tender and chicken is cooked, about 10-15 minutes more. Serve with rice.

SEAFOOD, SALMON, AND SPINACH MOUSSE LOAF *serves 6-8*

Slices of this loaf, with its stripes of white and pink and thin veined lines of deep spinachy green, are very beautiful—an elegant foodscape on the plate. And this delicious work of art is really quite easy to prepare. Serve with a simple steamed and buttered vegetable such as green beans and Buttery Brioche Twists or other homemade bread. Follow with a tossed green salad.

One 10-ounce package frozen chopped spinach, cooked and well squeezed
2 Tablespoons chopped scallion or finely minced shallot

2 Tablespoons (1/4 stick) butter
1 Tablespoon anchovy paste or 2 anchovies, mashed
  Salt and freshly ground pepper to taste
1 recipe Seafood Mousse IV (p. 249), using 2 cups heavy cream instead of 1 1/2 cups
1/2 recipe Mushroom Duxelles (p. 249)*
1 Tablespoon tomato paste
1 recipe Salmon Mousse (p. 249)
  Processor or Blender Hollandaise (p. 247), with dill added

Preheat the oven to 400°F.
  Chop the cooked spinach extra fine. Sauté the scallion or shallot in butter. Add the spinach, anchovy

---

*I prefer to cut the chicken into half-size pieces with a cleaver. If you cannot do this or cannot have a butcher do this, simply use regular cut-up parts—small pieces like thighs or wings or small drumsticks will work especially well—and if pieces are larger increase sautéing and cooking time accordingly.

*You can omit the duxelles and simply add the tomato paste to the Salmon Mousse mixture, creating a slightly darker pink center.

paste, and salt and pepper to taste. Mix well. Let cool completely.

Add ½ cup of the Seafood Mousse to the spinach mixture. Set aside. Combine the Mushroom Duxelles with the tomato paste and ¼ cup of the Salmon Mousse. Set aside.

Butter a 9 by 5-inch loaf pan generously. Line it with waxed paper, leaving an overhang on the 2 long sides. Butter the waxed paper. Spread one quarter of the remaining Seafood Mousse over the bottom of the loaf pan. Cover with one half of the spinach mixture, spreading it as thinly and evenly as possible over the mousse, then add the second quarter of Seafood Mousse. Cover with a little more than one half of the remaining Salmon Mousse. Form a narrow channel or trough down the center of the Salmon Mousse and fill it with the mushroom mixture. Cover with the remaining Salmon Mousse, smoothing it as evenly as possible. Then repeat the original sequence of Seafood Mousse, spinach mixture, and Seafood Mousse.

Cover the mousse loaf with a buttered sheet of waxed paper that is cut to fit the top of the pan, then cover with aluminum foil, pressing the foil around the edges of the pan to seal. Place the loaf in a 9 by 13-inch baking pan and pour boiling water into the larger pan to halfway up the sides of the loaf pan. Bake for 60–70 minutes. (The temperature of the loaf will register 150°F except in the very center, which will be a little lower.)

Let cool slightly. Pour off excess juices (save for sauces). Unmold onto a large platter and serve with Processor or Blender Hollandaise with dill, or cold with a lemony dilled mayonnaise.

Here are some delightful recipes for corn and flour tortillas with savory beef, chicken, and vegetarian fillings and toppings.

CHICKEN 'CHILADAS *serves 4–5*

Flour tortillas, with their chewy tenderness, seem to exist somewhere between pasta and pastry. Pair them with this mildly spicy, creamy chicken filling for a delightful meal.

2 cups diced cooked chicken
  One 1-pound can kidney beans, drained
½ cup sliced pimento-stuffed green olives
½ cup minced scallion

½ cup sour cream
1 teaspoon salt
6–8 drops Tabasco sauce, or to taste
¾ pound Cheddar or combination Cheddar and Jack cheese, grated or diced
1 recipe Mexican Tomato Sauce (p. 241)
  Ten 8-inch flour tortillas
  Finely minced scallion

Preheat the oven to 375°F.

Combine the chicken, beans, olives, the 1/2 cup scallion, sour cream, salt, Tabasco sauce, half the grated or diced cheese, and 3 Tablespoons of the Mexican Tomato Sauce. Place the remaining sauce in a sauté pan and add about 1/2 cup water. Bring the sauce to a simmer and place a tortilla on top of the sauce until it is softened and pliable. Lay the softened tortilla sauce side up on a work surface, place 1/2 cup of the filling mixture along one edge of the tortilla, and roll up tightly but gently. Repeat with the remaining tortillas.

Spread 2 Tablespoons sauce on a large ovenproof platter or in a lasagna pan then line up the 'Chiladas, flaps down, on it. Nap the 'Chiladas with the remaining sauce and distribute the remaining cheese and finely minced scallion over the sauce. Bake for 25 minutes, or until hot and bubbly.

CHICKEN (AND VEGETARIAN) TOSTADAS

This is a favorite quick lunch, snack, or dinner— easy to prepare if you have the ingredients on hand.

Corn tortillas
1 recipe Seasoned Bean Puree (p. 252)
1 recipe Mexican Tomato Sauce (p. 241)*
Minced cooked chicken (optional)
Grated Cheddar cheese
Alfalfa sprouts
Chopped tomato
Minced scallion

1 Tablespoon of the Mexican Tomato Sauce over the puree, top with minced cooked chicken and a generous Tablespoon of grated Cheddar. Return to the oven to melt the cheese. Place a moderate-size tuft of alfalfa sprouts on top of the tostada and return it to the oven to bake for 5 minutes more, or until the sprouts are softened. Distribute chopped tomato and minced scallion on top of the sprouts and serve. Allow 2 tostadas per person.

Preheat the oven to 500°F.

Arrange tortillas on baking sheets so that they are not touching, or only barely overlapping. Bake for about 5 minutes on each side, or until the tortillas are crisp, being careful not to brown or burn them. Spread each tortilla with a generous Tablespoon of Seasoned Bean Puree. Spread about

*You can substitute commercial salsa or canned tomatoes with green chilis, available in the Mexican food section of your supermarket.

TACO PICADILLO

Crisp corn tortillas, sweet-spicy meat, tender beans and cheese, meltingly warm then topped with cool bits of lettuce, tomato, and onion.

1 recipe Picadillo (p. 254)
 Cooked kidney beans
 Taco shells
 Chopped scallion
 Grated Cheddar cheese
 Shredded lettuce
 Chopped tomato
 Chopped onion

Warm the Picadillo and add the kidney beans to it. Spoon 1-2 Tablespoons of the Picadillo into each taco shell. Sprinkle with scallion and about 1 Tablespoon grated Cheddar. Place in a hot oven just until the cheese melts. Arrange the tacos on a platter, surround with shredded lettuce and mounds of chopped tomato and onion. Garnish also with sliced avocado and mounds of alfalfa sprouts, if you like them. Allow 2 tacos per person, plus a few extra for big eaters.

JACK'S FAMOUS CHILI AND BEANS *yields 9 cups*

This chili is adapted from the recipe of an old friend, Jack Zeman. When I first tasted it, I found myself standing at the door of his opened refrigerator with a spoon that just kept going from chili to mouth, chili to mouth. Delicious by itself, it is sublime in Mexican Lasagna with Chili and Beans and can be used to prepare enchiladas, tacos, and tostadas.

 1 medium onion, chopped
4-6 cloves garlic, minced
 2 Tablespoons oil
 2 pounds lean ground beef
 One 35-ounce can plum tomatoes
 Three 1-pound cans kidney beans
¼-⅓ cup chili powder
 1 teaspoon oregano

 1 teaspoon basil
 A few dashes garlic powder
4-6 very hot peppers, minced, or plenty of
 Tabasco sauce
 Cayenne pepper and salt to taste

In a large Dutch oven or casserole sauté the onion and garlic in oil until the onion is tender. Add the ground meat and sauté, breaking up with a wooden spoon, until the meat is crumbly and no longer pink. Add the tomatoes, breaking them up slightly, then the beans. Add the chili powder, oregano, basil, garlic powder, hot peppers or Tabasco sauce, cayenne, and salt. Simmer gently, uncovered, for 2-3 hours, stirring 2 or 3 times.

ENCHILADAS WITH CHILI AND BEANS *serves 4-5*

Hearty, simple, tasty food, great to make when you have a good supply of chili on hand. Serve with a tossed green salad with avocado slices and Salsa Vinaigrette, or slices of avocado nestled in lettuce leaves and napped lightly with Salsa Vinaigrette.

4 cups Jack's Famous Chili and Beans (preceding recipe)
1/2 pound Cheddar or combination Cheddar and Jack cheese, grated
1 recipe Mexican Tomato Sauce (p. 241)
8 corn tortillas
Sour cream
Minced scallion and/or chopped green chilis

Preheat the oven to 375°F.

Combine the Chili and Beans with half the grated cheese. Spread 2-3 Tablespoons of the Mexican Tomato Sauce over the bottom of a baking dish. Place 1/2 cup of the chili and cheese mixture on a tortilla and roll it up, then place the rolled tortillas flaps down on the sauce-covered baking dish. Smooth some sour cream over each tortilla roll. Nap each roll with a generous spoonful or two of the Mexican Tomato Sauce and sprinkle the rolls with the remaining grated cheese. Distribute minced scallion and/or chopped green chilis down the center of the rolls. Bake until hot and bubbly, 25-35 minutes.

PICADILLO AND BRIOCHE LOAF *yields 1 large round loaf*

Here is a meat loaf—not in the usual sense, though. This is a high, light round loaf of buttery brioche with a savory Picadillo and cheese filling nestled within. Served warm or at room temperature and cut in tall wedges, the loaf is wonderful as part of a brunch buffet, portable picnic, or informal dinner accompanying a crisp tossed salad or a more elaborate antipasto spread. It can be baked in advance, frozen, then defrosted and reheated.

1 recipe Picadillo (p. 254)
1 recipe Easy Processor Brioche (p. 7)
1/2 pound Cheddar cheese, grated
Egg wash (1 egg beaten with 1 Tablespoon milk or cream)
Cumin seeds

When preparing the Picadillo, make sure that as much liquid as possible is evaporated and blot up any excess fat with paper towels. Keep warm. Roll out the brioche that has risen, been punched down, and rested for 5 minutes to a circle about 20 inches in diameter, rolling the edges thinner than the center of the dough. Butter a 9-inch springform pan lightly. Fold the dough in half, then in half again, and fit it gently into the pan, opening it up and letting the excess dough hang over the sides.

There will be less of a gap between dough and filling if the Picadillo is warm when it goes into the loaf. Turn the Picadillo into the dough-lined pan. Top with grated cheese, and with your finger or a spoon blend some of the cheese gently into the meat. Bring one edge of the dough up and lay it over the meat and cheese mixture. Working around the loaf, lay the excess dough over the meat and cheese in neat folds or pleats. When all the dough has been folded in this manner, take the excess dough in the center, press it together gently to form a small knob, and twist it, causing the folds to swirl slightly. Place the pan on a baking sheet. Brush the top of the dough generously with egg wash and sprinkle generously with cumin seeds. Let the dough rise for 20 minutes. Meanwhile, preheat the oven to 350°F.

After 20 minutes (the dough will not have risen much) open the springform pan and release the sides to their greatest diameter, but leave them around the loaf. Place the bread in the hot oven and bake for 55–65 minutes, or until it is deeply golden. Place the bread on a rack to cool, slightly, removing the sides of the springform pan carefully.

Serve the bread warm. Or cool completely, wrap in heavy-duty aluminum foil, and freeze.

TORTA PICADILLO *serves 4-6 or more*

Here is another kind of picadillo loaf: savory corn bread with a flavorful center of Picadillo, beans, corn, and cheese. It is attractive and delicious—a rave at pot luck parties. Serve with a crisp spinach salad for a lovely light meal.

1 recipe Maple Corn Bread (p. 30) with the
   following changes:
   decrease all-purpose flour to 1 cup
   increase cornmeal to 1½ cups
   add ¼ cup grated Parmesan cheese
1 cup drained canned corn
6 ounces Cheddar cheese, grated (1½-1¾ cups,
   fairly well packed)
1 recipe Picadillo (p. 254) to which you have added
   1 cup cooked kidney beans
1 Tablespoon grated Parmesan cheese
   About 1 teaspoon chili powder
   About 1 teaspoon cumin seed

Preheat the oven to 350°F.

Butter a 9-inch springform pan. Spread half the corn bread batter in the bottom of the pan. Sprinkle on half of the corn and half of the Cheddar cheese. Spoon the Picadillo mixture as evenly as possible over the batter, corn, and cheese, leaving a small border of batter not covered with the meat. Sprinkle the Picadillo with the remaining Cheddar, then the corn. Spread the remaining batter carefully and evenly over everything. Sprinkle the top of the torta with the Parmesan, chili powder, and cumin seed.

Bake about 55 minutes or until a knife inserted in the center comes out clean. Serve hot, warm, or at room temperature.

STUFFED BRIOCHE LATTICE LOAF

This gourmet calzone makes a stunning and delicious addition to any table. Serve it as an hors d'oeuvre, or as part of a lunch (with soup) or dinner. Use one of these fillings or make up your own. The loaf can be made ahead and refrigerated (or frozen), then reheated wrapped in aluminum foil. These instructions make 1 large and very impressive loaf. You can form 2 smaller loaves, using 1¼ pounds cheese.

    1 recipe Easy Processor Brioche (p. 7)
       Egg wash (1 egg beaten with 1 Tablespoon
       milk or water)
       Poppy seeds (optional)

filling 1

1½ pounds dilled Havarti cheese, grated
  1 cup smoked mussels
1-2 bunches scallions, chopped
 ⅓ cup chopped pimento

filling 2

1½ pounds Havarti cheese, grated
  1 cup (about 8 ounces) thinly sliced pepperoni,
     each slice halved
     One 2½-ounce can sliced black olives,
     drained

Prepare Easy Processor Brioche, let rise, and punch down according to recipe directions. Place a large sheet of aluminum foil on a large cookie sheet or a 12 by 15-inch jelly-roll pan. Butter the foil. Roll out the brioche dough to form a rectangle 12 by 15 inches long, with one of the long (15-inch) sides closest to you. (If you like, you can roll out the dough directly on the buttered foil.) Combine the filling ingredients and mound this mixture along the center 3 inches of the dough, leaving at least an inch at the top and bottom and about 6 inches on either side.

You will be following instructions similar to those for forming a pastry lattice loaf (see p. 89). Using a sharp knife or pizza cutter, cut 4–5-inch-long strips about 1 inch wide on a downward diagonal, as shown in the lattice diagram. Stretch the top edge of dough up over the filling. Then bring the right lattice strip over the filling, partially covering and overlapping the dough border. Fold the left strip up and over the filling, and continue weaving and overlapping the strips, alternating sides. When you get to the bottom, bring the bottom dough border up over the filling, then overlap it with one or two of the bottom strips. The filling should be neatly and tightly enclosed in the dough, with the inch or so of uncut dough forming the sides of the loaf.

When the loaf is formed, very gently lift it onto the aluminum foil (if you haven't rolled it out on the foil). If you are using a jelly-roll pan, the loaf should fit perfectly end to end in the pan. Bring the aluminum foil up so that it forms a kind of sling and support for the loaf. The sides of the foil should not be so long that the top of the loaf is covered. Trim the foil if it is too long.

Preheat the oven to 350°F. Let the lattice loaf rest on top of the stove or in some other relatively warm place for about 20 minutes. (It will not rise.) Brush the loaf with egg wash then sprinkle with poppy seeds, if desired. Bake for about 55 minutes, or until golden.

SWEET–AND–SOUR MEATBALLS WITH BULGUR *serves 4–6*

My favorite accompaniment for these meatballs made with bulgar is cooked pasta or spaetzle and chickpeas tossed in butter or garlic butter with plenty of minced fresh parsley. The lamb and bulgur mixture can also be used to stuff peppers or cabbage leaves that are then baked in the sauce. Mashed potatoes are another delicious accompaniment.

1/2 cup bulgur
1/2 cup boiling chicken, lamb, or beef stock or
    boiling water
 1 pound lean ground lamb
1/2 pound lean ground beef
 2 eggs
1/2 cup minced scallion
1/4 cup (or more) minced fresh parsley
 2 teaspoons salt
1/2 teaspoon allspice
1/4 teaspoon powdered ginger

Freshly ground pepper to taste
 1 recipe Sweet-and-Sour Tomato Sauce
    with Orange (following recipe)

Rinse the bulgur quickly in a sieve. Place the bulgur in a bowl and pour the boiling liquid over it. Cover tightly with a plate or pot lid and let stand for 30 minutes or more.

Preheat the oven to 375°F.

Combine the bulgur, ground lamb, ground beef, eggs, scallion, parsley, salt, allspice, ginger, and pepper. Mix well and form into 14–16 balls (or size and number you prefer) and place in a 3-quart-capacity casserole. Pour in heated Sweet-and-Sour Tomato Sauce with Orange then cover and bake for 30 minutes. (The casserole can also be cooked on the stove top.) If possible, cool, refrigerate overnight, skim off congealed fat, and reheat.

SWEET–AND–SOUR TOMATO SAUCE WITH ORANGE *yields about 3 cups*

A pleasant sweet-and-sour sauce with the delightful flavors of orange and basil.

   One 35-ounce can imported tomatoes
   One 6-ounce can tomato paste
 4 Tablespoons brown sugar, or to taste
 4 Tablespoons vinegar
   Grated rind of 1 orange
 2 teaspoons salt
 1 teaspoon basil
   Freshly ground pepper to taste

Combine the ingredients in a saucepan. Bring to a boil, breaking up the tomatoes with the back of a wooden spoon. Simmer for a few minutes to blend the flavors if you will be baking the sauce with meatballs or stuffed cabbage. Simmer longer if you are using it for other purposes.

BULGUR AND ZUCCHINI CASSEROLE WITH MEAT *serves 4-5*

Simple, earthy, and good.

  1 pound (or more) sweet Italian sausage, boned
    chicken breast, or boned lamb
  4 Tablespoons (or more) olive oil
  1 large onion, chopped
  2 bell peppers, diced (red, if available)
  4 cloves garlic, minced
1½ cups bulgur, rinsed and drained
  2 teaspoons oregano
  2 teaspoons salt
    Freshly ground pepper to taste
  2 cups zucchini, cut into ¾-inch slices
  1 cup cooked kidney beans or chick-peas
2¼ cups chicken stock (see p. 50)

Preheat the oven to 350°F.

In an ovenproof casserole sauté the sausage in a little olive oil until it is browned and about half cooked. Let cool slightly and cut into ¾-inch slices. If using lamb or chicken, cut into bite-size pieces and sauté in oil over medium-high heat until lightly browned.

Remove the meat from the casserole. Add the remaining oil and sauté the onion and peppers until they are softened, adding the garlic during the last minute or two of cooking. Add the bulgur, oregano, salt, pepper, zucchini, and the meat and stir until the ingredients are well mixed. Add the beans and stock, bring to a boil, cover, and bake for 40–45 minutes, adding more liquid if necessary.

LAMB SHANKS WITH BARLEY AND TURNIPS *serves 4*

This is a delicious way to eat lamb. You can also remove the lamb from the bone, cut it up into small pieces, and bake it with the grain that way.

lamb stock
  4 small lamb shanks
    Oil
    Water
  1 beef bouillion cube (optional)
  1 clove garlic, crushed lightly
  2 teaspoons rosemary
    Salt and freshly ground pepper to taste
  1 small onion, sliced
  1 carrot, sliced
  1 stalk celery
    Handful parsley

casserole
1½ cups chopped onion
  1 large clove garlic, minced
  2 Tablespoons oil or lamb fat
1¼ cups whole pearled barley, rinsed
 ¼ cup split peas, rinsed
  1 yellow turnip (rutabaga), peeled and cut into
    ¾-inch chunks (about 3 cups)
 ½ pound carrots (1–2 large carrots), cut into
    ½-inch chunks
    Salt and freshly ground pepper

To make the stock, brown the lamb shanks in a little oil. Add water just barely to cover. Add the optional beef bouillion cube, garlic, rosemary, salt and pepper, and the soup vegetables: sliced onion, sliced carrot, celery, and parsley. Bring to a boil then simmer until the lamb is almost tender. Skim off the fat, or refrigerate overnight and lift off the fat that has congealed on the top.

Preheat the oven to 350°F. In an ovenproof casserole sauté the chopped onion and minced garlic in the 2 Tablespoons oil or lamb fat until the onion is softened. Add the barley and split peas

and stir until the grain is well coated with oil. Add the turnip and carrots, stirring to distribute them. Lift the lamb shanks out of the stock then nestle them in the barley-vegetable mixture. Season to taste with salt and pepper, then pour on 2½ cups of the stock, bring to a boil, and cover. Bake for 1 hour, adding additional stock as needed.

COUNTRY–STYLE RIBS WITH FIGS AND WHITE SWEETS *serves 4-6*

Hearty food with delicate, savory flavors.

    4-6 thick country-style ribs, or thick center-
         cut pork chops
         Salt and freshly ground pepper to taste
         Flour for light dusting
      4 Tablespoons olive or vegetable oil
      2 cups chopped onion or white of leek
      2 cloves garlic, minced
      2 teaspoons rosemary, crumbled
      1 large bay leaf
  1½-2 teaspoons salt
    6-8 dried figs, halved*
      1 cup dry white wine
  1½-2 pounds small white sweet potatoes, peeled
         and halved diagonally
      1 cup chicken stock (see p. 50)
     ¼ cup minced fresh parsley
         Brussels sprouts

Preheat the oven to 400°F.

Season the pork with salt and pepper and dust

lightly with flour. In a large ovenproof casserole sauté the pork in oil over medium-high heat until it is well browned on both sides. Remove. Sauté the onion or leek and garlic in the oil remaining in the pan until they are softened then return the pork to the pan. Add the rosemary, bay leaf, the 1½-2 teaspoons salt, and pepper to taste and scatter the figs around the seasoned pork. Pour white wine over the pork and figs, raise the heat to high, and boil down until the wine is almost completely evaporated. Turn the ribs over. Nestle the sweet potato halves in the casserole among the ribs and pour in the chicken stock. Sprinkle with parsley. Bring the stock to a boil again, cover, and bake for 25-35 minutes, or until the pork is cooked and the potatoes are tender. While it is baking, baste the pork once or twice with pan juices and leave uncovered for the last 5 minutes or so of baking to glaze and crisp the potatoes slightly. Steam Brussels sprouts to tender crunchiness and mix in or serve along with the pork.

*Choose dried figs that are plump and soft.

MAPLE BEANS *serves 8-10*

 1 pound dried Great Northern or pea beans
 1 medium onion, chopped
2-3 large cloves garlic, chopped coarse
 1/4 pound prosciutto fat or salt pork, cut into
     2-3 pieces
 1/2 cup maple syrup
 2 Tablespoons blackstrap molasses
 2 teaspoons salt
    Freshly ground pepper to taste
 1 teaspoon dry mustard
 1 teaspoon thyme
 1 bay leaf
4-6 dashes Tabasco sauce

Soak the beans overnight in a pot full of water. In the morning make sure there is enough water to cover the beans, bring to a boil, turn off the heat, cover the pot, and let the beans sit for 10 minutes. Drain, reserving the liquid. Meanwhile, preheat the oven to 325°F. Place the beans in a 3-quart casserole or bean pot and stir in the rest of the ingredients. Add enough reserved liquid just to cover the beans.

Bake, covered, for 4-5 hours, stirring occasionally and adding more liquid as needed to keep the beans covered.

MAPLE BEANS AND CORN BREAD *serves 8-12 or more*

This is a fun potluck picnic dish. The beans can be prepared ahead and the dish baked just before leaving the house. Then the beans can be reheated on top of a grill or a stove top if you are at a yard picnic. The dish can also be warmed in an oven, but be careful not to rewarm at too high a heat or you might dry out the corn bread. This will serve a lot of people—especially if there are lots of other foods to choose from.

 1 recipe Maple Beans (preceding recipe)
 1 pound small pork sausage links, cooked and
    sliced (optional)
 1 recipe Maple Corn Bread batter (p. 30)
    Minced fresh parsley

Preheat the oven to 375°F.

Warm the beans if they have been prepared ahead and refrigerated. Add the optional pork sausage and turn the mixture into a 9 by 13-inch baking pan. Spoon Maple Corn Bread batter over the beans and smooth it gently to cover them. Sprinkle with parsley. Bake for 45-50 minutes, or until the corn bread topping is crusty and golden.

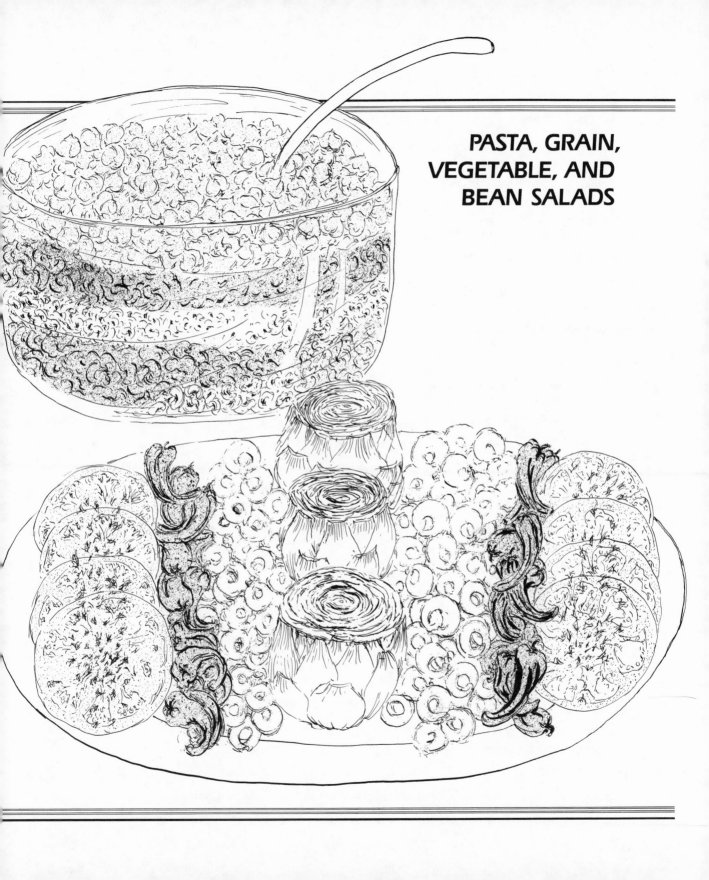

PASTA, GRAIN,
VEGETABLE, AND
BEAN SALADS

PASTA SALADS	Szechuan Pasta and Vegetable Salad
	Mexican Fiesta Pasta Salad
	Kung Pao Broccoli and Tofu Pasta Salad
	Spicy Szechuan Noodles
	Eggplant Tuna Pasta Salad
	Eggplant Walnut Pasta Salad
COLD STUFFED PASTAS	Guacamole-Filled Pasta Salad with Salsa
	Bean-Filled Pasta Salad with Salsa
	Cold Shrimp Won Tons with Broccoli in Szechuan Vinaigrette
	Szechuan Tortellini and Broccoli Salad
	Lemony Seafood Tortellini Salad
	Mexican Tortellini Salad
TABOULI	Grape Tabouli
	Carrot Raisin Walnut (or Peanut) Tabouli
	Tomato Tabouli
	Shrimp and Artichoke Tabouli
	Tabouli with Mixed Vegetables
VEGETABLE AND BEAN SALADS	Best Pickled Vegetables
	Broccoli with Tomatoes and Black Beans
	Ratatouille
	Sweet-and-Sour Zucchini
	Beet, Orange, and Onion Salad
	Carrot Rapee
	Green Beans Vinaigrette
	Szechuan Green Beans Vinaigrette
	Marinated White Beans with Capers, Anchovies, and Tuna
DRESSINGS	Basic Vinaigrette
	Szechuan Vinaigrette
	Salsa Vinaigrette
	Oriental Soy Sesame Vinaigrette
	Tarragon Orange Vinaigrette
	Basic Lemon Vinaigrette
	Mayonnaise and Yogurt Salad Dressing
	Norman Fine's Herb Sauce/Dip

PASTA, GRAIN, VEGETABLE, AND BEAN SALADS

One of my favorite ways to entertain, and to eat—especially in the warmer months—is to create mixed cold salad or antipasto platters vibrant with colors, textures, and tastes. Crisp raw vegetables and quartered hard-boiled eggs, along with pastas, vegetables, and beans in all manner of sauces and vinaigrettes, come together in a harmony of the simple and complex.

I prepare and refrigerate the salads the day before or early on the day I plan to serve them, then I leave them to come to flavor-enhancing room temperature on my kitchen counter. When we sit down to the table, a basket of warm homemade bread or rolls is passed, or crisp buttery garlic toast, or slices cut from a softly melting Cheese in Brioche. I serve each person a little of everything, creating a beautiful miniature still life on each plate.

I can make this platter as simple or as elaborate as I want to complement the meal. An elegant main course pasta may be preceded by a light appetite-inducing array of marinated, sweet-and-sour, and raw vegetables; beans in vinaigrette, hard-boiled eggs, and a wedge of a special cheese. I might even choose to make the main course itself this anytime picnic of marvelous tastes—going all out with a cold tortellini, won ton, or stuffed pasta salad, evocatively Szechuan or Mexican with the spirited flavors of salsa. I can serve a tabouli and a platterful of spicy Oriental chicken as a satisfying meaty accompaniment. I might include bright green beans marinated in dark, spicy Szechuan Vinaigrette and sprinkled with sesame seeds; and lots of raw vegetables for crisp color and taste; and a wonderful homemade bread—perhaps a beautiful and filling Brioche Lattice Loaf.

Cold salads are great anytime eating—delicious for lunches and parts of dinners, great for picnics and potluck parties. Tortellini and won ton salads served with toothpicks make unusual hors d'oeuvres, and guacamole and bean-filled pastas can be delicious first course openers. Leftovers, if there are any, merely deepen in flavor for great next-day lunches or the best standing-at-the-refrigerator eating imaginable.

PASTA SALADS

These first 2 pasta salads are simply among the best I have ever tasted. Each is a celebration of bright colors and vivid tastes. They are unusual, satisfying, and delicious.

SZECHUAN PASTA AND VEGETABLE SALAD *yields about 10 cups*

If you wish to prepare this several hours ahead, add broccoli and peas at the last minute, as their bright color fades in contact with the vinaigrette.

1 head broccoli
4 carrots, peeled and cut into julienne strips
   One 10-ounce package frozen peas, defrosted
2 red bell peppers, cut into thin strips (or use green when red is not available)
1 recipe Szechuan Vinaigrette (p. 235)
2 cups shredded red cabbage
1 bunch scallions, minced fine
1 pound long pasta such as spaghetti or linguini, or short pasta such as rotini or spirals
1 can whole baby corn, drained (optional)
2 cups very fresh bean sprouts
1 cup roasted peanuts (I use dry roasted unsalted), chopped medium fine

Divide the broccoli into small flowerets, leaving at least an inch or so of stem on each. Blanch in boiling water until crisp-tender. Rinse under cold water and drain well. Repeat the blanching process with the carrots. Blanch the peas and red pepper strips very briefly. Rinse and drain.

Combine the Szechuan Vinaigrette, carrot strips, red pepper strips, shredded cabbage, and minced scallions in a bowl and toss.

Cook the pasta until it is al dente, rinse quickly with cold water, and drain well. Toss the pasta with the marinated vegetables (this can be done up to an hour or two ahead). Just before serving, cut the optional baby corn in halves and add it to the bowl with the blanched peas (and blanched pea pods, if you like), the bean sprouts, and the broccoli flowerets. Toss, then sprinkle with chopped peanuts.

MEXICAN FIESTA PASTA SALAD *yields about 12 cups*

Sometimes I add ½ cup (or to taste) of a spicy commercial salsa for extra impact.

1 recipe Salsa Vinaigrette (p. 236)
8 ounces pepper Jack cheese (Monterey Jack cheese with bell and jalapeño peppers added), cut into small dice
   One 17-ounce can corn, drained
   One 16-ounce can black beans, rinsed and drained

2/3-1 cup minced scallion
2/3-1 cup chopped tomato pulp
   1   pound rotini (rigoletti or spirals), cooked
       al dente

Combine the ingredients for Salsa Vinaigrette in a large mixing bowl. Add the pepper Jack cheese, corn, black beans, minced scallion, and chopped tomato pulp. Add the pasta and toss. Season with salt and pepper to taste, adding a little minced

Salt and freshly ground pepper to taste
Additional minced garlic, or garlic powder
(optional)
Additional cumin seeds (optional)

garlic or garlic powder and cumin seeds if needed. Refrigerate for several hours, turning the ingredients occasionally. This allows the flavors to ripen and penetrate the pasta. Serve cold or at room temperature.

My dear friend and business partner, Norman Fine, created this cold pasta salad using a Kung Pao stir-fry sauce. It is a juicy-sweet/spicy-hot taste experience with the marvelous crunch of broccoli, red peppers, and peanuts.

KUNG PAO BROCCOLI AND TOFU PASTA SALAD *yields about 10 cups*

For a change of texture, deep fry the tofu cubes and simply toss them in the sauce with the red pepper and blanched broccoli. Sprinkle the salad with additional minced scallion, if you like.

sauce
   1   cup hoi sin sauce
   6   Tablespoons ground bean sauce*
   4   Tablespoons dry sherry or Gingered Sherry
       (p. 258)
   4   Tablespoons red wine vinegar
 1-2   Tablespoons chili paste with garlic, or to taste
   2   Tablespoons sugar

*Ground bean sauce is available in Oriental markets and keeps for a long time stored in a glass or plastic container in the refrigerator.

   4   Tablespoons oil
 6-8   cloves garlic, minced fine or pressed
   1   large or 2 regular bunches scallions,
       chopped
   1   pound firm-style tofu, cut into about
       1/2-inch cubes
8-10   cups small broccoli flowerets, blanched till
       crisp-tender (2 medium-size heads broccoli)
   1   large or 2 medium red bell peppers, diced
       or cut into thin strips (do not substitute
       green pepper)
   1   pound small pasta forms (rotini, ziti, shells,
       oversize elbow macaroni), cooked al dente
   1   cup (or more) roasted or dry roasted
       peanuts (unsalted)
       Dark sesame oil (optional)

Combine the hoi sin sauce, ground bean sauce, sherry, red wine vinegar, chili paste with garlic, and sugar.

Heat the oil in a wok or sauté pan. Add the finely minced or pressed garlic and cook briefly, being careful that the garlic does not brown. Add the sauce, stirring well. When the sauce begins to bubble add the chopped scallions and tofu. Cook for a minute or two. Allow the mixture to cool.

Add the broccoli, red pepper, and pasta and toss to distribute the sauce. Just before serving, add the peanuts and drizzle on a little sesame oil. Toss to mix. Serve warm, at room temperature, or cold.

SPICY SZECHUAN NOODLES *serves at least 4 as a main course or 6–8 as a first course*

Here it is. The Szechuan noodle of my past re-created as delicious as remembered—seductively smooth, exhilaratingly fiery, and with just the right crunch and bite. Because of its intensity it works best served by itself rather than as part of an assortment of dishes for a Chinese dinner, but it is also fun to bring as a potluck dish.

3/4–1 cup unsweetened chunky peanut butter*
   8 Tablespoons soy sauce or tamari
   6 Tablespoons dark sesame oil
   4 Tablespoons red wine vinegar
   2 Tablespoons minced preserved radish, or to taste (optional)**
   4 teaspoons sugar
2–4 teaspoons chili paste with garlic
6–8 Tablespoons hot water (use pasta cooking water), or as needed

   1 pound thin spaghetti, cooked al dente
3/4–1 cup finely minced scallion
  1/4 cup chopped roasted peanuts (optional)

Combine the peanut butter, soy sauce or tamari, sesame oil, red wine vinegar, optional minced preserved radish, sugar, and chili paste with garlic. Add 6 Tablespoons hot water gradually, stirring until the ingredients are well mixed. Drain the cooked noodles, rinse quickly under cool water, and drain. Add the noodles to the sauce along with half the minced scallion and toss until they are coated evenly with sauce. Add additional hot water if the mixture is too thick and sticky. Turn into a serving bowl and sprinkle with the remaining minced scallion and the optional chopped peanuts. Serve at room temperature.

*You can use smooth rather than chunky peanut butter if that is what you have on hand, but if you do, use the smaller amount of peanut butter and add more chopped roasted peanuts.
**If you are omitting the minced preserved radish, you may want to add a generous pinch of salt.

EGGPLANT TUNA PASTA SALAD *yields about 8¹/2-9 cups*

This is a superb cold pasta salad, creamy and rich tasting. Rotini is my favorite choice of pasta because of the rich convolutions of pasta surface. This salad is also delightful stuffed into scooped-out tomatoes —a lovely accompaniment for grilled meats or fish or an attractive and satisfying luncheon main course. An equally delicious warm pasta sauce can be prepared from this same recipe: Cook spaghetti, or pasta of choice, al dente. Drain and add the steaming pasta to the sauce. Toss and serve immediately, passing additional grated cheese.

       One 10-ounce package frozen peas
1 pound rotelle (rotini) or other pasta
1 recipe Eggplant Tuna Parmesan, omitting parsley and pimento (p. 71)
¹/2 cup (or more) freshly grated Parmesan cheese
¹/4–¹/3 cup mayonnaise, preferably homemade or Hellman's
1 small jar diced pimento, drained

garnish
    ¹/4 cup reserved peas
       Whole pimento cut into strips
       Olive oil (virgin olive oil adds extra flavor)

Bring a large pot of salted water to a boil. Before you use it to cook the pasta, blanch the peas. Put the peas in a strainer and dip them briefly into the boiling pasta water. Reserve ¹/4 cup of the peas for the garnish. Then cook the pasta until it is al dente and rinse it quickly under cold water.

Combine the Eggplant Tuna Parmesan with additional Parmesan, mayonnaise, peas, and pimento. Add the cooked pasta to the sauce and toss to mix well and coat pasta evenly with sauce. Taste for seasoning and add additional cheese if needed. Garnish with the reserved peas and whole pimento cut into strips.

Serve at room temperature or chilled. If chilled, moisten it with olive oil as needed.

EGGPLANT WALNUT PASTA SALAD *yields about 8¹/2-9 cups*

If you love basil pesto, consider this as a less oily alternative with its own unique texture and taste. Like the preceding pasta salad, Eggplant Walnut Pasta Salad can be served chilled, at room temperature, or hot.

1 pound pasta (rotini), cooked al dente
2 recipes Eggplant Walnut Pesto (p. 71)

garnish
    Grated cheese
    Minced fresh parsley or basil
    Chopped walnuts

Combine the pasta with Eggplant Walnut Pesto. Taste for seasoning. Garnish with grated cheese, minced fresh herbs, and chopped nuts.

COLD
STUFFED
PASTAS

Here are 3 magnificent cold stuffed pasta salads that use commercial pasta shells or won ton wrappers. These pastas with their robust Salsa or Szechuan Vinaigrettes and guacamole, bean, or shrimp fillings will surprise and delight all eaters.

Serve them as part of an antipasto platter or dinner buffet of mixed salads or as a light dinner or special lunch. They are exquisite fare for picnics and make memorable potluck dishes.

GUACAMOLE-FILLED PASTA SALAD WITH SALSA *yields about 24 stuffed shells*

This is also delicious with cold cooked shrimp scattered among the stuffed pasta shells.

> One 12-ounce package jumbo shells
> for stuffing
> 2½ cups Guacamole (about 1½ recipes, using
> 3 avocados) (p. 69)
> 1 cup cooked black beans, rinsed and drained
> 1 recipe Salsa Vinaigrette (p. 236)

Cook the shells until they are tenderly al dente. Rinse in cold water and let drain. Pick out the shells that are intact—you will probably get about 24 that are usable. Open each shell and fill with a generous kitchen teaspoonful of Guacamole. Close the shell so that the edges overlap and the filling is well enclosed. Place the shells in a single or double layer on a serving platter or in a bowl. Sprinkle with black beans and pour on the Salsa Vinaigrette.

Shells can be served immediately or, better yet, refrigerated for several hours so that the flavors in the vinaigrette can penetrate the pasta. (Shells can even be prepared the day before and refrigerated.)

Baste the top shells with vinaigrette using a spoon or ball baster once or twice (or more), being careful to keep the attractive pattern of beans, tomatoes, scallions, and green chilis that collect on top of the shells.

Allow 2–4 shells per person for a light lunch or as part of an antipasto platter.

BEAN-FILLED PASTA SALAD WITH SALSA *yields about 24 stuffed shells*

> One 12-ounce package jumbo shells for stuffing
> 2 recipes (3 cups) Seasoned Bean Puree (p. 252)
> ½ cup freshly grated Parmesan cheese
> 1 recipe Salsa Vinaigrette (p. 236)

Cook the shells until they are tenderly al dente. Rinse in cold water and let drain. Pick out the shells that are intact—you will probably get about 24 that are usable. Prepare the Seasoned Bean Puree and when it is hot, add the grated Parmesan to it. Open each shell and fill with a generous kitchen teaspoonful of Seasoned Bean Puree. Close the shell so that the edges overlap and the filling is well enclosed. Place the shells in a single or double layer on a serving platter or in a shallow bowl. Pour on the Salsa Vinaigrette. Let stand an hour to let

vinaigrette flavors penetrate the pasta or refrigerate for several hours or overnight.

Baste the top shells with vinaigrette using a spoon or ball baster once or twice (or more), being careful to keep the attractive pattern of tomatoes, scallions, and green chilis that collect on top of the shells. Serve cold or at room temperature.

COLD SHRIMP
WON TONS WITH BROCCOLI IN SZECHUAN VINAIGRETTE *yields about 8¹/2-9 cups*

These will be gobbled up. No matter how many you have. My favorite way to serve them is as an hors d'oeuvre. I just put out a large bowl of won tons with napkins and toothpicks, or forks and small plates. They are a sensation when taken to a potluck party. You can use more or less broccoli, depending on whether you want just a touch of color or a vegetable complement.

Flowerets with longish stems from 1 small head broccoli
1/2 recipe Shrimp and Tofu Won Tons (about 55 won tons) (p. 61)
1 recipe Szechuan Vinaigrette (p. 235)

Cook the broccoli briefly in boiling water until it is crisp-tender (more on the crisp side). Remove with a slotted spoon, run under cold water, and drain well. Boil the won tons in batches in gently boiling water until cooked through (3-5 minutes, longer by

2-3 minutes if the won tons were frozen). Remove the won tons with a slotted spoon to a colander and rinse quickly under cool water. Place in a bowl and toss with a little bit of oil (preferably dark sesame oil) to prevent the won tons from sticking together.

Just before serving, or even an hour or more before serving, combine the won tons, broccoli flowerets, and Szechuan Vinaigrette. Stir carefully once or twice before serving.

Note: The won ton skins from Chinese markets are slightly thicker and hold up much better than those sold in supermarkets. They can even be boiled a day ahead. If you can get wrappers only in a supermarket, boil them no more than a few hours before serving and be sure not to overcook them.

Pasta
Salads

Tortellini make impressive pasta salads and elegant hors d'oeuvres. Smaller tortellini work best. Use 2½-3-inch round cutters.

SZECHUAN TORTELLINI AND BROCCOLI SALAD *yields about 8½-9 cups*

Flowerets from 1 head broccoli, blanched
1 recipe Seafood Tortellini (p. 154)
1 recipe Szechuan Vinaigrette (p. 235)

Bring a large pot of salted water to a boil. Before using it to cook the pasta you can blanch your broccoli. Cook the flowerets for a few minutes until they are crisp-tender then remove them with a slotted spoon to a colander and run under cold water. Drain well. Then cook the tortellini until they are tenderly al dente. Drain them under cold water. Place tortellini in a bowl and pour on the Szechuan Vinaigrette. Refrigerate until the tortellini are cold. Add broccoli flowerets and toss just before serving.

LEMONY SEAFOOD TORTELLINI SALAD *yields about 8½-9 cups*

You can toss minced cooked shrimp in along with the tortellini. You can also prepare the tortellini with spinach pasta.

1 recipe Seafood Tortellini (p. 154)
1 recipe Basic Lemon Vinaigrette (p. 237), using all or mostly lemon juice instead of vinegar
½ cup (or more) minced red onion
½ cup (or more) minced fresh parsley

Cook the tortellini until they are tenderly al dente. (Remember, they won't continue cooking under a hot sauce.) Run quickly under cold water and drain well. Toss with Lemon Vinaigrette, onion, and parsley and refrigerate for several hours before serving.

MEXICAN TORTELLINI SALAD *yields about 8½-9 cups*

1 recipe Bean Tortellini (p. 155)
1 recipe Salsa Vinaigrette (p. 236)
Minced scallion

Boil the tortellini until they are tenderly al dente. Drain under cold water. Place the tortellini in a bowl and pour on the Salsa Vinaigrette. Let cool several hours, turning the tortellini occasionally. Sprinkle with minced scallion for color.

TABOULI

Tabouli is one of my favorite things to eat. It's refreshing, filling, and healthful—and relatively low calorie. It's great for lunch, dinners, snacks, and as a perfect no-wilt salad to bring to picnics. Include it in antipasto or party platters for entertaining or take along to someone else's party as a no-fail potluck dish.

Tabouli is made with bulgur—cracked wheat that has been precooked and dried. Bulgur is avail-able in most health-food and Middle Eastern stores. It needs only the barest of "cooking" to bring it to delicious tenderness. For the tabouli recipes in this cookbook, measure out 1½ cups bulgur and rinse it quickly in a colander. Place in a bowl and pour in an equal amount of boiling water. Cover tightly and let stand for 30 minutes or longer.

GRAPE TABOULI *yields 6–7 cups*

Sweet, crisp grapes and softly chewy kidney beans in a subtle vinaigrette—a popular and unusual combination.

  1 cup seedless green grapes, halved
  1 cup cooked drained kidney beans
  1 cup finely minced fresh parsley (1 large bunch)
½ cup minced red onion
  1 recipe Basic Lemon Vinaigrette (p. 237)
  2 teaspoons sugar
1½ cups bulgur, prepared according to the
     directions above

Combine the grapes, kidney beans, parsley, onion, Lemon Vinaigrette, and sugar. Refrigerate while preparing the bulgur. Combine the prepared bulgur with the grape mixture, taste for seasoning, and serve cold or at room temperature.

CARROT RAISIN WALNUT (OR PEANUT) TABOULI *yields 6–7 cups*

Raises carrot and raisin salad to new heights.

  1 cup (or more) finely diced or shredded
     carrots (up to 1 pound carrots)
½ cup coarsely chopped walnuts (or peanuts)
½ cup raisins
½ cup minced scallion
  1 cup minced fresh parsley (1 large bunch)
½ cup feta cheese, crumbled (optional)
  1 recipe Basic Lemon Vinaigrette (p. 237)
  2 teaspoons sugar
1½ cups bulgur, prepared according to the
     directions above

Combine the carrots, walnuts or peanuts, raisins, scallion, parsley, feta, Lemon Vinaigrette, and sugar. Refrigerate while preparing the bulgur. Combine the prepared bulgur with the carrot mixture, taste for seasoning, and serve at room temperature or chilled.

TOMATO TABOULI *yields about 9 cups*

This is my most-made tabouli. The balance of tastes and textures is very pleasing.

2-3 unpeeled, good-size vine-ripened tomatoes
(about 2 cups chopped tomato pulp),
or 1 container cherry tomatoes, halved
1 large bunch parsley, minced fine
One 1-pound can kidney beans, drained
About 4-6 ounces feta cheese, crumbled
1 recipe Basic Lemon Vinaigrette (p. 237)
1½ cups bulgur, prepared according to the
directions on page 229
Lightly toasted sunflower seeds

Combine the chopped tomato pulp or halved cherry tomatoes, minced parsley, kidney beans, feta cheese, and Lemon Vinaigrette. Let the mixture marinate (in the refrigerator, if you wish) while you prepare the bulgur.

When the bulgur is ready, combine it with the tomato mixture and taste for seasoning. Sprinkle generously with toasted sunflower seeds just before serving. Serve cold or at room temperature.

SHRIMP AND
ARTICHOKE TABOULI *yields about 7 cups*

This is a classy tabouli. You can increase the amount of shrimp if your budget can take it. Mix them whole or chopped into the tabouli and use them whole to garnish the tabouli, placing them around the edges of the salad or in a line down the center.

> One 6-ounce jar marinated quartered artichoke hearts, drained
> 1 recipe Basic Lemon Vinaigrette (p. 237)
> 1 pound small whole shrimp, cooked, peeled, and deveined, or larger shrimp, cooked and diced
> 1/2 teaspoon oregano, or to taste
> 1/2 teaspoon Dijon mustard, or to taste
> One 4-ounce jar sliced pimento, drained
> About 1 cup finely minced parsley (1 large bunch)
> 1 1/2 cups bulgur, prepared according to the directions on page 229

Reserve the marinade drained from the artichoke hearts and cut the artichoke quarters into smaller pieces. Prepare the Lemon Vinaigrette using the reserved artichoke marinade instead of the 1/4 cup olive oil and adding the oregano and Dijon mustard. Combine the shrimp, chopped artichoke, pimento, parsley, and revised Lemon Vinaigrette. Refrigerate while preparing the bulgur. Combine the prepared bulgur and the shrimp mixture. Taste for seasoning. Serve cold or at room temperature.

TABOULI WITH
MIXED VEGETABLES *yields 7-8 cups*

> 1/2 large cucumber, peeled and cut into small or medium dice
> 1 medium tomato, unpeeled, excess juice and seeds squeezed, cut into small or medium dice
> 1 small green pepper, diced
> 1/2 cup diced green cabbage
> 1/2-1 cup cooked drained kidney beans, or chick-peas, if you prefer
> About 1/2 cup feta cheese, crumbled
> About 1 cup finely minced fresh parsley (1 large bunch)
> 1/4 cup finely minced scallion
> 1 recipe Basic Lemon Vinaigrette (p. 237)
> 1/2 teaspoon oregano
> 1 1/2 cups bulgur, prepared according to the directions on page 229

Combine the cucumber, tomato, green pepper, cabbage, kidney beans, feta cheese, parsley, scallion, Lemon Vinaigrette, and oregano. Let marinate in or out of the refrigerator while you are preparing the bulgur. Combine the prepared bulgur with the vegetable mixture and taste for seasoning. Serve at room temperature or chilled.

BEST PICKLED VEGETABLES

These colorful, crunchy, tart-sweet vegetables are great as is, for a low-cal nibble or relish or a zippy addition to a tossed green salad. They raise sandwiches to new heights, adding wonderful flavor and bite to meat loaf or hummus or cheese and sprout sandwiches or any stuffed pita bread "meal." I generally prepare a mixture of onions, pepper, and cabbage for "sandwich pickles" and a more color-contrasting mixture such as broccoli and carrots or cauliflower and onion for an antipasto platter. Sometimes I toss the pickled vegetables and beans with a little olive oil, salt, pepper, and herbs. The oil mellows the flavor a bit, creating a wonderful marinated salad and a delicious addition to any antipasto platter. Pickled yellow squash with kidney beans and minced fresh dill, moistened with olive oil, makes a particularly nice salad.

pickling liquid
      2 cups cider vinegar
    3/4 cup water
      1 Tablespoon salt
      2 Tablespoons sugar
    3-4 cloves garlic, unpeeled and crushed lightly
      1 teaspoon tarragon
      1 teaspoon dried dill, or several sprigs fresh
    3-4 black peppercorns
      1 large bay leaf

vegetables
        Red or green pepper, sliced or diced
        Onions, quartered and separated, or small whole onions
        Zucchini or yellow squash, sliced
        Carrots, sliced or cut into julienne strips
        Cabbage, cut into squares or slices
        Green beans
        Cauliflowerets

        Brussels sprouts, whole or halved
        Broccoli flowerets
        Beets
        Chick-peas and/or kidney beans
        (optional)

Combine the cider vinegar, water, salt, and sugar in an enamel or stainless steel saucepan. Tie the garlic, tarragon, dill, peppercorns, and bay leaf into a square of cheesecloth. Add this bouquet garni to the pot and bring the liquid to a boil, stirring once or twice to dissolve the sugar and salt. (You can add the herbs directly to the liquid, but each time you remove batches of vegetables you will be removing the herbs as well.)

Clean and slice the vegetables you wish to use—this can be one or many different kinds. If you are using different vegetables, arrange them in separate batches because cooking times will vary, although I often pickle onions, peppers, and cabbage together. Add the vegetables to the pickling bath and simmer each batch just until the vegetables are crunchy-tender. Remove to a bowl with a slotted spoon and continue pickling. (If you are processing a large amount of vegetables you will need a double or triple recipe of pickling liquid.) If you are pickling cauliflower, Brussels sprouts, or broccoli, do these at the end since they impart a flavor to the liquid. And if you are processing beets, reserve these for the very last as they color the liquid and any vegetable cooked in it with a pinkish hue.

As the vegetables are cooked, either stir them together in a bowl or arrange them in different-colored layers in glass jars or a glass soufflé dish. Add cooked chick-peas and/or kidney beans, if you like. Pour the pickling liquid over the vegetables and refrigerate until cold.

BROCCOLI WITH TOMATOES AND BLACK BEANS *yields about 8 cups*

Turn this into a delicious cold pasta salad by adding 1/2 pound or so cooked small pasta forms such as rotini or shells. If you have full-flavored tomatoes during the summer, by all means use them, peeled and cut up, instead of the canned.

1	large Spanish onion, diced or sliced fairly thin
3-4	Tablespoons olive oil
1	large red bell pepper, cut into thin strips (do not use green pepper. If red is not available, just omit)
	About 6 cups small broccoli flowerets (from 1 good-size head broccoli)
4	large cloves garlic, minced
	One 28-ounce can tomatoes
3	teaspoons basil
1	teaspoon oregano
1	teaspoon sage
	Salt and freshly ground pepper to taste
	A few drops Tabasco sauce
1	cup (or more) cooked black beans (half a 1-pound can, drained)
	Freshly grated Parmesan cheese (optional)

In a wok or large frying pan sauté the onion in olive oil until it begins to soften, adding the red pepper toward the end of the sauté time. Add the broccoli and garlic and continue cooking over medium heat for about 5 minutes, stirring and tossing the ingredients occasionally. Add the tomatoes, basil, oregano, sage, salt, pepper, Tabasco, and beans and cook over medium-high heat until the broccoli is cooked crisp-tender and most of the liquid is reduced. This will take just a few minutes more. Add additional water if the liquid cooks away before the broccoli is done. Cool. Taste for seasoning. Add grated Parmesan, if desired. Serve cold or at room temperature.

RATATOUILLE *yields 6 cups*

You can make an excellent ratatouille by preparing Ratatouille Sauce (p. 244) using a 28-ounce can of tomatoes and omitting the tomato paste (add a little paste if you want a more tomato-y flavor) or using a 1-pound can of tomatoes and a small can of paste, adding additional water, if needed.

SWEET-AND-SOUR ZUCCHINI *yields 4-5 cups*

4	cups zucchini or yellow squash, cut into 1/2-inch slices
2	Tablespoons olive oil
1	large onion, cut into wedges
1/4	cup red wine vinegar
2	Tablespoons tomato paste
2	Tablespoons water
2	Tablespoons currants or raisins
1	Tablespoon capers
1	Tablespoon sugar
1/2	teaspoon salt, or to taste

In a wok or large frying pan sauté the zucchini or yellow squash and the onion in olive oil over high heat until the squash is browned lightly. Combine the remaining ingredients in a small saucepan and heat, stirring, until the sauce is well blended. Add to the zucchini and simmer for 10 minutes, stirring occasionally, until the zucchini are tender.

Serve chilled or at room temperature, as a salad or relish accompanying a meal or as part of an antipasto platter.

BEET, ORANGE, AND ONION SALAD *yields 3-4 cups*

1 large bunch beets
1 large onion, sliced
1 recipe Tarragon Orange Vinaigrette (p. 236)
1 large navel orange, peeled, halved, and sliced

Cook the beets until they are tender but still have a little crunch. Peel them and slice thin. Combine the beets and onion and toss with enough Tarragon Orange Vinaigrette to coat lightly. Garnish with orange slices.

Serve as a dinner salad or as part of an antipasto platter.

CARROT RAPEE

Carrot Rapee is a classic—simple, refreshing, and easy to prepare, adding a brilliant splash of color to any plate.

Grate carrots in the food processor (best) or by hand. Long shreds are best. Toss with enough Basic Vinaigrette (p. 235) to coat lightly. Toss with minced parsley, if desired, or sprinkle lightly with minced parsley. Serve chilled or at room temperature.

GREEN BEANS VINAIGRETTE

Steam or boil green beans until they are crisp-tender. Rinse under cold water and drain. Toss with Basic Vinaigrette (p. 235) and sprinkle with freshly grated Parmesan cheese, if desired.

SZECHUAN GREEN BEANS VINAIGRETTE

Toss steamed or boiled green beans with enough Szechuan Vinaigrette (p. 235) to coat lightly. Sprinkle with toasted sesame seeds. Serve immediately or very soon because the bright green color of the beans fades as it marinates in the vinaigrette.

MARINATED WHITE BEANS WITH CAPERS, ANCHOVIES, AND TUNA

Toss cooked navy or pea beans or drained canned cannelini beans with Basic Vinaigrette (p. 235). Add plenty of fresh minced parsley, 1-2 Tablespoons capers, and salt and freshly ground pepper to taste. Add drained, flaked canned tuna and refrigerate for several hours or overnight. Serve garnished with anchovy strips or rolled anchovies stuffed with capers.

DRESSINGS

Here are vinaigrettes and creamy dressings that shimmer their crisp, herby flavors over green salads and taboulis or help express the Mexican or Szechuan souls of exciting pasta salads. Follow these recipes or try making your own versions.

BASIC VINAIGRETTE *yields about 1 cup*

One of the joys of this dressing is that you can vary the flavors. Use half or all virgin olive oil or use walnut oil alone or in combination with olive or vegetable oil. Experiment with different flavored vinegars, too. I like to add a splash of raspberry vinegar along with red wine vinegar, and when I do I almost invariably add a spoonful of capers with a little caper juice. The various herb vinegars alter the tastes too, so try them.

2/3 cup olive oil or salad oil, or a combination
1/3 cup red wine vinegar, or a combination of vinegar and lemon juice
  1 clove garlic, minced fine
  1 teaspoon Dijon or grainy mustard, or to taste
    Dried or fresh herbs of choice (optional)
    Salt and pepper to taste

Combine the ingredients and whisk to mix well.

These next 2 dressings are nothing short of transformational, changing the raw materials of vegetables, pasta, and beans into fabulous-tasting dishes.

SZECHUAN VINAIGRETTE *yields about 1 1/2 cups*

This deeply flavorful, spicy vinaigrette makes a wonderful dressing for Chinese pasta, won ton, and tortellini salads and is an excellent marinade for fish, seafood, or chicken. It is terrific, too, as a dressing for blanched broccoli and carrots or blanched green beans.

2/3 cup salad oil
1/2 cup red wine vinegar
  2 Tablespoons dark sesame oil
  2 Tablespoons light soy sauce or tamari
  2 Tablespoons dark soy sauce
  2 Tablespoons chili paste with garlic, or to taste
1 1/2 Tablespoons sugar
  1 Tablespoon finely minced fresh gingerroot
  1 large clove garlic, minced fine
    Salt to taste

Combine the ingredients and mix thoroughly.

SALSA VINAIGRETTE *yields 2 1/2 cups*

I am not a fan of fresh coriander. If you are, however, by all means add some chopped fresh coriander to the Salsa Vinaigrette.

1/2 cup olive oil, or half unrefined corn oil
1/4 cup red wine vinegar
1/4 cup freshly squeezed lemon juice
 2 cloves garlic, minced fine
 1 Tablespoon cumin seeds
 2 teaspoons salt, or to taste
 1 teaspoon oregano
 2 drops Tabasco sauce, or to taste
   One 3-ounce can green chilis, undrained
2/3 cup (or more) chopped tomato pulp
2/3 cup (or more) minced scallion (about 1 bunch
   scallions)

Combine the oil, red wine vinegar, lemon juice, garlic, cumin seeds, salt, oregano, and Tabasco.

Now you will have to do some chopping. This should be done by hand to give the right vegetable-y texture. If the green chilis are whole, chop them and add them along with the liquid in the can to the vinaigrette. Chop enough tomato pulp to fill the chili can (this will measure 2/3 cup) and add to the vinaigrette. Measure the scallion in the same way. Stir well and taste for seasoning.

ORIENTAL SOY SESAME VINAIGRETTE *yields about 1 cup*

Serve tossed with salad greens to which you have added fresh bean sprouts and sliced water chestnuts, if you like. Mandarin orange slices are also a tasty addition.

2/3 cup olive oil or salad oil, or a combination
1/3 cup red wine vinegar
 1 clove garlic, minced fine
 1 Tablespoon soy sauce or tamari
 1 Tablespoon (or more) lightly toasted
   sesame seeds
1/2 Tablespoon dark sesame oil
   Grainy or Dijon mustard to taste

Combine the ingredients to mix thoroughly.

TARRAGON ORANGE VINAIGRETTE *yields about 1 cup*

Use for cold beet salads or tossed green salads with halved seedless grapes.

1/4-1/2 cup olive oil
   1/4 cup cider vinegar
   1/4 cup orange juice
    1 clove garlic, minced (optional)
    1 teaspoon tarragon
   1/2 teaspoon basil
      Salt and freshly ground pepper to taste
      Grated rind of 1 orange (optional)

Combine the ingredients to mix thoroughly.

BASIC
LEMON VINAIGRETTE *yields about 3/4 cup*

1/4 cup freshly squeezed lemon juice
(1 large lemon)
1/4 cup red wine vinegar
1/4 cup olive oil or salad oil
1 large clove garlic, minced
1 Tablespoon salt, for tabouli—use less if for a
salad dressing
Freshly ground pepper to taste

Combine the ingredients to mix well.

MAYONNAISE
AND YOGURT SALAD DRESSING

This simple, creamy dressing is one of my favorites.
I love to serve it on an abundant main course salad
with assorted greens, chopped tomato, hard-boiled
egg, cubes of cheese, and generous sprinklings of
peanuts and seeds.

2 parts mayonnaise
1 part (or more) unflavored yogurt
Grainy or Dijon mustard to taste (be generous)
Garlic powder to taste
Salt and freshly ground pepper to taste
Fresh or dried herbs (optional)
Crumbled blue cheese (optional)

Combine all the ingredients until well blended.

NORMAN FINE'S
HERB SAUCE/DIP *yields about 3 1/4 cups*

I consider this *the* dip for raw vegetables, delightfully fresh, herbed, and garlicky. It also makes a
first-rate potato salad dressing and an excellent
sauce for cold fish or seafood salads or cold pasta
salad with mixed vegetables and cooked chick-peas
or beans. Its consistency is pourable, so if you want
a thicker sauce (for potato salad), process the ingredients without the mayonnaise then stir the mayonnaise in.

2 cups Hellman's mayonnaise
1/2 cup sour cream
2 Tablespoons (or more) freshly squeezed
lemon juice
1 *heaping* Tablespoon grainy mustard
1/2 Tablespoon red wine vinegar
1/2 bunch watercress, leaves and top stems only
1/2 bunch parsley, leaves and top stems only
1 1/2–2 large scallions, chopped
Lots of minced fresh dill
2 medium cloves garlic
1 teaspoon sugar
3/4–1 teaspoon salt
1/4 teaspoon garlic powder
1/8 teaspoon Tabasco sauce
About 1/8 teaspoon freshly ground pepper

Place all the ingredients in a food processor and
process until the greens are minced very fine. The
mixture will be a pale green color with darker
green flecks.

SAUCES,
FILLINGS, AND
MARINADES

SAUCES	Basic Tomato Sauce	**FILLINGS**	Seafood Mousse I
	Mexican Tomato Sauce		Seafood Mousse II
	Marinara Sauce		Seafood Mousse III
	Seafood Marinara Sauce or Seafood Tomato Sauce		Seafood Mousse IV
	Favorite Meat Sauce		Salmon Mousse
	Ratatouille Sauce		Mushroom Duxelles
	Creamy Eggplant Tomato Sauce		Mushroom Pecan Filling
	Basic Béchamel		Mushroom Marsala Filling
	Thick Béchamel		Mushroom Marsala and Ricotta Filling
	Sesame Béchamel		Seasoned Bean Puree
	Mornay Sauce		Bean Filling
	Basil Béchamel		Cheese Bean Filling
	Seafood Velouté		Picadillo
	Crab Meat Velouté		Kasha with Herbs
	Pesto Sauce		Brown Rice
	Frozen Pesto Cubes		Potato Cheese Filling I
	Processor or Blender Hollandaise		Dilled Potato Cheese Filling II
			Rich Potato Cheese Filling III
			Parsnip Filling
			Parsnip and Spinach Filling
			Spinach Mornay
			Seasoned Eggplant Puree
		MARINADES	Special Szechuan Marinade
			Norman Fine's Chinese Marinade
			Gingered Sherry
			Mayonnaise Marinade for Fish

What is pasta without a sauce or strudel without a filling? Sauces, fillings, and marinades too pair so gracefully with other ingredients that they create a whole greater than any possible sum of its parts.

Here in this chapter are robust, fragrant red sauces and subtly varied whites. These enhance pastas, enrich crêpes, and transform or complete numberless dishes. And there are fillings of all kinds to grace the insides of pastas, pastries, crêpes, and even breads. And marinades—powerful silent partners that work their magic behind the scenes, lending special impact and finish to chicken, fish, and meat.

BASIC
TOMATO SAUCE *yields 3 cups*

    1 cup chopped onion or white of leek
  2-3 Tablespoons olive oil
  2-3 large cloves garlic, minced fine
      One 35-ounce can imported tomatoes
1 1/2 teaspoons salt
    1 teaspoon sugar
    1 teaspoon dried basil, or 2-3 Tablespoons
      minced fresh, or 1/2-1 Frozen Pesto Cube
      (p. 247)
    4 drops Tabasco sauce
      Freshly ground pepper to taste

In a wok or large frying pan sauté the onion or leek in olive oil until it is tender and translucent, adding the garlic toward the end of the sauté time. Add the tomatoes, salt, sugar, basil, Tabasco sauce, and pepper and cook over medium-high heat for about 20 minutes, or until the sauce is thickened, breaking up the tomatoes with the back of a wooden spoon.

MEXICAN
TOMATO SAUCE *yields about 3 cups*

    1 cup finely chopped onion
  3-4 cloves garlic, minced
    2 Tablespoons oil, preferably unrefined corn oil
      One 35-ounce can imported tomatoes
    2 Tablespoons red wine
    1 teaspoon oregano
    1 teaspoon chili powder
  1/2 teaspoon basil
    1 small hot pepper, cut up, or Tabasco sauce
      to taste
      About 1 1/2 teaspoons salt, or to taste

Sauté the onion and garlic in oil until the onion is translucent. Add the tomatoes, wine, oregano, chili powder, basil, hot pepper or Tabasco sauce, and salt. Simmer for 20-30 minutes, or until the sauce is thickened, stirring occasionally and breaking up the tomatoes with the back of a wooden spoon.

MARINARA SAUCE *yields about 3 cups*

Light, sweet, utterly delicious. Requires a little extra effort and it shows in the results.

1 1/2 cups chopped onion
  1 carrot, grated fine
  2 Tablespoons olive oil
  4 Tablespoons (1/2 stick) butter
  4 cloves garlic, minced fine
    One 35-ounce can imported tomatoes
1 1/2 teaspoons salt
  1 teaspoon dried basil, or 2-3 Tablespoons minced fresh, or 1/2-1 Frozen Pesto Cube (p. 247)
1/2-1 teaspoon oregano
    Freshly ground pepper to taste

In a wok or large frying pan sauté the onion and carrot in the olive oil and 2 Tablespoons of the butter until the onion is softened. Add the garlic toward the end of the sauté time. Blend the tomatoes then put them through a sieve or food mill to remove the seeds. Add them to the pan with the salt, basil, oregano, and pepper and cook over medium-high heat for 20-30 minutes, or until the sauce is thickened. Stir in the remaining 2 Tablespoons butter. Use as is or put through the food mill one more time.

SEAFOOD MARINARA SAUCE OR SEAFOOD TOMATO SAUCE *yields 3 cups*

A lovely, light, full-flavored sauce that enhances the seafood flavor in any recipe in which it is used.

1 recipe Marinara Sauce (preceding recipe) or Basic Tomato Sauce (p. 241)
1 cup (or more) bottled clam juice or fish stock (see p. 51)
    About 1 teaspoon thyme (optional)

Prepare Marinara Sauce or Basic Tomato Sauce. After sautéing the garlic and before adding the canned tomatoes, add the clam juice or rich fish stock. Boil this down over high heat until the liquid is almost completely evaporated then proceed with the recipe. Add the thyme along with the other herbs, if you like.

FAVORITE MEAT SAUCE *yields about 5 1/2 quarts*

This is like the sauce I grew up calling "spaghetti sauce," as if there were no other kind. When I make it I "sauce up," freezing 3-cup portions in empty yogurt containers—just the right amount for 8 ounces of spaghetti. I use it as a base of Meat and Sausage Lasagna with Eggplant, a sauce for Potato Drop Gnocchi, and for ricotta-cheese-filled ravioli, tortellini, and manicotti. Delicious.

1 very large onion, chopped
3 large peppers, preferably red and green, diced
1–2 ribs celery, chopped
1 large carrot, grated
4 Tablespoons olive oil, or a combination of olive oil and rendered prosciutto fat*

---

*Buy inexpensive prosciutto fat in an Italian market, cut it up into small dice, and render it down in the 2 Tablespoons of olive oil. If you don't use prosciutto fat, add a small smoked hock to the sauce as it simmers.

4 pounds ground meat*
  Four 35-ounce cans imported tomatoes
  Three 6-ounce cans tomato paste
2 Tablespoons red wine
1 Tablespoon red wine vinegar
1 Tablespoon sugar
1–2 large bay leaves
1 Tablespoon salt
  Lots of freshly ground pepper
1 large head garlic (10–15 cloves)
  Oregano
  Basil or Frozen Pesto Cubes (p. 247)

In a large sauté or frying pan sauté the onion, peppers, celery, and carrot in the olive oil or olive oil and prosciutto fat until the vegetables are softened. Remove to a large pot. In the sautéing pan sauté the ground meat, breaking it up with the back of a spoon, until it loses most of its pink color. Transfer the meat with a slotted spoon to the pot with the vegetables, leaving behind the fat. Add the tomatoes and tomato paste to the pot along with the wine, red wine vinegar, sugar, bay leaves, salt, and pepper. Bring the sauce to a boil, stirring constantly, then lower the heat and simmer, uncovered, for 2 hours, stirring occasionally and being careful that the sauce does not stick to the bottom of the pot and burn. If this is a danger, lower the heat further.

Peel and mince the cloves from 1 large head of garlic and add them to the sauce along with lots of oregano and basil (use Frozen Pesto Cubes for the basil, if you have them). Simmer for 30 minutes more and taste for seasoning.

---

*My suggestion is to use 2 pounds lean ground beef, 1 pound ground pork, and 1 pound sausage meat.

RATATOUILLE SAUCE *yields 8 cups*

A versatile sauce/filling. Freeze a 2–3-cup portion for Manicotti Ratatouille or Ratatouille Crêpes, a 3-cup portion for Garden Lasagna, and serve the remainder, thinned with a little water, as a sauce for 8 ounces spaghetti or linguini. And pass the Parmesan cheese, please.

       1 eggplant (about 1 pound)
          Salt
     ¼ cup olive oil
     ½ pound onions, diced
  10–12 cloves garlic, chopped (1 whole head)
          About 2 cups red and green bell peppers, cut into ½-inch dice
       1 pound (combined weight) zucchini and yellow squash, cut into ½-inch dice
     12 ounces mushrooms, left whole if small, halved or quartered if large
          One 35-ounce can imported tomatoes
          One 6-ounce can tomato paste
       4 Tablespoons minced fresh basil, or 4 teaspoons dried, or 2 (or more) Frozen Pesto Cubes (p. 247)
       4 teaspoons salt, or to taste
       2 Tablespoons (or more) minced fresh parsley
       1 Tablespoon dry red wine
       2 teaspoons oregano
       6 dashes Tabasco sauce
          Freshly ground pepper to taste
       1 bay leaf

Peel and slice the eggplant into ½-inch-thick slices and salt liberally. Let the slices sit on paper towels for 20–30 minutes then pat them dry and cut into ½-inch dice.

Heat the olive oil in a large wok or Dutch oven. Add the onions, garlic, peppers, and the zucchini and yellow squash and sauté over high heat for several minutes. Rinse and dry the eggplant then add it and the mushrooms and sauté for about 10 minutes more, turning the vegetables regularly and being careful they don't burn. Add the tomatoes, tomato paste, basil, salt, parsley, wine, oregano, Tabasco sauce, pepper, and bay leaf and bring the sauce to a boil. Lower the heat and simmer until the vegetables are tender, but *not* soft or mushy. You should be able to distinguish the different shapes and colors well. Taste and adjust the seasoning.

CREAMY EGGPLANT TOMATO SAUCE *yields 4 cups*

Eggplant puree lends these sauces an extra creamy richness and flavor wonderful on fresh ravioli, manicotti, drop gnocchi, etc. Serve with plenty of freshly grated cheese.

       3 cups (1 recipe) Basic Tomato Sauce (p. 241) or Favorite Meat Sauce (p. 243)
       1 cup Seasoned Eggplant Puree (p. 257)

Combine all the ingredients.

BÉCHAMEL

Basic Béchamel, or white sauce, can be varied in a number of subtly delicious ways. Sauté a small amount of minced shallot or onion in the butter before you add the flour. When your sauce has thickened, add ½ teaspoon dry mustard or a small amount of an excellent prepared mustard. Add cheese to the sauce and it becomes "Mornay." Use stock as all or part of the liquid, and you are creating a "velouté."

See page 142 for Garlic Béchamel and page 143 for Eggplant Béchamel.

BASIC BÉCHAMEL *yields 1¾ cups*

        3 Tablespoons butter
        3 Tablespoons all-purpose flour
    1½ cups milk or cream*
            Few drops Tabasco sauce
            Salt to taste

Melt the butter in a medium-size saucepan, preferably one with a stainless steel or enamel surface. Add the flour and whisk the gently bubbling mixture over medium heat for a minute or two, being careful that the mixture ("roux") keeps its golden color and does not burn. Add the milk or cream and whisk constantly until the mixture has thickened. Season with Tabasco sauce and salt to taste.

THICK BÉCHAMEL

Reduce the amount of milk or cream to 1 cup.

*If you warm the milk or cream before you add it, the sauce will thicken more quickly.

SESAME BÉCHAMEL

Add ¼ cup sesame tahini to the thickened sauce. If you like, you may also add grated Parmesan cheese and lightly toasted sesame seeds. Use as a sauce for fresh noodles or nap over fish, sprinkle with sesame seeds, and broil or bake.

MORNAY SAUCE

When the Basic Béchamel has thickened, stir in grated cheese of choice. This can be Cheddar, Swiss, Parmesan, Brie, or an emphatic garlic and herb cheese. Begin with a small amount of cheese. Let it melt into the sauce, taste, and see if you want to add more. You are aiming for a subtle, not overpowering, cheese flavor. Often a generous sprinkling of Parmesan is all that is needed to round out the taste. If the sauce becomes too thick, thin with a little milk or cream.

BASIL BÉCHAMEL *yields 2 1/2 cups*

  4 Tablespoons (1/2 stick) butter
  4 Tablespoons all-purpose flour
2-2 1/4 cups milk or cream
  1/3 cup freshly grated Parmesan cheese
  1/3 cup finely chopped fresh basil, or
    1-2 Tablespoons dried, or to taste, or
    1-2 Frozen Pesto Cubes (p. 247)

Prepare according to directions for Basic Béchamel (p. 245).

SEAFOOD VELOUTÉ *yields 1 3/4 cups*

The addition of a little fresh crab meat or finely minced raw shrimp or clams creates a lovely, special sauce with a nice texture. A squeeze of lemon juice or a dash of the liquid from a jar of capers gives a fuller flavor.

  3 Tablespoons butter
  3 Tablespoons all-purpose flour
  1 cup reduced clam juice or fish stock (see p. 51)
  1/2 cup heavy cream
 1-2 teaspoons tomato paste
    Salt and freshly ground pepper to taste
    Tabasco sauce to taste

Prepare according to the directions for Basic Béchamel (p. 245).

CRAB MEAT VELOUTÉ *yields about 3 cups*

Use this wonderful sauce with Seafood Mousse Pockets or Seafood Mousse Strudel Slices.

  4 Tablespoons (1/2 stick) butter
  4 Tablespoons all-purpose flour
  1 cup reduced clam juice or reduced fish stock simmered with shrimp shells*
  1 cup heavy cream
  1 Tablespoon tomato paste
  1 teaspoon lemon juice, or to taste
    A few drops Tabasco sauce
    Salt to taste
 6-8 ounces crab meat, preferably fresh

Melt the butter in a medium-size saucepan with a stainless steel or enamel surface. Add the flour and whisk the gently bubbling mixture over medium heat for a minute or two, being careful that the mixture or "roux" keeps its golden color and does not burn. Add the clam juice or stock and cream and whisk constantly until the mixture thickens to the desired sauce consistency. Add tomato paste, lemon juice, Tabasco, and salt, stirring until the tomato paste is mixed in evenly. Stir in the crab meat. Taste for seasoning.

*For the best flavor, simmer shrimp shells in 2 cups (16 ounces) clam juice. Drain the liquid and reduce it to 1 cup.

PESTO SAUCE *yields enough for 1 pound of pasta*

Toss your pasta with 2–4 Tablespoons butter before adding pesto.

  2 cloves garlic
  1 cup basil leaves, packed
½ cup olive oil
¾ cup freshly grated Parmesan cheese
  1 cup finely chopped walnuts
½ teaspoon salt

Place the garlic in the work bowl of a food processor and process until it is minced fine. Add the basil leaves and process. Add the oil gradually through the feed tube while the motor is running. When the basil is minced fine add the grated Parmesan, walnuts, and salt and process just until mixed.

FROZEN PESTO CUBES *yields 6 cubes*

4 cloves garlic
2 cups basil leaves, packed
1 teaspoon salt
    About ½ cup olive oil

Prepare according to the directions for Pesto Sauce (preceding recipe), adding just enough olive oil to mix and bind the fresh basil. Spoon into plastic ice cube trays and freeze. Remove the frozen cubes and store in plastic bags. Use half or whole cubes when basil is called for in a recipe.

PROCESSOR OR BLENDER HOLLANDAISE *yields about ¾ cup*

Additional flavorings for your Hollandaise might include minced dill or minced capers. Consider using 1 Tablespoon raspberry vinegar instead of lemon juice.

4 egg yolks
1 Tablespoon freshly squeezed lemon juice
8 Tablespoons (1 stick) butter, melted and
    bubbling hot
    Salt to taste
    Tabasco sauce to taste

Place the yolks in the work bowl of a food processor along with the lemon juice. With the motor running add the bubbling hot butter gradually through the feed tube in a thin stream. Season with salt and Tabasco sauce to taste. If you are not using the Hollandaise immediately, keep it warm in a bowl set over simmering water.

FISH AND SEAFOOD MOUSSES

Years ago when I purchased my first food processor, there was included a recipe for a seafood paste bound with egg and lightened with heavy cream then formed into nuggets rolled in crumbs and sautéed in butter. The result was airy and velvety smooth, the flavor rich yet elusive. The uncooked paste was so easy to make and to work with that it inspired me to all kinds of creative uses: stuffing pasta and phyllo and flaky pastry as well as producing beautifully layered loaves of different-colored mousse mixtures. Until the advent of the food processor, mousses existed almost entirely in professional kitchens. Now, mousses and the wonderful uses to which they can be put are well within the reach of any home cook who owns this tool.

Seafood mousse begins with raw fish or seafood or a combination of the two. For fish mousse choose flounder or sole or chowder fish (which is inexpensive and often a lovely combination of pieces from different white fishes). If you use chowder fish, try to pick out pieces without bones or skin. For seafood mousse, use a combination of shrimp and scallops (and chowder fish—which will cut the expense a little). And for a softly shaded pink mousse choose salmon.

Put the fish or seafood, cut up into chunks, into the work bowl of your processor and process until it is the consistency of a paste. Add egg, egg yolk, or egg white as called for in the recipe and process until well blended. Next, with the processor running add heavy cream in a thin stream through the feed tube. If you are using shrimp in your mousse, cook the shrimp shells in clam juice or fish stock, strain, then reduce to about 1 Tablespoon. When it is cool, add enough cream to measure what is called for in the recipe. Use this "fortified" cream to lend an extra depth of flavor to any mousse.

After you have added the cream, stir down any unprocessed fish that is adhering to the sides of the work bowl. Process to mix. Add the flavorings or seasonings called for and again process to mix. Taste a small amount of the raw mixture or sauté a tiny mousse pancake to see what flavor adjustments or additions are needed.

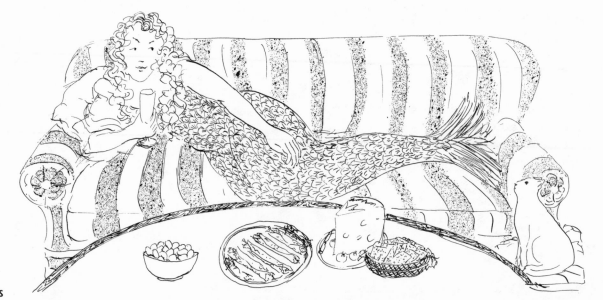

SEAFOOD MOUSSE I *yields 1 cup*

6 ounces white fish, such as flounder, sole, or
  chowder fish*
1 egg white
1/4 cup plus 2 Tablespoons heavy cream
2-4 drops Tabasco sauce
  About 1/2 teaspoon salt, or to taste
2 ounces smoked salmon, minced fine, plus
  1 Tablespoon minced capers or minced fresh
  dill to taste
        or
4 anchovies, minced, plus 2 Tablespoons
  (or more) minced fresh dill

Prepare according to the directions on page 248.

*You can also use a mixture of white fish and shrimp.

SEAFOOD MOUSSE III *yields about 3 cups*

1 recipe Seafood Mousse II (preceding recipe)
1-2 anchovies, rinsed, patted dry, and minced
1/4 cup freshly grated Parmesan cheese
4 ounces scallops, diced*
4 ounces mushrooms, sliced thin
1 Tablespoon butter

Add to the Seafood Mousse II the anchovies and
grated Parmesan. Sauté the scallops and mushrooms in the butter. When they are cool, fold the
scallops and mushrooms into the mousse mixture.

*You can substitute fresh crab meat for the scallops.

SEAFOOD MOUSSE II *yields 2 cups*

12 ounces mixed seafood:
  4 ounces white fish, such as flounder, sole,
  or chowder fish, cut up into pieces
  4 ounces raw shrimp, shelled and deveined
  4 ounces scallops
1 egg
1/2 cup heavy cream
1 1/2 teaspoons salt, or to taste
6 drops Tabasco sauce

Prepare according to the directions on page 248.

SEAFOOD MOUSSE IV *yields about 4 1/2 cups*

1/2 pound uncooked shelled shrimp*
1/2 pound scallops
1/2 pound chowder fish, sole, or flounder
1 egg plus 1 white
1 1/2 cups heavy cream
2 teaspoons freshly squeezed lemon juice
2 teaspoons salt
6-8 drops Tabasco sauce

Prepare according to directions on page 248.

*Buy a little more than 1/2 pound unshelled shrimp and use the shells to
prepare stock.

SALMON MOUSSE *yields 2 cups*

12 ounces skinned and boned fresh salmon fillet,
   cut into pieces
1 egg yolk or egg white
1 cup heavy cream
1 teaspoon salt
1 teaspoon freshly squeezed lemon juice, or
   to taste
   Dash Tabasco sauce

Prepare according to the directions on page 248.

MUSHROOM DUXELLES *yields 1 1/2 cups*

Duxelles are simple to prepare, freeze perfectly in plastic-wrap packages, and provide an intensity of mushroom that glorifies any recipe that calls for them. Tamari or soy sauce heightens the musky mushroom flavor of duxelles, and wines and herbs broaden and give it depth.

1 pound mushrooms, rinsed and well drained
2 Tablespoons (1/4 stick) butter
1/4 cup finely minced onion, or 1-2 Tablespoons
   minced shallot
1-2 Tablespoons soy sauce or tamari
1 Tablespoon sherry, Madeira, or Marsala
1 teaspoon freshly squeezed lemon juice or
   tarragon vinegar
   Salt and freshly ground pepper to taste
   Tabasco sauce to taste
1 teaspoon dried herb of choice, such as
   tarragon, chive, dill (optional)

Chop the mushrooms medium fine by hand or in the food processor. (If using the processor, break the mushrooms up by hand directly into the food processor and chop in 2-3 batches.) Melt the butter in a wok or large sauté pan and sauté the onion or shallot until tender. Raise the heat to high. Add the chopped mushrooms and sauté until the mushrooms begin to lose their raw color and exude liquid. Add the soy sauce or tamari, wine, and lemon juice or tarragon vinegar and cook over high heat until all the liquid is evaporated and the mushroom mixture is fairly dry. Season with salt and pepper, a drop or two of Tabasco sauce, and herbs, if you like.

MUSHROOM
PECAN FILLING *yields 2¹/2-3 cups*

A delicious and versatile mushroom filling for turn-overs, strudels, crêpes, and tortellini—anywhere you would like a mushroom filling, including mushrooms.

1 pound mushrooms, rinsed and well drained
2 Tablespoons (¹/4 stick) butter
1 cup (or more) chopped scallion
1 large clove garlic, minced
1 Tablespoon soy sauce or tamari
1 Tablespoon sherry or Madeira
1 teaspoon freshly squeezed lemon juice, or to taste
3 ounces cream cheese, softened and broken up
¹/2 cup (2 ounces) grated Cheddar or Swiss cheese
¹/2 cup freshly grated Parmesan cheese
1 cup finely chopped but not powdered pecans
1 egg yolk
Salt and freshly ground pepper to taste

Prepare according to the directions for Mushroom Duxelles (preceding recipe), substituting the scallion for the onion and adding garlic. When the excess mushroom liquid has been cooked off and the duxelles are dry, add the cream cheese, grated Cheddar or Swiss, and grated Parmesan and stir until the cheese is completely mixed in then mix in the pecans. When the mushroom mixture has cooled, stir in the egg yolk and season with salt and pepper.

MUSHROOM
MARSALA FILLING *yields about 1 ³/4 cups*

Another fine mushroom filling. Add a little grated Bruder Basil cheese for a lovely smoky flavor.

¹/4 cup finely minced onion
2 Tablespoons (¹/4 stick) butter
1 pound mushrooms, chopped, but not too fine
2 Tablespoons Marsala
1 Tablespoon soy sauce or tamari
1 teaspoon freshly squeezed lemon juice, or to taste
A few drops Tabasco sauce
Salt and freshly ground pepper to taste
3 ounces cream cheese, softened
1 small bunch parsley leaves, minced fine
¹/4 cup freshly grated Parmesan cheese
¹/4 cup bread crumbs
1 egg yolk

In a wok or large sauté pan sauté the onion in butter until it is tender. Add the mushrooms and sauté over high heat until they begin to lose their raw color and exude their liquid. Add the Marsala, soy sauce or tamari, lemon juice, Tabasco sauce, and salt and pepper and continue cooking over high heat until all the liquid is evaporated and the mushroom mixture is dry. Reduce the heat. Add the cream cheese, stirring gently until it is melted. Remove the pan from the heat and stir in the parsley, grated Parmesan, and bread crumbs. When the mixture has cooled, stir in the egg yolk. Taste for seasoning.

MUSHROOM MARSALA AND RICOTTA FILLING *yields 5 cups*

Use 2¹/2 cups to stuff tortellini, ravioli, or cannelloni made with spinach pasta.

- 1 medium onion, minced fine
- 2 large cloves garlic, minced
- 2 Tablespoons (¹/4 stick) butter
- 1 pound mushrooms, chopped fine
- 2 Tablespoons Marsala
- 1 Tablespoon soy sauce or tamari (optional)
- 1 bunch parsley leaves, minced fine
  Salt and freshly ground pepper to taste
- 1 pound ricotta cheese, or use the 15-ounce container if that is what you have (about 2 cups)
- ¹/2 pound grated Italian fontina or mozzarella
- 1 cup freshly grated Parmesan or other hard grating cheese
- 1 egg plus 1 yolk
  A few gratings of fresh nutmeg

Sauté the onion and garlic in butter until the onion is tender. Add the chopped mushrooms and sauté over high heat until they lose their raw color and exude their liquid. Add the Marsala and optional soy sauce or tamari and continue to cook the mushroom mixture over high heat until all the liquid is evaporated. Mix in the minced parsley and season with salt and pepper to taste. Set aside to cool.

Combine the ricotta, grated fontina and Parmesan cheeses, egg and egg yolk, and nutmeg. Stir in the cooled mushroom mixture. Taste for seasoning, adding additional salt and pepper as needed.

SEASONED BEAN PUREE *yields 1¹/2 cups*

This healthy unfried version of refried beans contributes to mouth-watering tostadas, savory Mexican hors d'oeuvres and main course pastries, and an unusual Mexican stuffed pasta salad. For flavor and texture variations add grated cheese, chopped scallion, chopped green chilis, chopped green or black olives, and tomato paste.

- ¹/2 cup chopped onion
- ¹/4-¹/2 cup chopped green or red bell pepper
- 2 large cloves garlic, minced
- 1 Tablespoon oil
- 1 teaspoon cumin seed
- 1 teaspoon chili powder
  One 1-pound can kidney or black beans
  Salt to taste
  Tabasco sauce to taste

In a wok or medium sauté pan sauté the onion, green or red pepper, and garlic in the oil until they are softened. Add the cumin and chili powder and sauté briefly. Add the beans and cook, covered, over medium heat for 5 minutes to blend flavors. Uncover, raise the heat to medium-high or high and cook, stirring frequently, until the mixture is very thick. Mash the beans with the back of a wooden spoon or puree in the food processor. Adjust the seasoning and add salt and Tabasco sauce to taste.

BEAN FILLING *yields 3 cups*

1 cup finely chopped onion
2 large cloves garlic, minced
2 Tablespoons olive oil
1 teaspoon thyme
1 teaspoon oregano
1 teaspoon basil
  Two 1-pound cans kidney beans, drained of most excess liquid
1/3 cup freshly grated Parmesan cheese
1 Tablespoon tomato paste
  Salt and freshly ground pepper to taste
1 egg yolk

Sauté the onion and garlic in the olive oil until the onion is tender. Add the herbs and sauté an additional few seconds. Add the kidney beans and some of the liquid from the can. Cover and cook over medium-high heat for 5 minutes to blend flavors and soften the beans further. Remove the cover and cook, stirring often, until the liquid is completely evaporated and the beans are beginning to stick to the pan.

Add the beans to the bowl of a food processor and process until they are smooth and creamy or mash by hand or with an electric mixer. Add the grated Parmesan, tomato paste, and salt and pepper to taste. When the mixture has cooled slightly, mix in the egg yolk.

CHEESE BEAN FILLING *yields about 2 cups*

1 cup Seasoned Bean Puree (p. 252)
4 ounces Cheddar cheese, grated
1/4 cup chopped green chilis or minced green olives, or to taste
2-4 Tablespoons minced scallion
2 Tablespoons freshly grated Parmesan cheese
1 Tablespoon tomato paste
  Salt to taste
  Tabasco sauce to taste
  Chili powder to taste (optional)
  Garlic powder to taste (optional)

Combine all the ingredients. Use in hors d'oeuvre pastries or as a spread for tostadas or Mexican crêpes.

PICADILLO *yields about 3 1/2 cups*

A versatile meat mixture—delicious in pastry, surrounded by brioche, or simply glorifying a tortilla. I often add a 1-pound can of drained kidney beans when I add the tomatoes.

1 1/2 cups chopped onion
   1 large red or green pepper, diced fine
1–2 large cloves garlic, minced fine
   2 tablespoons oil
   1 pound lean ground beef
      One 1-pound can tomatoes
  1/4 cup raisins
  1/4 cup pimento-stuffed olives
   2 Tablespoons red wine
   1 Tablespoon A-1 or Worcestershire sauce
   1 Tablespoon capers
   2 teaspoons salt
   6 dashes Tabasco sauce, or to taste

Sauté the onion, pepper, and garlic in oil until they are softened. Add the ground beef and sauté, breaking it up with a wooden spoon, until it loses its raw color. (If there is excess fat from the beef, pour it off.) Add the tomatoes, raisins, olives, red wine, A-1 or Worcestershire sauce, capers, salt, and Tabasco sauce and simmer, uncovered, over medium-high heat for about 30 minutes, or until the excess liquid is evaporated.

KASHA WITH HERBS *yields 3 cups*

Use in Kasha and Potato Pie or as a stuffing for chicken or turkey. Add slightly more stock to the kasha (1 1/2 cups) and serve as a side dish with bluefish brochettes or crispy fried fish.

   1 bunch scallions, minced
   1 medium onion, chopped fine
   1 large red bell pepper, diced (use green pepper if red are not available)
   2 Tablespoons (or more) oil, butter, or chicken fat
  3/4 teaspoon tarragon
  1/2 teaspoon basil
   1 cup medium kasha (buckwheat groats)
1 1/4 cups (or more) chicken stock (see p. 50), heated
   1 teaspoon salt
      Freshly ground pepper to taste

Sauté the scallions, onion, and bell pepper in oil, butter, or chicken fat until the onion begins to color slightly. Add the tarragon, basil, and kasha and sauté until all the grains are coated with oil and give off a slightly roasted aroma. Stir in hot stock, salt, and pepper. Cover and cook over low heat for 5–10 minutes.

BROWN RICE *serves 2-3*

This is my favorite way to prepare rice. It comes out dry, not mushy, and tenderly al dente. If you happen to prefer a softer grain, add a little more water and increase the cooking time.

3/4 cup short-grain brown rice, rinsed
1 1/4 cups water

Bring the rice and water to a boil in a small saucepan. Cover. Turn the heat to low and cook for 20-25 minutes. Turn the heat off and let sit for at least 10-15 minutes.

POTATO CHEESE
FILLING I *yields about 3 cups, enough to fill 14-18 pierogin*

1 1/2 pounds potatoes
4 ounces mild cheese, such as Muenster or Jack, grated
1/2 cup cottage cheese
Salt and freshly ground pepper to taste

Scrub or peel the potatoes. Slice then cook until tender in enough water to cover. Boil off the excess water or drain it and save it for bread making, soup, etc. Continue to dry out the potatoes over heat until they are about to stick to the pan—to ensure that the filling will not have excess liquid and be too loose. Add the cheeses and mash, or beat with an electric mixer until smooth and creamy. Season with salt and pepper to taste. The filling is easiest to stuff pierogin with if it is cold, so refrigerate it for several hours or overnight.

DILLED POTATO
CHEESE FILLING II *yields about 3 cups*

Both this filling and the following recipe are delicious for phyllo turnovers and individual strudels.

1 1/2 pounds potatoes
4 ounces dilled Havarti, grated
3 ounces cream cheese, softened
Salt and freshly ground pepper to taste
Fresh or dried dill (optional)

Peel and cut up the potatoes. Cook until tender, draining or boiling off the excess water. Add the Havarti and cream cheese and beat with an electric mixer or mash until the cheese is melted and the mixture is smooth and creamy. Season with salt and pepper to taste. Add dill if you would like a more definitive dill flavor.

RICH POTATO
CHEESE FILLING III *yields about 3 cups*

1 1/2 pounds potatoes
2 ounces Bruder Basil (smoked cheese), grated
4 ounces cream cheese, softened
Salt and freshly ground pepper to taste

Prepare according to the directions for Dilled Potato Cheese Filling II (preceding recipe).

PARSNIP FILLING *yields about 3 cups*

½ cup finely diced onion
2 Tablespoons (¼ stick) butter
1½–1¾ pounds parsnips, peeled and cut
    into chunks
½ cup cottage cheese
¼ cup minced parsley
1 teaspoon sugar
Salt and freshly ground pepper to taste

Sauté onion in butter until translucent and tender. Set aside. Cook parsnips in water until tender. Boil or drain off excess water, continuing to cook parsnips over medium heat until they are quite dry and almost beginning to stick to the pan. Mash or process parsnips together with the sautéed onion and cottage cheese until the mixture is smooth and creamy. Add parsley, sugar, and salt and pepper and mix or process just until well combined.

PARSNIP AND SPINACH FILLING *yields about 3 cups*

Use as a filling for strudels, turnovers, and tortellini.

1¾–2 pounds parsnips, peeled and cut into chunks
    Dry or cream sherry
3 ounces cream cheese
    One 10-ounce package frozen chopped spinach, cooked, rinsed, and well squeezed
    Generous pinch of sugar
    Salt and freshly ground pepper to taste

Cook the parsnips until tender in enough water to cover. Add a splash of sherry to the cooking water for extra flavoring. Boil off or drain the excess cooking water then continue to cook the parsnips over medium heat until they are quite dry and beginning to stick. Add the cream cheese and beat with an electric mixer or process in a food processor until the parsnips are smooth and creamy. Mix in half the spinach and season with sugar, salt, and pepper to taste.

SPINACH MORNAY *yields about 2 cups*

2 Tablespoons (¼ stick) butter
2 Tablespoons all-purpose flour
⅔ cup heavy cream
2 Tablespoons freshly grated Parmesan cheese
    Dash garlic powder
    Salt and freshly ground pepper to taste
    Two 10-ounce packages frozen chopped spinach, cooked and well squeezed

Melt the butter in a small stainless steel or enamel saucepan. Add the flour and whisk over medium heat for several minutes, letting the "roux" bubble gently. Be careful that it does not lose its golden color or burn. Add the cream and whisk constantly while the mixture thickens. Add the Parmesan cheese, garlic powder, and salt and pepper. Combine this mixture with the spinach. Taste for seasoning.

SEASONED EGGPLANT PUREE *yields 3 cups*

This puree is an excellent way to process and preserve eggplants when they are abundant and beautifully firm and ripe. Freeze the puree in 1-cup portions in plastic wrap. Use in sauces for pasta, as a filling for crêpes, and in the superb Eggplant Mushroom Quiche on page 82.

2 medium eggplants
 Salt
1 medium onion, chopped
2–3 cloves garlic, minced
3–4 Tablespoons olive oil
1 Tablespoon minced fresh basil, or
 1 teaspoon dried
2–3 Tablespoons water (use as little
 as possible)

Peel the eggplant and slice into 1/2-inch-thick slices. Salt both sides generously and lay them on paper towels for 30 minutes to drain. Pat them dry and cut into cubes.

 In a wok or large sauté pan sauté the onion and garlic in olive oil until the onion is softened. Add the eggplant cubes and sauté until the eggplant begins to color. Before the particles on the bottom of the pan get too brown, add the basil and water. Stir, cover, and steam until the eggplant is tender. Puree in a food processor or blender.

SPECIAL SZECHUAN MARINADE *yields about 1 cup*

Use in preparing Hoi Sin Spicy Chicken on a Skewer or as a marinade for seafood and fish. Multiply the recipe as needed.

3 Tablespoons soy sauce
1 Tablespoon hoi sin sauce
1 Tablespoon sugar
1 Tablespoon sesame oil
1 Tablespoon chili paste with garlic
1 teaspoon minced fresh gingerroot

Combine the ingredients.

NORMAN FINE'S CHINESE MARINADE *yields about 2 1/2 cups*

Use to marinate chicken or pork for 24 hours. This is enough marinade for 2 1/2–4 pounds of meat.

3/4 cup dry sherry
1 cup hoi sin sauce
1/4 cup soy sauce or tamari
1 medium onion, diced
5 large cloves garlic, smashed or chopped coarse
2 Tablespoons sugar
1 heaping teaspoon (or more) chili paste
 with garlic

Combine the ingredients.

GINGERED SHERRY

This is my foolproof method for always having available mild fresh ginger flavor for my stir-fry and Chinese hors d'oeuvre recipes. I don't have to worry about fresh ginger becoming moldy or dried out, and I never begin a Chinese recipe only to find out I don't have any or any usable ginger.

Buy 1 good-size piece of gingerroot. Peel the ginger and slice it any old way and put it in a clean jar. Fill the jar with dry sherry and refrigerate. Use in any recipe that calls for sherry.

If you would like a stronger ginger flavor, shave off a small piece of the ginger, mince, and add to the recipe. Preserved in this way, ginger keeps indefinitely, but generally when I get low on sherry I discard the old ginger and replenish with a new piece of ginger, more sherry, etc.

MAYONNAISE MARINADE FOR FISH *yields about 1/2 cup*

This marinade is particularly good with darker, full-flavored fish such as swordfish, bluefish, mackerel, and shark. Simply spread the fish fillets or steaks with the marinade and broil or bake. Or let the fish marinate, in fillets or in cubes for brochettes, in the mayonnaise for several hours. The marinade imparts a lovely flavor—and a beautiful crisp finish.

1/3 cup mayonnaise
  1 Tablespoon grainy or Dijon mustard
1/2 Tablespoon soy sauce or tamari
1/2 teaspoon tarragon, rosemary, or dill
    Dash garlic powder, or to taste
    Freshly ground pepper to taste

Combine the ingredients. Double or triple the recipe as needed.

DESSERTS

PIES AND TARTS	Sweet Pastry	

PIES AND TARTS
Sweet Pastry
Sweet Lattice Tart Pastry
Blueberry Praline Tart
Cranberry Praline Tart
Plum Praline Tart
Favorite Apple Pie
Lattice Summer Fruit Tart
Amaretto Pear Tart
Fresh Blueberry or Strawberry Almond Tart
Fresh Fruit and Custard Pie with a Difference
Pastry Cream
Chocolate Velvet Pie
Chocolate-flavored Whipped Cream
Honey Rum Ricotta and Pecan Pie
Honey Rum Sauce with Fruit
Raisin d'Être
Banana Raisin Walnut Lattice Tart

CAKES
Double Chocolate Bourbon Cake
Bourbon Cream Cheese Frosting
Double Chocolate Mousse Cake
Walnut Ultimate
Walnut Ultimate with Chocolate Mousse
Pastry for Cheesecakes
Amaretto Cheesecake with Chocolate Sour Cream Glaze
Chocolate Sour Cream Glaze
Orange Praline Cheesecake
Prune Marvel Loaf for Colleen
Peach Torte
Plum Kuchen
Banana Nut Roll
Rum Cream Cheese Filling
Chocolate Cream Cheese Filling
Carrot Nut Roll
Orange Cream Cheese Filling

Orange Buttercream
Marsala Raisin Pound Cake
Orange Poppy Seed Cake

DESSERT BARS AND SQUARES
Pecan Buttercrunch Bars
Luscious Chocolate Nut Bars
Linzer Almond Shortbread Squares
Orange Lemon Coconut Squares
Aunt Clara's Brownies
Rum Raisin Squares

MISCEL-LANEOUS TREATS
Praline
Orange Praline
Chocolate Praline or Orange Praline with Chocolate
Praline Parfait Cloud
Chocolate Mousse
Chocolate Mousse Praline Parfait
Chocolate-dipped Stuffed Prunes
Chocolate Banana Nut Strudel
Zabaglione

Whether to eat desserts, and how much, seems to me to be a very personal matter, one that each of us works out in a quiet (or unquiet) place of the soul. Desserts simply have no justification for being other than sheer deliciousness, so above all they should taste sublime. If one is going to surrender, surrender should be sweet indeed.

SWEET PASTRY *yields 9-inch crust*

- 1 cup all-purpose flour
- 6 Tablespoons (3/4 stick) butter
- 1 Tablespoon sugar
- 1/2 teaspoon salt
- 1 Tablespoon kirsch, Grand Marnier, rum, brandy, or liqueur of choice
- 1 egg, or 2 Tablespoons heavy cream

For directions on making this pastry, see general pastry directions on pages 75–76.

SWEET LATTICE TART PASTRY *yields 9-inch crust plus lattice*

- 1 1/2 cups all-purpose flour
- 10 Tablespoons (1 1/4 sticks) butter
- 1 Tablespoon sugar
- 1/2 teaspoon salt
- 1 egg
- 1 Tablespoon (or more) kirsch, Grand Marnier, rum, brandy, or liqueur of choice

For directions on making this pastry, see general pastry directions on pages 75–76.

BLUEBERRY PRALINE TART *serves 6-8*

This is one of my favorite desserts. It is elegant and sensuous with its buttery pastry, thin vein of praline, velvety kirsch-touched custard, and sweet-tart fruit counterpoint. I prepared it for a friend, a serious critic and taster of all things that go in the mouth, who called me back after her dinner party exclaiming that the tart was simply orgasmic—her highest compliment. It is at its best served warm. If the tart has been prepared ahead and refrigerated, warm in a slow oven (about 300°F). Serve plain or, as my friend did, with crème fraîche. This dessert freezes well.

   1 recipe Sweet Pastry, prepared with kirsch (p. 261)
  3/4 cup plus 2 Tablespoons Praline (p. 286)*
 1 1/3 cups heavy cream
 1 1/4 cups confectioners sugar
   2 eggs plus 1 yolk
 1 1/2 Tablespoons kirsch**
   2 Tablespoons all-purpose flour
     Pinch of salt
1 1/2-2 cups blueberries, preferably fresh
     Additional confectioners sugar (optional)

Preheat the oven to 400°F. Butter the bottom and sides of a 9-inch springform pan or removable-bottom cake pan.

Prepare Sweet Pastry and pat it onto the bottom of the pan, pushing the pastry dough up the edges of the pan very slightly. Prick the dough with a fork and bake for 10 minutes. Spread 3/4 cup of the Praline over the crust, reserving 2 Tablespoons. Pat down gently but firmly and bake for an additional 10 minutes. Remove from the oven and reduce the heat to 375°F.

Prepare the filling. Place the heavy cream, confectioners sugar, eggs and egg yolk, kirsch, flour, and salt in the container of a blender or food processor and blend or process until smooth.

Cover the Praline-coated pastry completely with blueberries, then pour in the custard filling gently (the blueberries will float on top), sprinkle with the remaining 2 Tablespoons Praline, and bake for 40-50 minutes, or until the custard is golden and a knife inserted into the center comes out clean. Sprinkle lightly with confectioners sugar, if you wish, before serving.

CRANBERRY PRALINE TART

Follow directions for Blueberry Praline Tart but substitute 1 1/4-1 1/2 cups chopped cranberries for the blueberries, prepare Orange Praline, and use orange liqueur in the filling. Sprinkle the top of the tart generously with confectioners sugar while it is still warm from the oven.

Note: Although blueberry is my favorite, cranberries make an attractive winter tart.

PLUM PRALINE TART

Substitute 4 large *ripe* purple plums for the blueberries. (You might like to experiment with plum varieties to see which you like best—the purple

---

*If you are preparing the Praline fresh for this recipe, swirl some of the heavy cream or kirsch in the Praline pan over medium heat after you have removed the Praline. The caramel left in the pan will melt into the cream or kirsch and add additional flavor to the tart.
**I'm *very* partial to kirsch with custards, but brandy, rum, or orange liqueur can also be used.

plums seem to have the best color when baked.) Cut the plums in half and remove the pits. Arrange 7 of the plum halves, cut side up, around the circumference of the pan, leaving 1/2–3/4 inch space between the plums and the pan. Place the remaining plum half in the center. Pour in the custard filling

gently until it reaches, but does not cover, the tops of the plums.

Note: This tart is a visual work of art. The purple plums, when baked, become shimmering deeps of color and are wonderful tart-sweet mouthfuls.

FAVORITE APPLE PIE *yields 9-inch pie*

I am absolutely powerless before this apple-y, buttery, juicy, golden pie.

  2 recipes Sweet Pastry (p. 261)*
6–7 large tart apples, or Cortlands sprinkled with
      lemon juice
  1 cup sugar
  3 Tablespoons all-purpose flour
      Pinch of salt
      Butter

Preheat the oven to 450°F.

Roll out slightly more than half the dough and line a 9-inch pie pan, allowing the dough to hang over the edge of the pan. Peel, core, and slice the apples thin. Combine the sugar, flour, and salt and

sprinkle a few Tablespoons of this mixture into the bottom of the pie shell. Alternately layer the sliced apples, sugar mixture, and generous dots of butter until all the ingredients are used, ending with a sprinkling of sugar and dots of butter. Roll out the remaining pastry and cover the pie with it. Trim and crimp the edges. Make a few decorative slits in the top crust with a sharp knife.

Wrap a small piece of aluminum foil around a wooden spoon handle to form a tube and place this foil tube, still wrapped around the handle, in the center of the pie. Remove the spoon handle and you have formed a steam escape.

Bake the pie for 10 minutes at 450°F then reduce the temperature to 350°F and bake for 40 minutes more, or until the pastry is golden. Serve warm.

*Omit liqueur. Instead use 1 egg beaten with 3–4 Tablespoons cream.

LATTICE SUMMER FRUIT TART *yields 9-inch tart*

Light and fruity—a lovely summer tart.

- 1 recipe Sweet Lattice Tart Pastry (p. 261)
- 1 Tablespoon kirsch, rum, or brandy
- 1 teaspoon cornstarch
- 1/3 cup plus 1 Tablespoon granulated sugar
- 2 Tablespoons sour cream
- 1/4 teaspoon vanilla extract
  Pinch of salt
- 3 cups ripe fruit:
  6 peaches, peeled and sliced, or
  5 peaches, peeled and sliced, plus 1 cup
  blueberries or raspberries, or
  6 plums, sliced thin
- 1 Tablespoon butter
  Confectioners sugar

Preheat the oven to 400°F.

Roll out two thirds of the pastry dough and fit it into a 9-inch removable-bottom tart pan or spring-form pan, forming sides about 1 inch high. Prick the bottom of the dough with a fork, press aluminum foil in over the dough, and fill the foil with rice or beans, then bake for 10 minutes. Remove the foil and rice or beans and bake for an additional 10 minutes.

Mix together the kirsch and cornstarch until the cornstarch is dissolved. Add 1/3 cup of the granulated sugar, the sour cream, vanilla, and salt and stir until they are well combined. Add the fruit and stir gently until all fruit is coated lightly. Turn the fruit into the prebaked shell. Sprinkle with the remaining Tablespoon of the granulated sugar and dot with the butter.

Roll out the remaining one third of pastry dough and cut strips 1/2 inch wide. Use the strips to form a lattice crust or a shell pattern with "spokes" radiating from the center of the pie. Trim the excess pastry, but attach the edge of each strip to the prebaked crust by pressing gently with the back of the tines of a fork.

Bake for 40-45 minutes. Let cool slightly and dust with confectioners sugar before serving. If the tart is prepared ahead and refrigerated, warm slightly before serving.

AMARETTO PEAR TART *yields 9-inch tart*

1 recipe Sweet Pastry (p. 261), prepared with
   Amaretto plus cream and 1/2 teaspoon
   almond extract
3 large almost-ripe pears
1 lemon, cut into wedges
4 Tablespoons (1/2 stick) butter
4 Tablespoons granulated sugar
2 Tablespoons Amaretto
1 cup light cream
2 egg yolks
1/4 cup confectioners sugar
   Grated chocolate or Praline (p. 286) made
   with unblanched almonds

Preheat the oven to 400°F.

Roll out the dough and fit it into a 9-inch removable-bottom tart pan. Prick the bottom of the dough with a fork, press aluminum foil in over the dough, and fill with rice or beans. Bake for 10 minutes, remove the foil and rice or beans then bake for 10 minutes more. Remove the crust from oven and reduce the heat to 375°F.

Peel and halve the pears. Using a melon baller remove the center part with the seeds then, with a melon baller or a sharp knife, cut away the pithy part that runs down the length of the pear. Rub the pears all over with a cut lemon wedge to keep them from discoloring.

Melt the butter and granulated sugar together in a sauté pan. Mix in the Amaretto, add the pear halves, and sauté them over medium-high heat, turning occasionally, for 10–15 minutes. (The amount of time will depend on the ripeness of your pears. Pears are done when they are tender but not mushy.) Remove the pears with a slotted spoon and slice each pear half into 1/8-inch crosswise slices, holding them together to keep their original shape. Lift each sliced pear half carefully with a spatula and transfer it to the pastry shell. Arrange the pears, rounded sides up, so that the narrow (stem) ends of each meet in the center of the tart. When all the pears are in place push each one gently from the center to the rim so that the slices separate slightly and you end up with the pear shape kept intact but with overlapping, slightly angled slices. This makes a very pretty pattern after the custard is baked.

Boil the butter-sugar-Amaretto mixture down to a thick syrup. Add the light cream and whisk until well mixed. Beat together the egg yolks with a little of the warm cream mixture, then whisk the egg yolks and the confectioners sugar into the cream. Pour this custard slowly around the pears, using as much as you need to bring the custard almost to the top of the pears. (You want to be able to see the attractive pattern of the slices.) Bake the tart for 35 minutes, or until a knife inserted into the center of the custard comes out clean. You can decorate the tart by grating chocolate lightly over it when it has cooled or sprinkling with almond Praline.

FRESH BLUEBERRY OR STRAWBERRY ALMOND TART *yields 9-inch tart*

Ambrosial—nutty, crisp, juicy, and fresh. Blueberries are my favorite fruit choice for it.

1 recipe Sweet Pastry (p. 261)
2 cups (2 recipes) Praline (p. 286), made with unblanched almonds*
2 eggs
1 Tablespoon brandy or rum
Pinch of salt
1/3 cup apricot preserves
1 pint blueberries or halved strawberries
Additional brandy or rum
Whipped cream

Preheat the oven to 400°F.

Roll out the dough and fit it into a 9-inch removable-bottom tart pan, springform pan (allow for 1-inch sides), or a regular pie pan with dough coming just to, not out over, the top of the pan.

Prick the bottom of the dough with a fork, press aluminum foil in over the dough, fill the foil with rice or beans, and bake for 10 minutes. Remove the foil and rice or beans and return to the oven for 5 minutes. Remove the crust from oven and reduce the heat to 375°F.

Combine the Praline, eggs, brandy or rum, and salt and turn into the pastry shell, smoothing it evenly. Bake for 12–15 minutes, or until the praline filling is puffed and golden. Let cool.

Melt the apricot preserves and brush generously over the filling, but reserve a little bit to use as a glaze. Cover completely with blueberries or halved strawberries. (If you are using strawberries and have blueberries on hand you can put a blueberry in the spaces between each strawberry.) Thin the reserved melted preserves with a little brandy or rum and brush this glaze lightly over the fruit. Refrigerate until ready to serve. Serve with whipped cream.

FRESH FRUIT AND CUSTARD PIE WITH A DIFFERENCE *yields 9-inch pie*

The "difference" is the thin layer of smooth, rich chocolate. Use any combination of fruits you prefer or use a single fruit such as all strawberries or all kiwi.

1 recipe Sweet Pastry (p. 261)
4 Tablespoons (1/2 stick) butter, softened

1/4 cup sugar
1/4 cup unsweetened cocoa
1 egg
3/4 Tablespoon brandy, kirsch, or orange liqueur
1/2 teaspoon vanilla extract
1 recipe Pastry Cream (following recipe), cooled
Assorted fresh fruits: strawberries, blueberries, green grapes
Apricot preserves
Brandy, rum, or orange liqueur

*If you are making the Praline fresh for this recipe, swirl some orange liqueur in the pan after you have turned the Praline out and use the Praline-flavored liqueur and a little vanilla extract to flavor the whipped cream topping.

Preheat the oven to 400°F.

Roll out the dough and fit it into a 9-inch pie pan or removable-bottom tart pan. Prick the bottom of the dough with a fork. Press aluminum foil in over the dough and fill the foil with rice or beans. Bake for 10 minutes. Remove the foil and rice or beans and bake for an additional 12–15 minutes, or until the pastry is lightly golden. Cool.

Process the butter, sugar, cocoa, egg, liqueur, and vanilla until completely smooth and creamy. Spread the bottom of the cooled pastry shell evenly with this chocolate mixture and refrigerate until it is firm.

Smooth cooled Pastry Cream over the chocolate base then arrange fresh fruit in a decorative pattern over the custard. (One suggestion: 4 strawberry halves in the center and strawberry halves around the perimeter of the pie with a circle of green grapes, then blueberries, then green grapes in between. Place blueberries around the edge in the small spaces between strawberries.)

Melt some apricot preserves. Add a little brandy or other liqueur to thin the preserves and brush this glaze over the fruit. Refrigerate until ready to serve.

PASTRY CREAM

1/2 cup sugar
 4 Tablespoons cornstarch
   Pinch of salt
 2 cups light cream
 4 egg yolks
 1 teaspoon vanilla extract
   Butter

In a medium-size, stainless steel or enamel saucepan combine the sugar, cornstarch, and salt. Add about 1/4 cup of the light cream and whisk until smooth. Add all but 1/4 cup of the remaining cream and cook, whisking regularly, over medium-high heat until the mixture is quite thick. Reduce the

heat. Beat the egg yolks with the remaining 1/4 cup of the cream then add to the hot mixture, whisking constantly. Cook over low heat until thick, being careful that the mixture does not boil. Stir in the vanilla. Dot the top of the warm custard with butter to prevent a skin from forming. Let cool then refrigerate until chilled. (Chilling will thicken the mixture more.) If you find that the chilled custard is lumpy, force it through a fine-mesh sieve before turning it into the pie shell.

CHOCOLATE VELVET PIE *serves 8-12*

Very chocolaty, very smooth, *very* rich (serve small slices), and very easy to make. Serve with fresh strawberries.

  1 recipe Sweet Pastry (p. 261)
 12 Tablespoons (1½ sticks) unsalted butter, softened
 ¾ cup sugar
 ¾ cup unsweetened cocoa
  3 eggs
  2 Tablespoons rum or liqueur of choice
 ½ teaspoon vanilla extract
    Pinch of salt
    Chocolate-flavored Whipped Cream (following recipe)
    Semisweet or unsweetened chocolate

Preheat the oven to 400°F.

Roll out the dough and fit it into a 9-inch removable-bottom tart pan or pie pan. Prick the dough with a fork, cover with aluminum foil, and fill the foil with rice or beans. Bake for 10 minutes. Remove the foil and rice or beans and bake for an additional 12-15 minutes, or until the crust is lightly golden. Let cool.

Process the butter, sugar, and cocoa until smooth and no longer granular. Add the eggs one at a time, processing until well mixed, and scraping down the sides of the work bowl as needed. When the mixture is very smooth, add the rum, vanilla, and salt and process just to mix. (The filling can also be prepared in a blender. Just add all the ingredients at once and blend until smooth.) Pour the filling into the baked and cooled shell and refrigerate until firmed. Pipe or spread Chocolate-flavored Whipped Cream over the filling and grate semisweet or unsweetened chocolate lightly over the whipped cream.

If the pie has been prepared in a pan with a removable bottom and you are serving it free-standing, it looks elegantly and seriously chocolaty as is and can be cut into thin wedges and placed on dessert plates with a dollop of whipped cream spooned over each slice.

CHOCOLATE-FLAVORED WHIPPED CREAM

Gelatin keeps the whipped cream in shape—no leaking. The pie can then be totally prepared hours in advance. If you wish, you can make the chocolate-flavored whipped cream without the gelatin and spread or pipe it over the pie just before serving.

 ¾ teaspoon unflavored gelatin
  1 Tablespoon water
  1 cup heavy cream
2-4 Tablespoons confectioners sugar
  2 Tablespoons crème de cacao, preferably white
½-1 teaspoon vanilla extract, or to taste

In a small measuring cup sprinkle the gelatin over the water and let it soften. Place the measuring cup in a pan of simmering water and heat until the gelatin dissolves completely. Set aside.

Beat the cream until it begins to thicken then add the sugar gradually while continuing to beat then pour the dissolved gelatin in a fine stream right in the path of the moving beaters. Beat until the cream is whipped and thick, being careful not to overbeat. Fold in the crème de cacao and vanilla.

HONEY RUM RICOTTA AND PECAN PIE *yields 9-inch pie*

1 recipe Sweet Pastry, prepared with rum (p. 261)
1 pound ricotta cheese
1/2 cup honey*
2 eggs
2 Tablespoons rum
1 Tablespoon all-purpose flour
1 teaspoon vanilla extract
1/2 teaspoon salt
1/4 cup finely chopped pecans
   Honey Rum Sauce with Fruit (following recipe)

Preheat the oven to 400°F.

Roll out the dough and fit it into a 9-inch removable-bottom tart pan. Prick the bottom of the dough with a fork, press aluminum foil in over the dough and fill with rice or beans, and bake for 10 minutes. Remove the foil and rice or beans and bake for an additional 10 minutes. Remove the pastry from the oven and reduce the heat to 350°F.

Process or beat together the ricotta cheese, honey, eggs, rum, flour, vanilla, and salt. When the mixture is well combined and smooth, stir in the pecans or process just to mix through. (Be careful not to overprocess.) Pour the ricotta mixture into the prebaked crust and bake for 50-60 minutes, or until the top of the pie is golden and a knife inserted into the center comes out clean. Serve at room temperature with a small amount of Honey Rum Sauce with Fruit spooned over each slice.

HONEY RUM SAUCE WITH FRUIT

This recipe makes a small amount of sauce (less than a cup), but it is to be spooned sparingly over the pie. If you like more sauce, by all means increase the recipe.

1/2 cup honey
1 Tablespoon rum
1 teaspoon freshly squeezed lemon juice
1 cup fresh blueberries or diced kiwi fruit

Warm the honey, rum, and lemon juice, stirring. Let cool to room temperature then add the fruit.

*If you find the taste of honey too strong, use half honey and half corn syrup.

RAISIN D'ÊTRE *yields 9-inch pie*

This is the ultimate raisin pie. I developed it for my ex-husband, Jack Golden, whose second-favorite food is raisins. Chocolate is number one.

1 Tablespoon rum
1 Tablespoon Grand Marnier or other
   orange liqueur
1 cup raisins
1 recipe Sweet Pastry, prepared with rum (p. 261)
1 cup sugar
6 Tablespoons (¾ stick) butter, softened
2 eggs
½ cup buttermilk or unflavored yogurt*
1 Tablespoon all-purpose flour
1 Tablespoon finely grated orange rind
½ teaspoon vanilla extract

Preheat the oven to 400°F.
   Pour the rum and Grand Marnier over the rai-sins and let them macerate for at least 1 hour, stirring occasionally. Roll out the dough and fit into a 9-inch pie pan or removable-bottom tart pan. Prick the bottom of the dough with a fork, press aluminum foil in over the dough and fill the foil with rice or beans. Bake for 10 minutes. Remove the foil and bake for 10 minutes more. Remove the pastry from the oven and reduce the heat to 375°F.
   Process or beat together the sugar, butter, and eggs until smooth. Add the buttermilk or yogurt then the flour, grated orange rind, and vanilla and process or mix until they are blended. (You can also put all the ingredients in the jar of a blender and blend until smooth and creamy.) Pour the macerated raisins into the bottom of the prebaked pie shell, spreading them evenly over the bottom. Pour in the filling gently and bake for 40–45 minutes, or until the filling is puffed and brown and a knife inserted into the center comes out clean.

BANANA RAISIN WALNUT LATTICE TART *yields 9-inch tart*

½ cup raisins
2 Tablespoons rum
2 Tablespoons orange juice
2 Tablespoons honey
2 Tablespoons granulated sugar
1 teaspoon (or more) finely grated orange rind
1 recipe Sweet Lattice Tart Pastry, prepared
   with rum (p. 261)
1½ pounds (about 3 medium) ripe but not soft
   bananas

½ cup broken or coarsely chopped walnuts
2 Tablespoons (¼ stick) butter
   Confectioners sugar

Preheat the oven to 400°F.
   Combine the raisins, rum, orange juice, honey, granulated sugar, and orange rind. Let macerate for 30–60 minutes, stirring occasionally.
   Roll out two thirds of the dough and fit it into a 9-inch removable-bottom tart pan or regular pie pan. Prick the bottom of the dough with a fork, press foil in over the pastry, and fill with rice or

*You can vary the filling and make it slightly lighter and less sweet by increasing the buttermilk or yogurt to 1 cup.

beans. Bake for 10 minutes. Remove the foil and rice or beans and bake for 10 more minutes. Remove the pastry and reduce the heat to 375°F.

Peel the bananas and slice 1/2 inch thick. (You should have about 2 cups.) Add the bananas and the walnuts to the raisin mixture, stirring gently. Turn the banana mixture into the prebaked pastry shell and dot with 1 Tablespoon of the butter. Roll out the remaining one third of the dough and cut it into 8 strips 1/2 inch wide. Form a lattice over the filling with the strips, cut off the excess pastry, and attach the edge of each strip to the prebaked crust by pressing gently with the back of the tines of a fork. Bake for 35–45 minutes, or until the pastry is golden. Midway through the baking, dot with the remaining Tablespoon of the butter.

Let cool slightly and sprinkle with confectioners sugar. Serve with vanilla ice cream.

DOUBLE CHOCOLATE BOURBON CAKE *yields two 9-inch round layers, serving 12–20 people*

This recipe is adapted from Maida Heatter's 86-Proof Chocolate Cake. It makes one of the all-time best chocolate cakes and leaves lovers of chocolate either exclaiming excitedly or moaning in helpless ecstasy. The relatively thin batter and slow baking at low temperature (not to mention the high chocolate and butter content) create an incomparable texture that manages to be light and dense at the same time. And the Bourbon Cream Cheese Frosting is just—the icing on the cake. Doing all the melting and mixing in 1 saucepan makes this, incredibly, one of the fastest and easiest cakes to prepare as well.

This is a lovely cake to give as a holiday gift. One recipe makes three 3 by 5-inch loaves for gift giving.

Or you can create cupcakes the likes of which you never had as a child. Place 1/3 cup batter in 24 paper baking cups (or make 1/2 recipe for 12). Bake for 35–40 minutes, or until the cupcakes test done. Frost with Bourbon Cream Cheese Frosting. (An exquisite picnic dessert.)

1 3/4 cups strong coffee
1/4 cup bourbon
5 squares (5 ounces) unsweetened chocolate
2 sticks (1/2 pound) butter, cut up
2 cups sugar
2 cups all-purpose flour
1 1/4 teaspoons baking soda
1/2 teaspoon salt
2 eggs
1 teaspoon vanilla extract
Bourbon Cream Cheese Frosting (following recipe)
Semisweet chocolate

Preheat the oven to 275°F. Butter two 9-inch cake pans. Lay a 12 by 4-inch strip of waxed paper down the center of each pan and up the sides; butter the waxed paper. (This will ensure that the center of the cake does not stick to the pan.) Dust the pans with unsweetened cocoa or flour; shake out excess.

Place the coffee, bourbon, chocolate, and butter

in a 2½-quart saucepan. Stir or whisk occasionally over medium heat until the chocolate and butter are melted. Add the sugar. Turn off the heat and let cool for 10-15 minutes, stirring occasionally to dissolve the sugar.

Sift together the flour, baking soda, and salt. Add the flour gradually to the chocolate mixture, beating with a whisk or an electric hand mixer on medium speed. Beat in the eggs then the vanilla. Pour the batter into the prepared pans and rap the pans gently on the counter to break air bubbles. Bake for 45-50 minutes, or until a toothpick inserted into the center comes out clean. Let the layers cool completely in the pans on a wire rack before removing.

The cake is easiest to frost when it is chilled. Turn the layers out of the pans onto sheets of waxed paper. (Before upending the pan, pull a little on the waxed paper under the cake to loosen it.) Refrigerate the layers until they are firm. Transfer to a cake form or dish and fill and frost with Bourbon Cream Cheese Frosting. Grate semisweet chocolate lightly over the top of the cake.

BOURBON CREAM CHEESE FROSTING

8 ounces cream cheese, softened
8 Tablespoons (1 stick) butter, softened
1 Tablespoon bourbon
1 Tablespoon crème de cacao, preferably white

½ teaspoon vanilla extract
2 pounds (7½ cups) confectioners sugar

Process or beat together the ingredients until they are smooth and creamy.

DOUBLE CHOCOLATE MOUSSE CAKE *serves 20-25 or more*

Double Chocolate Bourbon Cake becomes an even more stunning dessert when filled and frosted with Chocolate Mousse (p. 287).

Follow directions for preparing Double Chocolate Bourbon Cake but form 3 thinner layers instead of 2 and decrease baking time accordingly (to about 25-30 minutes). If you don't have three 9-inch cake pans, use a 9-inch springform pan for one of the layers. Make sure you line your pans with a buttered and floured strip of waxed paper to facilitate removal of the cooled layers.

Prepare a double recipe of Chocolate Mousse* and refrigerate several hours or overnight. It is easiest to work with cold cake and firm, chilled mousse, so I always prepare mousse and cake the day before I am assembling it. Spread the cake

*I double the recipe *and* add an extra ounce (1 square) of unsweetened chocolate—using a total of 17 ounces chocolate.

layers generously with the mousse, then cover the top and sides of the cake with mousse and smooth with a metal spatula. Use a piping bag to cover the top of the cake completely with a decorative layer of mousse swirls. (If you don't have a pastry bag, continue with a knife or spatula.)

Refrigerate the cake for several hours, or overnight, to make sure mousse is firm again before cutting. Serve the cake with lightly sweetened and liqueur-flavored whipped cream or with Praline Parfait Cloud (see page 287). Leftover cake, if there is any, can be frozen and enjoyed at a later time.

WALNUT ULTIMATE *serves at least 10-12*

Dense and rich with subtly explosive sweet-nut flavors and velvety buttercream. Small slices will do. If you have only 1 springform pan, you can prepare each layer separately (preparing half the recipe each time), freeze, remove the layer from the pan, then make the next layer. Prepare the cake ahead and freeze it, in layers or assembled.

cake
  4 extra-large egg whites
  ¼ teaspoon salt
  4 cups confectioners sugar
  1 pound walnut halves (about 4¼-4½ cups)
  1 teaspoon vanilla extract

buttercream
  2 sticks (½ pound) butter, preferably unsalted
     Pinch of salt (if using unsalted butter)
  2 egg yolks
  2 Tablespoons kirsch, or brandy or rum
  4 cups confectioners sugar
     Unsweetened or semisweet chocolate

Preheat the oven to 300°F. Butter the bottoms and sides of two 9-inch springform pans.

In a large bowl beat the egg whites and salt into fairly stiff peaks. Add 3½ cups of the sugar, beat slowly to mix, then beat at high speed for 2 minutes. (The whites will be thick and will not peak.)

Process the walnuts with the remaining ½ cup of sugar until they are very fine and powdery. Add the nuts and vanilla to the egg white mixture and beat until well combined. Divide the mixture between the 2 prepared pans and spread evenly. Bake 40-45 minutes, or until the top is golden and somewhat firm to the touch. Remove from the oven, let the layers cool, then carefully remove the sides of the pans and place the layers on the pan bottoms in the freezer for 1 hour.

To make the buttercream, process the butter, salt, egg yolks, kirsch, and confectioners sugar until smooth. Take the layers from the freezer. Spread one with a thin layer of buttercream. With a thin knife or spatula remove the other nut layer carefully from its pan and place it on the iced layer. Spread buttercream over top and sides just to cover. Grate chocolate over the buttercream (a Mouli grater works well) and pipe tiny rosettes around the rim with the remaining buttercream. Refrigerate until 30-60 minutes before serving.

WALNUT ULTIMATE WITH CHOCOLATE MOUSSE *serves 18–24*

As with Double Chocolate Bourbon Cake, Walnut Ultimate is raised to astonishing heights when filled and frosted with Chocolate Mousse.

Prepare Chocolate Mousse (see page 287) and refrigerate until firm. Prepare 2 Walnut Ultimate layers. Refrigerate—or better, freeze—them so you are working with cold firm layers. The top of each layer will be sunken. Use most of the mousse to fill the cavity formed by putting these 2 tops of the layers together—one upside-down. Use the remaining mousse to cover the sides and top with a thin, smooth chocolate coating. If you want a thicker mousse covering and topping, you will need to prepare a larger amount of mousse.

Decorate the circumference of the cake with candied violets or small whipped cream rosettes. Serve with whipped cream flavored with orange liqueur and grated orange rind.

The cool, creamy thickness of cheesecake demands attention. It's impossible not to savor each substantial and melting bite. Here are 2 very special examples. The Amaretto Cheesecake is subtly almond flavored with a rich, dark bittersweet glaze. The Orange Praline Cheesecake has a thin bottom striation of orange praline with an orange- and rum-flavored filling.

PASTRY FOR CHEESECAKES

¾ cup all-purpose flour
 6 Tablespoons (¾ stick) butter, cut into pieces
 1 Tablespoon sugar
¼ teaspoon salt
 1 Tablespoon liqueur that corresponds with the flavors in the cheesecake, such as Amaretto for Amaretto Cheesecake and rum for Orange Praline Cheesecake

For directions on making this pastry, see general pastry directions on pages 75–76.

AMARETTO CHEESECAKE WITH CHOCOLATE SOUR CREAM GLAZE

1 recipe Pastry for Cheesecakes (preceding recipe), prepared with Amaretto
24 ounces (three 8-ounce packages) cream cheese, softened
1½ cups sugar
6 eggs
2 cups sour cream
¼ cup Amaretto
1 teaspoon cornstarch
1 teaspoon vanilla extract
½ teaspoon almond extract
¼ teaspoon salt
Chocolate Sour Cream Glaze (following recipe)*
20 almonds, blanched and lightly toasted

Preheat the oven to 400°F.

Pat the dough into the bottom of a 9-inch springform pan. Bake for 15 minutes. Remove the pastry and reduce the heat to 325°F.

Process or cream together the cream cheese and 1 cup of the sugar until they are smooth. Separate 4 of the eggs. Add the egg yolks and the 2 whole eggs one at a time, processing continuously or beating well after each addition. Add the sour cream, Amaretto, cornstarch, and vanilla and almond extracts, and process or mix until well combined. In a large bowl beat the egg whites and salt until soft peaks form. Continue beating, adding the remaining ½ cup of the sugar gradually, until the whites are stiff but not dry. Pour the cream cheese mixture carefully into the egg white mixture and fold and stir with a wire whisk or rubber spatula until the two are well combined. Pour into the springform pan and bake 75 minutes. Turn the oven off and leave the door ajar for another 60 minutes. Remove the cake from the oven and let it come completely to room temperature, then refrigerate.

When cool, top with Chocolate Sour Cream Glaze, if desired, and decorate the edge of the cake with the almonds. Refrigerate for several hours before serving. If refrigerated overnight, remove from the refrigerator 1–2 hours or more before serving.

CHOCOLATE SOUR CREAM GLAZE

This is not a thick frosting, but a semisoft shiny glaze.

1 cup sugar
½ cup sour cream
2 squares (2 ounces) unsweetened chocolate
2 Tablespoons (¼ stick) butter
½ teaspoon vanilla extract
½ teaspoon almond extract

Combine the sugar, sour cream, chocolate, and butter in a small saucepan. Melt them together over low heat, stirring often. (Do not allow the mixture to come to a boil or it will be granular rather than velvety and smooth.) Stir in the vanilla and almond extracts. Let cool at room temperature until of spreading consistency.

*Amaretto Cheesecake is also delicious unglazed, but go all the way.

ORANGE PRALINE CHEESECAKE

1 recipe Pastry for Cheesecakes, prepared with orange liqueur or rum (p. 274)

1 recipe Orange Praline, prepared with pecans (p. 286)

24 ounces (three 8-ounce packages) cream cheese, softened

1¼ cups sugar

6 eggs

2 cups sour cream

2 Tablespoons orange liqueur

2 Tablespoons rum

1 teaspoon cornstarch

1 teaspoon vanilla extract

½ teaspoon orange extract, or grated rind of 1 orange

¼ teaspoon salt

3 orange sections, skin and pith removed
Chopped pecans

Preheat the oven to 375°F.

Pat the dough into the bottom of a 9-inch springform pan. Bake for 10 minutes. Pour in the Orange Praline, smooth evenly over the crust, pat down gently and bake for an additional 5 minutes.

Remove the pastry from the oven and reduce the heat to 325°F.

Process or cream together the cream cheese and ¾ cup of the sugar until smooth. Separate 4 of the eggs. Add the egg yolks and the 2 whole eggs one at a time, processing continuously or beating well after each addition. Add the sour cream, orange liqueur, rum, cornstarch, vanilla, and orange extract or rind and process or mix until well combined. In a large bowl beat the egg whites and salt until soft peaks form. Continue beating, adding the remaining ½ cup of the sugar gradually, until the whites are stiff but not dry. Pour the cream cheese mixture into the egg white mixture and fold and stir with a wire whisk or rubber spatula until well combined. Pour into the springform pan and bake for 75 minutes. Turn off the oven and leave the door slightly ajar for another 60 minutes. Remove the cake from the oven, let it come completely to room temperature, then refrigerate. Decorate with 3 orange sections in the center and a light sprinkling of chopped pecans over them. Remove from the refrigerator 1–2 hours before serving.

Here are 3 fine fruity coffee cakes that use the same tender cake base, flavored with almond and orange.

PRUNE MARVEL LOAF FOR COLLEEN *yields 9 by 5-inch loaf*

My old friend Colleen told me about prune-filled muffins she had cherished as a child; this loaf and the Prune Marvel Muffins (p. 31) were my attempt to duplicate (she says surpassed!) her remembered experience. Colleen says she likes the loaf best wrapped in foil and eaten the second day because the prune filling moistens and flavors the cake even more.

8 Tablespoons (1 stick) butter
¾ cup sugar
2 eggs
½ cup buttermilk or unflavored yogurt
   Grated rind of 1 orange
1 teaspoon vanilla extract
½ teaspoon almond extract
¼ teaspoon salt
1 teaspoon baking powder
½ teaspoon baking soda
2 cups all-purpose flour (you can use ½ cup whole wheat)
   Orange Prune Filling (p. 31)

Preheat the oven to 350°F. Butter and flour a 9 by 5-inch loaf pan lightly.

Cream or process the butter and sugar until smooth and creamy. Add the eggs one at a time, beating or processing well after each addition, and scraping the work bowl as necessary. Add the buttermilk or yogurt, orange rind, vanilla and almond extracts, and salt. Process or mix briefly to combine. Add the baking powder, baking soda, and flour to the batter. Process in 2–3 quick on-off pulses, completing the mixing with a rubber scraper. Or beat just to combine with an electric mixer.

Smooth half the batter into the prepared pan. Spoon Orange Prune Filling evenly over the batter and cover with the remaining cake batter. Marble the cake slightly by running a knife lengthwise down the cake in 2 places. Then, beginning at one end, make 4 swirling side-to-side movements all the way down the length of the pan.

Bake for 55–65 minutes, or until a toothpick inserted into the center comes out clean.

PEACH TORTE

3 large freestone peaches (1¼–1½ pounds)
1 recipe Prune Marvel Loaf batter, omitting the orange rind (p. 276)
¼ cup sugar, or ½ cup Praline (p. 286), made with unblanched almonds
1–2 Tablespoons butter

Preheat the oven to 350°F. Butter a 9-inch springform pan.

Blanch, peel, and slice the peaches. Spread Prune Marvel Loaf batter into the prepared pan and arrange the peach slices over the batter (pressing down

slightly) in 2 concentric circles. Sprinkle the peaches with the sugar or Praline and dot with the butter.

Bake for 55–60 minutes, or until a toothpick inserted into the center comes out dry. Serve warm, with ice cream if you like.

PLUM KUCHEN

1 recipe Prune Marvel Loaf batter, orange rind optional (p. 276)
2 pounds ripe small purple plums, halved, or larger plums, quartered
1/4 cup sugar
1/2 teaspoon ground cinnamon
2 Tablespoons (1/4 stick) butter

Preheat the oven to 350°F. Butter a 9 by 13-inch baking pan.

Spread the batter into the prepared pan and arrange the plum halves over the batter, cut side up. Cover as much of the batter with the plums as possible. Combine the sugar and cinnamon and sprinkle over the plums. Dot with the butter.

Bake for 40–50 minutes, or until a toothpick inserted into the center of the cake comes out dry. (During the last 10 minutes of baking, tilt the pan so that the butter and plum juices can run over the cake.) Serve warm, with lightly whipped cream if you like.

Here are 2 rolled cakes—light, airy versions of banana and carrot cakes with luscious cream cheese and buttercream fillings. If you've never made a rolled cake before, this is a good place to start.

If you don't have a hand-held electric mixer as called for in the instructions you can warm the eggs over hot water, stirring gently, then proceed with the recipe, beating with an electric mixer on a stand. Longer beating may be necessary.

BANANA NUT ROLL *serves 10-15*

This cake will yield about 15 slices. If this is more than you need, freeze half for another time.

3 extra-large eggs, at room temperature
1/2 teaspoon salt
1 cup granulated sugar
1 cup banana puree (about 2 large bananas)
1 teaspoon vanilla extract
3/4 cup all-purpose flour
1 teaspoon baking powder
1/2-3/4 cup chopped walnuts or pecans
Confectioners sugar

Preheat the oven to 375°F. Butter the bottom and sides of a 10 by 15-inch jelly-roll pan then line the pan with waxed paper, letting the paper overhang at the ends. Butter the waxed paper generously.

Place the eggs and salt in a large mixing bowl and place the bowl in a large pot with enough simmering water to come at least halfway up the sides of the bowl. Beat the mixture at high speed with an electric hand mixer until the eggs become very foamy and begin to thicken. Add the granulated sugar gradually, beating continuously. When the eggs are very thick and form a ribbon (after about 10 minutes), add the banana puree and vanilla and beat at the lowest speed just to mix. Remove the bowl from the water. Sift the flour and baking powder together over the egg mixture and fold it in gently with a rubber spatula or wire whisk. Spread the batter evenly in the prepared pan and sprinkle with the chopped nuts.

Bake for 13-15 minutes, or until the top is a deep golden color and rebounds lightly to the touch. Remove the cake from the oven and let it cool for 5 minutes on a rack.

While the cake is cooling, sprinkle a kitchen towel generously with confectioners sugar then turn the pan over onto the prepared towel. If the cake does not come out, rap the pan and/or pull gently on the waxed paper. Lift off the pan and remove the waxed paper carefully, sprinkle the cake lightly with more confectioners sugar and, making sure to have a few inches of towel folded over the edge where you will begin your rolling, roll/fold the cake and towel up together into thirds as if for a jelly roll.

Let cool for at least 30 minutes then unroll carefully.

Spread the cake with Rum Cream Cheese Filling, Chocolate Cream Cheese Filling, or Chocolate Mousse Filling and reroll without the towel. Refrigerate to firm the filling but remove the cake from the refrigerator about 30 minutes before serving. Dust the top lightly with confectioners sugar.

RUM
CREAM CHEESE FILLING

I like the combination of rum and banana, but I have also prepared this filling with bourbon, using pecans in the cake recipe, with very good results.

6 ounces cream cheese, softened
4 Tablespoons (½ stick) butter, softened
1 cup confectioners sugar
1 Tablespoon rum
½ teaspoon vanilla extract

Beat or process the ingredients until they are smooth and creamy.

For an extra-fancy touch, prepare extra filling and pipe rosettes at intervals down the center of the top of the roll. Place a whole walnut or a pecan half in the center of each rosette.

CHOCOLATE
CREAM CHEESE FILLING

1 recipe Rum Cream Cheese Filling (preceding recipe)
1 square (1 ounce) unsweetened chocolate, melted

Beat or process the ingredients until they are smooth and creamy.

CHOCOLATE MOUSSE FILLING

1 recipe Chocolate Mousse (p. 287)

CARROT NUT ROLL *serves 10-15*

3 extra-large eggs, at room temperature
1/2 teaspoon salt
1 cup granulated sugar
1 Tablespoon orange liqueur (optional)
1/2 teaspoon vanilla extract
3/4 cup all-purpose flour
1 teaspoon baking powder
8 ounces (about 4 smallish) carrots,
    grated fine
    Confectioners sugar
1/2–3/4 cup chopped walnuts or pecans

Preheat the oven to 375°F. Butter the bottom and sides of a 10 by 15-inch jelly-roll pan. Line with waxed paper, letting the paper overhang the ends. Butter the waxed paper generously.

Place the eggs and salt in a large mixing bowl and place the bowl in a large pot with enough simmering water to come at least halfway up the sides of the bowl. Beat the mixture at high speed with an electric hand mixer until the eggs become very foamy and begin to thicken. Add the sugar gradually, beating continuously. When the eggs are very thick and form a ribbon (after about 10 minutes), add the optional liqueur and the vanilla. Remove the bowl from the water. Sift the flour and baking powder together over the egg mixture and fold it in gently with a rubber spatula or wire whisk. Fold in the grated carrots. Spread the batter evenly in the prepared pan and sprinkle with the chopped nuts.

Bake for 13–15 minutes, or until the top is a light golden color and rebounds to the touch. Remove the cake from the oven and let it cool for 5 minutes on a rack. While it is cooling, sprinkle a kitchen towel generously with confectioners sugar then turn the pan over onto the towel. (If the cake does not come out, rap the pan and/or pull gently on the waxed paper.) Lift off the pan, remove the waxed paper carefully, sprinkle the cake lightly with more confectioners sugar, then, making sure to have a few inches of towel folded over the edge where you will begin your rolling, fold/roll the cake and towel into thirds, as if for a jelly roll. Let cool for at least 30 minutes then unroll carefully.

Spread the cake with either of the following fillings and reroll without the towel. Refrigerate to firm the filling but remove the cake from the refrigerator at least 30 minutes before serving. Dust the top lightly with confectioners sugar.

ORANGE CREAM CHEESE FILLING

6 ounces cream cheese, softened
4 Tablespoons (1/2 stick) butter, softened
1 cup confectioners sugar
1/2 Tablespoon orange liqueur (optional)
    Grated rind of 1 orange
1/2 teaspoon vanilla extract

Beat or process ingredients until smooth and creamy.

ORANGE BUTTERCREAM

10 Tablespoons (1 1/4 sticks) butter, softened
1 cup confectioners sugar
    Grated rind of 1 orange
1/2 Tablespoon orange liqueur (optional)

Beat or process ingredients until smooth and creamy.

MARSALA RAISIN POUND CAKE (RAISIN AND WINE CAKE) *yields 9 by 5-inch loaf*

1 cup raisins
1/2 cup dry Marsala, or cream or medium sherry
2 sticks (1/2 pound) butter
1 1/2 cups sugar
4 eggs, separated
1 teaspoon vanilla extract
1 teaspoon baking powder
2 cups all-purpose flour
1/2 teaspoon salt

Preheat the oven to 350°F. Butter a 9 by 5-inch loaf pan.

Combine the raisins and wine in a saucepan. Warm slightly then let stand for 20–30 minutes.

Process or cream the butter and 1 cup of the sugar. Add the egg yolks. Drain the Marsala from the raisins and add with the vanilla to the batter. Process or beat to mix well. Add the baking powder and flour and process or beat just until mixed through. Beat the egg whites with the salt until soft peaks form. Add the remaining 1/2 cup of the sugar gradually, beating until the whites are stiff but not dry. Fold one third of the beaten whites into the cake batter (you can do this in the work bowl of the food processor). Then add the remaining egg whites and fold until well combined. (Do this by hand.)

Turn into the prepared pan and bake for 60–70 minutes, or until a toothpick inserted into the center of the loaf comes out dry.

ORANGE POPPY SEED CAKE *yields 8 by 4-inch loaf*

For a 9 by 5-inch loaf increase recipe by one half.

1/2 cup orange juice
1/2 cup poppy seeds
2 Tablespoons rum
Grated rind of 1 orange
8 Tablespoons (1 stick) butter
3/4 cup sugar
2 eggs
1/2 teaspoon vanilla extract
1/4 teaspoon salt
1 teaspoon baking powder
1 1/2 cups all-purpose flour

Combine the orange juice, poppy seeds, rum, and orange rind in a small saucepan. Bring to a boil. Cover and remove from the heat. Let steep for 1 hour.

Preheat the oven to 375°F. Butter an 8 by 4-inch loaf pan.

Process or cream the butter and sugar. Add the eggs one at a time, processing continuously or beating well after each addition. Scrape the work bowl occasionally as needed. Add the poppy seed mixture, vanilla, and salt and process to combine. Sprinkle on the baking powder then the flour and process in 2 quick on-off pulses, mixing with a spatula to complete. Or beat with an electric mixer until the ingredients are combined. Turn into the prepared pan.

Bake for 60–65 minutes, or until a toothpick inserted into the center of the loaf comes out dry.

PECAN BUTTERCRUNCH BARS *yields 20 large squares or 40–80 smaller bars or squares*

These bars are my favorites. They're a little like pecan pie, but crunchier and chewier. They freeze beautifully, but you can make ½ recipe in a 9-inch square pan. The smaller amount of pastry when processed will be soft rather than powdery—just pat it into the prepared pan.

crust
2¾ cups all-purpose flour
 ⅔ cup confectioners sugar
 ¾ teaspoon salt
  2 sticks (½ pound) butter, cut up
  2 Tablespoons rum, preferably dark, or bourbon

filling
1½ cups brown sugar (packed)
  8 Tablespoons (1 stick) butter
 ¼ cup honey
 ¼ cup corn syrup
  2 Tablespoons rum or bourbon
  2 Tablespoons sour cream or heavy cream
  1 teaspoon vanilla extract
  3 cups medium–coarsely chopped pecans
 ¾ cup coconut
     Grated rind of 1 orange

     Confectioners sugar

Preheat the oven to 375°F. Butter a 10 by 15-inch jelly-roll pan lightly.

To make the crust, combine the flour, confectioners sugar, salt, and butter in the work bowl of a food processor.* Process until the ingredients are powdery. With the motor running add the rum or bourbon. Transfer the mixture to the prepared pan,

*If you have only a small-capacity processor, divide ingredients in half and prepare in 2 batches.

smooth it out evenly in the pan, and use a spatula to compact it lightly. Bake for 15 minutes. The surface of the pastry may crack, but it should not be browned.

While the pastry is baking, make the filling. Combine the brown sugar, butter, honey, corn syrup, rum or bourbon, sour cream or heavy cream, and vanilla in a heavy saucepan. Bring to a boil over medium-high heat, stirring occasionally. When the mixture is bubbly and all the ingredients are melted, stir in the chopped pecans, coconut, and grated orange rind. Spoon the pecan mixture over the baked pastry, being careful that the nuts and the syrup are distributed fairly evenly over the surface. Return to the oven for 15 minutes more, or until the top is browned and bubbly, with tiny pinpricks all over the surface.

Do not bake longer than 20 minutes or it will burn. Let cool completely, sprinkle lightly with confectioners sugar, and cut into 20 large (2 by 3-inch) squares or 40–80 smaller bars or squares.

LUSCIOUS CHOCOLATE NUT BARS *yields 16–24 bars or squares*

Moist fudgy filling on a flaky shortbread base. Prepare 2 recipes in a 10 by 15-inch pan. These also freeze perfectly.

crust
1 cup all-purpose flour
8 Tablespoons (1 stick) butter
1/3 cup confectioners sugar
1/4 teaspoon salt

filling
3/4 cup light corn syrup
1/2 cup granulated sugar
3 eggs
6 Tablespoons unsweetened cocoa
6 Tablespoons (3/4 stick) butter, softened
1 teaspoon vanilla extract
1 cup coarsely chopped walnuts or pecans

Preheat the oven to 375°F. Butter a 9-inch square pan lightly.

To make the crust, process or blend the flour, butter, confectioners sugar, and salt until the consistency of fine meal. Pat into the prepared pan and bake for 15 minutes, or until lightly golden.

To make the filling, blend or process the corn syrup, granulated sugar, eggs, cocoa, butter, and vanilla until smooth. Pour the chocolate mixture over the crust. Sprinkle on the chopped nuts. Bake for 30–40 minutes, or until the filling is puffed across the top. Let cool completely and cut into 16–24 bars or squares.

Note: For extra chocolaty richness sprinkle 1/4 cup chocolate mini-chips over the filling before baking.

LINZER ALMOND SHORTBREAD SQUARES *yields 20 large squares or 40–80 smaller bars and squares*

A grainy, buttery mouthful—very pretty with its glistening raspberry surface. It freezes well, and the recipe can be halved and prepared in a 9-inch square pan.

crust
2 cups all-purpose flour
1 cup cornmeal
1 cup whole wheat flour
1 cup confectioners sugar
1 cup light brown sugar (packed)
1/2 cup chopped unblanched almonds
1 teaspoon ground cinnamon
1/4 teaspoon salt
4 sticks (1 pound) butter, cut into pieces

topping
2 cups (1 pound) raspberry preserves
1 teaspoon almond extract
1/2 cup coarsely chopped unblanched almonds

Preheat the oven to 325°F. Butter a 10 by 15-inch jelly-roll pan lightly.

To make the crust, place 1 cup of the all-purpose flour, 1/2 cup of the cornmeal, 1/2 cup of the whole wheat flour, 1/2 cup of the confectioners sugar, 1/2 cup of the brown sugar, 1/4 cup of the chopped almonds, 1/2 teaspoon of the cinnamon, 1/8 teaspoon of the salt, and 2 sticks of the butter in the work bowl of a food processor. Process until the

ingredients are powdery. (Or cut the butter in by hand using a pastry blender.) Transfer the dough to the prepared jelly-roll pan.

Repeat with the remaining all-purpose flour, cornmeal, whole wheat flour, confectioners sugar, brown sugar, chopped almonds, cinnamon, salt, and butter and add this to the dough in the pan. Smooth out this shortbread as evenly as possible and pat down with a spatula to compact and smooth it slightly. Bake for 45 minutes. Re-

move from the oven and raise the heat to 375°F.

To make the filling, warm the raspberry preserves in a small saucepan until melted. Stir in the almond extract. Smooth the preserves evenly over the surface of the baked pastry. Sprinkle with the coarsely chopped almonds and bake for 15 minutes, or until the surface is bubbling gently all over. Let cool completely before cutting into 20 large (2 by 3-inch) squares or 40–80 smaller bars and squares.

ORANGE LEMON COCONUT SQUARES *yields 20 large squares or 40–80 smaller bars and squares*

crust

    3 cups all-purpose flour*
    3/4 cup confectioners sugar
    1/2 cup sweetened or unsweetened coconut
    3 sticks (3/4 pound) butter, cut up

filling

    6 eggs
    2 1/4 cups granulated sugar
    9 Tablespoons freshly squeezed lemon juice
    6 Tablespoons all-purpose flour
    1 1/2 teaspoons baking powder
        Pinch of salt
        Grated rind of 1 orange
        Grated rind of 1 lemon
        Confectioners sugar (optional)

Preheat the oven to 350°F. Butter a 10 by 15-inch jelly-roll pan lightly.

*If you can get it, substitute 1/2 cup rice flour for 1/2 cup of the all-purpose flour.

To make the crust, combine the flour, confectioners sugar, coconut, and butter in the work bowl of a food processor. Process until the mixture is fine and powdery. (Or cut the butter in by hand using a pastry blender.) Transfer the dough to the prepared pan. Smooth out the dough evenly in the pan and pat down with a spatula to compact and smooth it slightly. Bake for 15–20 minutes, or until lightly golden. Reduce the heat to 325°F.

To make the filling, process or beat together the eggs and granulated sugar until smooth and well mixed. Add the lemon juice, flour, baking powder, salt, and orange and lemon rinds, and process or beat until well mixed. Pour over the hot pastry.

Bake for 45–55 minutes, or until a knife inserted into the center comes out clean. Let cool. Sprinkle with confectioners sugar, if desired, and cut into 20 large (2 by 3-inch) squares or 40–80 smaller bars or squares.

AUNT CLARA'S BROWNIES *yields about 24 brownies*

I've never tasted a better brownie. Even though I don't think these can be surpassed, I can't help fooling with them. Sometimes I add brandy or crème de cacao instead of the milk.

12 ounces semisweet chocolate (chips will do fine)
11 Tablespoons (2/3 cup) butter
 3 eggs
 1 cup sugar
 2 Tablespoons milk
 1 teaspoon vanilla extract
 1 cup all-purpose flour
 1 teaspoon baking powder
   Pinch of salt
2/3 cup chopped walnuts

Preheat the oven to 350°F. Butter and flour a 9 by 13-inch pan.

Melt the chocolate and butter together over low heat then let cool. Beat or process the eggs and sugar together. Add the cooled chocolate mixture, milk, and vanilla. Beat or process just to combine. Add the flour, baking powder, and salt and process or beat, being careful not to overmix (if using a processor, 2 quick on-off pulses will do), then use a rubber spatula to complete the mixing. Stir in the walnuts. Pour the mixture into the prepared pan.

Bake for 35–40 minutes or until a toothpick inserted into the center comes out clean.

RUM RAISIN SQUARES *yields 16 squares*

1 1/2 cups raisins
  2 Tablespoons rum plus enough water to measure 1/2 cup
  2 Tablespoons (1/4 stick) butter
    Pinch of salt
1 1/4 cups confectioners sugar
  1/2 cup chopped walnuts
  1 recipe Sweet Lattice Tart Pastry, prepared with an extra 1/2 Tablespoon rum (p. 261)

Preheat the oven to 375°F. Butter an 8- or 9-inch square pan lightly.

Combine the raisins, rum and water, butter, and salt in a small saucepan. Bring to a boil, cover, remove from the heat and let sit for 30 minutes then puree in a food processor. Add the confectioners sugar and walnuts and process to mix and chop the walnuts to the desired consistency.

Adding the extra rum to the pastry recipe for a soft and malleable dough. Pat two thirds of the dough into the prepared pan. Spread with the raisin filling. Roll out the remaining dough and cut strips to form a lattice topping.

Bake for 40–45 minutes, or until golden.

Bar Cookies

PRALINE *yields 1 cup*

I wish I hadn't waited so long before attempting praline. I've had a few goofs where the sugar crystallizes, but once ground up, "failed" praline turns out just fine. The only mistake you can really make is to burn the caramel. Just avoid this and you can create a topping and filling for desserts with a deep nut-rich flavor that is incomparable. Although praline will keep indefinitely in your freezer, it's certain not to stay there for very long. Make sure that whenever you prepare praline and remove the hot nut mixture from the pan, you swirl and heat some brandy or liqueur in the pan right away. Be careful, though. If the pan is on a flame the liqueur may ignite. Let it burn off the alcohol if you wish. The flame will eventually burn out or you can extinguish it by covering the saucepan with a lid. Save this praline-flavored syrup to add to whipped creams or buttercream, or any recipe that calls for a liqueur flavoring.

1/2 cup sugar
2 Tablespoons water
1/2 cup coarsely chopped walnuts, pecans, or unblanched almonds

Butter a cookie sheet. Set it aside.

In a small, heavy saucepan dissolve the sugar and water over medium heat, swirling the mixture occasionally or stirring with the handle of a wooden spoon. (I use the handle of a wooden spoon because the wood doesn't change the temperature of the caramel the way metal would, and it just works well. Also, if you use the spoon end, too much caramel sticks to it and is lost to the praline.) When the sugar is dissolved, raise the heat and boil the mixture, paying close attention when it begins to color. (If sugar crystals form on the side of your pan, take a brush, dip it in cold water, and brush the sides of the pan—the crystals will dissolve back into the syrup.) When the syrup turns a consistent golden color, add the nuts, then lower the heat. Stir for a few seconds with the wooden spoon handle then turn the praline out onto the buttered cookie sheet. Let it cool completely and harden then break it into pieces and pulverize it in a food processor or blender. Store in a plastic bag or container in the refrigerator. It will keep indefinitely in the freezer.

ORANGE PRALINE

Grate the rind of 1 orange rough (or peel it with a potato peeler and chop it up). Add the rind to the syrup along with the nuts.

CHOCOLATE PRALINE OR
ORANGE PRALINE WITH CHOCOLATE

Prepare Praline or Orange Praline. When pulverized and completely cool, add 2 ounces finely or coarsely grated semisweet or bittersweet chocolate.

PRALINE PARFAIT CLOUD *serves 8-12*

This is very easy to make, absolutely gorgeous to look at, and people just go nuts when they taste it. I like to serve it with Double Chocolate Mousse Cake and fresh strawberries (for larger parties) or as a dessert by itself with a bowl of fresh berries or other fruit. "Cloud" can also be prepared in individual wineglasses—1/2 recipe to serve 4-5, a full recipe for 8-9. If you wish to extend it, place fresh sliced strawberries in the bottom of a wineglass, top with the cream mixture, angled slightly, Chocolate Praline, another layer of cream, then a lighter sprinkle of praline: more fruit, fewer layers of "Cloud."

  1 envelope unflavored gelatin
  4 Tablespoons water
  4 cups heavy cream
  1/2 cup confectioners sugar
  2 Tablespoons crème de cacao, preferably white
  2 Tablespoons rum
  2 Tablespoons orange liqueur
  2 teaspoons vanilla extract
  1 1/2-2 cups Chocolate Praline or Orange Praline with Chocolate (preceding recipe)

In a 1/2-cup metal measuring cup soften the gelatin in water. Place the measuring cup in a small amount of simmering water until the gelatin is completely melted and clear.

Whip the cream, adding the confectioners sugar as the cream begins to thicken. While beating the cream, pour in the gelatin in a thin stream, right into the track of the rotating beaters. Beat until the cream is quite thick, being careful not to overbeat. Fold in the crème de cacao, rum, orange liqueur, and vanilla. Using a glass bowl or straight-sided pitcher (9-10-cup capacity), spoon a thick layer of the whipped cream mixture, angling it or mounding it unevenly. Cover the whipped cream with a little more than one third of the praline, creating a beautiful nutty-chocolate or orange curving vein. Cover with more mounds of whipped cream and more praline, end with whipped cream and a generous sprinkling of praline in the center and a few gratings of orange rind if you wish. (If you are using a tall pitcher instead of a bowl, you may wish to make 4 layers of cream/praline.) Chill until ready to serve.

CHOCOLATE MOUSSE *yields 3 2/3 cups*

This wonderfully smooth, dense, rich mousse is based on Craig Claiborne's Marquis de Chocolat. It is an elegant filling and frosting, and wonderful eaten as just mousse. A single recipe will fill and frost one Walnut Ultimate, a double recipe will fill and frost Double Chocolate Bourbon Cake. One recipe will fill one Banana Nut Roll with about half left over (use it to decorate the top).

8 squares (8 ounces) semisweet chocolate
2 sticks (1/2 pound) butter (I use 1 salted, 1 unsalted)
5 eggs, separated
1/4 cup superfine sugar
1 Tablespoon rum, bourbon, or flavoring of choice
1/4-1/2 teaspoon vanilla extract

Melt the chocolate and butter together over low heat, whisking occasionally until the mixture is smooth. Beat the egg yolks with an electric mixer on high speed, adding the chocolate mixture gradually. Continue beating on high speed for 5-10 minutes.

While the chocolate and yolks are beating in my stand model mixer, I use an electric hand mixer to beat the egg whites. Beat the whites on high speed until soft peaks form. Gradually add the sugar, beating until the whites are stiff. Add the egg whites to the chocolate mixture, along with the rum and vanilla, and beat at high speed for 5-10 minutes more.

Refrigerate for several hours or overnight before serving or using as a filling or frosting.

CHOCOLATE MOUSSE PRALINE PARFAIT

Here is a way to intensify your chocolate mousse experience.

Prepare Praline, Chocolate Praline, or Orange Praline with Chocolate (p. 286) and prepare 1 recipe Chocolate Mousse (p. 287). In 6 wineglasses or goblets layer mousse and praline. Top the Chocolate Mousse Praline Parfait with a dollop of whipped cream, lightly flavored with liqueur and lightly sweetened with confectioners sugar.

You can also prepare this in a 4-5-cup capacity glass soufflé dish. If you would like to serve more than 6, double the amount of praline you are using and create lovely thick veins of praline and a thick praline topping. For an even larger number of people, 10-15, double the mousse recipe as well. For layering suggestions, see Praline Parfait Cloud (p. 287).

CHOCOLATE-DIPPED STUFFED PRUNES *yields 40-42 prunes*

The idea of chocolate-dipped prunes really turns some people on—and really turns others off. But the actual eating always elicits sounds of surprised pleasure from everyone. If you would like to experiment with different fillings, use 8 ounces Neufchâtel cheese in various fruit flavors—strawberry, pineapple, peach, and mandarin orange—and omit the other filling flavoring.

filling

     6 ounces cream cheese, softened
     4 Tablespoons (1/2 stick) butter, softened
  1/4 cup confectioners sugar
  1/2-1 teaspoon very finely minced fresh
        gingerroot*, or grated rind of 1 orange
        One 12-ounce package pitted prunes

glaze

     6 squares (6 ounces) semisweet chocolate
     3 Tablespoons butter
        Roughly grated orange rind or grated
        semisweet chocolate

To make the filling, process or beat together the cream cheese, butter, confectioners sugar, and minced ginger or orange rind until the mixture is smooth and creamy. Refrigerate until firm but flexible. Open the prunes gently with thumb and forefinger. Fit a pastry bag with a plain tip or the plastic insert without a tip (my choice). Fill the bag with the firmed cream cheese mixture and pipe some into each prune, mounding the mixture slightly at the opening. Place the prunes on a baking sheet lined with waxed paper and refrigerate or freeze until the cream cheese mixture is quite firm and the prunes are very cold.

To make the glaze, in a small saucepan melt together the chocolate and butter over low heat, stirring occasionally. Let cool to thicken slightly. Dip the cold prunes, lengthwise, into the chocolate so that half the prune and a small part of the filling are covered with chocolate. Place the prunes on the waxed paper chocolate side up and refrigerate until the chocolate is firm.

If you have made ginger-stuffed prunes, grate chocolate, using a Mouli grater, over filling and prunes. If yours are orange-stuffed prunes, dip the exposed filling part of the prune into grated orange rind so that each picks up a few pieces of rind. Place the prunes in paper petits fours cups and serve as a dessert or candy.

CHOCOLATE BANANA NUT STRUDEL *serves 4*

This is an unusual strudel that is very easy to prepare. It's moist and best eaten within a few hours of baking. If you are preparing it for a company dessert, form it hours ahead of time, refrigerate it, bake it just before dinner, and let it cool while dinner is being eaten. The baked banana center surrounded by melted chocolate and nuts then delicate strudel leaves is very attractive and is especially appealing arranged in a double-circle flower or sunburst pattern on a round platter.

  1/2 cup well-chopped but not powdery pecans
     2 squares (2 ounces) semisweet chocolate, grated
     2 long, straight, ripe, but not overly soft bananas
        Bourbon, rum, or brandy
        Honey
    10 sheets phyllo
     8 Tablespoons (1 stick) butter, melted

*Or instead you can use minced crystallized ginger (6-8 slices, or to taste) and eliminate or decrease the sugar.

Combine the pecans and grated chocolate and set aside on a sheet of waxed paper.

Peel the bananas and brush them lightly with the bourbon, rum, or brandy and then brush generously all over with honey. Combine leftover honey and liquor to use as a glaze while baking. Immediately roll the honeyed bananas in the chocolate and nut mixture, making sure that the mixture adheres well over the entire banana.

Cover a work surface with waxed paper then place on it 1 sheet of phyllo with a short side facing you. Brush the phyllo lightly with melted butter. Repeat until you have 5 buttered layers. Place the coated banana about 1 inch from the bottom of the short end nearest you. Sprinkle half of any remaining chocolate-nut bits around on the pastry then trim the sides with scissors if there is more than 1/2 inch excess. Fold the 1-inch border up over the banana, tuck in the sides, and roll the strudel. (Don't worry if the banana breaks as it straightens out in the rolling.) Place the roll on a baking sheet and brush with melted butter. Form a second roll in the same manner. Refrigerate until you are ready to bake.

When you are ready to bake, preheat the oven to 375°F. Bake for about 30–35 minutes, or until the rolls are golden. Turn the rolls midway through the baking time so that they brown evenly. As the rolls bake they will flatten somewhat and a small amount of filling may ooze out. About 5–10 minutes before the end of the baking time, brush any remaining honey/liquor over the top of the strudels. When the rolls are done let them cool then slice them on a diagonal into about fourteen 1-inch pieces. Serve with cut sides up.

ZABAGLIONE *serves 4-6*

Zabaglione is an amazement of tastes—warm, nutty flavored, rich yet light. Although it requires last-minute preparation, I still find it simple and gratifying to serve. It is excellent over sliced strawberries. If you use enough berries you can stretch this recipe to serve 6, especially if you use the whole egg, which will give you a slightly less rich zabaglione with a higher volume.

  6 egg yolks, or 4 egg yolks and 1 whole egg
1/3 cup dry Marsala
1/4 cup sugar

Combine the egg yolks, Marsala, and sugar in a 1 1/2-quart (minimum) stainless steel bowl, preferably one with high sides. (I use the small bowl from my electric stand mixer.) Place the bowl in a large saucepan filled with enough simmering water to come halfway up the sides of the bowl. Over low heat beat the yolk mixture over the simmering water at high speed with an electric hand mixer until the yolks are very light, thick, and gently warmed. Spoon into wineglasses and serve immediately.

INDEX

Agnolotti. *See also recipes for* Tortellini
  forming, 153-4
Almond
  Blueberry or Strawberry Tart, Fresh, 266
  and Carrot Bisteeya, 96-7
  Carrot Bisteeya Hors d'Oeuvre Pastries,
    100
  Raspberry Bread, Best Ever, 24
  Shortbread Squares, Linzer, 283
Amaretto Cheesecake with Chocolate Sour
    Cream Glaze, 275
Amaretto Pear Tart, 265
Anchovies: Marinated White Beans with
    Capers, Tuna, and, 234
Appetizers (Hors d'oeuvres), 55-71
  about, 55
  Carrot Almond Bisteeya Hors d'Oeuvre
    Pastries, 100
  Chatham Clam Crêpes, 116
  Cheese in Brioche, 68
  cheeses in pastry
    about, 66
    Brie en Croûte, 66-7
    En Croûte pastry for, 66
    Miniature Brie or Camembert en
      Croûte, 67
  Chinese, 56-61
    Dipping Sauce for, 60
    Dumplings, about, 58
    Dumplings, Homemade Dough for,
      59
    Dumplings, Pork and Shrimp
      (Jao-Tze), 59
    Dumplings: Shrimp, Scallop, or Fish,
      with Spinach, 60
    Hoi Sin Spicy Beef on a Skewer, 194
    Hoi Sin Spicy Chicken (or Turkey) on
      a Skewer, 194
    Mustard for, 60
    Shrimp and Tofu Won Tons, 61
    Spring Rolls, Emmy's, 57
    Spring Rolls II, 58
    Sweet-and-Sour Walnut Chicken
      Crisps, 199
  dips
    Eggplant Tuna Parmesan, 71
    Eggplant Walnut Pesto, 71
    Guacamole, 69
    Guacamole, Party, 70

Appetizers (*continued*)
  Hummus, 69
  Fish Bites, Crispy Fried, 200
  Gravlaks, 201-2
  Huevos Rancheros, Golden, 102
  Mexican Cheese Bean Pinwheel Tarts,
    103
  Mushroom Marsala or Mushroom Pecan
    Phyllo Strudels, 99
  Pastry, 62-5
    Empanadas (Mexican Meat
      Turnovers), 64
    Empanada Tarts, 64
    Kasha and Potato Tarts, 65
    Kasha Knishes, 64-5
    Mexican Cheese Bean Turnovers,
      63-4
    Mushroom Marsala Turnovers, 63
    Mushroom Pecan Turnovers, 63
    Seafood Mousse Turnovers, 62-3
    Sour Cream Pastry for Turnovers, 62
    Turnover Pastry for, 62
  Picadillo Pinwheel Tarts, 103
  Sausage Crêpe Rolls, 117
  Seafood Mousse in Phyllo, 99
  Stuffed Brioche Lattice Loaf, 214
Apple Pie, Favorite, 263
Apricot and Cheese Cornmeal Crêpes, 111
Artichoke
  Quiche, Elegant, 78
  and Shrimp Tabouli, 231
Asparagus
  Noodles with Beef and, 189
  Spaghetti and Eggs with Mushrooms
    and, 132
  in Spring Celebration Lasagna, 141
  Stir-Fry, 182
    with Ground Beef, 182
Aunt Clara's Brownies, 285
Aunt Clara's Fruit Soup, 47
Avocado
  Guacamole, 69
    -Filled Pasta Salad with Salsa, 226
    Party, 70
  and Spinach Torte, 80

Bacon
  Broccoli Crêpe Roll-Ups with Cheddar
    Cheese and, 115

Bacon (*continued*)
  Mushroom Crêpe Roll-Ups with
    Cheddar Cheese and, 115
Banana
  Bread, Best Ever
    Master Recipe, 24
    Variations, 24-6
  Chocolate Nut Strudel, 289-90
  Nut Roll, 278-9
  puree, in breads, 16
  Raisin Walnut Lattice Tart, 270-1
Barley, Lamb Shanks with Turnips and,
    216-17
Bars. *See also* Squares
  Luscious Chocolate Nut, 283
  Pecan Buttercrunch, 282
Basil
  Béchamel, 246
  Pesto Cubes, Frozen, 247
  Pesto Sauce, 247
    Pasta with, 135
  and Zucchini Tart, 85
Bean(s). *See also* Black Beans;
    Kidney Beans
  Cheese Filling, 253
    in Mexican Cheese Bean Turnovers,
      63-4
  Cheese Pinwheel Tarts, Mexican, 103
  Chicken (and Vegetarian) Tostadas with,
    210
  in Crêpes à la Mexicaine, 112
  Curd. *See* Tofu
  -Filled Pasta Salad with Salsa, 226-7
  Filling, 253
    Pierogin with, 159
  Maple, 218
    and Corn Bread, 218
  Marinated White, with Capers,
    Anchovies, and Tuna, 234
  and Pasta Rolls, Mexican, 152
  Puree, Seasoned, 252
  Soup, Multi-, 38
  Tortellini
    with Egg Sauce, 155
    Salad, Mexican, 228
Béchamel
  Basic, 245
  Basil, 246
  Eggplant, 143

Béchamel (*continued*)
 Garlic, 142
 Sesame, 245
 Thick, 245
Beef
 Chili and Beans, Jack's Famous, 211
  Enchiladas with, 212
  Mexican Lasagna with, 142
 Ground, Stir-Fry Asparagus with, 182
 Hoi Sin Spicy, 195
  Kebobs, 194
  on a Skewer, 194
 Noodles with
  Asparagus (or Broccoli) and, 189
  Sesame, Scallions, and, Spicy, 190
 Picadillo, 254
  and Brioche Loaf, 212-13
  Pinwheel Tarts, 103
  Taco, 211
  Torta, 213
 Sesame Szechuan Kebobs, 198
 Stock, 51
Beet
 and Orange, and Onion Salad, 234
 Soup
  Borscht, Chilled Fresh, 48
  with Dilled Meatballs, Hot, 45
  Orange and, Quick, 48
Bisque
 Curried Butternut, 42
 Gingered Carrot and Pear, 41
 Spinach Walnut, 43
Bisteeya, Carrot and Almond, 96-7
Bisteeya, Carrot Almond Hors d'Oeuvre
  Pastries, 100
Black Beans
 Broccoli with Tomatoes and, 233
 fermented, in stir-fry dishes, 170
 in Mexican Fiesta Pasta Salad,
  222-3
 Pasta with Broccoli, Tomatoes, and
  (*Vipasśtana*), 134
Blintz(es), 118-22
 about, 118
 Batter
  Basic, 119
  Whole Wheat, 119
 Cheese
  with Feta and Dill, Savory, 120

Blintz(es) (*continued*)
  Strawberry-, Joe Lazar's, 119
  Sweet, with Raisins, 120
 Herbed Kasha and Potato, 121
 Soufflé
  Savory Kasha, 122
  Sweet, 121
 Strawberry Cheese, Joe Lazar's, 119
Blueberry
 Almond Tart, Fresh, 266
 Banana Bread, Best Ever, 25
 Bread, 29
 Grape Soup, Summer, 47
 Muffins, 32
  Extraordinary, 32
 Praline Tart, 262
Blue Cheese
 and Broccoli Quiche, 81
 Spaghetti and Eggs with Sunflower Seeds
  and, 131
Bluefish
 Gravlaks, 201-2
 Sauce, Linguini with, 136
Borscht
 Beet, Chilled Fresh, 48
 Tomato, Fresh, 49
Bourbon
 Cake, Double Chocolate, 271-2
 Cream Cheese Frosting, 272
Bran Muffins, Raisin and, for Jack,
  33
Breads
 Quick, 23-33
  about, 23
  Almond Raspberry Bread, Best Ever,
   24
  Banana Bread, Best Ever:
   Master Recipe, 24
  Banana Bread, Best Ever: Variations,
   24-6
  Blueberry Banana Bread, Best Ever,
   25
  Blueberry Bread, 29
  Blueberry (or Cranberry) Muffins,
   Extraordinary, 32
  Buckwheat and Maple Walnut Muffins,
   32
  Buckwheat Banana Bread, Best Ever,
   25

Breads (*continued*)
  Caraway Rye Banana Bread,
   Best Ever, 25
  Carrot Bread, Best Ever, 26
  Chocolate Banana Bread, Best Ever,
   25
  Cornmeal Banana Bread, Best Ever,
   25
  Corn. *See* Corn Bread
  Cottage Health Loaf for Faye, 30
  Cranberry Banana Bread, Best Ever,
   25
  Cranberry Raisin Bread, 29
  Cranberry Raisin or Blueberry Muffins,
   32
  Cream Cheese Banana Bread,
   Best Ever, 25
  Fruit Bread, Four Season, 26-7
  Fruited Soda Bread with Nuts and
   Caraway, 28
  Maple Corn Bread, 30
  Nutted Soda Bread with Herbs, 28
  Peanut Banana Bread, Best Ever, 25
  Poppy Seed Banana Bread, Best Ever,
   24
  Prune Marvel Muffins, 31
  Raisin and Bran Muffins for Jack, 33
  Sesame Banana Bread, Best Ever, 25
  Three Seed and Nut Bread, Best Ever,
   25
  Velvet Pumpkin Bread, 27
  Zucchini Bread, Best Ever, 26
 Yeast, 3-22
  banana puree in, 16
  Brioche, Easy Processor, 7
  Brioche, Whole Wheat Processor, 7
  Brioche Twists, Buttery, 8
  Brioche with Savory Cheese Filling,
   9
  Brioche with Whole Grains and
   Seeds, Rich Herbed, 10
  Buckwheat Dill Bread, 18
  English Muffins, 22
  flours for, 6
  freezing, 5-6
  Fruit and Nut, Farmhouse, 11
  Herbed Walnut Cheese Swirl, 19
  Oatmeal Dill Bread, 18
  Oatmeal Dill Bread, with Onion, 18

Breads (*continued*)
    Oatmeal Dill Rolls, 18
    process of making, 3–5
    Raisin Bread, Buckwheat Honey, 20
    Raisin Bread, Wonderful, 17
    Rye, Braided, 16
    Swirls, Rich Sweet, 13
    Swirls, Savory, 14–15
    Three Grain Loaf, 12
    Whole Wheat and Rye Rolls, 21
Brie
    En Croûte, 66–7
        Miniature, 67
    Herbed Crêpes with, 112
Brioche
    Cheese in, 68
    Lattice Loaf, Stuffed, 214
    and Picadillo Loaf, 212–13
    Processor
        Easy, 7
        Whole Wheat, 7
    with Savory Cheese Filling, 9
    Twists, Buttery, 8
    with Whole Grains and Seeds,
        Rich Herbed, 10
Broccoli
    and Blue Cheese Quiche, 81
    Crêpes, 110
        Roll-Ups with Cheddar Cheese and
        Bacon, 115
    Noodles with Beef and, 189
    Pasta with Tomatoes, Black Beans, and
        (*Vipassana*), 134
    in salads
        Kung Pao Broccoli and Tofu Pasta
        Salad, 223–4
        Shrimp Won Tons with Broccoli in
        Szechuan Vinaigrette, Cold, 227
        Szechuan Pasta and Vegetable Salad,
        222
        Szechuan Tortellini and, Salad, 228
        Tomatoes and Black Beans,
        Broccoli with, 233
    Stalk Soup, Cream of, 41
    Stir-Fry Tofu and (Number 97), 176
    Vinegar Chicken with Kielbasa and, 208
Broth, Scotch, 46
Brownies, Aunt Clara's, 285
Brown Rice, 255

Buckwheat. *See also* Kasha
    Banana Bread, Best Ever, 25
    Crêpes, 109
        Maple-buttered Triangles, 111
    Dill Bread, 18
    Honey Raisin Bread, 20
    and Maple Walnut Muffins, 32
    Pasta, 150
    Spaetzle, 160
Bulgur. *See also* Tabouli
    Sweet-and-Sour Meatballs with, 215
    and Zucchini Casserole with Meat,
        216
Buttercream, Orange, 280
Buttercrunch Bars, Pecan, 282
Butternut Squash Bisque, Curried, 42
Buttery Brioche Twists, 8

Cabbage
    Stir-Fry Tofu, Ground Pork, and,
        in Oyster Sauce, 174
    Stir-Fry Tofu and, in Oyster Sauce, 175
Cake. *See also* Cheesecake
    Banana Nut Roll, 278–9
    Carrot Nut Roll, 280
    Double Chocolate Bourbon, 271–2
    Double Chocolate Mousse, 272–3
    Filling. *See* Filling—Cake
    Orange Poppy Seed, 281
    Peach Torte, 277
    Plum Kuchen, 278
    Pound, Marsala Raisin (Raisin and Wine
        Cake), 281
    Prune Marvel Loaf for Colleen, 276–7
    Walnut Ultimate, 273
        with Chocolate Mousse, 274
Camembert en Croûte, Miniature, 67
Cannelloni Seafood Mousse, 144
Caper(s)
    and Eggplant Sauce, Vermicelli with, 138
    Marinated White Beans with Anchovies,
        Tuna, and, 234
Caraway
    Onion Twists, 8
    Rye Banana Bread, Best Ever, 25
Carrot(s)
    and Almond Bisteeya, 96–7
    Almond Bisteeya Hors d'Oeuvre Pastries,
        100

Carrot(s) (*continued*)
    Bread, Best Ever, 26
    and Dill Quiche, 81
    Nut Roll, 280
    Pasta, 149
    and Pear Bisque, Gingered, 41
    -Raisin Walnut (or Peanut) Tabouli, 229
    Rapee, 234
Casserole, Bulgur and Zucchini, with Meat,
    216
Cauliflower and Cheddar Cheese Soup,
    Cream of, 42
Charlotte's Pasta, 138
Chatham Clam Crêpes, 116
Cheddar Cheese
    Broccoli Crêpe Roll-Ups with Bacon and,
        115
    and Cauliflower Soup, Cream of, 42
    Mushroom Crêpe Roll-Ups with Bacon
        and, 115
Cheese
    Bean Filling, 253
        in Mexican Cheese Bean Turnovers,
        63–4
    Bean Pinwheel Tarts, Mexican, 103
    Blintzes
        Savory, with Feta and Dill, 120
        Strawberry-, Joe Lazar's, 119
        Sweet, with Raisins, 120
    in Brioche, 68
    Brioche Lattice Loaf Stuffed with, 214
    Brioche Twists with Herbs and, 8
    Brioche with Savory Filling of, 9
    in Crêpes à la Mexicaine, 112
    Gnocchi with Semolina, Eggs, and
        (Semolina Squares), 162–3
    and Herb Filling for Savory Bread Swirls,
        15
    for pasta, 128
    in pastry
        Brie en Croûte, 66–7
        En Croûte pastry for, 66
        Miniature Brie or Camembert en
        Croûte, 67
    Potato Filling
        I, 255
        II, Dilled, 255
        III, Rich, 255
        Pierogin with, 159

Cheese (*continued*)
  and Potato Turnovers, 95
  Spaetzle, 161
  in Spanokopita
    Pie, 97
    Turnovers, 94–5
  Swirl, Herbed Walnut, 19
  in Torta Rustica, 86
  in Tostada Pie, 87
Cheesecake
  Amaretto, with Chocolate Sour Cream
    Glaze, 275
  Orange Praline, 276
  Pastry for, 274
Chicken
  with Broccoli and Kielbasa, Vinegar, 208
  Bulgur and Zucchini Casserole with, 216
  'Chiladas, 209–10
  Crisps, Sweet-and-Sour Walnut, 199
  Double-Cooked, 177
  Fettucini, 137
  Hoi Sin, Gentle, 196
  Hoi Sin Spicy, 195
    on a Skewer, 194
  Marrakech, 206
  Mixed Vegetables with, in Oyster Sauce,
    173–4
  Mu Shu, 180
  Noodles with Sesame, Scallions, and,
    Spicy, 190
  Norman's Chinese, 195
  with Peaches and Peanuts, 179
  Sesame Szechuan, 197
  Stock, 50–1
Chick-peas, in Hummus, 69
Chili
  and Beans, Jack's Famous, 211
    Enchiladas with, 212
    Mexican Lasagna with, 142
  paste with garlic, for stir-fry dishes,
    170
Chinese dishes, 193–9
  about, 193
  Gentle Hoi Sin Chicken, 196
  Gentle Hoi Sin Duck, 196
  Gentle Hoi Sin Pork (Chinese [Not So
    Spare] Ribs), 197
  Hoi Sin Spicy Beef on a Skewer,
    194

Chinese dishes (*continued*)
  Hoi Sin Spicy Chicken, 195
  Hoi Sin Spicy Chicken (or Turkey) on a
    Skewer, 194
  Hoi Sin Spicy Kebobs, 194
  Hors d'oeuvres. *See* Appetizers—
    Chinese
  Marinade, Norman Fine's, 257
  Norman's Chinese Chicken, 195
  Pancakes, 181
  Sesame Szechuan Beef, Lamb, or Pork
    Kebobs, 198
  Sesame Szechuan Chicken, 197
  Sesame Szechuan Seafood or Fish,
    198
  Stir-fry dishes. *See* Stir-fry dishes
  Sweet-and-Sour Walnut Chicken Crisps,
    199
  Sweet Szechuan Seafood, 198
Chocolate
  Banana Bread, Best Ever, 25
  Bourbon Cake, Double, 271–2
  Cream Cheese Filling, 279
  Crêpes, 110
  -dipped Stuffed Prunes, 288–9
  -flavored Whipped Cream, 268–9
  Mousse, 287–8
    Cake, Double, 272–3
    Praline Parfait, 288
    Walnut Ultimate with, 274
  Nut Bars, Luscious, 283
  Orange Praline with, 286
  Praline, 286
  Sour Cream Glaze, 275
    Amaretto Cheesecake with, 275
  Velvet Pie, 268
Chowder, Nantucket Scallop, 43
Claiborne, Craig, 287
Clam(s)
  Crêpes, Chatham, 116
  in Fruits of the Sea Pasta, 135
Coconut Orange Lemon Squares,
  284
Corn, in Mexican Fiesta Pasta Salad,
  222–3
Corn Bread
  Maple, 30
  Maple Beans and, 218
  in Torta Picadillo, 213

Cornmeal
  Banana Bread, Best Ever, 25
  Crêpes, 109
    Cheese and Apricot, 111
    Mexican, 109
    Sweet, 109
  Pastry, 77
    Tart and Turnover, 77
Cornstarch, in stir-fry dishes, 168–9
Cottage Cheese
  Pancakes, 122
    with Herbs, 123
  Pastry, 77
Cottage Health Loaf for Faye, 30
Couscous with Turkey and Ported Prunes,
  207
Crab Meat
  in Fruits of the Sea Pasta, 135
  Rice Sticks with Pork, Vegetables, and,
    188
  in Seafood Lasagna, 140
  in Spring Celebration Lasagna, 141
  Velouté, 246
    Seafood Mousse Pockets with, 93
    Seafood Mousse Strudel Slices with,
      92
Cranberry
  Banana Bread, Best Ever, 25
  Muffins, Extraordinary, 32
  Praline Tart, 262
  Raisin Bread, 29
Cream
  Pastry, 267
  Whipped, Chocolate-flavored, 268–9
Cream Cheese. *See also* Cheesecake
  Banana Bread, Best Ever, 25
  Bourbon Frosting, 272
  Chocolate Filling, 279
  Orange Filling, 280
  Rum Filling, 279
Crêpe(s), 107–17. *See also* Blintz(es)
  about, 107–8
  à la Mexicaine, 112
  Batter, Basic, 108
  Broccoli, 110
    Roll-Ups with Cheddar Cheese and
      Bacon, 115
  Buckwheat, 109
  Cheese and Apricot Cornmeal, 111

Crêpe(s) (*continued*)
  Chocolate, 110
  Clam, Chatham, 116
  Cornmeal, 109
    Mexican, 109
    Sweet, 109
  Eggplant Pockets, 114
  Herbed, 110
    with Brie, 112
  Maple-buttered Buckwheat Triangles, 111
  Mushroom, 110
    Pecan, 113
    Roll-Ups with Cheddar Cheese and
      Bacon, 115
  Ratatouille, 114
  Sausage Rolls, 117
  Seafood Mousse Stuffed, Elegant, 115
  Spinach and Mushroom, 113
  Sweet, 110
Curried Butternut Bisque, 42
Custard and Fresh Fruit Pie with a
    Difference, 266–7

Desserts, 261–90. *See also* Bars; Cake;
    Pie; Squares; Tart(s)
  Blintz(es)
    Cheese, with Raisins, 120
    Soufflé, 121
    Strawberry Cheese, Joe Lazar's, 119
  Brownies, Aunt Clara's, 285
  Chocolate Banana Nut Strudel, 289–90
  Chocolate-dipped Stuffed Prunes, 288–9
  Chocolate Mousse, 287–8
    Praline Parfait, 288
  Crepes
    Cheese and Apricot Corn, 111
    Chocolate, 110
    Hana's Palatchinken, 117
    Maple-buttered Buckwheat Triangles,
      111
    Sweet, 110
  Zabaglione, 290
Dill(ed)
  Bread
    Buckwheat, 18
    Oatmeal, 18
    Oatmeal, with Onion, 18
  Cheese Blintzes with Feta and, Savory,
    120

Dill(ed) (*continued*)
  Green Soup, Summer Chilled, 49
  Mayonnaise, 202
  Meatballs, 45
    Hot Beet Soup with, 45
  Mushroom Tofu Tart, 84
  Potato Cheese Filling II, 255
  Quiche, Carrot and, 81
  Rolls, Oatmeal, 18
Dip
  Guacamole, 69
  Herb, Norman Fine's, 237
  Hummus, 69
Dipping Sauce, Chinese, 60
Double Chocolate Bourbon Cake, 271–2
Double Chocolate Mousse Cake, 272–3
Double-Cooked Chicken, 177
Double-Cooked Pork, 177
Double-Cooked Tofu, 177
Dressing
  Mayonnaise and Yogurt, 237
  Vinaigrette
    Basic, 235
    Lemon, Basic, 237
    Oriental Soy Sesame, 236
    Salsa, 236
    Szechuan, 235
    Tarragon Orange, 236
Duck, Gentle Hoi Sin, 196
Dumplings, Chinese
  about, 58
  Homemade Dough for, 59
  Pork and Shrimp (Jao-Tze), 59
Duxelles, Mushroom, 250

Eggplant
  Béchamel, 143
  and Caper Sauce, Vermicelli with,
    138
  Manicotti Stuffed with Mushrooms and,
    145
  Meat and Sausage Lasagna with, 143
  Mushroom Quiche, 82
  Pockets, 114
  Puree, Seasoned, 257
  in Ratatouille, 233
    Sauce, 244
  Tomato Sauce, Creamy, 244
  Tuna Parmesan, 71

Eggplant (*continued*)
  Tuna Pasta Salad, 225
  Walnut Pasta Salad, 225
  Walnut Pesto, 71
Egg(s)
  Crêpe(s). *See* Crêpe(s)
  Gnocchi with Semolina, Cheese, and
    (Semolina Squares), 162–3
  Golden Huevos Rancheros, 102
  Jacobson, 101–2
  Pasta, Homemade, 148
  Sauce, Bean Tortellini with, 155
  Spaghetti and
    about, 130
    with Asparagus and Mushrooms, 132
    Basic, 131
    with Blue Cheese and Sunflower
      Seeds, 131
    with Mushrooms, 131
    Pesto, 133
  Zabaglione, 290
Elegant Artichoke Quiche, 78
Emmy's Spring Rolls, 57
Empanada(s) (Mexican Meat Turnovers), 64
  Tarts, 64
Enchiladas with Chili and Beans, 212
En Croûte Pastry, 66
  Brie in, 66–7
  Miniature Brie or Camembert in, 67
English Muffins, 22

Farmhouse Fruit and Nut Bread, 11
Feta Cheese, Blintzes with Dill and, Savory,
    120
Fettucini, Chicken, 137
Figs, Country-Style Ribs with White Sweets
    and, 217
Filling
  Bean, 253
  Bean Puree, Seasoned, 252
  Cake
    Chocolate Cream Cheese, 279
    Chocolate Mousse, 287
    Orange Buttercream, 280
    Orange Cream Cheese, 280
    Orange Prune, 31
    Rum Cream Cheese, 279
  Cheese Bean, 253
  Cheese and Herb, 15

Filling (continued)
    Eggplant Puree, Seasoned, 257
    Garlic Tahini, 15
    Honey Poppy Seed, 15
    Honey Sesame, 15
    Jam and Praline, 15
    Kasha with Herbs, 254
    Mushroom Duxelles, 250
    Mushroom Marsala, 251
    Mushroom Marsala and Ricotta, 252
    Mushroom Pecan, 251
    Parsnip, 256
    Parsnip and Spinach, 256
    Picadillo, 254
    Potato Cheese
        I, 255
        II, Dilled, 255
        III, Rich, 255
    Salmon Mousse, 250
    Seafood Mousse, 249
        about, 248
    Spinach Mornay, 256
Fine, Norman, 134, 223
Fish. See also Bluefish; Salmon; Seafood;
    Sole; Tuna
    Bites, Crispy Fried, 200
    Brochettes, Favorite, 200
    Dumplings with Spinach, Chinese, 60
    Gravlaks, 201-2
    Mayonnaise Marinade for, 258
    Mousse. See also Seafood—Mousse
        about, 248
    Sesame Szechuan, 198
    Soup, Simple and Simply Beautiful, 44
    Stock, 51-2
    Sweet Szechuan, 198
    with Vegetables, Sweet-and-Sour, 178
Four Season Fruit Bread, 26-7
Frosting, Bourbon Cream Cheese, 272
Fruit(-s,-ed). See also specific fruits
    Bread
        Farmhouse Nut and, 11
        Four Season, 26-7
        Soda, with Nuts and Caraway, 28
        and Custard Pie with a Difference, Fresh,
           266-7
    Honey Rum Sauce with, 269
    Soup, Aunt Clara's, 47
    Tart, Lattice Summer, 264

Fruits of the Sea Pasta, 135
Fungus, Dried Black, 170

Garden Lasagna, 139-40
    Ricotta Cheese Filling for, 140
Garlic
    Béchamel, 142
    chili paste with, for stir-fry dishes,
        170
    Tahini Filling for Savory Bread Swirls,
        15
Gentle Hoi Sin Chicken, 196
Gentle Hoi Sin Duck, 196
Gentle Hoi Sin Pork (Chinese [Not So
    Spare] Ribs), 197
Ginger(ed)
    Carrot and Pear Bisque, 41
    Sherry, 258
Glaze, Chocolate Sour Cream, 275
    Amaretto Cheesecake with, 275
Gnocchi
    about, 161
    Potato Drop, 161-2
    with Semolina, Eggs, and Cheese
        (Semolina Squares), 162-3
Golden, Jack, 270
Golden Huevos Rancheros, 102
Grape
    Blueberry Soup, Summer, 47
    Tabouli, 229
Gravlaks, 201-2
Green Beans Vinaigrette, 234
    Szechuan, 234
Guacamole, 69
    -Filled Pasta Salad with Salsa, 226
    Party, 70

Hana's Palatchinken, 117
Heatter, Maida, 271
Herb(-s,-ed). See also specific herbs
    Brioche Twists with Cheese, 8
    Brioche with Whole Grains and Seeds,
        Rich, 10
    and Cheese Filling for Savory Bread
        Swirls, 15
    Cottage Cheese Pancakes with, 123
    Crêpes with Brie, 112
    Kasha and Potato Blintzes, 121
    Kasha with, 254

Herb(-s,-ed) (continued)
    Nutted Soda Bread with, 28
    Pasta, 150
    Pastry with Wine, 76
    Sauce/Dip, Norman Fine's, 237
    Spaetzle, 160-1
    Walnut Cheese Swirl, 19
High-Protein Griddle Cakes, 123
High-Protein Waffles, 123
Hoi Sin Chicken, Gentle, 196
Hoi Sin Duck, Gentle, 196
Hoi Sin Sauce, 170
Hoi Sin Spicy Beef on a Skewer, 194
Hoi Sin Spicy Chicken, 195
Hoi Sin Spicy Chicken (or Turkey) on a
    Skewer, 194
Hoi Sin Spicy Kebobs, 194
Hollandaise, Processor or Blender, 247
Honey
    Poppy Seed Filling for Rich Sweet Swirls,
        15
    Raisin Bread, Buckwheat, 20
    Rum Ricotta and Pecan Pie, 269
    Rum Sauce with Fruit, 269
    Sesame Filling for Rich Sweet Swirls,
        15
Hors d'oeuvres. See Appetizers
Huevos Rancheros, Golden, 102
Hummus, 69

Jack's Famous Chili and Beans, 211
    Enchiladas with, 212
    Mexican Lasagna with, 142
Jam and Praline Filling for Rich Sweet
    Swirls, 15
Jao-Tze (Chinese Steamed Dumplings),
    59
Joe Lazar's Strawberry Cheese Blintzes,
    119

Kasha
    Blintz Soufflé, Savory, 122
    with Herbs, 254
    Knishes, 64-5
    and Potato Blintzes, Herbed, 121
    and Potato Pie, 88
    and Potato Tarts, 65
Kebobs
    Hoi Sin Spicy, 194

Kebobs (*continued*)
  Sesame Szechuan Beef, Lamb, or Pork, 198
Kidney Beans
  in Chicken 'Chiladas, 209–10
  Chili and, Jack's Famous, 211
    Enchiladas with, 212
    Mexican Lasagna with, 142
  Grape Tabouli with, 229
  in Lasagna
    Garden, 139–40
    Mexican, with Chili and Beans, 142
  in Taco Picadillo, 211
  Tomato Tabouli with, 230
Kielbasa, Vinegar Chicken with Broccoli and, 208
Knishes, Kasha, 64–5
Kung Pao Broccoli and Tofu Pasta Salad, 223–4

Lamb
  Bulgur and Zucchini Casserole with, 216
  Hoi Sin Spicy, 195
    Kebobs, 194
  Kebobs, Sesame Szechuan, 198
  Marrakech, 206
  Meatballs with Bulgur, Sweet-and-Sour, 215
  Shanks with Barley and Turnips, 216–17
  with Zucchini and Onions, Spicy, 183
Lasagna
  Garden, 139–40
    Ricotta Cheese Filling for, 140
  Mexican, with Chili and Beans, 142
  Seafood, 140
  Spring Celebration, 141
Lattice Loaf Pastry, 90
  Sole or Seafood and Spinach in, 89–90
Lattice Summer Fruit Tart, 264
Lemon
  Lentil Soup, 39
  Orange Coconut Squares, 284
  Poppy Seed Twists, 8
  Seafood Tortellini Salad, 228
  Spaetzle, 161

Lemon (*continued*)
  Vinaigrette, Basic, 237
Lentil Soup, Lemon, 39
Linguini
  with Bluefish Sauce, 136
  with Broccoli, Tomatoes, and Black Beans (*Vipasśtana*), 134
Linzer Almond Shortbread Squares, 283
Lo Mein Outside Chinatown, The Best, 186

Manicotti
  Ratatouille, 144
  Stuffed with Eggplant and Mushrooms, 145
Maple
  Beans, 218
    and Corn Bread, 218
  -buttered Buckwheat Triangles, 111
  Corn Bread, 30
  Walnut and Buckwheat Muffins, 32
Marinade
  Chinese, Norman Fine's, 257
  Mayonnaise, for Fish, 258
  Special Szechuan, 257
Marinara Sauce, 242
  Seafood, 242
    Fruits of the Sea Pasta with, 135
  Spaghetti with, 133
Marsala
  Mushroom and Ricotta Filling, 252
    Tortellini with, 157
  Mushroom Filling, 251
    in Phyllo Strudels, 99
    Turnovers, 63
  Raisin Pound Cake (Raisin and Wine Cake), 281
  Zabaglione with, 290
Mayonnaise
  Dilled, 202
  Marinade for Fish, 258
  and Yogurt Pastry, Pat-In, 76
  and Yogurt Salad Dressing, 237
Meat. *See also* Beef; Lamb; Pork; Veal
  Bulgur and Zucchini Casserole with, 216
  Sauce, Favorite, 243
    Spaghetti with, 133
  and Sausage Lasagna with Eggplant, 143

Meatballs
  Dilled, 45
    Hot Beet Soup with, 45
  Sweet-and-Sour, with Bulgur, 215
Mexican Cheese Bean Pinwheel Tarts, 103
Mexican Cheese Bean Turnovers, 63–4
Mexican Cornmeal Crêpes, 109
Mexican Fiesta Pasta Salad, 222–3
Mexican Lasagna with Chili and Beans, 142
Mexican Meat Turnovers (Empanadas), 64
Mexican Pasta and Bean Rolls, 152
Mexican Tomato Sauce, 241
Mexican Tortellini Salad, 228
Monkfish with Vegetables, Sweet-and-Sour, 178
Mornay
  Sauce, 245
  Spinach, 256
Mousse
  Chocolate, 287–8
    Cake, Double, 272–3
    Praline Parfait, 288
    Walnut Ultimate with, 274
  Loaf: Seafood, Salmon, and Spinach, 208–9
  Salmon, 250
  Seafood, 249
    about, 248
    Cannelloni, 144
    Crêpes Stuffed with, Elegant, 115
    Pasta Rolls, 152
    in Phyllo, 99
    Pockets with Crab Meat Velouté, 93
    Strudel Slices with Crab Meat Velouté, 92
    Turnovers, 62–3
Muffins
  Blueberry (or Cranberry), Extraordinary, 32
  Buckwheat and Maple Walnut, 32
  Cranberry Raisin or Blueberry, 32
  English, 22
  Prune Marvel, 31
  Raisin and Bran, for Jack, 33
Multi-Bean Soup, 38
Mushroom(s)
  Crêpes, 110
    Roll-Ups with Cheddar Cheese and Bacon, 115

Mushroom(s) (*continued*)
dried black, in stir-fry dishes,
170
Duxelles, 250
Eggplant Quiche, 82
Manicotti Stuffed with Eggplant and,
145
Marsala and Ricotta Filling, 252
Tortellini with, 157
Marsala Filling, 251
in Phyllo Strudels, 99
Turnovers with, 63
Pecan Filling, 251
Crêpes with, 113
in Phyllo Strudels, 99
Tortellini with, 157
Turnovers with, 63
Spaetzle with, 160
Spaghetti and Eggs with, 131
and Asparagus, 132
and Spinach Crêpes, 113
-Tofu Tart, Dilled, 84
Mu Shu Chicken, 180
Mu Shu Pork My Way, 180
Mustard, Chinese, 60

Nantucket Scallop Chowder, 43
Nests, Phyllo, 100–1
Eggs Jacobson in, 101–2
Noodles
Spicy Szechuan, 224
stir-fry dishes with, 184–90
about, 184–5
The Best Lo Mein Outside Chinatown,
186
Noodles with Beef and Asparagus
(or Broccoli), 189
Number 97, 176
Rice Sticks with Crab Meat (or Tofu),
Pork, and Vegetables, 188
Rice Sticks with Scallops and
Vegetables, 187
Spicy Noodles with Sesame, Scallions,
and Chicken or Beef, 190
Norman Fine's Chinese Marinade, 257
Norman Fine's Herb Sauce/Dip, 237
Norman's Chinese Chicken, 195
Number 97 (Stir-Fry Tofu and Broccoli),
176

Nut(-s,-ted). *See also* Praline
Banana Roll, 278–9
Bread
Farmhouse Fruit and, 11
Fruited Soda Bread with Nuts and
Caraway, 28
Soda, with Herbs, 28
Carrot Roll, 280
Chocolate Banana Strudel,
289–90
Chocolate Bars, Luscious, 283

Oatmeal
Dill Bread, 18
with Onion, 18
Dill Rolls, 18
Onion(s)
and Beet, and Orange Salad, 234
Caraway Twists, 8
Lamb with Zucchini and, Spicy, 183
Orange
and Beet, and Onion Salad, 234
and Beet Soup, Quick, 48
Buttercream, 280
Cream Cheese Filling, 280
Lemon Coconut Squares, 284
Poppy Seed Cake, 281
Praline, 286
Cheesecake, 276
with Chocolate, 286
-Prune Filling, 31
Sweet-and-Sour Tomato Sauce with, 215
Tarragon Vinaigrette, 236
Oriental Soy Sesame Vinaigrette, 236
Oyster Sauce, 171
Mixed Vegetables with Tofu or Chicken
in, 173–4
Stir-Fry Cabbage, Tofu, and Ground Pork
in, 174
Stir-Fry Cabbage and Tofu in, 175
Oysters with Vegetables, Sweet-and-Sour,
178

Palatchinken, Hana's, 117
Pancakes
Chinese, 181
Cottage Cheese, 122
with Herbs, 123
High-Protein Griddle Cakes, 123

Parmesan, about, 128
Parsnip
Filling, 256
Pierogin with, 159
and Spinach Filling, 256
Tortellini with, 156
Turnovers with, 95
Party Guacamole, 70
Pasta, 127–63. *See also* Noodles
about, 127–8
with Broccoli, Tomatoes, and Black
Beans (*Vipasśtana*), 134
Cannelloni Seafood Mousse, 144
Charlotte's, 138
cheese for, 128
Fettucini, Chicken, 137
Fruits of the Sea, 135
Gnocchi
about, 161
Potato Drop, 161–2
with Semolina, Eggs, and Cheese
(Semolina Squares), 162–3
Homemade, 146–57. *See also* Rolls
below; Tortellini
about, 146–7
Buckwheat, 150
Carrot, 149
Egg, 148
Herbed, 150
machine for, 147, 148
Spinach, 149
Tomato, 149
Lasagna
Garden, 139–40
Meat and Sausage, with Eggplant,
143
Mexican, with Chili and Beans, 142
Seafood, 140
Spring Celebration, 141
Lemon Lentil Soup as sauce for, 39
Linguini with Bluefish Sauce, 136
Manicotti
Ratatouille, 144
Stuffed with Eggplant and
Mushrooms, 145
Multi-Bean Soup as sauce for, 38
with Pesto, 135
Pierogin, 158–9
Ricotta and Walnut Sauce for, 129

Pasta (*continued*)
Rolls
about, 150
Mexican Bean and, 152
Seafood Mousse, 152
Spinach and Ricotta, 151
Salad
Bean-Filled, with Salsa, 226-7
Eggplant Tuna, 225
Eggplant Walnut, 225
Guacamole-Filled, with Salsa, 226
Kung Pao Broccoli and Tofu, 223-4
Lemony Seafood Tortellini, 228
Mexican Fiesta, 222-3
Mexican Tortellini, 228
Shrimp Won Tons with Broccoli in
Szechuan Vinaigrette, 227
Spicy Szechuan Noodles, 224
Szechuan Tortellini and Broccoli,
228
Szechuan Vegetable and, 222
Spaetzle, 160-1
Spaghetti and Eggs
about, 130
with Asparagus and Mushrooms, 132
Basic, 131
with Blue Cheese and Sunflower
Seeds, 131
with Mushrooms, 131
Pesto, 133
Spaghetti with Favorite Meat Sauce, 133
Spaghetti with Marinara Sauce, 133
Spaghetti with Ratatouille Sauce, 135
Spanakugel, 163
with Squid, Squash, and Tomato Sauce,
136-7
Tortellini. *See* Tortellini
Vermicelli with Eggplant and Caper
Sauce, 138
Pastry Cream, 267
Pastry(-ies)
about making, 75-6
Carrot Almond Bisteeya Hors d'Oeuvre,
100
for cheesecakes, 274
Cornmeal, 77
Tart and Turnover, 77
Cottage Cheese, 77
en Croûte, 66

Pastry(-ies) (*continued*)
Brie in, 66-7
Miniature Brie or Camembert in,
67
Herbed, with Wine, 76
Lattice Loaf, 90
Sole or Seafood and Spinach in,
89-90
Pat-In Yogurt and Mayonnaise, 76
Phyllo. *See* Phyllo
Ricotta, 77
Sweet, 261
Sweet Lattice Tart, 261
Turnover, 62
Sour Cream, 62
Peach(es)
Chicken with Peanuts and, 179
in Lattice Summer Fruit Tart, 264
Torte, 277
Peanut(s)
Banana Bread, Best Ever, 25
-Carrot Raisin Tabouli, 229
Peanuts, Chicken with Peaches and, 179
Pear
and Carrot Bisque, Gingered, 41
Tart, Amaretto, 265
Pecan
Buttercrunch Bars, 282
and Honey Rum Ricotta Pie, 269
Mushroom Filling, 251
Crêpes with, 113
in Phyllo Strudels, 99
Tortellini with, 157
Turnovers, 63
Pesto
Cubes, Frozen, 247
Eggplant Walnut, 71
Pasta with, 135
Sauce, 247
Pasta with, 135
Spaghetti and Eggs, 133
Phyllo
about, 90-2
Carrot and Almond Bisteeya in,
96-7
Carrot Almond Bisteeya Hors d'Oeuvre
Pastries, 100
to form cigars of, 91-2
to form rolls of, 91

Phyllo (*continued*)
Nests, 100-1
Eggs Jacobson in, 101-2
Seafood Mousse in, 99
Spanokopita Pie in, 97
Strudel(s)
Mushroom Marsala or Mushroom
Pecan, 99
Potato, Individual, 98
Seafood Mousse, Pockets with Crab
Meat Velouté, 93
Seafood Mousse, Slices with Crab
Meat Velouté, 92
Turnovers
Parsnip and Spinach, 95
Potato and Cheese, 95
Spanokopita, 94-5
Picadillo, 254
and Brioche Loaf, 212-13
Pinwheel Tarts, 103
Taco, 211
Torta, 213
Pickled Vegetables, Best, 232
Pie
Apple, Favorite, 263
Carrot and Almond Bisteeya,
96-7
Chocolate Velvet, 268
Fresh Fruit and Custard, with a
Difference, 266-7
Honey Rum Ricotta and Pecan, 269
Kasha and Potato, 88
Pastry dough for. *See* Pastry
Raisin d'Être, 270
Ricotta Basil, 84-5
Spanokopita, 97
Torta Rustica, 86
Tostada, 87
Pierogin, 159
about, 158
Plum
Kuchen, 278
Praline Tart, 262-3
Poppy Seed
Banana Bread, Best Ever, 24
-Honey Filling for Rich Sweet Swirls, 15
Lemon Brioche Twists, 8
Orange Cake, 281
Spaetzle, 161

Pork. *See also* Ribs; Sausage
    Chops, with Figs and White Sweets,
        217
    Double-Cooked, 177
    Gentle Hoi Sin (Chinese [Not So Spare]
        Ribs), 197
    Ground, Stir-Fry Cabbage, Tofu, and, in
        Oyster Sauce, 174
    Hoi Sin Spicy, 195
    Kebobs, 194
    Kebobs, Sesame Szechuan, 198
    Mu Shu, My Way, 180
    Rice Sticks with Crab Meat (or Tofu),
        Vegetables, and, 188
Potato(es)
    Cheese Filling
        I, 255
        II, Dilled, 255
        III, Rich, 255
        Pierogin with, 159
    and Cheese Turnovers, 95
    Gnocchi, 161
        Drop, 161-2
    and Kasha Blintzes, Herbed, 121
    and Kasha Pie, 88
    and Kasha Tarts, 65
    Strudels, Individual, 98
Poultry. *See* Chicken; Duck; Turkey
Pound Cake, Marsala Raisin (Raisin and
        Wine Cake), 281
Praline, 286
    Chocolate, 286
    and Jam Filling for Rich Sweet Swirls,
        15
    Orange, 286
        Cheesecake, 276
        with Chocolate, 286
    Parfait
        Chocolate Mousse, 288
        Cloud, 287
    Tart
        Blueberry, 262
        Cranberry, 262
        Plum, 262-3
Prune(s)
    Chocolate-dipped Stuffed, 288-9
    Marvel Loaf for Colleen, 276-7
    Marvel Muffins, 31
    -Orange Filling, 31

Prune(s) (*continued*)
    Ported, Couscous with Turkey and, 207
Pumpkin Bread, Velvet, 27

Quenelle Quiche, Salmon, 79
Quiche
    Artichoke, Elegant, 78
    Broccoli and Blue Cheese, 81
    Carrot and Dill, 81
    Eggplant Mushroom, 82
    Salmon Quenelle, 79

Raisin(s)
    Banana Walnut Lattice Tart,
        270-1
    Bread
        Buckwheat Honey, 20
        Cranberry, 29
        Wonderful, 17
        -Carrot Walnut (or Peanut) Tabouli,
            229
    d'Être Pie, 270
    Marsala Pound Cake (Raisin and Wine
        Cake), 281
    Muffins
        Bran and, for Jack, 33
        Cranberry, 32
        Cranberry, Extraordinary, 32
    Rum Squares, 285
Raspberry Almond Bread, Best Ever, 24
Ratatouille, 233
    Sauce, 244
        Crêpes with, 114
        Garden Lasagna with, 139-40
        Manicotti with, 144
        Spaghetti with, 135
        in Torta Rustica, 86
Ravioli. *See also recipes for* Tortellini
    forming, 154
Ribs, Country-Style
    Chinese (Not So Spare) (Gentle Hoi Sin
        Pork), 197
    with Figs and White Sweets, 217
    Hoi Sin Spicy, 195
Rice, Brown, 255
Rice Sticks
    with Crab Meat (or Tofu), Pork, and
        Vegetables, 188
    with Scallops and Vegetables, 187

Ricotta
    Basil Pie, 84-5
    Filling
        Tortellini with, 156
    Filling, for Garden Lasagna, 140
    and Mushroom Marsala Filling, 252
        Tortellini with, 157
    Pastry, 77
    and Pecan Pie, Honey Rum, 269
    and Spinach Pasta Rolls, 151
        Tortellini with, 156
    and Walnut Sauce for Pasta, 129
Rolls
    Oatmeal Dill, 18
    Pasta. *See* Pasta—Rolls
    Whole Wheat and Rye, 21
Rum
    Cream Cheese Filling, 279
    Honey Ricotta and Pecan Pie, 269
    Honey Sauce with Fruit, 269
    Raisin Squares, 285
Rye
    Bread, Braided, 16
    Caraway Banana Bread, Best Ever, 25
    Rolls, Whole Wheat and, 21

Salad, 221-34
    about, 221
    Beet, Orange, and Onion, 234
    Broccoli with Tomatoes and Black Beans,
        233
    Carrot Rapee, 234
    Green Beans Vinaigrette, 234
        Szechuan, 234
    Marinated White Beans with Capers,
        Anchovies, and Tuna, 234
    Pasta
        Bean-Filled, with Salsa, 226-7
        Eggplant Tuna, 225
        Eggplant Walnut, 225
        Guacamole-Filled, with Salsa, 226
        Kung Pao Broccoli and Tofu, 223-4
        Lemony Seafood Tortellini, 228
        Mexican Fiesta, 222-3
        Mexican Tortellini, 228
        Shrimp Won Tons with Broccoli in
            Szechuan Vinaigrette, 227
        Spicy Szechuan Noodles, 224
        Szechuan Tortellini and Broccoli, 228

Salad (*continued*)
    Szechuan Vegetables and, 222
    Ratatouille, 233
    Sweet-and-Sour Zucchini, 233
    Tabouli
        about, 229
        Carrot-Raisin Walnut (or Peanut), 229
        Grape, 229
        with Mixed Vegetables, 231
        Shrimp and Artichoke, 231
        Tomato, 230
Salad dressing. *See* Dressing
Salmon
    Gravlaks, 201-2
    Mousse, 250
    Quenelle Quiche, 79
    and Seafood, and Spinach Mousse Loaf,
        208-9
Salsa Vinaigrette, 236
    Bean-Filled Pasta Salad with, 226-7
    Guacamole-Filled Pasta Salad with, 226
    Mexican Fiesta Pasta Salad with,
        222-3
Sauce
    Béchamel
        Basic, 245
        Basil, 246
        Eggplant, 143
        Garlic, 142
        Sesame, 245
        Thick, 245
    Bluefish, Linguini with, 136
    Dipping, Chinese, 60
    Egg, Bean Tortellini with, 155
    Eggplant
        and Caper, Vermicelli with, 138
        Tomato, Creamy, 244
    Herb, Norman Fine's, 237
    Hoi Sin, 170
    Hollandaise, Processor or Blender, 247
    Honey Rum, with Fruit, 269
    Lemon Lentil Soup as, for pasta, 39
    Marinara, 242
        Seafood, 242
        Spaghetti with, 133
    Meat, Favorite, 243
        Spaghetti with, 133
    Mornay, 245
    Multi-Bean Soup as, for pasta, 38

Sauce (*continued*)
    Oyster, 171
        Mixed Vegetables with Tofu or
            Chicken in, 173-4
        Stir-Fry Cabbage, Tofu, and Ground
            Pork in, 174
        Stir-Fry Cabbage and Tofu in, 175
    Pesto, 247
        Pasta with, 135
    Ratatouille, 244
        Crêpes with, 114
        Garden Lasagna with, 139-40
        Manicotti with, 144
        Spaghetti with, 135
        in Torta Rustica, 86
    Ricotta and Walnut, for Pasta, 129
    for Stir-Fry Vegetables, Basic, 184
    Tomato. *See also* Marinara Sauce
        Basic, 241
        Mexican, 241
        Pasta with Squid, Squash, and, 136-7
        Seafood, 242
        Sweet-and-Sour, with Orange, 215
    Velouté
        Crab Meat, 246
        Seafood, 246
Sausage
    Crêpe Rolls, 117
    Italian, Bulgur and Zucchini Casserole
        with, 216
    Kielbasa, Vinegar Chicken with Broccoli
        and, 208
    Maple Beans and Corn Bread with, 218
    and Meat Lasagna with Eggplant, 143
Scallions
    Spicy Noodles with Sesame, Chicken or
        Beef, and, 190
Scallop(s)
    Chowder, Nantucket, 43
    Dumplings with Spinach, Chinese, 60
    in Fruits of the Sea Pasta, 135
    Rice Sticks with Vegetables and, 187
    Sesame Szechuan, 198
    with Vegetables, Sweet-and-Sour,
        178
Scotch Broth, 46
Seafood. *See also specific fish or shellfish*
    Bites, Crispy Fried, 200
    Lasagna, 140

Seafood (*continued*)
    Marinara Sauce, 242
        Fruits of the Sea Pasta with, 135
    Mousse, 249
        about, 248
        Cannelloni, 144
        Crêpes Stuffed with, Elegant, 115
        Pasta Rolls, 152
        in Phyllo, 99
        Pockets with Crab Meat Velouté, 93
        Salmon, Spinach, and, Loaf, 208-9
        Strudel Slices with Crab Meat Velouté,
            92
        Turnovers, 62-3
    Sesame Szechuan, 198
    and Spinach Pastry Lattice Loaf,
        89-90
    Sweet Szechuan, 198
    Tomato Sauce, 242
    Tortellini, 154
        Salad, Lemony, 228
        Salad, Szechuan Broccoli and, 228
    with Vegetables, Sweet-and-Sour, 178
    Velouté, 246
Seasoned Bean Puree, 252
Semolina Squares (Gnocchi with Semolina,
        Eggs, and Cheese), 162-3
Sesame (Seed)
    Banana Bread, Best Ever, 25
    Béchamel, 245
    -Honey Filling for Rich Sweet Swirls, 15
    Oil, 171
    Spaetzle, 161
    Spicy Noodles with Scallions, Chicken
        or Beef, and, 190
    Szechuan Beef, Lamb, or Pork Kebobs,
        198
    Szechuan Chicken, 197
    Szechuan Seafood or Fish, 198
    Tahini. *See* Tahini
    Vinaigrette, Oriental Soy, 236
Sherry, Gingered, 258
Shortbread Squares, Linzer Almond, 283
Shrimp
    and Artichoke Tabouli, 231
    Dumplings with Spinach, Chinese, 60
    in Fruits of the Sea Pasta, 135
    Sesame Szechuan, 198
    and Tofu Won Tons, 61

Shrimp (*continued*)
  with Broccoli in Szechuan Vinaigrette,
    Cold, 227
  with Vegetables, Sweet-and-Sour, 178
Soda Bread
  Fruited, with Nuts and Caraway, 28
  with Herbs, Nutted, 28
Sole and Spinach Pastry Lattice Loaf, 89-90
Soufflé, Blintz
  Savory Kasha, 122
  Sweet, 121
Soup, 37-49. *See also* Bisque
  about, 37
  Beet
    Hot, with Dilled Meatballs, 45
    and Orange, Quick, 48
  Blueberry Grape, Summer, 47
  Borscht
    Beet, Chilled Fresh, 48
    Tomato, Fresh, 49
  Broccoli Stalk, Cream of, 41
  Cauliflower and Cheddar Cheese, Cream
    of, 42
  Dilled Green, Summer Chilled, 49
  Fish, Simple and Simply Beautiful, 44
  Fruit, Aunt Clara's, 47
  Lemon Lentil, 39
  Multi-Bean, 38
  Scallop Chowder, Nantucket, 43
  Scotch Broth, 46
  Split Pea
    Favorite, 40
    Vegetarian, 40
  Won Ton, 46
Sour Cream Glaze, Chocolate, 275
  Amaretto Cheesecake with, 275
Soy Sauce (or Tamari), 171
Spaetzle, 160
  about, 160
  Buckwheat or Whole Wheat, 160
  Cheese, 161
  Herbed, 160-1
  Lemon, 161
  with Mushrooms, 160
  Seeded, 161
Spaghetti
  and Eggs
    about, 130
    with Asparagus and Mushrooms, 132

Spaghetti (*continued*)
  Basic, 131
  with Blue Cheese and Sunflower
    Seeds, 131
  with Mushrooms, 131
  Pesto, 133
  with Favorite Meat Sauce, 133
  with Marinara Sauce, 133
  with Ratatouille Sauce, 135
Spanakugel, 163
Spanokopita
  Pie, 97
  Turnovers, 94-5
Spareribs, Hoi Sin Spicy, 195
Spinach
  and Avocado Torte, 80
  Mornay, 256
  and Mushroom Crêpes, 113
  and Parsnip Filling
    Tortellini with, 156
    Turnovers with, 95
  Pasta, 149
  and Ricotta Pasta Rolls, 151
  and Seafood, and Salmon Mousse Loaf,
    208-9
  Shrimp, Scallop, or Fish Dumplings with,
    60
  and Sole or Seafood Pastry Lattice Loaf,
    89-90
  Spanokopita
    Pie, 97
    Turnovers, 94-5
  and Tofu Tart, 83
  Walnut Bisque, 43
Split Pea Soup
  Favorite, 40
  Vegetarian, 40
Spring Celebration Lasagna, 141
Spring Rolls
  Emmy's, 57
  II, 58
Squares. *See also* Bars
  Linzer Almond Shortbread, 283
  Orange Lemon Coconut, 284
  Rum Raisin, 285
Squash. *See also* Zucchini
  Butternut, Bisque, Curried, 42
  Yellow, in Ratatouille Sauce,
    244

Squid: Pasta with Squash, Tomato Sauce,
    and, 136-7
Stir-fry dishes
  Asparagus Stir-Fry, 182
    with Ground Beef, 182
  Cabbage, Tofu, and Ground Pork in
    Oyster Sauce, 174
  Cabbage and Tofu in Oyster Sauce,
    175
  Chicken with Peaches and Peanuts, 179
  Double-Cooked Chicken, 177
  Double-Cooked Pork, 177
  Double-Cooked Tofu, 177
  ingredients for, 170-1
  Mixed Vegetables with Tofu or Chicken
    in Oyster Sauce, 173-4
  Mu Shu Chicken, 180
  Mu Shu Pork My Way, 180
  noodle dishes, 184-90
    about, 184-5
    The Best Lo Mein Outside Chinatown,
      186
    Noodles with Beef and Asparagus
      (or Broccoli), 189
    Number 97 Noodles, 176
    Rice Sticks with Crab Meat (or Tofu),
      Pork, and Vegetables, 188
    Rice Sticks with Scallops and
      Vegetables, 187
    Spicy Noodles with Sesame, Scallions,
      and Chicken or Beef, 190
  Number 97 Noodles, 176
  Number 97 (Stir-Fry Tofu and Broccoli),
    176
  protein for, 168-9
  sauces for, 169-71
    Basic Sauce for Vegetables, 184
  Spicy Lamb with Zucchini and Onions,
    183
  Sweet-and-Sour Fish or Seafood with
    Vegetables, 178
  vegetables for, 167-8
  woks for, 172
Stock
  about making, 50
  Beef, 51
  Chicken, 50-1
    for stir-fry dishes, 170
  Fish, 51-2

Strawberry(-ies)
  Almond Tart, Fresh, 266
  Cheese Blintzes, Joe Lazar's, 119
Strudel(s)
  Chocolate Banana Nut, 289–90
  Mushroom Marsala or Mushroom Pecan,
    99
  Potato, Individual, 98
  Seafood Mousse
    Pockets with Crab Meat Velouté, 93
    Slices, with Crab Meat Velouté, 92
Stuffing. See Filling
Summer Blueberry Grape Soup, 47
Sunflower Seeds, Spaghetti and Eggs with
    Blue Cheese and, 131
Sweet-and-Sour Fish or Seafood with
    Vegetables, 178
Sweet-and-Sour Meatballs with Bulgur, 215
Sweet-and-Sour Tomato Sauce with
    Orange, 215
Sweet-and-Sour Walnut Chicken Crisps, 199
Sweet-and-Sour Zucchini, 233
Sweet Potatoes, White, Country-Style Ribs
    with Figs and, 217
Szechuan Beef, Lamb, or Pork Kebobs,
    Sesame, 198
Szechuan Chicken, Sesame, 197
Szechuan Green Beans Vinaigrette, 234
Szechuan Marinade, Special, 257
Szechuan Noodles, Spicy, 224
Szechuan Pasta and Vegetable Salad, 222
Szechuan Seafood, Sweet, 198
Szechuan Seafood or Fish, Sesame, 198
Szechuan Tortellini and Broccoli Salad, 228
Szechuan Vinaigrette, 235
    Cold Shrimp Won Tons with Broccoli
    in, 227

Tabouli
  about, 229
  Carrot-Raisin Walnut (or Peanut), 229
  Grape, 229
  with Mixed Vegetables, 231
  Shrimp and Artichoke, 231
  Tomato, 230
Taco Picadillo, 211
Tahini
  Garlic Filling for Savory Bread Swirls,
    15

Tahini (continued)
  in Sesame Béchamel, 245
Tarragon Orange Vinaigrette, 236
Tart(s)
  Amaretto Pear, 265
  Banana Raisin Walnut Lattice, 270–1
  Blueberry or Strawberry Almond, Fresh,
    266
  Blueberry Praline, 262
  Cranberry Praline, 262
  Dilled Mushroom Tofu, 84
  Empanada, 64
  Kasha and Potato, 65
  Lattice Summer Fruit, 264
  Mexican Cheese Bean Pinwheel, 103
  Pastry dough for. See Pastry
  Picadillo Pinwheel, 103
  Plum Praline, 262–3
  Spinach and Tofu, 83
  Zucchini and Basil, 85
Three Grain Loaf, 12
Three Seed and Nut Bread, Best Ever, 25
Tofu
  about, 171–2
  Double-Cooked, 177
  Mixed Vegetables with, in Oyster Sauce,
    173–4
  -Mushroom Tart, Dilled, 84
  Pasta Salad, Kung Pao Broccoli and,
    223–4
  Rice Sticks with Pork, Vegetables, and,
    188
  and Shrimp Won Tons, 61
    with Broccoli in Szechuan Vinaigrette,
    Cold, 227
  and Spinach Tart, 83
  Stir-Fry Broccoli and (Number 97), 176
  Stir-Fry Cabbage, Ground Pork, and, in
    Oyster Sauce, 174
  Stir-Fry Cabbage and, in Oyster Sauce,
    175
  in stir-fry dishes, 168
Tomato(es)
  Borscht, Fresh, 49
  Broccoli with Black Beans and, 233
  Eggplant Sauce, Creamy, 244
  Pasta, 149
  Pasta with Broccoli, Black Beans, and
    (Vipasśtana), 134

Tomato(es) (continued)
  Sauce. See also Marinara Sauce
    Basic, 241
    Mexican, 241
    Pasta with Squid, Squash, and, 136–7
    Seafood, 242
    Sweet-and-Sour, with Orange, 215
  Tabouli, 230
Torta Picadillo, 213
Torta Rustica, 86
Torte
  Peach, 277
  Spinach and Avocado, 80
Tortellini
  Bean
    with Egg Sauce, 155
    Salad, Mexican, 228
  forming, 153–4
  Mushroom Marsala Ricotta, 157
  Mushroom Pecan, 157
  with Parsnip and Spinach Filling, 156
  with Ricotta, 156
  Seafood, 154
    Salad, Lemony, 228
    Salad, Szechuan Broccoli and,
    228
Tortilla Crisps, 70
Tostada Pie, 87
Tostadas, Chicken (and Vegetarian),
    210
Tuna
  Eggplant Parmesan, 71
  Eggplant Pasta Salad, 225
  Marinated White Beans with Capers,
    Anchovies, and, 234
Turkey
  Couscous with Ported Prunes and,
    207
  Hoi Sin Spicy
    on a Skewer, 194
    Kebobs, 194
Turnips, Lamb Shanks with Barley and,
    216–17
Turnovers
  Mexican Cheese Bean, 63–4
  Mexican Meat (Empanadas), 64
  Mushroom Marsala, 63
  Mushroom Pecan, 63
  Parsnip and Spinach, 95

Turnovers (*continued*)
    Pastry for, 62
        Cornmeal, 77
        Sour Cream, 62
    Potato and Cheese, 95
    Seafood Mousse, 62–3
    Spanokopita, 94–5
Twists, Buttery Brioche, 8

Vegetable(s). *See also specific vegetables*
    in Charlotte's Pasta, 138
    Fish or Seafood with, Sweet-and-Sour,
        178
    and Pasta Salad, Szechuan, 222
    Pickled, Best, 232
    Rice Sticks with Crab Meat (or Tofu),
        Pork, and, 188
    Rice Sticks with Scallops and, 187
    in stir-fry dishes, 167–8
        Basic Sauce for, 184
        Mixed Vegetables with Tofu
            or Chicken in Oyster Sauce,
            173–4
    Tabouli with Mixed, 231
Vegetarian Split Pea Soup, 40
Vegetarian Tostadas, 210
Velouté
    Crab Meat, 246

Velouté (*continued*)
    Seafood, 246
Velvet Pumpkin Bread, 27
Vermicelli with Eggplant and Caper Sauce,
    138
Vinaigrette
    Basic, 235
    Lemon, Basic, 237
    Salsa, 236
    Szechuan, 235
    Tarragon Orange, 236
Vinegar Chicken with Broccoli and Kielbasa,
    208
Vipasśtana (Pasta with Broccoli, Tomatoes,
    and Black Beans), 134

Waffles, High-Protein, 123
Walnut(s)
    Banana Raisin Lattice Tart,
        270–1
    Cake, Ultimate, 273
        with Chocolate Mousse, 274
    -Carrot Raisin Tabouli, 229
    Cheese Swirl, Herbed, 19
    Chicken Crisps, Sweet-and-Sour, 199
    Eggplant Pasta Salad, 225
    Eggplant Pesto, 71
    Maple, and Buckwheat Muffins, 32

Walnut(s) (*continued*)
    and Ricotta Sauce for Pasta, 129
    in Spaghetti and Eggs Pesto, 133
    Spinach Bisque, 43
Wei, Emmy and Kuo, 56
Woks, 172
Won Ton(s)
    Shrimp and Tofu, 61
        with Broccoli in Szechuan Vinaigrette,
        Cold, 227
    Soup, 46

Yogurt
    and Mayonnaise Dressing, 237
    and Mayonnaise Pastry, Pat-In, 76

Zabaglione, 290
Zeman, Jack, 211
Zucchini
    and Basil Tart, 85
    Bread, Best Ever, 26
    and Bulgur Casserole with Meat,
        216
    Pasta with Squid, Tomato Sauce, and,
        136–7
    in Ratatouille Sauce, 244
    Spicy Lamb with Onions and, 183
    Sweet-and-Sour, 233

A NOTE ABOUT THE AUTHOR

Sherry Lazar Golden was born in Pittsburgh, Penn-
sylvania. She and her 15-year-old son, Jamie, now
live in Brookline, Massachusetts. With her friend and
partner, Norman Fine, she owns a catering company,
Fine and Golden.

A NOTE ON THE TYPE

The text of this book was set in Souvenir Gothic, a type
face designed by George Brian in 1977 in Dallas, Texas.
Souvenir Gothic is based on Souvenir, a face originally
drawn by Morris Fuller Benton in 1914 for American
Type Founders.
  In 1970, Edward Benguiat updated Souvenir for International Typeface Corporation. The original Souvenir con-
sisted of a single roman face; Benguiat transformed the
roman into four different weights and added an italic for
each of these weights.
  George Brian created Souvenir Gothic for the full ex-
panded range. The resulting face is a most useful addition
to film composition, for the Gothic version of Souvenir,
while maintaining the many virtues of the original, is free
of its ornateness.

Composed by Superior Type, Champaign, Illinois
Printed and bound by Halliday Lithographers,
West Hanover, Massachusetts
Designed by Betty Anderson